T0127836

Get the eBook FREE!

(PDF, ePub, Kindle, and liveBook all included)

We believe that once you buy a book from us, you should be able to read it in any format we have available. To get electronic versions of this book at no additional cost to you, purchase and then register this book at the Manning website.

Go to https://www.manning.com/freebook and follow the instructions to complete your pBook registration.

That's it!
Thanks from Manning!

Graph-Powered Machine Learning

Graph-Powered Machine Learning

ALESSANDRO NEGRO

FOREWORD BY DR. JIM WEBBER

MANNING

SHELTER ISLAND

For online information and ordering of this and other Manning books, please visit
www.manning.com. The publisher offers discounts on this book when ordered in quantity.
For more information, please contact

Special Sales Department
Manning Publications Co.
20 Baldwin Road
PO Box 761
Shelter Island, NY 11964
Email: orders@manning.com

Manning Publications Co.
20 Baldwin Road
PO Box 761
Shelter Island, NY 11964

Development editor:	Dustin Archibald
Technical development editors:	Michiel Trimpe & Al Krinker
Review editor:	Ivan Martinović
Production editor:	Andy Marinkovich
Copy editor:	Keir Simpson
Proofreader:	Katie Tennant
Technical proofreader:	Alex Ott
Typesetter:	Gordan Salinovic
Cover designer:	Marija Tudor

ISBN 9781617295645

Printed in the United States of America

To Filippo and Flavia:
I hope you are as proud of your father
as I am always proud of you.

brief contents

contents

foreword

The technology world is abuzz with machine learning. Every day we are bombarded with articles on its applications and advances. But there is a quiet revolution brewing among practitioners, and that revolution puts graphs at the very heart of machine learning.

Alessandro wrote this book after almost a decade of practice, at the confluence of graphs and machine learning. Had Alessandro worked for one of the Web giants distilling the knowledge of an army of PhDs working on special one-off systems, this would be an interesting book, but for the majority of us it would satisfy our curiosity rather than being a practical guide. Fortunately for us, while Alessandro does have a PhD, he works in the enterprise space and has deep empathy and understanding for the kinds of systems that enterprises build. The book reflects this: Alessandro ably addresses the kinds of practical design and implementation challenges that software engineers and data professionals building contemporary systems outside of the hyperscale Web giants must circumvent.

Graph-Powered Machine Learning demonstrates how important graphs are to the future of machine learning. It shows not only that graphs provide a superior means of fuelling contemporary ML pipelines, but also how graphs are a natural way of organizing, analyzing, and processing data for machine learning. The book offers a rich, curated tour of graph machine learning, and each topic is underpinned with detailed examples drawing on Alessandro's deep experience and the easy, refined confidence of a long-term practitioner.

The book eases us in, providing an overall framework to reason about machine learning and integrate it into our data systems. It follows up immediately with a practical approach to recommendations covering a variety of approaches, such as collaborative filtering, content- and session-based recommendations, and hybrid styles. Alessandro calls out the problems which lack explainability in state-of-the-art techniques and shows that this isn't an issue with the graph approach. He then continues to tackle fraud detection, taking in concepts like proximity and social network analysis, where we relearn the maxim that "birds of a feather flock together" in the context of criminal networks. Finally, the book deals with knowledge graphs: the ability of graph technology to consume documents and distil connected knowledge from them, disambiguate terms, and handle ambiguous query terms. The breadth of topics is vast, but the quality of information is always excellent.

Throughout the book, Alessandro gently guides the reader, building up from the basics to advanced concepts. With the examples and companion code, practically minded readers are able to get examples working quickly, and from there to adapt them for their own needs. You will finish this book armed with a variety of practical tools at your disposal and, if you like, some dirt under your fingernails. You will be ready to extract graph features to make your existing models perform better today, and you'll be equipped to work natively with graphs tomorrow. I promise it's going to be a wonderful journey.

—DR. JIM WEBBER, CHIEF SCIENTIST @ NEO4J

The summer of 2012 was one of the warmest I can remember in southern Italy. My wife and I were awaiting our first son, who was going to be delivered quite soon, so we had few chances to go out or take any refreshment in the awesomely fresh, clean water of Apulia. Under those conditions, you can get crazy with DIY (not my case), or you can keep your mind busy with something challenging. Because I'm not a great fan of Sudoku, I started working on a night and weekend project: attempting to build a generic recommendation engine that could serve multiple scopes and scenarios, from small and simple to complex and articulated datasets of user-item interactions, eventually with related contextual information.

This was the moment when graphs forcefully entered my life. Such a flexible data model allowed me to store in the same way not only the users' purchases, but also all the corollary information (later formally defined as contextual information) together with the resulting recommendation model. At that time, Neo4j 1.x was recently released. Although it didn't have Cypher or the other advanced query mechanisms it has now, it was stable enough for me to select it as the main graph database for my project. Adopting graphs helped me unblock the project, and after four months, I released the alpha version of reco4j: the first graph-powered recommendation engine in history!

It was the beginning of a true and passionate love story. For three years, I experimented on my own, trying to sell the reco4j idea here and there (not so successfully, to be honest) when I had a call with Michal Bachman, CEO of GraphAware. A few days later, I flew to London to sign my contract as the sixth employee of this small consultancy firm, which helped companies succeed in their graph projects. Finally, graphs had become my *raison d'etre* (after my two children, of course ☺).

After that, the graph ecosystem changed a lot. More and bigger companies started to adopt graphs as their core technology to deliver advanced services to their customers or solve internal problems. At GraphAware, which had grown significantly and where I had become Chief Scientist, I had the opportunity to help companies to build new services and improve existing ones with the help of graphs. Graphs were capable not only of solving classical problems—from basic search facilities to recommendation engines, from fraud detection to information retrieval—but also became prominent technology for improving and enhancing machine learning projects. Network science and graph algorithms provided new tools for performing different types of analysis of naturally connected data and unconnected data.

In many years of consultancy, speaking with data scientists and data engineers, I found a lot of common problems that could have been solved by using graph models or graph algorithms. This experience of showing people a different way to approach machine learning projects led me to write the book you have in your hands. Graphs don't pretend to solve all problems, but they could be another arrow in your quiver. This book is where your own love story could begin.

acknowledgments

This book took more than three years to be released. It required a lot of work—definitely more than what I thought when this crazy idea hit my mind. At the same time, it has been the most exciting experience of my career up until now. (And, yes, I am planning a second book.) I enjoyed crafting this book, but it was a long journey. That's why I'd like to thank quite a few people for helping me along the way.

First and foremost, I want to thank my family. My poor wife, Aurora, had to sleep alone during all my long nights and early-starting mornings, and my kids rarely saw my face except on the laptop screen for countless weekends. Thank you for your understanding and your unconditional love.

Next, I'd like to acknowledge my development editor at Manning, Dustin Archibald. Thank you for working with me and teaching me all I know about writing. I especially thank you for being so patient when I was late month after month. Your commitment to the quality of this book has made it better for everyone who reads it. Another big thank you goes to all the other people at Manning who worked with me at each stage of the publishing process. Your team is a great and well-oiled machine, and I enjoyed working with each of you.

To all the reviewers: Alex Ott, Alex Lucas, Amlan Chatterjee, Angelo Simone Scotto, Arnaud Castelltort, Arno Bastenhof, Dave Bechberger, Erik Sapper, Helen Mary Labao Barrameda, Joel Neely, Jose San Leandro Armendáriz, Kalyan Reddy, Kelvin Rawls, Koushik Vikram, Lawrence Nderu, Manish Jain, Odysseas Pentakalos, Richard Vaughan, Robert Diana, Rohit Mishra, Tom Heiman, Tomaz Bratanic, Venkata Marrapu, and Vishwesh Ravi Shrimali; your suggestions helped make this a better book.

Last but not least, this book would not exist without GraphAware and especially without Michal—not only because he hired me and allowed me to grow in such an amazing company, but also because when, over a beer, I told him I was thinking about writing a book, he said, "I think you should do it!" This book also would not exist without Chris and Luanne, who have been my greatest fans from day one; without KK, who always had the right words at the right moment to cheer me up and motivate me; without Claudia, who helped me review the images; and without my awesome colleagues with whom I had the most interesting and challenging discussions. You all made this book happen!

about this book

Graph-Powered Machine Learning is a practical guide to using graphs effectively in machine learning applications, showing you all the stages of building complete solutions in which graphs play a key role. It focuses on methods, algorithms, and design patterns related to graphs. Based on my experience in building complex machine learning applications, this book suggests many recipes in which graphs are the main ingredient of a tasty product for your customers. Across the life cycle of a machine learning project, such approaches can be useful in several aspects, such as managing data sources more efficiently, implementing better algorithms, storing prediction models so that they can be accessed faster, and visualizing the results in a more effective way for further analysis.

Who should read this book?

Is this book the right book for you? If you are a data scientist or a data engineer practitioner, it could help you complete or start your learning path. If you are a manager who has to start or drive a new machine learning project, it could help you suggest a different perspective to your team. If you are an advanced developer who's interested in exploring the power of graphs, it could help you discover a new perspective on the role of the graph not only as a kind of database, but also as an enabler technique for AI.

   This book is not a compendium on machine learning techniques in general; it focuses on methods, algorithms, and design patterns related to graphs, which are the prominent topic here. Specifically, the book focuses on how graph approaches can help you develop and deliver better machine learning projects. Graph model techniques are presented in great detail, and multiple graph-based algorithms are described. The most complex concepts are illustrated with concrete scenarios, and concrete applications are designed.

This book aims to be a practical guide that will help you install a working application in the production environment. Hence, it describes optimization techniques and heuristics to help you deal with real data, real problems, and real users. The book discusses not only toy examples, but also end-to-end applications from real-world use cases, with some suggestions for dealing with concrete problem.

If these scenarios piqued your interest, this book is definitely the right book for you.

How this book is organized

The book has 12 chapters organized in four parts. The first part introduces the main topics in the book, starting with generic machine learning and graph concepts, and then moving to the advantages of combining these concepts:

- Chapter 1 introduces machine learning and graphs and covers the basic concepts necessary to understand the following chapters.
- Chapter 2 lists the main challenges related to big data as input to machine learning and discusses how to deal with them by using graph models and graph databases. It also introduces the main features of a graph database.
- Chapter 3 provides a detailed description of the role of graphs in the machine learning workflow and describes a system for large-scale graph processing.

Part 2 discusses several real use cases in which graphs supported the development of a machine learning project and improved the final outcome, specifically focusing on recommendations:

- Chapter 4 introduces the most common recommendation techniques and describes how to design proper graph models for one of them: the content-based recommendation engine. It shows in detail how to import existing (non-graph) datasets into the graph models and implement working content-based recommendation engines.
- Chapter 5 describes how to design proper graph models for a collaborative filtering approach and how to implement fully working collaborative filtering recommendation engines.
- Chapter 6 introduces session-based recommendation algorithms and describes a graph model that is capable of capturing the user session data. It illustrates how to import a sample dataset into the designed model and implement a real recommendation engine on top of it.
- Chapter 7 drives the reader through the implementation of a recommendation engine that takes into account the user's context. It describes the graph models for context-aware recommendation engines and shows how to import existing datasets into the graph models. Moreover, the chapter illustrates how to combine multiple recommendation approaches in a single engine.

Part 3 addresses fraud detection:

- Chapter 8 introduces fraud detection and describes the different types of fraud in different domains. It also specifies the role of graphs in modeling data to reveal frauds faster and more easily, as well as some techniques and algorithms to use in a simple graph model for fighting fraud.
- Chapter 9 moves to more advanced algorithms for fighting fraud based on anomaly detection. It shows how to use graphs to store and analyze the k-NN of transactions and to identify transactions that are anomalous.
- Chapter 10 describes how to use social network analysis (SNA) to classify fraudsters and fraud risks. It lists the different graph algorithms for SNA-based fraud analytics and shows how to derive a proper graph from the data.

Part 4 covers natural language processing (NLP):

- Chapter 11 introduces the concepts related to graph-based NLP. In particular, it describes a simple approach for decomposing a text and storing it in a graph by extracting the hidden structure of unstructured data via NLP.
- Chapter 12 provides an introduction to knowledge graphs, describing in detail how to extract entities and relationships from text and create a knowledge graph from them. It lists the postprocessing techniques used with knowledge graphs, such as semantic network building and automatic topic extraction.

The book doesn't have to be read cover to cover, even though reading it that way will maximize learning. It can be used as a reference for whenever a new challenge is knocking at the door. For beginners in this field, I recommend starting with the first three chapters to get a clear understanding of the key concepts and then jumping to chapters on specific topics of interest. If you are interested in a specific topic or application, it is better to start with the first chapter of the part you are interested in: chapter 4 for recommendations, chapter 8 for fraud detection, and chapter 11 for natural language processing. If you are an expert on graphs and machine learning, and are only looking for suggestions, you can read the chapters of interest to you. Each chapter suggests material to read in other chapters.

About the code

This book contains many examples of source code, both in numbered listings and inline with normal text. In both cases, source code is formatted in a `fixed-width font like this` to separate it from ordinary text.

In many cases, the original source code has been reformatted; we've added line breaks and reworked indentation to accommodate the available page space in the book. In some cases, even this was not enough, and listings include line-continuation markers (➥). Additionally, comments in the source code have often been removed from the listings when the code is described in the text. Code annotations accompany many of the listings, highlighting important concepts.

Source code for the examples in this book is available for download from the publisher's website at https://www.manning.com/books/graph-powered-machine-learning, or you can clone it from my Git repository at https://github.com/alenegro81/gpml.

liveBook discussion forum

Purchase of *Graph-Powered Machine Learning* includes free access to a private web forum run by Manning Publications where you can make comments about the book, ask technical questions, and receive help from the author and from other users. To access the forum and subscribe to it, point your web browser to https://livebook.manning.com/book/graph-powered-machine-learning. You can also learn more about Manning's forums and the rules of conduct at https://livebook.manning.com/discussion.

Manning's commitment to our readers is to provide a venue where a meaningful dialogue between individual readers, and between readers and the author, can take place. It is not a commitment to any specific amount of participation on the part of the author, whose contributions to the forum remain voluntary (and unpaid). We suggest that you ask him challenging questions, lest his interest stray! The forum and the archives of previous discussions will be accessible from the publisher's website as long as the book is in print.

Online resources

Need additional ideas and support?

The GraphAware website (https://www.graphaware.com) is always full of new blog posts, video, podcasts, and case studies related to using graphs to solve problems.

The Neo4j website (https://neo4j.com) also constantly publishes new material on graphs to show how to use graph databases properly in multiple contexts.

If you run into trouble while installing, querying, or managing your Neo4j instance or other graph databases, Stack Overflow (https://stackoverflow.com) is always the best resource for finding solutions to your problems.

about the author

First and foremost, I am immensely passionate about computer science and data research. I specialize in NLP, recommendation engines, fraud detection, and graph-aided search.

After pursuing computer engineering academically and working in various capacities in the domain, I pursued my PhD in Interdisciplinary Science and Technology. With my interest in graph databases peaking, I founded a company called Reco4, which aimed to support an open source project called reco4j—the first recommendation framework based on graph data sources.

Now I'm Chief Scientist at GraphAware, where we are all driven by the goal of being the first name in graph technologies. With clients such as LinkedIn, the World Economic Forum, the European Space Agency, and Bank of America, we are singularly focused on helping clients gain a competitive edge by transforming their data into searchable, understandable, and actionable knowledge. In the past few years, I have spent my time leading the development of Hume (our knowledge graph platform) and speaking at various conferences around the world.

about the cover illustration

The image on the cover of *Graph-Powered Machine Learning* has been extracted from *Roman Tarantella Dancer with Tambourine and a Mandolin Player* (1865). The artist is Anton Romako (1832-1889), an Austrian nineteenth-century painter who fell in love with Italy during one of his travels, moved to Rome in 1857, and started painting portions of everyday life in Italy. The painting shows a tarantella dancer, dancing and playing a tambourine (together with a man playing a mandolin). The image was chosen as a tribute to the author's own origins in southern Italy, specifically in south Apulia, where this is still a living tradition. The tarantella is a traditional dance where the performer simulates what happens after the bite of a locally common type of Lycosa tarantula spider, named "tarantula" (not to be confused with what is commonly known as a tarantula today). This spider was popularly believed to be highly venomous and its bite would cause a hysterical condition known as *tarantism*. The original form of this dance is disordered and free-flowing to simulate such a condition. Others believe the dance was invented because the continuous movements, by causing intense sweating, can help to expel the spider's venom from the body.

Whatever the real origin of this dance might be, the music and rhythm are pleasant and irresistible. It is still very common to see and hear local people performing it today.

Part 1

Introduction

We are surrounded by graphs. Facebook, LinkedIn, and Twitter are the most famous examples of social networks—that is, graphs of people. Other types of graphs exist even though we don't think of them as such: electrical or power networks, the tube, and so on.

Graphs are powerful structures useful not only for representing connected information, but also for supporting multiple types of analysis. Their simple data model, consisting of two basic concepts such as nodes and relationships, is flexible enough to store complex information. If you also store properties in nodes and relationships, it is possible to represent practically everything of any size.

Furthermore, in a graph every single node and every single relationship is an access point for analysis, and from an access point, it is possible to navigate the rest in an endless way, which provides multiple access patterns and analysis potentials.

Machine learning, on the other side, provides tools and techniques for making representations of reality and providing predictions. Recommendation is a good example; the algorithm takes what the users interacted with and is capable of predicting what they will be interested in. Fraud detection is another one, taking the previous transactions (legit or not) and creating a model that can recognize with a good approximation whether a new transaction is fraudulent.

The performance of machine learning algorithms, both in terms of accuracy and speed, is affected almost directly from the way in which we represent our training data and store our prediction model. The quality of algorithm prediction is as good as the quality of the training dataset. Data cleansing and feature selection, among other tasks, are mandatory if we would like to achieve a reasonable level of trust in the prediction. The speed at which the system provides prediction affects the usability of the entire product. Suppose that a recommendation algorithm for an online retailer produced recommendations in 3 minutes. By that time, the user would be on another page or, worse, on a competitor's website.

Graphs can support machine learning by doing what they do best: representing data in a way that is easily understandable and easily accessible. Graphs make all the necessary processes faster, more accurate, and much more effective. Moreover, graph algorithms are powerful tools for machine learning practitioners. Graph community detection algorithms can help identify groups of people, page rank can reveal the most relevant keywords in a text, and so on.

If you didn't fully understand some of the terms and concepts presented in the introduction, the first part of the book will provide you all the knowledge you need to move further in the book. It introduces the basic concepts related to graphs and machine learning as single, independent entities and as powerful binomials. Let me wish you good reading!

Machine learning and graphs: An introduction

This chapter covers

- An introduction to machine learning
- An introduction to graphs
- The role of graphs in machine learning applications

Machine learning is a core branch of artificial intelligence: it is the field of study in computer science that allows computer programs to learn from data. The term was coined in 1959, when Arthur Samuel, an IBM computer scientist, wrote the first computer program to play checkers [Samuel, 1959]. He had a clear idea in mind:

> *Programming computers to learn from experience should eventually eliminate the need for much of this detailed programming effort.*

Samuel wrote his initial program by assigning a score to each board position based on a fixed formula. This program worked quite well, but in a second approach, he had the program execute thousands of games against itself and used the results to refine the board scoring. Eventually, the program reached the proficiency of a human player, and machine learning took its first steps.

An entity—such as a person, an animal, an algorithm, or a generic computer agent[1]—is *learning* if, after making observations about the world, it is able to improve its performance on future tasks. In other words, learning is the process of converting *experience* to *expertise* or *knowledge* [Shalev-Shwartz and Ben-David, 2014]. Learning algorithms use training data that represents experience as input and create expertise as output. That output can be a computer program, a complex predictive model, or tuning of internal variables. The definition of performance depends on the specific algorithm or goal to be achieved; in general, we consider it to be the extent to which the prediction matches specific needs.

Let's describe the learning process with an example. Consider the implementation of a spam filter for emails. A pure programming solution would be to write a program to *memorize* all the emails labeled as spam by a human user. When a new email arrives, the pseudoagent will search for a similar match in the previous spam emails, and if it finds any matches, the new email will be rerouted to the trash folder. Otherwise, the email will pass through the filter untouched.

This approach could work and, in some scenarios, be useful. Yet it is not a learning process because it lacks an important aspect of learning: the ability to *generalize,* to transform the individual examples into a broader model. In this specific use case, it means the ability to label unseen emails even though they are dissimilar to previously labeled emails. This process is also referred to as *inductive reasoning* or *inductive inference.*[2] To generalize, the algorithm should scan the training data and extract a set of words whose appearance in an email message is indicative of spam. Then, for a new email, the agent would check whether one or more of the suspicious words appear and predict its label accordingly.

If you are an experienced developer, you might be wondering, "Why should I write a program that learns how to program itself, when I can instruct the computer to carry out the task at hand?" Taking the example of the spam filter, it is possible to write a program that checks for the occurrence of some words and classifies an email as spam if those words are present. But this approach has three primary disadvantages:

---

[1] According to Russell and Norvig [2009], an agent is something that acts. (*Agent* comes from the Latin *agere*, to do.) All computer programs do something, but computer *agents* are expected to do more: operate autonomously, perceive their environment, persist over a prolonged period, adapt to change, and create and pursue goals.

[2] According to the Stanford Encyclopedia of Philosophy website (https://plato.stanford.edu/entries/logic-inductive), in *inductive* logic, the premises should provide support for the conclusion to some extent. By contrast, in *deductive* reasoning, the premises logically entail the conclusion. For this reason (although some people disagree with this definition), *induction* is sometimes defined as the process of deriving general principles from specific observation.

- A developer cannot anticipate all possible situations. In the spam-filter use case, all the words that might be used in a spam email cannot be predicted up front.
- A developer cannot anticipate all changes over time. In spam emails, new words can be used, or techniques can be adopted to avoid easy recognition, such as adding hyphens or spaces between characters.
- Sometimes, a developer cannot write a program to accomplish the task. Even though recognizing the face of a friend is a simple task for a human, for example, it is impossible to program software to accomplish this task without the use of machine learning.

Therefore, when you face new problems or tasks that you would like to solve with a computer program, the following questions can help you decide whether to use machine learning:

- Is the specific task too complex to be programmed?
- Does the task require any sort of adaptivity throughout its life?

A crucial aspect of any machine learning task is the training data on which the knowledge is built. Starting from the wrong data leads to the wrong results, regardless of the potential performance or the quality of the learning algorithm used.

The aim of this book is to help data scientists and data engineers approach the machine learning process from two sides: the *learning algorithm* and the *data*. In both perspectives, we will use the graph (let me introduce it now as a set of nodes and relationships connecting them) as a valuable mental and technological model. A lot of learning algorithms based on data represented as graphs can deliver efficient predictive models, and other algorithms can be improved by using either data represented as graphs or graph algorithms in the workflow. The use of graphs also provides many other benefits: graphics are a valuable storage model for representing knowledge from the input of the process, managing the training data, and storing the output of the predictive model, providing multiple ways to access it quickly. This book walks the reader through the entire machine learning project life cycle, showing step by step all cases in which graphs could be valuable and reliable friends.

But graphs are not a panacea for all machine learning projects. In stream analytics, in which it is necessary to process a stream of data to reveal short-term anomalies, storing data in the form of a graph could be useless. Furthermore, other algorithms require data in a format that cannot fit in a graph, either during training or for model storage and access. This book gives the reader the capability to discern whether using a graph in the process would be an advantage or a burden.

1.1 *Machine learning project life cycle*

A machine learning project is a human process as well as a software project. It involves a large number of people, a lot of communication, a great deal of work, and a mixed set of skills, and it requires a well-defined approach to be effective. We'll start our long journey by defining a workflow with clear steps and components that will be used throughout the book. The mental schema proposed here, which is one of many possible schemas, will help you better understand the role of graphs in the development and deployment of a successful machine learning project.

Delivering machine learning solutions is a complex process that requires more than selecting the right algorithm(s). Such projects include numerous tasks related to [Sculley, 2015]

- Selecting the data sources
- Gathering data
- Understanding the data
- Cleaning and transforming the data
- Processing the data to create ML models
- Evaluating the results
- Deploying

After deployment, it is necessary to monitor the application and tune it. The entire process involves multiple tools, a lot of data, and different people.

One of the most commonly used processes for data mining projects is the Cross-Industry Standard Process for Data Mining, or CRISP-DM [Wirth and Hipp, 2000]. Although the CRISP-DM model was designed for data mining, it can also be applied to generic machine learning projects. Key features of the CRISP-DM that make it attractive as part of the base workflow model are

- It is not proprietary.
- It is application, industry, and tool neutral.
- It explicitly views the data analytics process from both an application-focused and a technical perspective.

This method can be used for project planning and management, for communicating, and for documentation purposes.

The CRISP-DM reference model offers an overview of the life cycle of a machine learning project. This schema or mental model helps in approaching the machine learning project from a data perspective before taking an algorithmic point of view and provides the baseline for the definition of a clear workflow. Figure 1.1 shows the six phases of the process. It is worth noting that data is at the core of this process.

Looking at figure 1.1, we see that the sequence of the phases is fluid. The arrows indicate only the most important and frequent dependencies between phases; in a particular project, the outcome of each phase determines which phase, or which particular task of a phase, has to be performed next.

The outer circle symbolizes the cyclic nature of the process, which is not finished when a solution is deployed. Subsequent machine learning processes can benefit not only from the experiences of previous ones (the virtuous cycle of Linoff and Berry [2011]), but also from the outcomes of the previous processes. Let's outline each phase in more detail.

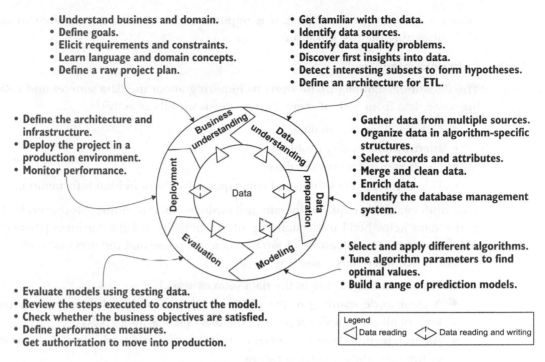

- Understand business and domain.
- Define goals.
- Elicit requirements and constraints.
- Learn language and domain concepts.
- Define a raw project plan.

- Get familiar with the data.
- Identify data sources.
- Identify data quality problems.
- Discover first insights into data.
- Detect interesting subsets to form hypotheses.
- Define an architecture for ETL.

- Define the architecture and infrastructure.
- Deploy the project in a production environment.
- Monitor performance.

- Gather data from multiple sources.
- Organize data in algorithm-specific structures.
- Select records and attributes.
- Merge and clean data.
- Enrich data.
- Identify the database management system.

- Select and apply different algorithms.
- Tune algorithm parameters to find optimal values.
- Build a range of prediction models.

- Evaluate models using testing data.
- Review the steps executed to construct the model.
- Check whether the business objectives are satisfied.
- Define performance measures.
- Get authorization to move into production.

Legend
◁| Data reading   ◁|▷ Data reading and writing

Figure 1.1   The six phases of the CRISP-DM process

1.1.1   *Business understanding*

The first phase requires defining the goals of the machine learning project. These objectives are often expressed in general terms: increase revenue, improve the customer experience, get better and customized search results, sell more products, and so on. To convert these high-level problem definitions to concrete requirements and constraints for the machine learning project, it is necessary to understand the business and the domain.

Machine learning projects are software projects, and during this phase, it is also important to learn the language and domain concepts. This knowledge will not only help with communication between the data scientist and the internal team during subsequent phases, but also improve the quality of the documentation and the presentation of the results.

The outcomes of this phase are

- A clear understanding of the domain and the business perspective
- A definition of the goals, requirements, and constraints
- The conversion of this knowledge to a machine learning problem definition
- A preliminary and reasonable project plan designed to achieve the objectives

The goals of the first iteration shouldn't be too broad, because this round requires a lot of effort related to the injection of the machine learning process into the existing infrastructure. At the same time, it is important to keep future extensions in mind while designing the first iteration.

1.1.2   *Data understanding*

The data-understanding phase starts by inquiring about the data sources and collecting some data from each of them, and proceeds with these activities:

- Get familiar with the data.
- Identify data quality problems.
- Get first insights into the data.
- Detect interesting subsets to form hypotheses about hidden information.

Data understanding requires domain and business understanding. Moreover, looking at the data helps build understanding of the domain and the business perspective, which is why there is a feedback loop between this phase and the previous one.

The outcomes of this phase are

- A clear understanding of the data sources available
- A clear understanding of the different kinds of data and their content (or at least of all the significant parts of the machine learning goals)
- An architecture design to get or extract this data and feed it into the next steps of the machine learning workflow

1.1.3   *Data preparation*

This phase covers all the activities to gather data from multiple sources and organize it in the specific kind of structure required by the algorithm in the modeling phase. Data preparation tasks include record and attribute selection, feature engineering, data merging, data cleaning, construction of new attributes, and enrichment of existing data. As pointed out before, the quality of the data has an enormous impact on the final results of the next phases, so this phase is crucial.

The outcomes of this phase are

- One or more data structure definitions, using adequate design techniques
- A well-defined data pipeline for feeding the machine learning algorithm training data
- A set of procedures for merging, cleaning, and enriching data

Another outcome of this phase is the identification of the database management system where this data will be stored while waiting to be processed.

For the sake of completeness, it is not always required to have an explicit data store for persisting data before further processing. It is possible to extract data and convert it before the processing phase. Having such an intermediate step, however, has a lot of advantages related to performance and data quality as well as to further extensibility.

1.1.4 Modeling

The modeling phase is where machine learning occurs. Different algorithms are selected and applied, and their parameters are calibrated to optimal values. The algorithms are used to build a range of prediction models from which the best is selected for deployment when the evaluation phase is complete. An interesting aspect is that some algorithms produce a prediction model, but others do not.[3]

The outcomes of this phase are

- The set of algorithms to be tested in the next phase
- The related predictive models (where applicable)

There is a close link between data preparation and modeling, because you often identify problems with the data and get ideas for constructing new data points while modeling. Moreover, some techniques require specific data formats.

1.1.5 Evaluation

At this stage in a machine learning project, you have built one or more predictive models that appear to be of high quality. Before a model can be deployed, it is important to evaluate it thoroughly and review the steps executed to construct the model, so that you can be certain it properly achieves the business objectives defined at the beginning of the process.

This evaluation is conducted in a formal way, such as splitting the available data into a training set (80%) and a testing set (20%). Another primary objective is to determine whether any important business issues have not been sufficiently considered.

The outcomes of this phase are

- A set of values that allows measurement of performance. (The specific measure of success depends on the algorithm type and the scope.)
- A thorough evaluation of whether the business goals are achieved.
- Authorization for using the solution in a production environment.

1.1.6 Deployment

Because machine learning models are built to serve some purpose in an organization, the creation of a model is generally not the end of the project. Depending on the requirements, the deployment phase can be as simple as generating a report or as complex as releasing a complete infrastructure that delivers a service to end users. In many cases, the customer—not the data scientist—carries out the deployment steps. In any event, it is important to understand up front what actions will need to be carried out to make use of the created models.

The outcomes of this phase are as follows:

---

[3] Appendix A (about machine learning taxonomy) contains some examples of algorithms that create a prediction model.

- One or multiple reports with the results of the prediction models
- The predictive models themselves, used for predicting the future and supporting decisions
- An infrastructure to provide a specific set of services to the end users

When the project is in production, it is necessary to monitor it constantly (evaluating performance, for example).

1.2   Machine learning challenges

Machine learning projects have some intrinsic challenges that make them complex to accomplish. This section summarizes the main aspects you need to take into account when approaching a new machine learning project.

1.2.1   The source of truth

The CRISP-DM model puts data at the center of the machine learning process by describing the life cycle from a data perspective. The training data represents the *source of truth* from which any insight can be extracted and any prediction can be made. Managing the training requires a lot of effort. To quote Jeffrey Heer, professor of computer science at the University of Washington, "It's an absolute myth that you can send an algorithm over raw data and have insights pop up." As a case in point, it has been estimated that data scientists spend up to 80% of their time on data preparation [Lohr, 2014].

I often use the following statement to shift the focus to data before discussing the details of the algorithms:

> *Even the best learning algorithm on the wrong data produces the wrong results.*

The seminal papers by Banko and Brill [2001] and Halevy, Norvig, and Pereira [2009] point out how, for complex problems, data often matters more than algorithms. Both articles consider natural language processing, but the concept can be generalized to machine learning in general [Sculley, 2015].

Figure 1.2, from Banko and Brill [2001], shows the learning curves for a set of learners, considering the average performance of each on different sizes of training data (up to 1 billion words). The specific algorithms used are not important here; the key takeaway is that, as is clear from the image, increasing the amount of data available during the training phase improved the performance of all the learners. These results suggest that it's worth reconsidering spending time and money on corpus development versus spending it on algorithm development. From another perspective, as a data scientist you can focus on the vertical dimension—finding a better algorithm—but the graph shows that there is more room for improvement in the horizontal direction—gathering more data. As proof, the worst-performing algorithm in figure 1.2 performs much better with 10 million elements than the best one with 1 million elements.

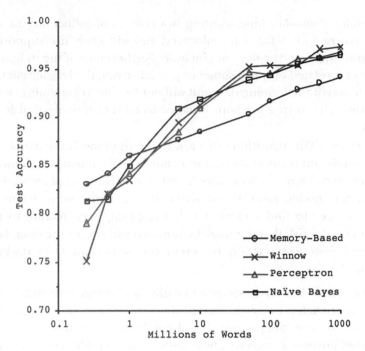

Figure 1.2 Learning curves for confusion set disambiguation

Collecting data from multiple sources allows you not only to access a huge set of data, but also to improve the quality of the data, solving problems such as sparsity, misspellings, correctness, and so on. Gathering data from a variety of sources is not an issue; we live in the big data era, and an abundance of digital data is available from the web, sensors, smartphones, corporate databases, and open data sources. But if there is value in combining different datasets, there are problems too. Data from different sources comes in different formats. Before the learner can analyze it, the data must be cleaned up, merged, and normalized into a unified and homogeneous schema that the algorithm can understand. Furthermore, obtaining additional training data has a nonzero cost for many problems, and for supervised learning, this cost may be high.

For these reasons, the data represents the first big challenge in the machine learning process. Data concerns can be summarized in four categories:

- *Insufficient quantity of data*—Machine learning requires a lot of training data to work properly. Even for simple use cases, it needs thousands of examples, and for complex problems such as deep learning or for nonlinear algorithms, you may need millions of examples.
- *Poor quality of data*—Data sources are always full of errors, outliers, and noise. Poor data quality directly affects the quality of the results of the machine learning process because it is hard for many algorithms to discard wrong (incorrect, unrelated, or irrelevant) values and to then detect underlying patterns in this mess.

- *Nonrepresentative data*—Machine learning is a process of induction: the model makes inferences from what it has observed and will likely not support edge cases that your training data does not include. Furthermore, if the training data is too noisy or is related only to a subset of possible cases, the learner might generate bias or overfit the training data and will not be able to generalize to all the possible cases. This is true for both instance-based and model-based learning algorithms.

- *Irrelevant features*—The algorithm will learn in the right way if the data contains a good set of relevant features and not too many irrelevant features. Although it is often a useful strategy to select more features, with the goal of increasing the accuracy of the model, more is not always better. Using more features will enable the learner to find a more detailed mapping from feature to target, which increases the risk that the model computed will overfit the data. Feature selection and feature extraction represent two important tasks during the preparation of data.

To overcome these issues, data scientists have to gather and merge data from multiple sources, clean it, and enrich it by using external sources. (Moreover, it often happens that data is prepared for a certain purpose, but along the way, you discover something new, and the desired purpose changes.) These tasks are not simple ones; they require not only a significant amount of professional skill, but also a data management platform that allows the changes to be performed in a convenient way.

The issues related to the quality of the training examples determine a set of data management constraints and requirements for the infrastructure of the machine learning project. The problems can be summarized as follows:

- *Managing big data*—Gathering data from multiple data sources and merging it into a unified source of truth will generate a huge dataset, and as pointed out before, increasing the amount of (quality) data will improve the quality of the learning process. Chapter 2 considers the characteristics of a big data platform and shows how graphs can play a prominent role in taming such a beast.

- *Designing a flexible schema*—Try to create a schema model that provides the capabilities to merge multiple heterogeneous schemas into a unified and homogeneous data structure that satisfies the informational and navigational requirements. The schema should evolve easily according to changes in the purpose of the machine learning project. Chapter 4 introduces multiple data model schemas and best practices to model the data for several scenarios.

- *Developing efficient access patterns*—Fast data reads boost the performance, in terms of processing time, of the training process. Tasks such as feature extraction, filtering, cleaning, merging, and other preprocessing of the training data will benefit from the use of a data platform that provides multiple and flexible access patterns.

1.2.2 Performance

Performance is a complex topic in machine learning because it can be related to multiple factors:

- *Predictive accuracy*, which can be evaluated by using different performance measures. A typical performance measure for regression problems is the *root mean squared error* (RMSE), which measures the standard deviation[4] of the errors the system makes in its predictions. In other words, it looks at the difference between the estimated value and the known value for all the samples in the test dataset and calculates the average value. I present other techniques for measuring performance later in the book, when discussing the different algorithms. Accuracy depends on several factors, such as the amount of data available for training the model, the quality of the data, and the algorithm selected. As discussed in section 1.2.1, the data plays a primary role in guaranteeing a proper level of accuracy.

- *Training performance*, which refers to the time required to compute the model. The amount of data to be processed and the type of algorithm used determine the processing time and the storage required for computing the prediction model. Clearly, this problem affects more the algorithms that produce a model as a result of the training phase. For instance-based learners,[5] performance problems will appear later in the process, such as during prediction. In batch learning, the training time is generally longer, due to the amount of data to be processed (compared with the online learning approach, in which the algorithm learns incrementally from a smaller amount of data). Although in online learning, the amount of data to be processed is small, the speed at which it is crunched affects the capacity of the system to be aligned with the latest data available, which directly affects the accuracy of the predictions.

- *Prediction performance*, which refers to the response time required to provide predictions. The output of the machine learning project could be a static one-time report to help managers make strategic decisions or an online service for end users. In the first case, the time required to complete the prediction phase and compute the model is not a significant concern, so long as the work is completed in a reasonable time frame (that is, not years). In the second case, prediction speed does matter, because it affects the user experience and the efficacy of the prediction. Suppose that you are developing a recommendation engine that recommends products similar to what the user is currently viewing according to their interests. The user navigation speed is quite high, which implies the need for a significant number of predictions in a short time interval; only a few milliseconds are available to suggest something useful before the user proceeds to the next item. In this scenario, the speed of prediction is the key to success.

---

[4] *Standard deviation* is a measure expressing how much the members of a group differ from the mean value for the group.

[5] If concepts such as instance-based algorithms and batch learning are new to you, please refer to appendix A, which covers machine learning taxonomy.

These factors can be translated into multiple requirements for machine learning projects, such as fast access to the data source during training, high data quality, an efficient access pattern for the model to accelerate predictions, and so on. In this context, graphs could provide the proper storage mechanism for both source and model data, reducing the access time required to read data as well as offering multiple algorithmic techniques for improving the accuracy of the predictions.

1.2.3 Storing the model

In the model-based learner approach, the output of the training phase is a model that will be used for making predictions. This model requires time to be computed and has to be stored in a persistence layer to avoid recomputation at every system restart.

The model's structure is related directly to the specific algorithm or the algorithm class employed. Examples include

- Item-to-item similarities for a recommendation engine that uses a nearest-neighbor approach
- An item-cluster mapping that expresses how the elements are grouped in clusters

The sizes of the two models differ enormously. Consider a system that contains 100 items. As a first effort, item-to-item similarities would require 100 x 100 entries to be stored. Taking advantage of optimizations, this number can be reduced to consider only the top k similar items, in which case the model will require 100 x k entries. By contrast, item-cluster mapping requires only 100 entries; hence, the space required to store the model in memory or on disk could be huge or relatively modest. Moreover, as pointed out earlier, model access/query time affects global performance during the prediction phase. For these reasons, model storage management represents a significant challenge in machine learning.

1.2.4 Real time

Machine learning is being used more and more frequently to deliver real-time services to users. Examples run the full spectrum from simple recommendation engines that react to the user's last clicks all the way to self-driving cars that have been instructed not to injure a pedestrian crossing the street. Although the outcomes in case of failure are vastly different in these two examples, in both cases the capability of the learner to react quickly (or in an appropriate timely manner) to new stimuli coming from the environment is fundamental for the quality of the final results.

Consider a recommendation engine that provides real-time recommendations for anonymous users. This anonymity (the user is not registered or logged in) means that there is no long-term history of previous interactions—only short-term, session-based information provided by the use of cookies. This task is a complex one that involves multiple aspects and affects several phases of a machine learning project. The approaches taken could differ according to the learner(s) used, but the goals can be described as follows:

- *Learn fast.* The online learner should be able to update the model as soon as new data is available. This capability will reduce the time gap between events or generic feedback, such as navigational clicks or interaction with a search session and updating of the model. The more the model is aligned to the latest events, the more it is able to meet the current needs of the user.

- *Predict fast.* When the model is updated, the prediction should be fast—a maximum of a few milliseconds—because the user may navigate away from the current page or even change their opinion quite rapidly.

Both of these goals require algorithms that can align the model quickly, as well as a storage mechanism (in memory, on disk, or a combined version) that provides fast memorization and efficient access patterns.

1.3   Graphs

As stated at the introduction of this chapter, graphs provide models and algorithms that can heavily support machine learning projects. Even though a graph is a simple concept, it is important to understand how to represent it and how to use the main concepts around it. This section introduces the key elements of the graph world. If you already dominate such concepts, you can skip this part.

1.3.1   What is a graph?

A *graph* is a simple and quite old mathematical concept: a data structure consisting of a set of vertices (or nodes/points) and edges (or relationships/lines) that can be used to model relationships among a collection of objects. Legend says that the lazy Leonhard Euler first started talking about graphs in 1736. While visiting Königsberg in Prussia (now Kaliningrad, Russia), Euler didn't want to spend too much time walking in the city, which sat on both sides of the Pregel River and included two large islands that were connected to each other and to the two mainland portions of the city by seven bridges. Euler formalized the problem as planning a walk through the city that would cross each of those bridges once and only once. He proved that doing so was impossible, which led to the invention of graphs and graph theory [Euler, 1736]. So he stayed home instead. Figure 1.3 shows an old map of Königsberg and a representation of the graph that Euler used to prove his thesis.

More formally, a graph is a pair $G = (V, E)$, where V is a collection of vertices $V = \{V_i, i = 1,n\}$ and E is a collection of edges over V, $E_{ij} = \{(V_i, V_j), V_i \in V, V_j \in V\}$. $E \subseteq [V]^2$; thus, the elements of E are two-element subsets of V [Diestel, 2017].

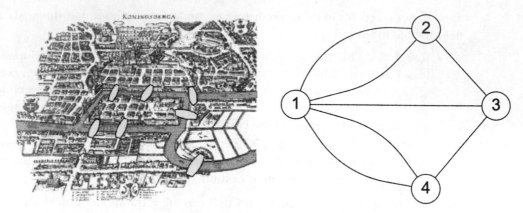

Figure 1.3   The bridges in Königsberg that led to the invention of graph theory

The simplest way to represent a graph is to draw a dot or a small circle for each vertex and then join two of those vertices by a line if they form an edge. This more formalized description is shown in figure 1.4.

Graphs can be directed or undirected, depending on whether a direction of traversal is defined on the edges. In *directed* graphs, an edge E_{ij} can be traversed from V_i to V_j but not in the opposite direction; V_i is called the *tail*, or *start node*, and V_j is called the *head*, or *end node*. In *undirected* graphs, edge traversals in both directions are valid. Figure 1.4 represents an undirected graph, and figure 1.5 represents a directed graph.

The arrow indicates the direction of the relationship. By default, edges in a graph are unweighted; thus, the corresponding graphs are said to be *unweighted.* When a weight—a numerical value used to convey some significance—is assigned to the edges, the graph is said to be *weighted.* Figure 1.6 shows the same graphs as figures 1.4 and 1.5 with a weight assigned to each edge.

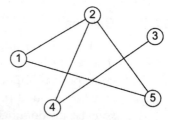

Figure 1.4   The undirected graph on V = {1, 2, 3, 4, 5} with edge set E = {(1,2), (1,5), (2,5), (2,4), (4,3)}

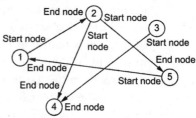

Figure 1.5   The directed graph on V = {1, ..., 5} with edge set E = {(1,2), (2,5), (5,1), (2,4), (3,4)}

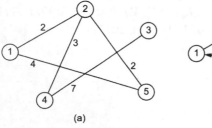

(a)

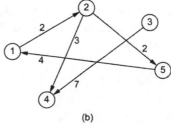

(b)

Figure 1.6   An undirected weighted graph (a) and a directed weighted graph (b)

Two vertices *x* and *y* of *G* are defined as *adjacent,* or *neighbors,* if {*x,y*} is an edge of *G*. The edge E_{ij} connecting them is said to be *incident on* the two vertices V_i and V_j. Two distinct edges *e* and *f* are adjacent if they have a vertex in common. If all the vertices of *G* are pairwise adjacent, *G* is *complete.* Figure 1.7 shows a complete graph in which each vertex is connected to all the other vertices.

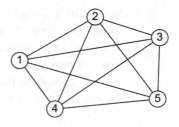

Figure 1.7   A complete graph in which each vertex is connected to all the others

One of the most important properties of a vertex in a graph is its *degree*, defined as the total number of edges incident to that vertex, which is also equal to the number of neighbors of that vertex. In the undirected graph of figure 1.4, for example, the vertex 2 has degree 3 (it has the vertices 1, 4, and 5 as neighbors); the vertices 1 (neighbors are 2, 5), 4 (neighbors are 2, 3), and 5 (neighbors are 1, 2) have degree 2, whereas vertex 3 has degree 1 (is connected only with 4).

In a directed graph, the degree of a vertex V_i is split into the *in-degree* of the vertex, defined as the number of edges for which V_i is their end node (the head of the arrow) and the *out-degree* of the vertex, which is the number of edges for which V_i is their start node (the tail of the arrow). In the directed graph of figure 1.5, vertices 1 and 5 have an in-degree and out-degree of 1 (they each have two relationships, one ingoing and one outgoing), vertex 2 has an in-degree of 1 and an out-degree of 2 (one ingoing relationship from 1 and two outgoing to 4 and 5), vertex 4 has an in-degree of 2 and an out-degree of 0 (two ingoing relationships from 2 and 3), and vertex 3 has an out-degree of 1 and in-degree of 0 (one outgoing relationship to 4).

The average degree of a graph is computed as follows,

$$ a = \frac{1}{N} \sum_{i=1..N} degree(Vi) $$

where *N* is the number of vertices in the graph.

A sequence of vertices with the property that each consecutive pair in the sequence is connected by an edge is called a *path*. A path with no repeating vertices is called a *simple path*. A *cycle* is a path in which the first and the last vertex coincide. In figure 1.4, [1,2,4], [1,2,4,3], [1,5,2,4,3], and so on are paths; in particular, the path of vertices [1,2,5] represents a cycle.

1.3.2   *Graphs as models of networks*

Graphs are useful for representing how things are either physically or logically linked in simple or complex structures. A graph in which we assign names and meanings to the edges and vertices becomes what is known as a *network*. In these cases, a graph is the mathematical model for describing a network, whereas a network is a set of relations between objects, which could include people, organizations, nations, items found in a Google search, brain cells, or electrical transformers. This diversity illustrates the great power of graphs and their simple structure (which also means that they require a small amount of disk storage capacity) that can be used to model[6] a complex system.

Let's explore this concept by using an example. Suppose that we have the graph shown in figure 1.8.

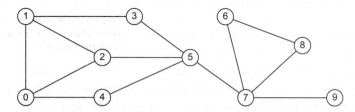

Figure 1.8   A nontrivial
generic graph

This graph, which is pure in the mathematical definition, can be used to model several types of networks, according to the types of edges and vertices:

- A *social network*, if the vertices are people and each edge represents any sort of relationship between humans (friendship, family member, coworker)
- An *informational network*, if the vertices are information structures such as web pages, documents, or papers and the edges represent logical connections such as hyperlinks, citations, or cross-references
- A *communication network*, if the vertices are computers or other devices that can relay messages and the edges represent direct links along which messages can be transmitted
- A *transportation network*, if the vertices are cities and the edges represent direct connections using flights or trains or roads

This small set of examples demonstrates how the same graph can represent multiple networks by assigning different semantics to edges and vertices. Figure 1.9 illustrates different types of networks.

Looking at figure 1.9, we can spot another interesting characteristic of graphs: they are highly communicative. Graphics are able to display information in a clear manner, which is why they are often used as *information maps*. Representing data as networks and using graph algorithms, it is possible to

- Find complex patterns
- Make them visible for further investigation and interpretation

When the power of machine learning is combined with the power of the human brain, it enables efficient, advanced, and sophisticated data processing and pattern recognition. Networks are useful for displaying data by highlighting connections

---

[6] In this context, the verb *model* is used in terms of representing a system or phenomenon in a simplified way. Modeling also aims at representing the data in such a way that it can be processed easily by a computer system.

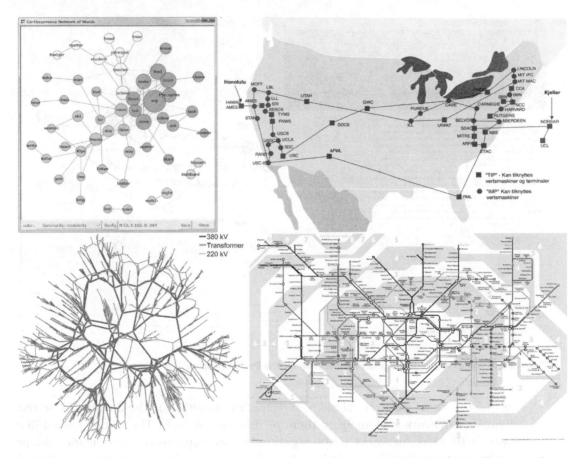

Figure 1.9   Clockwise from top left: a co-occurrence network,[7] ARPA network 1974,[8] London Tube network,[9] and electrical grid[10]

among elements. Newspapers and news websites are increasingly using networks, not only to help people navigate the data, but also as a powerful investigation tool. Recently (at the time of this writing), the Panama Papers[11] showcased the astonishing features of networks. The International Consortium of Investigative Journalists (ICIJ) analyzed the leaked financial documents to expose highly connected networks of offshore tax structures used by the world's richest elites. The journalists extracted the entities (people, organizations, and any sort of intermediaries) and relationships

---

[7] Higuchi Koichi—Co-occurrence screen shot of KH Coder (https://en.wikipedia.org/wiki/Co-occurrence_network).

[8] Yngvar—Symbolic representation of the ARPANET as of September 1974 (https://en.wikipedia.org/wiki/ARPANET).

[9] Courtesy Transport for London (http://mng.bz/G6wN).

[10] Paul Cuffe—Network diagram of a high voltage transmission system, showing the interconnection between the different voltage levels (https://en.wikipedia.org/wiki/Electrical_grid).

[11] https://panamapapers.icij.org.

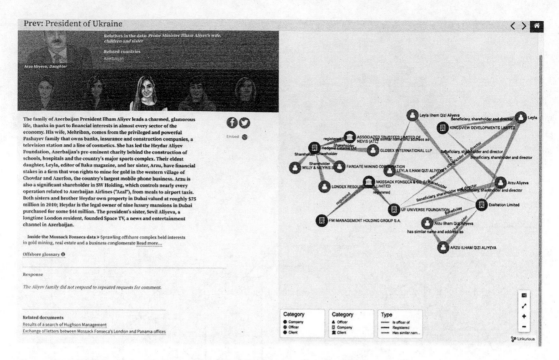

Figure 1.10   An example of the graph visualization for the Panama Papers

(protector, beneficiary, shareholder, director, and so on) from the documents, stored them in a network, and analyzed them by using visual tools. The results looked like figure 1.10. Here, networks, graph algorithms, and graph visualization made evident something that otherwise would have been impossible to discover by using traditional data mining tools.

A lot of interesting examples in this direction are also available in blog posts by Valdis Krebs,[12] an organization consultant who specializes in social network applications. His work contains examples of mixing graph-powered machine learning with the human mind, passing through graph visualization. Here, we consider one of the most famous examples.

The data in figure 1.11 was gathered from Amazon.com and represents its list of the top political books purchased in the United States in 2008 [Krebs, 2012]. Krebs employed network analysis principles to the data to create a map of books related to that year's presidential election. Two books are linked if they were often purchased by the same customer. These books are known as *also-bought* pairs (in that a customer who bought this book *also bought* that book).

---

[12] http://www.thenetworkthinkers.com.

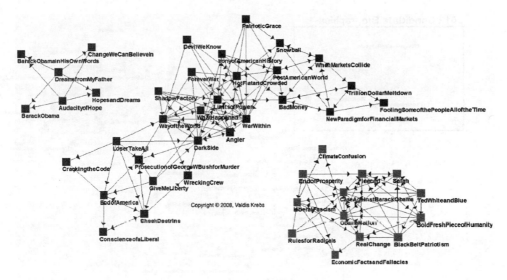

Figure 1.11 Network map of US political books in 2008 (Krebs, 2012)

There are three different and nonoverlapping clusters:

- An Obama cluster of books in the top-left corner
- A Democratic (blue) cluster in the middle
- A Republican (red) cluster in the bottom-right corner

In 2008, the US political climate was highly polarized. This fact is mirrored in Amazon's political-book data, with figure 1.11 showing a deep divide between conservative and liberal voters. There were no connections or intermediaries between red and blue books; each cluster was completely distinct from the others. As mentioned, there was a separate cluster of people reading biographies of presidential hopeful Barack Obama, but they were apparently not interested in reading or purchasing other political books.

Four years later, in 2012, the same analysis produced a network that appeared to be substantially different (figure 1.12). This network shows a lot of books that act as bridges between clusters. Moreover, potential voters appear to be reading books about both major candidates. The result is a more complex network that has no isolated clusters.

The example of a network of political books introduces an important aspect of networks. If a graph is a pure mathematical concept that lives in its own Platonic world,[13] networks, as abstractions of some concrete system or ecosystem, are subjected to *forces* that, acting on them, change their structure. We refer to these forces as *surrounding contexts*: factors that exist outside the vertices and edges of a network but nonetheless affect how the network's structure evolves over time. The nature of such contexts and

---

[13] Mathematical *Platonism* (http://mng.bz/zG2Z) is the metaphysical view that there are abstract mathematical objects whose existence is independent of us and our language, thought, and practices.

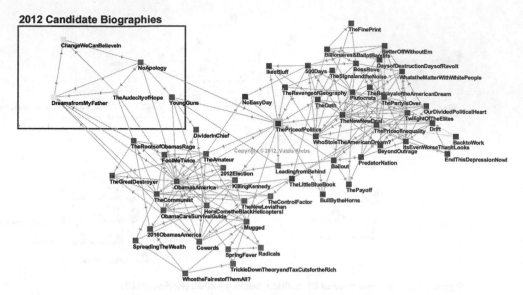

Figure 1.12   Network map of US political books in 2012 [Krebs, 2012]

the types of forces are specific to the kind of network. In social networks, for example, each individual has a distinctive set of personal characteristics, and similarities and compatibilities between two people's characteristics influence link creation or deletion [Easley and Kleinberg, 2010].

One of the most basic notions governing the structure of social networks is *homophily* (from the Greek, meaning love of the same): links in a social network tend to connect people who are similar. More formally, if two people have characteristics that match in a proportion greater than expected in the population from which they are drawn or the network of which they are part, they are more likely to be connected [Verbrugge, 1977]. The converse is also true: if two people are connected, they are more likely to have common characteristics or attributes. For this reason, our friends on Facebook (for example) don't look like a random sample of people, but are generally similar to us along ethnic, racial, and geographic dimensions; they tend to be similar to us in age, occupation, interests, beliefs, and opinions. This observation has a long history, with origins long before Mark Zuckerberg wrote his first line of code. The underlying idea can be found in the writings of Plato ("Similarity begets friendship") and Aristotle (people "love those who are like themselves"), as well as in folk propositions such as "Birds of a feather flock together." The homophily principle also applies to groups, organizations, countries, or any aspect of social units.

Understanding the surrounding contexts and the related forces that act on a network helps with machine learning tasks in multiple ways:

- Networks are conduits for both wanted and unwanted flows. Marketers are always trying to reach and persuade people. Personal contact is most effective, if one can find a way to start a snowball rolling. This concept is at the base of so-called *viral marketing*.

- Understanding such forces allows the prediction of how the network will evolve over time, and enables data scientists to proactively react to such changes or use them for specific business purposes.

- Findings in sociological and psychological disciplines point to the relevance of a person's social network in determining their tastes, preferences, and activities. This information is useful for building recommendation engines. One of the problems related to recommendation engines is the cold-start problem: you can't predict anything for a new user because you have no history for them. Social networks and the homophily principle can be used to make a recommendation based on the tastes of connected users.

1.4 The role of graphs in machine learning

Graphs are used to characterize interactions between objects of interest, to model simple and complex networks, or in general to represent real-world problems. Because they are based on a rigorous but straightforward formalism, they are used in many scientific fields, from computer science to historical sciences. We shouldn't be surprised to see them being widely used in machine learning as a powerful tool that can enable intuition and power a lot of useful features. Graph-based machine learning is becoming more common over time, transcending numerous traditional techniques.

Many companies of all sizes are using this approach to provide more advanced machine learning features to their customers. One prominent example is Google, which is using graph-based machine learning as the core of its Expander platform. This technology is behind many of the Google products and features you may use every day, such as reminders in your Gmail inbox or the latest image-recognition system in Google Photos.[14]

Building a graph-powered machine learning platform has numerous benefits, because graphs can be valuable tools not only for overcoming the previously described challenges, but also for delivering more advanced features that are impossible to implement without graph support.

Figure 1.13 illustrates the main contact points between machine learning and graphs, considering the goals of the different tasks.

---

[14] http://mng.bz/0rzz

DATA MANAGEMENT

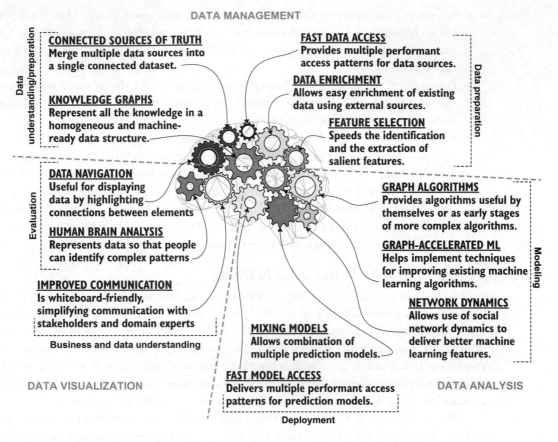

CONNECTED SOURCES OF TRUTH
Merge multiple data sources into
a single connected dataset.

KNOWLEDGE GRAPHS
Represent all the knowledge in a
homogeneous and machine-
ready data structure.

FAST DATA ACCESS
Provides multiple performant
access patterns for data sources.

DATA ENRICHMENT
Allows easy enrichment of existing
data using external sources.

FEATURE SELECTION
Speeds the identification
and the extraction of
salient features.

DATA NAVIGATION
Useful for displaying
data by highlighting
connections between elements

HUMAN BRAIN ANALYSIS
Represents data so that people
can identify complex patterns

IMPROVED COMMUNICATION
Is whiteboard-friendly,
simplifying communication with
stakeholders and domain experts

Business and data understanding

GRAPH ALGORITHMS
Provides algorithms useful by
themselves or as early stages
of more complex algorithms.

GRAPH-ACCELERATED ML
Helps implement techniques
for improving existing machine
learning algorithms.

NETWORK DYNAMICS
Allows use of social
network dynamics to
deliver better machine
learning features.

MIXING MODELS
Allows combination of
multiple prediction models.

FAST MODEL ACCESS
Delivers multiple performant access
patterns for prediction models.

Deployment

Data understanding/preparation

Evaluation

Data preparation

Modeling

DATA VISUALIZATION

DATA ANALYSIS

Figure 1.13   Graph-powered machine learning mind map

This mind map can be used to immediately visualize conceptually the role of graphs
in the machine learning panorama. In figure 1.13, graph features are grouped into
three main areas:

- *Data management*—This area contains the features provided by graphs that help
  machine learning projects deal with the data.
- *Data analysis*—This area contains graph features and algorithms useful for
  learning and predicting.
- *Data visualization*—This area highlights the utility of graphs as a visual tool that
  helps people communicate, interact with data, and discover insights by using
  the human brain.

The schema also shows the mapping between the graph-based techniques and the
phases in the CRISP-DM model.

1.4.1   Data management

Graphs allow the learning system to explore more of your data, to access it faster, and to clean and enrich it easily. Traditional learning systems train on a single table prepared by the researcher, whereas a graph-native system can access more than that table.

Graph-powered data management features include

- *Connected sources of truth*—Graphs allow you to merge multiple data sources into a single uniform, connected dataset ready for the training phase. This feature represents a great advantage by reducing data sparsity, increasing the amount of data available, and simplifying data management.
- *Knowledge graphs*—Building on the previous idea, knowledge graphs provide a homogeneous data structure for combining not only data sources, but also prediction models, manually provided data, and external sources of knowledge. The resulting data is machine ready and can be used during training, prediction, or visualization.
- *Fast data access*—Tables provide a single access pattern related to row and column filters. Graphs, on the other hand, provide multiple access points to the same set of data. This feature improves performance by reducing the amount of data to be accessed to the baseline minimum for the specific set of needs.
- *Data enrichment*—In addition to making it easy to extend existing data with external sources, the schemaless nature of graphs and the access patterns provided within graph databases help with data cleaning and merging.
- *Feature selection*—Identifying relevant features in a dataset is key in several machine learning tasks, such as classification. By providing fast access to data and multiple query patterns, graphs speed feature identification and extraction.

Connected sources of truth and knowledge graphs are valuable aids during the data understanding and data preparation phases of the CRISP-DM model, whereas fast data access, data enrichment, and feature selection are useful in the data preparation phase.

1.4.2   Data analysis

Graphs can be used to model and analyze the relationships between entities as well as their properties. This aspect brings an additional dimension of information that graph-powered machine learning can harness for prediction and categorization. The schema flexibility provided by graphs also allows different models to coexist in the same dataset.

Graph-powered data analysis features include

- *Graph algorithms*—Several types of graph algorithms, such as clustering, page ranking, and link analysis algorithms, are useful for identifying insights in the data and for analysis purposes. Moreover, they can be used as a first data preprocessing step in a more complex analysis process.

- *Graph-accelerated machine learning*—The graph-powered feature extraction discussed earlier is an example of how graphs can speed or improve the quality of the learning system. Graphs can help in filtering, cleaning, enriching, and merging data before or during training phases.
- *Network dynamics*—Awareness of the surrounding contexts and related forces that act on networks allows you not only to understand network dynamics, but also to use them to improve the quality of the predictions.
- *Mixing models*—Multiple models can coexist in the same graph, taking advantage of flexible and fast access patterns, provided that they can be merged during the prediction phase. This feature improves final accuracy. Moreover, the same model sometimes can be used in different ways.
- *Fast model access*—Real-time use requires fast predictions, which implies a model that can be accessed as fast as possible. Graphs provide the right patterns for these scopes.

Graph algorithms, graph-accelerated machine learning, and network dynamics are involved principally in the modeling phase because they are connected to the learning process more than other features. The deployment phase makes use of mixing models and fast model-access methods because they operate during the prediction stage.

1.4.3 *Data visualization*

Graphs have high communication power, and they can display multiple types of information at the same time in a way the human brain can easily understand. This feature is greatly important in a machine learning project, whether for sharing results, analyzing them, or helping people navigate the data.

Graph-powered data visualization features include

- *Data navigation*—Networks are useful for displaying data by highlighting connections between elements. They can be used both as aids to help people navigate the data properly and as powerful investigation tools.
- *Human-brain analysis*—Displaying data in the form of a graph unleashes the power of machine learning by combining it with the power of the human brain, enabling efficient, advanced, and sophisticated data processing and pattern recognition.
- *Improved communication*—Graphs—in particular, property graphs—are "whiteboard friendly," which means they are conceptually represented on a board as they are stored in the database. This feature reduces the gap between the technicalities of a complex model and the way in which it is communicated to the domain experts or stakeholders. Effective communication improves the quality of the final results because it reduces issues with the comprehension of the domain, the business goals, and the needs and constraints of the project.

Improved communication is particularly important during the business and data understanding phases, whereas data navigation and human-brain analysis are related mostly to the evaluation phase.

1.5   *Book mental model*

The mind map presented in this chapter helps you visualize easily where graphs fit in machine learning projects. It doesn't mean that, in all the projects, you will use graphs for everything listed there. In several examples throughout this book, graphs are used to overcome some issues or improve performance (both in terms of quality and quantity); it would be useful to have a mental model that helps you understand, by looking at a simple image, the role of graphs in that specific case.

The next schema organizes the key features (*contact points*) in the graph-powered machine learning mind map into the four main tasks of a machine learning workflow:

- *Managing the data sources*, which refers to all the tasks of gathering, merging, cleaning, and preparing the training dataset for the learning phase
- *Learning*, which involves the application of machine learning algorithms to the training dataset
- *Storing and accessing the model*, which includes approaches for storing the predictive model and the access pattern for providing predictions
- *Visualizing*, which refers to the way in which data can be visualized to support the analysis

These points are summarized in the mental map shown in figure 1.14.

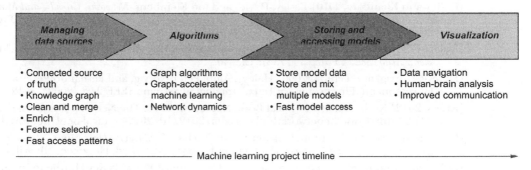

Figure 1.14   A mental model describing the four stages of a machine learning project

This figure will recur often in the book. The schema will help you figure out immediately where the current discussion fits in the project workflow.

This mental model presents the machine learning project from a process perspective and is the best way to figure out where you are in the life cycle. But it is also useful to think about the project from a broader, task-oriented perspective.

Summary

- Machine learning aims to develop computer programs that gain experience from sample data autonomously, converting it to expertise without being explicitly programmed.

- A machine learning project is not only a software project, but also a human process that involves a bunch of people with different skills and a lot of work. It requires a well-defined and systematic approach to succeed. CRISP-DM provides the formal project life cycle to drive such a project, helping deliver the right results.

- The challenges that any machine learning project has to deal with are related mostly to data management—either in terms of the training dataset or the prediction model—and the performance of the learning algorithm.

- Graphs are simple mathematical concepts that can be used to model and analyze complex networks. The surrounding context outside the network operates on it, determining how it evolves.

- Graphs and networks can empower machine learning projects in several ways, in three dimensions: data management, data analysis, and data visualization.

References

[Banko and Brill, 2001] Banko, Michele, and Eric Brill. "Scaling to Very Very Large Corpora for Natural Language Disambiguation." Proceedings of the 39th Annual Meeting on Association for Computational Linguistics (2001): 26–33.

[Diestel, 2017] Diestel, Reinhard. *Graph Theory.* 5th ed. New York: Springer, 2017.

[Easley and Kleinberg, 2010] Easley, David, and Jon Kleinberg. *Networks, Crowds, and Markets: Reasoning About a Highly Connected World.* Cambridge, UK: Cambridge University Press, 2010.

[Euler, 1736] Euler, Leonhard. "Solutio Problematis ad Geometriam Situs Pertinentis." *Comment. Acad. Sci. U. Petrop* 8 (1736): 128–40.

[Halevy, Norvig, and Pereria, 2009] Halevy, Alon, Peter Norvig, and Fernando Pereira. "The Unreasonable Effectiveness of Data." Intelligent Systems, IEEE 24:2 (2009): 8–12.

[Krebs, 2012] Krebs, Valdis. "Political Book Networks." TNT: The Network Thinkers, October 2012. http://www.thenetworkthinkers.com/2012/10/2012-political-book-network.html.

[Linoff and Berry, 2011] Linoff, Gordon S., and Michael J. A. Berry. *Data Mining Techniques: For Marketing, Sales, and Customer Relationship Management.* 3rd ed. Hoboken, NJ: Wiley, 2011.

[Lohr, 2014] Lohr, Steve. "For Big-Data Scientists, 'Janitor Work' Is Key Hurdle to Insights." New York Times, August 15, 2014. http://mng.bz/K4wn.

[Mihalcea et al., 2011] Mihalcea, Rada, and Dragomir Radev. *Graph-Based Natural Language Processing and Information Retrieval.* Cambridge, UK: Cambridge University Press, 2011.

[Russell and Norvig, 2009] Russell, Stuart J., and Peter Norvig. *Artificial Intelligence: A Modern Approach.* 3rd ed. Upper Saddle River, NJ: Pearson, 2009.

[Samuel, 1959] Samuel, Arthur L. "Some Studies in Machine Learning Using the Game of Checkers." *IBM Journal of Research and Development* 3:3 (July 1959): 210–229.

[Sculley, 2015] Sculley, D. , Gary Holt, Daniel Golovin, Eugene Davydov, Todd Phillips, Dietmar Ebner, Vinay Chaudhary, Michael Young, Jean-Francois Crespo, and Dan Dennison. 2015. "Hidden technical debt in Machine learning systems." In Proceedings of the 28th International Conference on Neural Information Processing Systems—Volume 2 (NIPS15). MIT Press, Cambridge, MA, USA, 2503–2511.

[Shalev-Shwartz and Ben-David, 2014] Shalev-Shwartz, Shai, and Shai Ben-David. *Understanding Machine Learning: From Theory to Algorithms*. Cambridge, UK: Cambridge University Press, 2014.

[Verbrugge, 1977] Verbrugge, Lois M. "The Structure of Adult Friendship Choices." *Social Forces* 56 (1977): 576–597.

[Wirth and Hipp, 2000] Wirth, R., and J. Hipp. "CRISP-DM: Towards a Standard Process Model for Data Mining." Proceedings of the Fourth International Conference on the Practical Application of Knowledge Discovery and Data Mining (2000): 29–39.

Graph data engineering

2

This chapter covers

- The main challenges related to big data as input to machine learning
- How to handle big data analysis with graph models and graph databases
- The shape and features of a graph database

Chapter 1 highlighted the key role played by data in a machine learning project. As we saw, training the learning algorithm on a larger quantity of high-quality data increases the accuracy of the model more than fine tuning or replacing the algorithm itself. In an interview about big data [Coyle, 2016], Greg Linden, who invented the now widely used item-to-item collaborative filtering algorithm for Amazon, replied:

> Big data is why Amazon's recommendations work so well. Big data is what tunes search and helps us find what we need. Big data is what makes web and mobile intelligent.

In the past few years, we have been experiencing an exponential growth in the amount of data generated in a broad range of sectors: information technology, industry, healthcare, the Internet of Things (IoT), and others. Back in 2013, IBM estimated that 2.5 quintillion bytes of data were being created every day—which meant that 90% of the data in the world had been created in the previous two years [Johnson, 2013]. This data comes from everywhere: sensors used to gather climate information, posts to social media sites, digital pictures and videos, purchase transaction records, and cell-phone GPS signals, to name a few sources. This data is *big data*. Figure 2.1 presents some statistics on the current volume of data generated from well-known applications or platforms every single minute [Domo, 2020].

What caused the dramatic change over the past decade was neither the explosion of the internet-using population nor the creation of new systems like data sensors. The change was generated by a greater awareness of the importance of data as a

Figure 2.1   The data generated every minute in 2020 (courtesy of Domo, Inc.)

source of knowledge. The strong desire to know more about users, customers, businesses, and organizations of all kinds generated new needs and new requirements for data collection, gathering, and processing. This desire has led to a change in the way in which data scientists collect data for analysis. Years ago, they had to scrabble around in unorganized and dirty data silos for data in some weird format. Now that companies have discovered the value hidden in the data they produce, data scientists lead the data generation and collection efforts.

Whereas a travel website once might have collected only the star ratings for a simple recommendation engine, for example, now it uses the informational power available in every user-provided review as a more detailed source of knowledge. This mental process generates a kind of virtuous loop (figure 2.2) that is capable of collecting more data in each cycle.

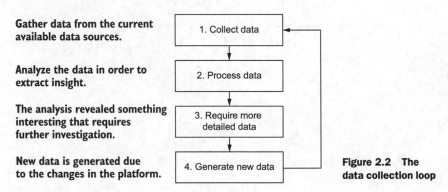

Gather data from the current available data sources.

1. Collect data

Analyze the data in order to extract insight.

2. Process data

The analysis revealed something interesting that requires further investigation.

3. Require more detailed data

New data is generated due to the changes in the platform.

4. Generate new data

Figure 2.2   The data collection loop

This unprecedented availability of data sources allows the machine learning practitioner to access a tremendous amount of data, available in multiple shapes. But if finding and accessing this data is relatively easy, storing and managing it can be a completely different story. Specifically, for machine learning processes, it is necessary to identify and extract the set of relevant *features*, or measurable properties or characteristics of the observed phenomenon. Choosing informative, discriminating, and independent features is a crucial step in creating effective learning algorithms, because these features define the input structure for the training phase of the algorithm and determine the accuracy of the predictions. The requirements for the list of features change according to the class of the algorithm, but in general terms, more accurate data generates better models. If you could run a forecast taking into account 300 factors rather than 6, you could predict demand better. With more factors, however, you run into the risk of overfitting.

The life cycle of the systems that analyze big data is composed of a series of steps that start with collecting data from multiple data sources. Specialized tools and frameworks are required to ingest the data from different sources into the defined big data storage. The data is stored in specific storage solutions (such as distributed filesystems or nonrelational databases) that are designed to scale. More formally, the steps required to accomplish these tasks can be summarized as follows:

- *Collect.* Data from multiple data sources is gathered and collected.
- *Store.* The data is stored in a proper way in a single (or occasionally more than one) easy-to-access data store so that it's ready for the next phases.
- *Clean.* The data is merged, cleaned, and (whenever possible) normalized by using a unified and homogeneous schema.
- *Access.* The data is available. Multiple views or access patterns are provided to simplify and speed access to the dataset that will be used for training purposes.

This chapter focuses on the last three of these four steps: storing, cleaning, and accessing the data. The chapter describes the main characteristics of big data and discusses the methods to handle it. Specific approaches based on graph models and graph databases are illustrated in detail, with best practices.

2.1   Working with big data

To tame the beast—to define the requirements for a big data analytics platform—we need to know it. Let's consider the underlying characteristics that qualify big data as *big*.

In 2001 (yes, more than 20 years ago!), Doug Laney, an analyst with the META Group, published a research note titled "3D Data Management: Controlling Data Volume, Velocity, and Variety" [Laney, 2001]. Although the term itself does not appear in Laney's note, a decade later the *three Vs*—volume, velocity, and variety—have become the generally accepted three defining dimensions of big data.

Later, another dimension was added: *veracity,* referring to the quality, accuracy, or truthfulness of the dataset or data source. With the advent of new, untrusted, and unverified data sources, such as the user-generated content in Web 2.0, the reliability and quality of the information gathered became a big concern, leading to the general acceptance of veracity as a valuable, important dimension of big data platforms. Figure 2.3 recaps the main aspects of the *four Vs,* which are described in more detail in the following sections.

Over the years, as the term *big data* began to gather a lot of attention and become trendy, analysts and tech journalists added more and more Vs to the list of dimensions. At last check, the count stood at 42 [Shafer, 2017]; as time goes on, more will undoubtedly be added.

We will focus on the original three Vs plus veracity, because they remain the most commonly accepted. These dimensions are used throughout the book to highlight the role of graph models and databases in managing large amounts of data.

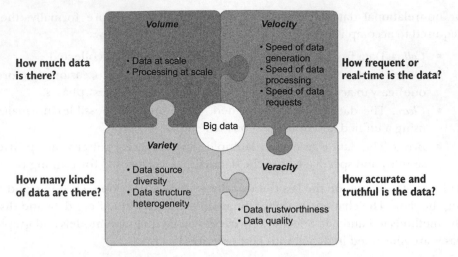

Figure 2.3   The four Vs of big data

2.1.1   *Volume*

The benefits gained from *volume* (figure 2.4)—the ability to process large amounts of information—are the main attractions of big data for machine learning. Having more and better data beats having better models. Simple mathematical operations can be incredibly effective given large amounts of data.

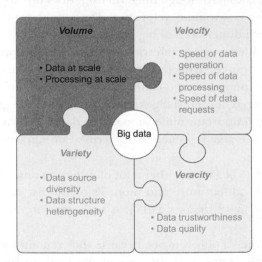

Figure 2.4   Volume in big data

Suppose that you would like to use a machine-learning approach that employs a wide variety of electronic health record (EHR) data to make real-time predictions regarding the kinds of treatments necessary for different symptoms. The amount of patient health data is increasing exponentially, which means that the amount of legacy EHR data is skyrocketing as well. According to Health Data Archiver [2018]:

A report from EMC and the research firm IDC offers a few imaginative ways at visualizing the health information proliferation, anticipating an overall increase in health data of 48 percent annually. The report pegs the volume of healthcare data at 153 Exabytes in 2013. At the projected growth rate, that figure will swell to 2,314 Exabytes by 2020.

As stated previously, the volume of data generated by modern IT, industrial, healthcare, IoT, and other systems is growing exponentially. This growth is driven on the one side by the lowering costs of data storage and processing architectures and on the other side by the capabilities (which create new needs) to extract valuable insights from the data—insights that improve business processes, efficiency, and the services delivered to end users or customers. Although there is no fixed threshold for a volume of data to be considered "big," typically the term denotes data of a scale that is "difficult to store, manage, and process using traditional relational database systems and data processing architectures" [Bahga and Madisetti, 2016].

Trying to continuously collect and analyze this big data has become one of the leading challenges across all of IT. The solutions to this challenge fall into two main categories:

- *Scalable storage*—*Scaling storage* generally refers to adding more machines and distributing the load (reads, writes, or both) over them. This process is known as scaling *horizontally*. Scalability can also be achieved through query or access mechanisms that provide multiple access points to a subset of the full data store, without the need to go over the entire dataset by using filters or index lookups. Native graph databases belong in this second group, which will be discussed in section 2.3.4.

- *Scalable processing*—The horizontal scaling of processing doesn't only mean having multiple machines executing tasks in parallel; it also requires a distributed approach to querying, a protocol for effective communication over the network, orchestration, monitoring, and a specific paradigm for distributed processing (such as divide and conquer, iterative, and pipeline).

During the data understanding and data preparation phases of the CRISP-DM life cycle (figure 2.5), it is necessary to identify the data sources and the size and structure of each phase to design the model and identify the database management system (DBMS) that will be used.

Graphs can provide valuable support during these phases, helping solve issues related to volume. A graph-based model enables data from multiple data sources to be stored in a single, highly connected, and

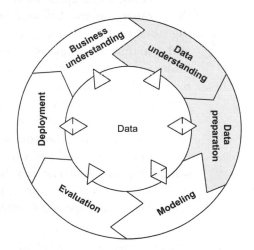

Figure 2.5 Data understanding and data preparation in the CRISP-DM model

homogeneous source of truth that offers multiple fast access patterns. Specifically, in a big data platform, graphs can help address volume issues by playing two roles:

- *Main data source*—In this case, the graph contains all data with the lowest granularity. The learning algorithms access the graph directly to perform their analyses. In this sense, according to the type of analysis, a proper graph database for big data has to expose
  - An indexing structure (common in other SQL and NoSQL databases) to support random access
  - An access pattern for accessing only a small portion of the graph, eliminating the need for complex index lookups or database scanning
- *Materialized views*—In this case, the graph represents a subset of the main dataset or an aggregated version of data in it, and is useful for analysis, visualization, or results communication. The views could be either the input or the output of an analytic process, and the global and local access patterns provided by the graph also provide valuable help in this case.

Section 2.2 illustrates these opposite approaches by presenting two example scenarios and their related implementations.

2.1.2 Velocity

Velocity (figure 2.6) refers to how rapidly data is generated, accumulated, or processed. Receiving and processing 1,000 search requests in an hour, for example, is different from receiving and processing the same number of requests in a fraction of a second. Some applications have strict time constraints for data analysis, including stock trading, online fraud detection, and real-time applications generally. The importance of data velocity has followed a pattern similar to that of volume. Problems previously restricted to particular segments of industry are now presenting themselves in a much broader setting.

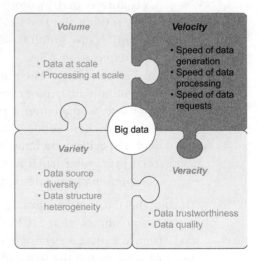

Figure 2.6   Velocity in big data

Suppose that you are working on a self-driving car. Each car that should drive autonomously has access to many sensors, such as cameras, radar, sonar, GPS, and lidar.[1] Each sensor generates a lot of data every second, as reported in table 2.1 [Nelson, 2016].

---

[1] "Lidar works much like radar, but instead of sending out radio waves it emits pulses of infrared light—aka lasers invisible to the human eye—and measures how long they take to come back after hitting nearby objects." Source: http://mng.bz/jBZ9.

Table 2.1 Data generated every second by a self-driving car's sensors

Sensor	Amount of data generated every second
Cameras	~20-40 MB/s
Radar	~10-100 KB/s
Sonar	~10-100 KB/s
GPS	~50 KB/s
Lidar	~10-70 MB/s

In such a scenario, the system you are designing should be able not only to process this data at speed, but also to generate a prediction as fast as possible to avoid, for example, hitting a pedestrian crossing the street.

But the velocity of the incoming data is not the only issue: it is possible to solve this problem by streaming fast-moving data into bulk storage for later batch processing, for example. The importance of velocity lies in the overall speed of the *feedback loop* (figure 2.7), which involves taking data from input to a decision:

> With a feedback loop, the system learns continuously by monitoring the effectiveness of predictions and retraining when needed. Monitoring and using the resulting feedback are at the core of machine learning.[2]

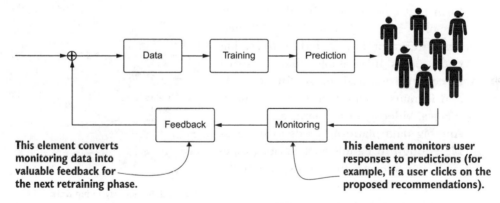

Figure 2.7 An example of a feedback loop

An advertisement for IBM makes the point that you wouldn't cross the road if all you had to go on was a five-minute-old snapshot of the traffic. This example illustrates the fact that at times, you won't be able to wait for a report to run or a Hadoop job to complete. In other words, "the tighter the feedback loop, the greater the competitive advantage" [Wilder-James, 2012]. Ideally, a real-time machine learning platform should be able to analyze data instantly, as it is generated.

---

[2] Puget and Thomas [2016].

Over time, machine learning architectural best practices have emerged for the management of big data. The Lambda Architecture [Marz and Warren, 2015], an architectural pattern for building real-time data-intensive systems, is one of these practices; we'll look at a graph-based implementation in section 2.2.1.

A data infrastructure that copes with velocity has to provide quick access to the necessary data, which could be a portion of the whole data. Suppose that you are going to implement a real-time recommendation engine for renting holiday homes. The learning algorithm uses the user's most recent clicks and searches to suggest houses. In such a case, the engine doesn't have to access the entire dataset; it checks the last N number of clicks or the clicks in the last X size of time frame and makes the prediction. A native graph database (described in section 2.3.4) maintains the list of relationships for each node. Starting from the last click—and having a proper graph model—the engine can navigate back through the previous clicks, following the relationships of each node back. This example is one illustration of the highly performant access to small portions of the dataset that graphs provide to serve velocity.

2.1.3   *Variety*

Variety (figure 2.8) has to do with the different types and nature of the data that is analyzed. Data varies in format, structure, and size; rarely does it present itself in a form that's perfectly ordered and ready for processing. Because it is collected from different and varied sources, big data comes in multiple shapes (structured, unstructured, or semistructured) and formats; it can include textual data, images, videos, sensor data, and so on. Any big data platform needs to be flexible enough to handle such variety, especially considering the data's potentially unpredictable evolution.

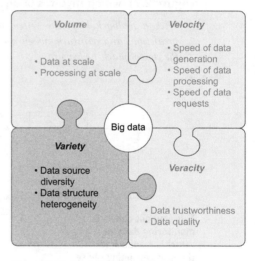

Figure 2.8   Variety in big data

Suppose that you would like to organize all of a company's knowledge, distributed across multiple data silos, to create a knowledge base for an insight engine.[3] The data could be in different formats, from well-structured relational databases to unstructured user reviews for products or services offered by the company, from PDF documents to social network data. To be processed by a machine learning platform, the data needs to be organized, stored, and managed as a unit in an homogeneous way.

---

[3] "Insight engines apply relevancy methods to describe, discover, organize and analyze data. This allows existing or synthesized information to be delivered proactively or interactively, and in the context of digital workers, customers or constituents at timely business moments." (Source: http://mng.bz/WrwX.)

Despite the popularity and familiarity of relational databases, they are no longer the destination of choice for big data platforms. Certain data types are better suited to certain types of databases than others. Social network relations, for example, are graphs by nature and so are well adapted to storage in graph databases such as Neo4j (described in appendix B), which make operations on connected data simple and efficient. Additionally, other classes of data fit well in a graph model due to the graph's versatility in managing connected data. As Edd Wilder-James [2012] puts it:

> *Even where there's not a radical data type mismatch, a disadvantage of the relational database is the static nature of its schemas. In an agile, exploratory environment, the results of computations will evolve with the detection and extraction of more signals. Semi-structured NoSQL databases meet this need for flexibility: they provide enough structure to organize data, but do not require the exact schema of the data before storing it.*

Graph databases, as a type of NoSQL database, are no exception. The simple model based on nodes and edges provides great flexibility in terms of data representation. Furthermore, new types of nodes and edges can appear later in the design process without affecting the previously defined model, giving graphs a high level of extensibility.

2.1.4 *Veracity*

Veracity (figure 2.9) is related to the quality and/or trustworthiness of the data collected. Data-driven applications can reap the benefits of big data only when the data is correct, meaningful, and accurate.

Suppose that you would like to create a recommendation engine for a travel website by using reviews. This type of engine is the new trend in the recommendation field, because reviews contain much more information than the old-style star ratings do. The issue resides in the veracity of such reviews:

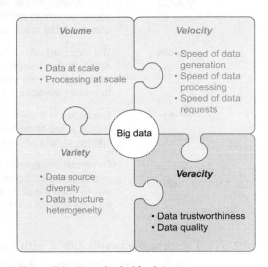

Figure 2.9 Veracity in big data

> *For online retailers, the war on the fake-review industry is now a major part of the business. Today, when a review is submitted to TripAdvisor, it goes through a tracking system that examines hundreds of different attributes, from basic data points, such as the IP address of the reviewer, to more detailed information, such as the screen resolution of the device that was used to submit the review.[4]*

As discussed in chapter 1, the combination of the quality and quantity of data in the training dataset directly affects the quality of the model inferred. The wrong data could affect the entire processing pipeline. The resulting predictions are definitely affected.

---

[4] Parkin [2018].

Data rarely comes wholly accurate and complete, which is why a cleaning process is necessary. This task can be accomplished with graph approaches. Specifically, graph access patterns make it easy to spot issues based on the relationships among elements. Moreover, by combining multiple sources in a single connected source of truth, it is possible to merge information, reducing data sparsity.

2.2   *Graphs in the big data platform*

Working with big data is a complex task. A machine learning platform requires access to data to extract insights and deliver predictive services to end users. Table 2.2 summarizes the challenges related to the four Vs, pairing each with the requirements for storing, managing, accessing, and analyzing data.

Table 2.2   Big data challenges

Big data Vs	Challenge
Volume	The database should be able to store large amounts of data, or the model defined should be able to compress the data through aggregation so that it can be accessed quickly but the model can perform all the analysis required.
Velocity	The data generally comes at a high rate, which requires a queue for decoupling the data ingestion from the storage mechanism. The ingestion rate and storage rate must be adequately balanced such that data can be transformed and stored quickly enough to prevent the accumulation of elements in the queue.
Variety	The database schema needs to be sufficiently flexible to store multiple kinds of information at the same time, using a model that allows the storage of all the current classes of data and any classes that could appear later in the project.
Veracity	The model designed and the database selected should allow for easy, fast navigation of data and identification of incorrect, invalid, or undesirable data. There should be a way to clean the data, allowing for the removal of noise. The task of simplifying and merging data (to combat data sparsity) should also be supported.

The approaches that deal with these challenges can be grouped into two categories: methodological (or design) and technological. To get the best from both, you should use them in combination, harmonically.

Methodological approaches include all the design decisions that involve the architecture, algorithms, storage schema, and cleaning methods; we'll look at these approaches in this section in relation to some specific, concrete scenarios.

Technological approaches include the design aspects related to the DBMS to use, the cluster configuration to adopt, and the reliability of the solution to deliver. Those aspects are considered in section 2.3.

Two scenarios are presented here to show the value of graphs in managing big data as part of the machine learning project pipeline and extracting insights from it. Whereas both scenarios are related to the methodological approach, they also highlight some aspects of the technological approach that will be discussed later in the chapter.

2.2.1 Graphs are valuable for big data

To see the value provided by graphs in the big data panorama, we'll explore a complex use case that requires processing a lot of data to be effective. In this case, the graphs can handle the problem complexity, providing a complete set of features to store, process and analyze the data. Consider the following scenario:

> You are a police officer. How can you track a suspect by using cellular tower data collected from the continuous monitoring of signals every phone sends to (or receives from) all towers it can reach?

An interesting article by Eagle, Quinn, and Clauset [2009] addresses the problem of using cellular tower data collected from the continuous monitoring signals that cell phones exchange with every tower in reach (figure 2.10). The goal of our example scenario is to use such monitoring data to create a predictive model that identifies location clusters relevant for the subject's life and that predicts and anticipates subsequent movements according to the subject's current location.

The relevant aspect of this approach is that it uses a graph as a way to collapse and organize the data available from cellular towers and creates a *graph-based materialized view* of the subject's movements. The resulting graph is analyzed with a graph algorithm that identifies clusters of positions. Those positions are used in the next algorithm in the analytics pipeline to build the position prediction model. At this stage of the book,

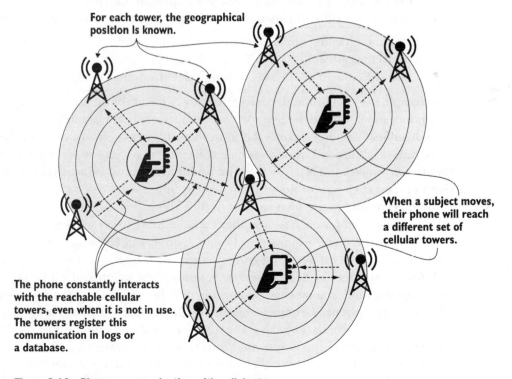

Figure 2.10 Phones communicating with cellular towers

I won't describe the details of the algorithms, because the purpose of the scenario is to show how to use a graph model as a valuable method for preprocessing and organizing the data in complex problems. The graph condenses information so that it is suitable for the analysis that has to be accomplished.

For the mental model in this scenario, a graph model is used to store and manage the data sources, a graph algorithm is used in the processing pipeline, and a graph is used to store the intermediate model (figure 2.11).

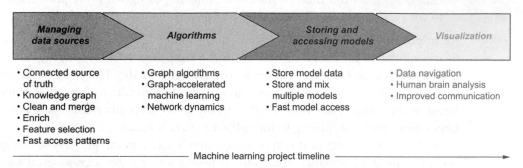

Figure 2.11   **The areas of our mental map relevant to this scenario**

Every mobile phone in use today has continuous access to information about the nearby cellular towers. Studying these data streams can provide valuable insight into a user's movements and behavior. The methods of obtaining continuous cellular tower data are

- Installing a logging application on the mobile phone itself to capture the continuous data stream
- Using (when available) raw continuous data from the cellular towers

This example uses a continuous data aggregation process for merging data about a specific phone, so we will use the first use case in this scenario to simplify the description.

Each subject's phone records the four nearest towers—the towers with the strongest signal—at 30-second intervals. Once collected, this data can be represented as a *cellular tower network* (CTN), in which the nodes are unique cellular towers. An edge exists between each pair of nodes that co-occur in the same record, and each edge is weighted according to the total amount of time the pair co-occurred over all records. A CTN is generated for each subject that includes every tower logged by the subject's phone during the monitoring period [Eagle, Quinn, and Clauset, 2009]. Figure 2.12 shows an example of the resulting graph for a single subject.

A node's strength is determined by summing the weights of all its edges. The nodes with the highest total edge weights identify the towers that are most often close to the subject's phone. Groups of highly weighted nodes, therefore, should correspond to locations where the subject spends a significant amount of time. Building on this idea, the graph can be segmented into clusters by means of different clustering algorithms. (We'll discuss these algorithms throughout the book, starting in part 2.) The result of such a clustering process will look something like figure 2.13.

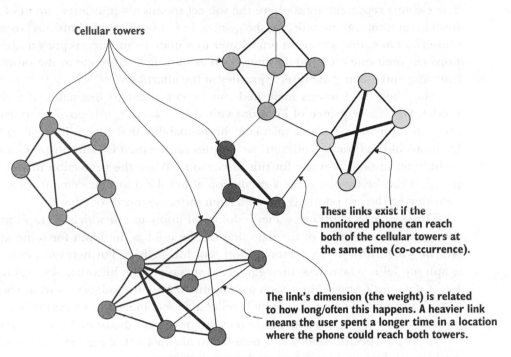

Cellular towers

These links exist if the monitored phone can reach both of the cellular towers at the same time (co-occurrence).

The link's dimension (the weight) is related to how long/often this happens. A heavier link means the user spent a longer time in a location where the phone could reach both towers.

Figure 2.12   A graph representation of a CTN for a single subject

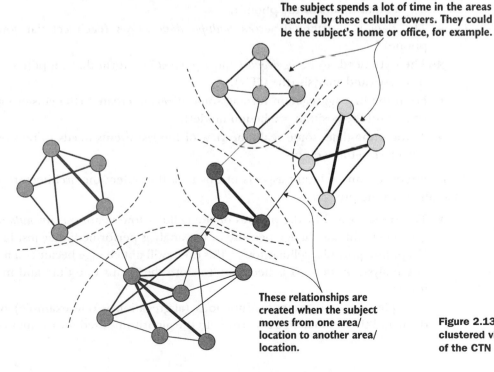

The subject spends a lot of time in the areas reached by these cellular towers. They could be the subject's home or office, for example.

These relationships are created when the subject moves from one area/ location to another area/ location.

Figure 2.13   A clustered view of the CTN

The clusters represent areas where the subject spends a significant amount of time—perhaps at home, at the office, at the gym, or in a shop. The relationships crossing the clusters, connecting a node in one cluster to a node in another, represent the transitions between one area and another, such as moving from home to the office in the morning and making the reverse journey in the afternoon.

The clusters of towers identified can be converted to the states of a dynamic model. Given a sequence of locations visited by a subject, it is possible to learn patterns in their behavior and calculate the probability that they will move to various locations in the future. (Different techniques can be used for this purpose, but these techniques are out of scope for this discussion.) When the prediction model is computed, it can be used to make a prediction about the future movements of a subject, considering the last positions revealed from the same source of data.

This scenario illustrates a methodological approach in which a graph model is used as a powerful view of the data that can be used as the input for some machine learning algorithm or as a visualization tool for analysts. Furthermore, because the graph model is schemaless, the aggregated version of the historical data (generally a lot of data, indicating things such as how much time the subject spent in each location) and the real-time value (which cellular towers the subject's phone is currently able to reach, which indicates where they are now) can coexist in the same model.

From the specific model, it is possible to abstract a more generic approach. The problem and process can be generalized as follows:

- There is a lot of data in the form of *events* (the monitoring data available from the cellular towers or the phone).
- The data is distributed across *multiple data sources* (each cellular tower or phone).
- The data needs to be *aggregated* and *organized* in a form that simplifies further processes and analysis (the CTN).
- From the first aggregation format, some *views* are created (the clustering algorithm and the position prediction model).
- At the same time, some real-time view of the last events needs to be stored to react fast to those events.

Some important and relevant aspects of this data flow affect the architecture of the machine learning project:

- The *events* logged by the phones or the cellular towers are *raw*, *immutable*, and *true*. They will not change because of the analysis performed; they just happen. If a phone pinged a cellular tower, this event will not change because of a different analysis purpose. It is necessary to store the events one time and in a raw format.
- Multiple *views* are created as functions (aggregation is one example) on this data, and they can change according to the algorithms used for the analysis.

- The *view-building process* generally operates on the entire set of data, and this process can take time, especially when it operates on a large amount of data, as in our specific use case. The time required to process the data creates a gap between the view of current events and previous events.
- To have a *real-time* view of the data, it is necessary to fill this gap. The real-time view requires a kind of streaming process that reads the events and appends information to the views.

The architectural problems described here are addressed by a specific type of architecture introduced by Nathan Marz and James Warren in their book *Big Data: the Lambda Architecture*, which "provides a general-purpose approach to implementing an arbitrary function on an arbitrary dataset and having the function return its results with low latency" [Marz and Warren, 2015]. The primary concept of the Lambda Architecture is to build big data systems as a series of three layers: batch, serving, and speed. The architectural schema is presented in figure 2.14.

Each layer satisfies a subset of the requirements and builds on the functionality provided by the other layers. Everything starts from the *query = function(all data)* equation. In our example scenario, the query is "Get the locations where the user spends a significant amount of time."

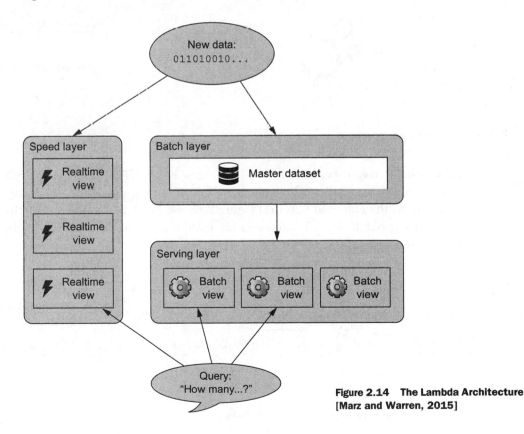

Figure 2.14 The Lambda Architecture [Marz and Warren, 2015]

Ideally, we could run the query on the fly to get the results. But this approach is generally infeasible due to the amount of data to be processed and the distributed nature of the data sources to be accessed. Moreover, it would take a huge amount of resources, would be unreasonably expensive, and would take a long time. It would also be unsuitable for any real-time monitoring and prediction system.

The most obvious alternative approach is to precompute the result of the query function or an intermediate value that speeds the final query results. Let's call the precomputed query result, final or intermediate, the *batch view*. Instead of computing the query on the fly, we compute the results from this view, which needs to be stored in a way that provides quick access to it. Then the previous equation is split as follows:

$$batch\ view = function(all\ data)$$

$$query = function(batch\ view)$$

All the data in the raw format is stored in the batch layer. This layer is also responsible for the raw-data access and the batch-view computation and extraction. The resulting views are stored in the serving layer, where they are indexed in a proper way and accessed during the queries (figure 2.15).

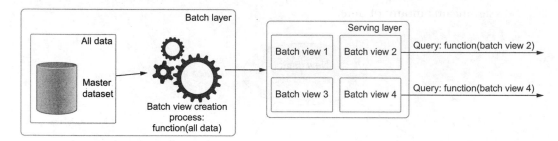

Figure 2.15   Batch-layer process

In the cellular tower scenario, a first batch view is the CTN, which is a graph. The function that operates on such a view is the graph cluster algorithm, which produces another view: the clustered network. Figure 2.16 shows the batch layer producing subject graphs as batch views. Those views are computed for each monitored subject as shown in figure 2.12.

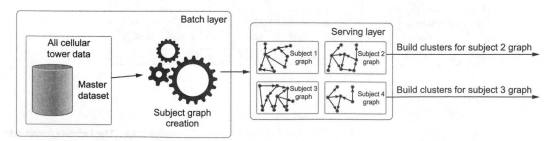

Figure 2.16   Batch-layer process producing graph views

The main difference in figure 2.16 is that both the batch views and, later, the real-time views are modeled as graphs. This modeling decision has advantages in several scenarios in which the graph representation not only allows us to reply faster to queries, but also facilitates analysis. In the specific scenario considered, the CTN is created as a function on all the raw cellular data collected and supports the clustering algorithm.

The serving layer is updated whenever the batch layer finishes precomputing a batch view. Because the precomputation requires time, the latest data to reach the architecture entry point is not represented in the batch view. The speed layer solves this issue by providing some views of the more recent data, filling the gap between the batch layer and the newest incoming data. These views could have the same structure as in the serving layer or could have a different structure and serve a different purpose.

One big difference between the two layers is that the speed layer only looks at recent data, whereas the batch layer looks at all the data. In the cellular tower scenario, the real-time views provide information on the last locations of the subjects and the transitions between locations.

The Lambda Architecture is *technology agnostic*; it is possible to use different approaches to realize it. The specific technologies you use might change depending on the requirements, but the Lambda Architecture defines a consistent approach to choosing those technologies and to wiring them together to meet your requirements.

The scenario presented in this section shows how to use a graph model as part of the serving layer and the speed layer. The resulting final architecture is represented in figure 2.17.

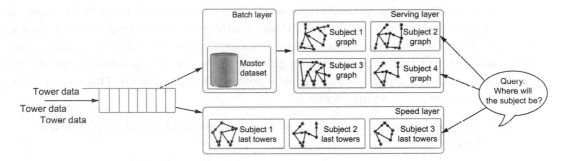

Figure 2.17 Graph-based Lambda Architecture

This new subtype of Lambda Architecture can be defined as a *graph-based Lambda Architecture*. In this scenario, the speed layer keeps track only of each subject's last known location based on the last cellular tower reached by their phone. Then this information is used in combination with the cluster and prediction model to predict where the subjects will be in the future.

The master dataset in the architecture in figure 2.17 can be stored by any database management system or a simple data store that can hold large amounts of data. The most commonly used data stores are HDFS, Cassandra, and similar NoSQL DBMSs.

In the specific scenario considered, it is necessary to merge the data before extracting it in the form of a graph. HDFS provides a basic access mechanism based on filesystem storage, whereas Cassandra offers more flexible access patterns. Storing the graph views requires a graph database. The generic features of such a database and a specific tool are presented in section 2.3.

The graph-based Lambda Architecture and the scenario described here are one example of the important role that graphs can play in the analysis of big data in the machine learning panorama. It is possible to use the same architecture in multiple scenarios, including the following:

- Analyzing bank transactions for fraud detection
- Analyzing server logs in a web farm to identify cyberattacks
- Analyzing phone-call data to identify communities of people

2.2.2 *Graphs are valuable for master data management*

In section 2.2.1, we saw how graphs can be used to create views on top of a master dataset (batch layer) or real-time (speed layer) representations of part of the data available. In that approach, the transactional data resides elsewhere: in the master dataset. That option is useful when you can query and perform analysis on aggregated data stored in the serving layer.

Other types of analysis, however, cannot be performed on an aggregate version of the data. Such algorithms require more detailed information to be effective; they need access to the fine-grained version of the data to accomplish their job. This type of analysis can also use the graph model as a way of representing connections and exploiting insights from the data. Understanding the connections between data and deriving meaning from these links provides capabilities not offered by classical analytical methods that are not based on graphs. In this case, the graph is the main source of knowledge, and it models a single connected source of truth. This concept brings us to our second example scenario:

> You would like to create a simple but effective fraud detection platform for banks.

Banks and credit card companies lose billions of dollars every year due to fraud. Traditional methods of fraud detection, such as rule-based, play an important role in minimizing these losses. But fraudsters constantly develop increasingly sophisticated methods to elude discovery, making rule-based fraud detection methods fragile and quickly obsolete. We will focus here on a specific type of fraud: credit card theft. Criminals can steal credit card data by using several methods, including Bluetooth-enabled data skimming devices installed in the cash machines, mass breaches by hackers, or small devices that cards are swiped through by checkout-line clerks or restaurant workers. People with legitimate access to your card can even surreptitiously jot down the relevant information on a piece of paper [Villedieu, n.d.]. To reveal such fraud, it is necessary to identify the source of the "breach": the credit card thieves and where they operate. By representing credit card transactions as a graph, we can look for commonalities and track down the point of origin of the scam. Unlike most other ways of looking at data, graphs are designed to express relatedness. Graph databases can uncover patterns that are difficult to detect using traditional representations such as tables.

Suppose that the transactions database in table 2.3 contains data for a subset of users who have disputed some transactions.

Table 2.3 User transactions[a]

User identifier	Timestamp	Amount	Merchant	Validity
User A	01/02/2018	$250	Hilton Barcelona	Undisputed
User A	02/02/2018	$220	AT&T	Undisputed
User A	12/03/2018	$15	Burger King New York	Undisputed
User A	14/03/2018	$100	Whole Foods	*Disputed*
User B	12/04/2018	$20	AT&T	Undisputed
User B	13/04/2018	$20	Hard Rock	Undisputed
User B	14/04/2018	$8	Burger King New York	Undisputed
User B	20/04/2018	$8	Starbucks	*Disputed*
User C	03/05/2018	$15	Whole Foods	Undisputed
User C	05/05/2018	$15	Burger King New York	Undisputed
User C	12/05/2018	$15	Starbucks	*Disputed*

[a] The merchant names here are used as examples to make the use case more concrete.

Starting from this transaction dataset, let's define a graph model. Each transaction involves two nodes: a person (the customer or user) and a merchant. The nodes are linked by the transactions themselves. Each transaction has a date and a status: *undisputed* for legitimate transactions and *disputed* for reported fraudulent transactions. Figure 2.18 presents the data as a graph.

In this figure, the red connections are disputed transactions; the others are regular (undisputed) transactions. The resulting graph is large, but the graph's dimensions do not affect the kind of analysis that has to be performed. Starting from such a dataset, the analysis steps to spot the source of fraud are

1 *Filter the fraudulent transactions.* Identify the people and the cards involved in the attack.
2 *Spot the point of origin of the fraud.* Search for all the transactions before the beginning of the fraud.
3 *Isolate the thieves.* Identify some common pattern, such as a merchant in common, that could be the origin of the fraud.

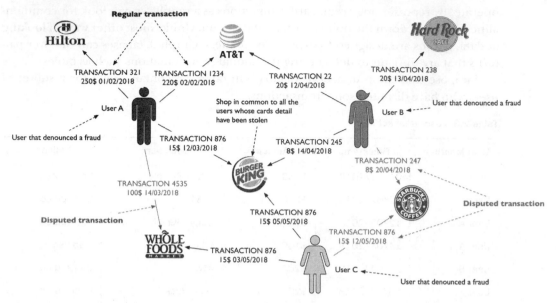

Figure 2.18   A sample graph model for credit card fraud detection

According to the sample graph in figure 2.18, the fraudulent transactions and the people affected are those listed in table 2.4.

Table 2.4   Disputed transactions

User identifier	Timestamp	Amount	Merchant	Validity
User A	14/03/2018	$100	Whole Foods	Disputed
User B	20/04/2018	$8	Starbucks	Disputed
User C	12/05/2018	$15	Starbucks	Disputed

All these transactions happened during different months. Now, for each user, let's consider all the transactions executed before the disputed transaction date, along with the related merchants. The results are shown in table 2.5.

Table 2.5   All transactions before the disputed transactions

User identifier	Timestamp	Amount	Merchant	Validity
User A	01/02/2018	$250	Hilton Barcelona	Undisputed
User A	02/02/2018	$220	AT&T	Undisputed
User A	12/03/2018	$15	Burger King New York	Undisputed
User B	12/04/2018	$20	AT&T	Undisputed
User B	13/04/2018	$20	Hard Rock	Undisputed

Table 2.5 All transactions before the disputed transactions *(continued)*

User identifier	Timestamp	Amount	Merchant	Validity
User B	14/04/2018	$8	Burger King New York	Undisputed
User C	03/05/2018	$15	Whole Foods	Undisputed
User C	05/05/2018	$15	Burger King New York	Undisputed

Let's group the transactions by store. The results are listed in table 2.6.

Table 2.6 Aggregated transactions

Merchant	Count	Users
Burger King New York	3	[User A, User B, User C]
AT&T	2	[User A, User B]
Whole Foods	1	[User A]
Hard Rock	1	[User B]
Hilton Barcelona	1	[User A]

It is clear from this table that the thief is operating in the Burger King restaurant, because it is the only merchant that all the users have in common and because in each case the fraud started after a transaction there.

Starting from this result, the analysis can go deeper, using the graph to search for other kinds of patterns, and the result can be converted to a decline action that will prevent any further transactions from the identified point of origin until further investigations have been conducted.

In this scenario, the graph is used to store the single source of truth on which analysis is performed by using graph queries. Furthermore, the data can be visualized in the form of a graph for further analysis and investigation. The related mental model is shown in figure 2.19.

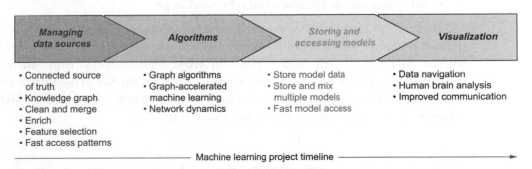

Figure 2.19 The areas of our mental map that are relevant to this scenario

This example is a simplification of the approach to revealing fraud, but it showcases some of the advantages of using a graph database for this type of analysis. Such advantages can be summarized as follows:

- *Multiple data sources,* such as geographical or GPS information, social network data, user personal profiles, family data, and the like, can be merged in a single connected source of truth.
- Existing data can be extended with *external sources of knowledge* (shop locations, people's addresses, and so on) or with *contextual information* (a new shop, other complaints, and the like) that can be used to improve the analysis.
- The same data model can support *several analysis techniques* (to uncover a fraud ring,[5] for example).
- Data can be *visualized as a graph* to speed the manual analysis.
- The analysis can be extended to multiple levels of interaction, considering *multiple hops.*
- The structure *simplifies the merging and cleaning* operation, thanks to the flexible access pattern provided by the graph model.

In the fraud-analysis scenario, the graph represents the *main source of knowledge* for the merged, cleaned, and extended data, on top of which the analysis is performed and based on which any decisions are taken. Unlike in the graph-based Lambda Architecture described in section 2.2.1, here the graph plays the role of master dataset and is the foundation for *master data management* (MDM)—the practice of identifying, cleaning, storing, and governing data [Robinson et al., 2015]. The key concerns of MDM include

- *Managing changes* over time as organizational structures change, businesses merge, and business rules evolve
- Incorporating *new sources* of data
- Supplementing existing data with *external data sources*
- Addressing the needs of reporting, compliance, and business intelligence consumers
- *Versioning data* as its values and schema change

MDM is not an alternative or modern version of data warehousing (DW), although the two practices have a lot in common. DW relates to the storage of historical data, whereas MDM deals with current data. An MDM solution contains the current and complete information for all business entities within a company. DW contains only historical data to be used for some kind of static analysis. When done correctly, MDM has numerous advantages that can be summarized as follows:

---

[5] According to the Law Dictionary (https://thelawdictionary.org/fraud-ring), a *fraud ring* is "an organization focused to defraud people. Forgery, false claims, stealing identities, counterfeiting checks and currencies are all fraudulent activities."

- *Streamlining* data sharing among personnel and departments
- *Facilitating* computing in multiple system architectures, platforms, and applications
- *Removing* inconsistencies and duplications from data
- *Reducing* unnecessary frustration when searching for information
- *Simplifying* business procedures
- *Improving* communication throughout the organization

Furthermore, when a proper MDM solution is in place, more faith can be placed in the data analysis provided by the system, improving confidence in decisions made based on that data. In this context, graph databases "don't provide a full MDM solution; they are, however, ideally suited to the modeling, storing, and querying of hierarchies, master data metadata, and master data models. Such models include type definitions, constraints, relationships between entities, and the mappings between the model and the underlying source systems" [Robinson et al., 2015].

Graph-based MDM has the following advantages:

- *Flexibility*—The data captured can be easily changed to include additional attributes and objects.
- *Extensibility*—The model allows the rapid evolution of the master data model in line with changing business needs.
- *Search capability*—Each node, each relationship, and all their related properties are search entry points.
- *Indexing capability*—Graph databases are naturally indexed by both relationships and nodes, providing faster access compared to relational data.

A graph-based MDM solution addresses different types of functionality. In the fraud-detection scenario, as well as in the rest of the book, it is considered to be part of the analytics/machine learning platform, operating as the main data source and extended by the resulting model, and represents an alternative approach to the graph-based Lambda Architecture.

Another interesting scenario in which graphs can represent MDM systems storing data for training purposes is in recommendation engines. In this case, the graph can store the user-to-item matrix containing the interaction history between the users and the items. We will consider this scenario in more detail in chapter 3.

2.3 Graph databases

Section 2.2 introduced some methodological machine learning approaches that use graphs and presented concrete examples illustrating how to use graphs as storage and access models for data to empower predictive analysis. To use such models in an optimal way, you have to be able to store, manipulate, and access the graphs in the same way that you are thinking about them in your data flow or in your algorithms. To accomplish this task, you need a graph database as a storage engine. A *graph database* allows you to store and manipulate entities (also known as *nodes*) and the connections between these entities (also known as *relationships*).

This section describes the technological aspects related to graph management. This perspective is relevant in a machine learning project's life cycle, during which you have to manipulate, store, and access real data. Furthermore, in most cases you will be working with big data, so you must take scalability issues into account. *Sharding* (splitting data horizontally across multiple servers) and *replication* (copying data across multiple servers, for high availability and scalability purposes) are presented in this context.

Many graph databases are available, but not all of them are *native* (built from the ground up for graphs); instead, they offer a graph "view" on top of a nongraph storage model. This nonnative approach leads to performance issues during storage and querying. A proper native graph database, on the other hand, uses a graph model for storing and processing the data, making graph manipulation straightforward, intuitive, and performant. The key differences are highlighted in section 2.3.4.

In many cases, I would say almost always, because you need at least a node identification, it could be useful to add some properties to nodes and relationships. In other words, it is necessary to group nodes in the same class. These "features" dramatically improve the expressivity and modeling capability of graph databases. Label property graphs, which satisfy such needs, are introduced in section 2.3.5.

Although all the theories, examples, and use cases presented in the book are completely technology agnostic, we will use Neo4j (introduced in appendix B) as the reference database platform. Neo4j not only is one of the few proper graph databases available that provide high performance, but also has a powerful and intuitive query language called Cypher.[6]

2.3.1   *Graph database management*

Using graphs in a machine learning project requires you to store, access, query, and manage each of those graphs. All those tasks fall into the general category of graph database management, as depicted in figure 2.20.

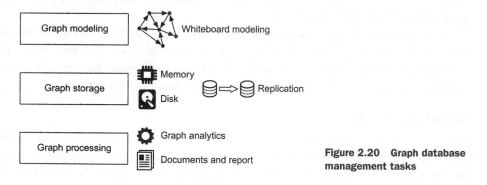

Figure 2.20   **Graph database management tasks**

---

[6] https://www.opencypher.org.

This figure shows the three main areas into which graph data management tasks can be grouped:

- *Graph modeling*—In general terms, the graph model is the fundamental abstraction behind a database system—the conceptual tool used to model representations of real-world entities and the relationships among them. One of the main features of a graph structure is the simplicity of modeling unstructured data. In graph models, the separation between schema and data is less substantial than in the classical relational model [Angles and Gutierrez, 2017]. At the same time, a graph model is flexible and extensible. The same aspect of reality or the same problem can be mapped in multiple ways in a graph model. Different models can address different problems from different perspectives, so defining the right model requires effort and experience. Luckily, the "schemaless" nature of graphs means that the models, even those defined during the early stages of a project, can be changed with relatively little effort. When you're using other types of NoSQL databases or relational databases, on the other hand, a change in the model could require a complete reingestion. This operation on big data could be an expensive task in terms of money, time, and effort. Furthermore, the model design affects the performance of all the queries and analyses performed on the graph. Therefore, modeling is a crucial aspect of data management. Some model examples are described earlier in this chapter, and in the following chapters, we'll look at several more use cases and consider the advantages and drawbacks of the related models.
- *Graph storage*—When the model is defined, the data has to be stored in a persistent layer. Graph DBMSs are specifically designed to manage graphlike data, following the common principles of database systems: persistent data storage, memory use, caching, physical/logical data independence, query languages, data integrity and consistency, and so on. Additionally, the graph database vendor has to take care of all the aspects related to scalability, reliability, and performance, such as backup, recovery, horizontal and vertical scalability, and data redundancy. We will discuss the key concepts of graph DBMSs in this section—specifically, those that affect the model and the way in which data is accessed during processing.
- *Graph processing*—These tasks involve frameworks (such as tools, query languages, and algorithms) for processing and analysis of graphs. Sometimes, processing graphs involves using multiple machines to improve performance. Some processing features, such as query languages and some graph access patterns, are available in the graph DBMS itself; others are available as algorithms or external platforms that have to be implemented on top of the graphs and the graph DBMS.

Graph processing is a wide-ranging topic, and the related tasks can be broadly divided into a few categories. Özsu [2015] presents an interesting way of classifying graph processing, organized along three dimensions: graph dynamism, algorithm types, and workload types (see figure 2.21).

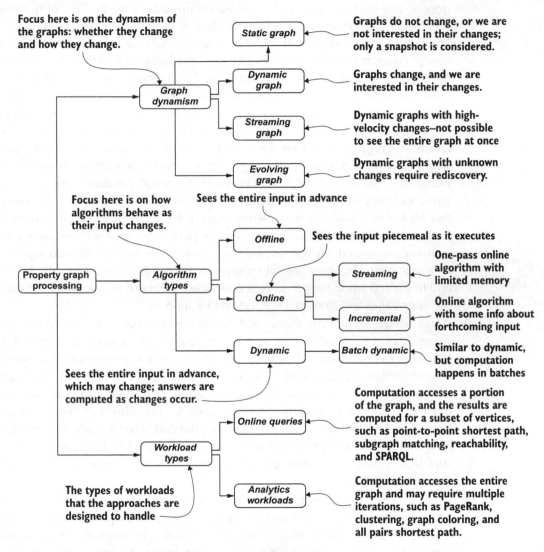

Figure 2.21   Property graph processing taxonomy [Özsu, 2015]

The complex topic of graph processing will be discussed throughout the book. Different algorithms will be presented along the way, and they will be mapped with specific real use cases or examples of applications in which they are useful for extracting insight.

2.3.2 Sharding

Looking at big data applications from a pure data storage perspective, the main four Vs challenges are

- *Volume*—The volume of the data involved is so large that it is hard to store the data on a single machine.
- *Velocity*—A single machine can serve only a limited number of concurrent users.

Although vertical scaling—such as the addition of increased compute, storage, and memory resources—can be a temporary solution to handle large volumes of data and improve the response times for multiple concurrent users, the data will ultimately become too large to be stored on a single node and the number of users too high to be handled by a single machine.

In NoSQL databases, one common scaling technique is *sharding*, wherein a large dataset is split, and subsets are distributed across several shards on different servers. These shards or subsets are typically replicated across multiple servers to increase reliability and performance. A *sharding strategy* determines which data partitions should be sent to which shards. Sharding can be accomplished by means of various strategies, which can be managed by the application or by the data storage system itself.

For aggregate-oriented data models like key/value, column family, and document databases [Fowler and Sadalage, 2012], in which the only way to express relations between concepts is to aggregate them in a single data entry by using a value or document, this solution is a sensible one. In these kinds of stores, the key used to retrieve any item is known and stable, and the lookup mechanism is fast and predictable, so directing clients that want to store or retrieve data to an appropriate shard is straightforward [Webber, 2011].

The graph data model, on the other hand, is highly relationship-oriented. Each node can be related to any other node, so a graph doesn't have predictable lookups. It also has a highly mutable structure: with few new links and few new nodes, the connection structure can change heavily. In these circumstances, sharding a graph database isn't straightforward at all [Webber, 2011]. One possible solution would be to colocate related nodes and, hence, the related edges. This solution would boost graph traversal performance, but having too many connected nodes on the same database shard would make it heavily loaded, because a lot of data will be on the same shard, making it unbalanced. Figures 2.22 and 2.23 illustrate these concepts.

Figure 2.22 shows how navigating a graph could involve crossing shard boundaries multiple times. This cross-shard traversal is quite expensive because it requires many network hops, resulting in substantially increased query times. In such a scenario, performance degrades quickly compared with the case in which everything happens on the same shard.

In figure 2.23, to overcome this issue, the related nodes are stored on the same shard. The graph traversal is faster, but the load between shards is highly unbalanced. Moreover, due to the dynamic nature of the graphs, graphs and their access patterns

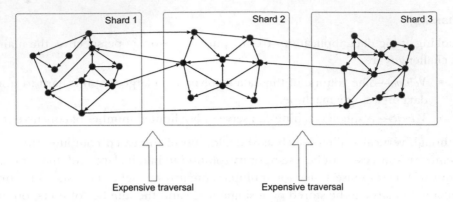

Figure 2.22   Traversing relationships belonging to different shards

can change rapidly and unpredictably at run time, making this solution inconvenient to implement in practice.

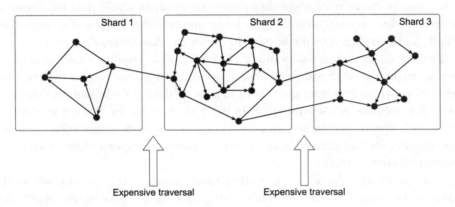

Figure 2.23   Overloading of a single shard (shard 2)

With these challenges in mind, generally speaking, there are three techniques for scaling a graph database:

- *Application-level sharding*—In this case, the sharding of the data is accomplished on the application side by using domain-specific knowledge. For a global business, nodes that relate to North America can be created on one server, and nodes that relate to Asia can be on another. This application-level sharding needs to understand that nodes are stored on physically different databases. The sharding could also be based on the different types of analysis or graph processing that have to be performed on the data. In such cases, each shard contains all the data required to execute the algorithm, and some nodes can be replicated across the shards. Figure 2.24 depicts application-level sharding.

- *Increasing the RAM or using cache sharding*—It is possible to scale the server vertically, adding more RAM so that the entire database fits in memory. This solution makes graph traversal extremely fast but is both unreasonable and unfeasible for large databases. In such a case, it is possible to adopt a technique called *cache sharding* to maintain high performance with a dataset whose size far exceeds the main memory space. Cache sharding isn't sharding in the traditional sense, because we expect the full dataset to be present on each database instance. To implement cache sharing, we partition the workload undertaken by each database instance to increase the likelihood of hitting a warm cache for a given request. (Warm caches in graph databases like Neo4j are highly performant.)
- *Replication*—It is possible to achieve scaling of the database by adding more (identical) copies of the database that act as followers with read-only access. When you pair a relatively high number of follower database instances, which are read-only, with a small number of leader database instances, you can achieve a high level of scalability. This technique is described in section 2.3.3. Other techniques have other pros and cons and are not discussed here.

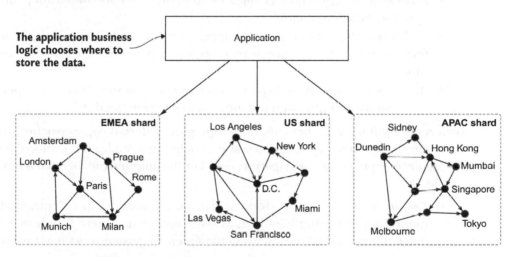

Figure 2.24 Application-level isolation of sharding

Sharding is more effective in some situations than others. Consider the two scenarios discussed earlier in this chapter:

- In the cellular tower monitoring example, a graph is created for each monitored subject, so the machine learning model produces multiple independent graphs that will be accessed in isolation. In this case, application-level sharding is an easy task, because all the graphs are isolated. To generalize, in the graph-based Lambda Architecture scenario, with multiple graph views created on the same dataset, we can store the views in multiple database instances because they are accessed in an independent way.

- In the second use case (fraud detection), sharding would be tricky because in theory, all the nodes can be connected. Some heuristics can be applied to reduce cross-shard traversals or to keep nodes that are frequently accessed together on the same shard, but the graph cannot be divided into multiple isolated graphs, as in the preceding use case. In such cases, another option is to use replication to scale read performance and speed analysis time.

2.3.3   *Replication*

As discussed in section 2.3.2, sharding is a difficult task in graph databases. A valid alternative for dealing with velocity and availability is replication. Data replication consists of maintaining multiple copies of data, called *replicas*, on separate computers. Replication has several purposes [Özsu and Valduriez, 2011]:

- *System availability*—Replication removes single points of failure from distributed DBMSs by making data items accessible from multiple sites. Even when some cluster nodes are down, data should remain available.
- *Performance*—Replication enables us to reduce latency by locating the data closer to its access points.
- *Scalability*—Replication allows systems to grow, both geographically and in terms of the number of access requests, while maintaining acceptable response times.
- *Application requirements*—As part of their operational specifications, applications may require multiple copies of the data to be maintained.

Data replication has clear benefits, but keeping the different copies synchronized is a challenge. A fundamental design decision in defining a replication protocol is where the database updates are first performed. The techniques can be characterized as follows:

- *Centralized* if they first perform updates on a master copy. Centralized techniques can be further identified as *single master* when there is only one master database copy for all data items in the system or *primary copy* when there can be a single master copy for each data item or set of data items.
- *Distributed* if they allow updates to any replica.

Due to the highly connected nature of graphs, implementing either a centralized primary copy protocol or a distributed protocol is a difficult task, one that has serious effects on performance and data consistency, to mention the most critical. (In a graph, a data item could be a node or a relation; a relation is connected, by definition, to two other data items—the nodes—and a node is likely to be connected to other nodes through multiple relationships.) Therefore, we will focus on the centralized approach with a single master, also described as *master/slave replication*.

In this approach, one node is designated as the authoritative source for the data, known as the *master*, *leader*, or *primary*. This node is typically responsible for processing any updates to that data. Even when slaves accept writes, those operations have to pass through the master to be performed (see figure 2.25). Master/slave replication is most useful if most of your data access is reads. By adding more slave nodes and routing all read requests to the slaves, you can scale horizontally. Master/slave replication also provides read resilience: if the master fails, the slaves can still handle requests [Fowler and Sadalage, 2012].

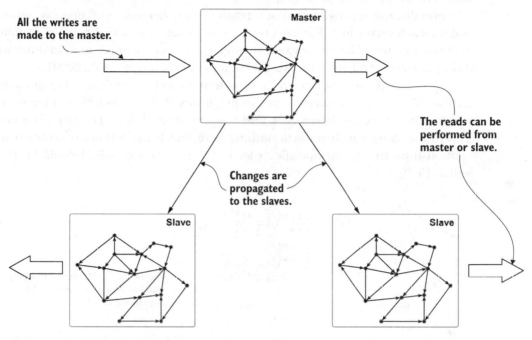

Figure 2.25   Replication based on a master/slave protocol

Most implementations of the master/slave protocol allow the slaves to vote for a different master if the current one becomes unavailable. This approach increases the availability and the reliability of the architectural stack. Specifically, in a machine learning project, replication allows the reading load to be spread across all the nodes during the training or prediction phase.

2.3.4   Native vs. non-native graph databases

This book describes multiple methods by which graphs can empower a machine learning project. To get the greatest advantages from the graph model, a proper graph DBMS for storing, accessing, and processing graphs is required. Although the model itself is reasonably consistent across the multiple graph database implementations, there are numerous ways to encode and represent graphs in the different database engines. A DBMS built to handle graph workloads across the entire computing stack, from the query language to the database management engine and filesystem and from clustering to backup and monitoring, is called a *native graph database* [Webber,

2018]. Native graph databases are designed to use the filesystem in a way that not only understands but also supports graphs, which means that they are both highly performant and safe for graph workloads. In more detail, a native graph DBMS exhibits a property called *index-free adjacency,* which means that each node maintains direct references to its adjacent nodes. The adjacency list representation is one of the most common ways to represent sparse graphs.

Formally, this representation of a graph $G = (V, E)$ consists of an array Adj of lists, one for each vertex in V. For each vertex u in V, the adjacency list $Adj[u]$ contains all the vertices v for which there exists an edge E_{uv} between u and v in E. In other words, $Adj[u]$ consists of all the vertices adjacent to u in G [Cormen et al., 2009].

Figure 2.26(b) is an adjacency list representation of the undirected graph in figure 2.26(a). Vertex 1, for example, has two neighbors, 2 and 5, so $Adj[1]$ is the list [2,5]. Vertex 2 has three neighbors, 1, 4, and 5, so $Adj[2]$ is [1,4,5]. The other lists are created in the same way. It is worth nothing here that because there is no order in the relationships, there is no specific order in the lists; hence, $Adj[1]$ could be [2,5] as well as [5, 2].

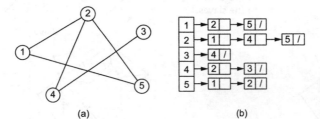

Figure 2.26 An undirected graph (a) and the related representation as an adjacency list (b)

Similarly, figure 2.27(b) is an adjacency list representation of the directed graph in figure 2.27(a). Such a list is visualized as a linked list, in which each entry contains a reference to the next one. In the adjacency list for node 1, the first element is node 2 and the reference to the next one is the element for node 5. This approach is one of the most common for storing the adjacency list, because it makes addition and deletion elements efficient. In this case, we consider only the outgoing relationships, but we can do the same thing with the ingoing relationships; what is important is to choose a direction and keep it consistent during the creation of the adjacency list. Here, vertex 1 has only one outgoing relationship, with vertex 2, so $Adj[1]$ will be [2]. Vertex 2 has two outgoing relationships, with 4 and 5, so $Adj[2]$ is [4,5]. Vertex 4 has no outgoing relationships, so $Adj[4]$ is empty ([]).

If G is a directed graph, the sum of the lengths of all the adjacency lists is $|E|$. Because every edge can be traversed in a single direction, E_{uv} will appear only in $Adj[u]$. If G is an undirected graph, the sum of the lengths of all the adjacency lists is $2 \times |E|$ because if E_{uv} is an undirected edge, E_{uv} appears in $Adj[u]$ and $Adj[v]$. The memory required by an adjacency list representation of either a directed or an undirected graph is directly proportional to $|V| + |E|$.

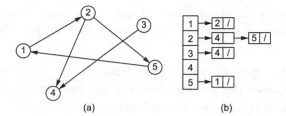

Figure 2.27 A directed graph (a) and the related representation as an adjacency list (b)

Adjacency lists can be easily adapted to represent weighted graphs by storing the weight w of the edge E_{uv} in $Adj[u]$. The adjacency list representation can be similarly modified to support many other graph variants too. In such a representation, each node acts as a microindex of other nearby nodes, which is much cheaper than using global indexes. A traversal across a relationship in such a database has a constant cost, irrespective of the size of the graph. Also, the query times are independent of the total size of the graph; instead, they are proportional to the amount of the graph searched.

The alternative is a *nonnative graph database*. Database systems in this group can be divided into two categories:

- Those that layer a graph API on top of an existing different data structure, such as key/value, relational, document, or column-based store
- Those that claim multimodel semantics, in which one system purportedly can support several data models

A nonnative graph engine is optimized for an alternative storage model, such as columnar, relational, document, or key/value data, so when dealing with graphs, the DBMS has to perform costly translations to and from the primary model of the database. Implementers can try to optimize these translations through radical denormalization, but this approach typically leads to high latency when querying graphs. In other words, a nonnative graph database will realistically never be as performant as a native graph database, for the simple reason that a translation process will need to occur.

Understanding how the graph is stored helps you define a better model for it, with the "native" nature of a graph database being of critical importance. This concern is also related to the philosophy of this book:

> In a successful machine learning project, every single aspect is relevant to delivering an efficient and performant service to the end user, where *efficient* and *performant* mean not only *accurate*, but also *delivered on time*.

A highly accurate recommendation on a website, for example, would be useless if it were delivered in 30 seconds, as by that time, the user would likely be elsewhere.

Sometimes, those aspects are considered to be secondary. A common misconception is that nonnative graph technology is good enough. To better understand the value of native support for graphs in the database engine for a machine learning project, let's consider an example:

You have to implement a supply chain management system that analyzes the entire chain to predict stock inventory issues in the future or spot bottlenecks in the network.

The Council of Supply Chain Management Professionals defines supply chain management as a system that "encompasses the planning and management of all activities involved in sourcing and procurement, conversion, and all logistics management activities."[7] A supply chain can be modeled naturally as a graph, as shown in figure 2.28.

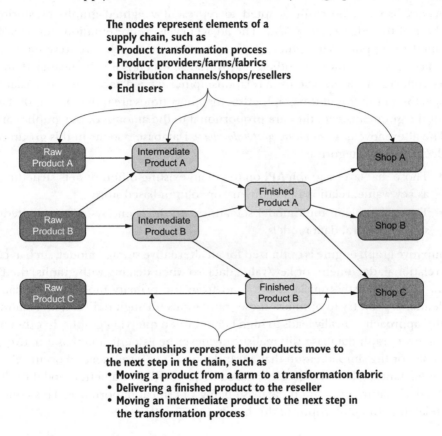

The nodes represent elements of a supply chain, such as
• **Product transformation process**
• **Product providers/farms/fabrics**
• **Distribution channels/shops/resellers**
• **End users**

The relationships represent how products move to the next step in the chain, such as
• **Moving a product from a farm to a transformation fabric**
• **Delivering a finished product to the reseller**
• **Moving an intermediate product to the next step in the transformation process**

Figure 2.28 A supply chain network

Suppose now that you would like to store the supply chain network model by using a relational database or any other NoSQL database based on a global index. The relationships among the elements in the supply chain are represented in figure 2.29.

As the figure shows, these indexes add a layer of indirection to each traversal, thereby incurring greater computational cost. To find where Finished Product B will

---

[7] http://mng.bz/8WXg.

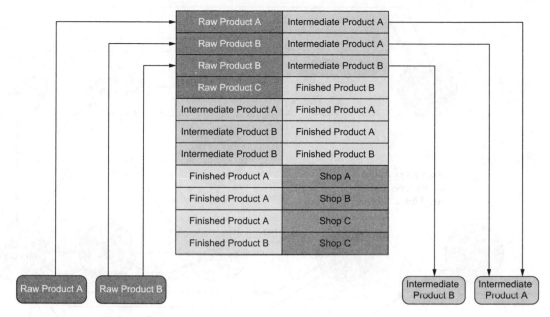

Figure 2.29 A tabular model for storing the supply chain network

be delivered after it is produced, we first have to perform an index lookup, at cost $O(\log n)$,[8] and then get the list of next nodes in the chain. This approach may be acceptable for occasional or shallow lookups, but it quickly becomes intolerably expensive when we reverse the direction of the traversal (to find the intermediate steps required to create Finished Product C, for example).

Suppose now that Raw Product A is contaminated or not available anymore, and we need to find all the products or shops affected by this issue in the chain. We would have to perform multiple index lookups, one for each node that is potentially in the chain between the raw product and the shops, which makes the cost far more onerous. Whereas it's $O(\log n)$ cost to find out where Finished Product B will be delivered, to traverse a network of m steps, the cost of the indexed approach is $O(m \log n)$. In a native graph database with index-free adjacency, bidirectional joins are effectively pre-computed and stored in the database as relationships, as represented in figure 2.30.

In this representation, the cost of traversing a relationship when you have the first node is $O(1)$, and it points directly to the next node. Performing the same traversal required before now costs only $O(m)$. Not only is the graph engine faster, but also, the cost is related only to the number of hops (m), not to the total number of relationships (n).

---

[8] Big O notation "is used in computer science to describe the performance or complexity of an algorithm. Big O specifically describes the worst-case scenario, and can be used to describe the execution time required or the space used (e.g. in memory or on disk) by an algorithm." (Source and examples: https://mng.bz/8WXg.)

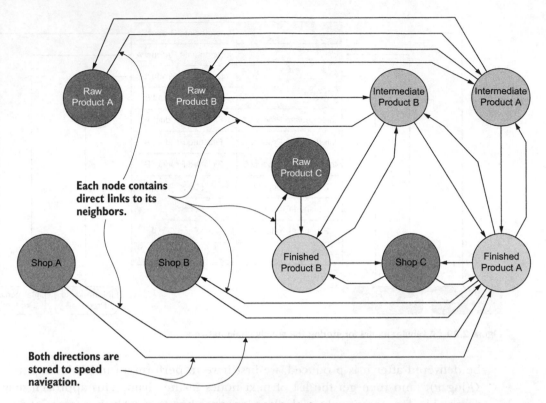

Figure 2.30   A graph-based model for storing the supply chain

Imagine now that you need to identify bottlenecks in the supply chain. One common method for spotting bottlenecks in a network is *betweenness centrality*, which is a measure of centrality (importance) in a graph based on calculating the shortest paths between nodes. The betweenness centrality of each node is the number of these shortest paths that pass through that node. In this case, the impact of the cost for an index lookup—$O(\log n)$—will greatly affect the performance of the computation.

To recap, a native graph architecture provides many advantages that make it generally superior to a nonnative approach to managing graph models. We can summarize these advantages as follows:

- *"Minutes-to-milliseconds" performance*—Native graph databases handle connected data queries far faster than nonnative graph databases. Even on modest hardware, native graph databases can easily handle millions of traversals per second between nodes in a graph on a single machine and many thousands of transactional writes per second [Webber, 2017].

- *Read efficiency*—Native graph databases can deliver constant-time traversals with index-free adjacency without complex schema design and query optimizations. The intuitive property graph model eliminates the need to create any additional, and often complex, application logic to process connections [Webber, 2017].

- *Disk space optimization*—To improve performance in a nonnative graph, it is possible to denormalize indexes or create new indexes, or a combination of both, affecting the amount of space required to store the same amount of information.
- *Write efficiency*—Index denormalization also has an effect on write performance because all those additional index structures need to be updated as well.

2.3.5   Label property graphs

A graph that is used to represent complex networks needs to store more information than a simple list of nodes and relationships. Fortunately, such simple structures can be easily extended to a richer model that contains additional information in the form of *properties*. Moreover, it is necessary to group nodes in classes and assign different types of relationships. Graph database management system providers introduced the *label property graph model* to tie a set of attributes to graph structures (nodes and relationships) and add classes or types to nodes and relationships. This data model allows a more complex set of query features typical of any DBMS, such as projection, filtering, grouping, and counting.

According to the openCypher project,[9] a label property graph is defined as "a directed, vertex-labeled, edge-labeled multigraph with self-edges,[10] where edges have their own identity." In a property graph, we use *node* to denote a vertex and *relationship* to denote an edge.

A property graph has the following properties (defined here in a platform-agnostic way):

- The graph consists of a set of *entities*. An entity represents either a *node* or a *relationship*.
- Each entity has an *identifier* that uniquely identifies it across the entire graph.
- Each relationship has a *direction*, a *name* that identifies the type of the relationship, a *start node*, and an *end node*.
- An entity can have a set of *properties*, which are typically represented as key/value pairs.
- Nodes can be tagged with one or more *labels*, which group nodes and indicate the roles they play within the dataset.

A property graph is still a graph, but the communication capability is greater than before. In figure 2.31, you can easily see that the `Person` Alessandro `WORKS_FOR` the `Company` GraphAware, as do Michal and Christophe. `name` is a property of the node `Person`, whereas `start_date` and `role` are properties of the relationship `WORKS_FOR`. The nationality of each `Person` is stored by using the relationship `HAS_NATIONALITY`, which connects the `Person` to a `Country` node that has the property `name` for storing the country name.

---

[9] http://mng.bz/N8wX.

[10] *Self-edges*, also referred to as *sloops*, are edges for which the source and destination nodes are the same.

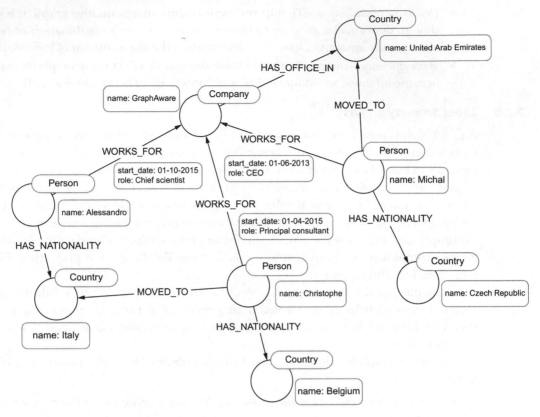

Figure 2.31   A property graph

As for relational databases, there are some best practices or style rules for defining a model for a graph. The labels for nodes should be singular, for example, because they represent a specific entity, whereas the names for the relationships should reflect the direction.

Obviously, there are multiple ways of representing the same set of concepts. In the model in figure 2.31, for example, the nationality could be stored as a property of the Person nodes. The schema could change significantly according to the specific needs in terms of access patterns and the underlying graph DBMS. In the second part of the book, we will see numerous models for representing data, each of which has a specific scope and satisfies the specific requirements of a target application.

Summary

This chapter described some of the challenges related to management of data in machine learning applications and discussed how the graph model helps address those challenges. The chapter illustrated specific aspects by using concrete scenarios with descriptions of related graph-based solutions. You learned the following:

- How to deal with the four Vs of big data: volume, velocity, variety, and veracity. The four-Vs model describes the multiple critical issues a machine learning project faces with regard to the scale of the data, the speed at which new data is generated, the heterogeneous structure the data exhibits, and the uncertainty of the sources.

- How to design architectures to handle large amounts of training data. Predictive analytics and machine learning in general require a lot of data during training to be effective. Having more data beats having better models.

- How to design a proper Lambda Architecture that uses graphs for storing views of the data. In the graph-based Lambda Architecture, a graph model is used for storing and accessing batch or real-time views. These views represent precomputed and easy-to-query views of the master dataset, which contains raw data in the original format.

- How to plan your MDM platform. MDM is the practice of identifying, cleaning, storing, and, (most important) governing data. In this context, graphs expose more flexibility and extensibility in the data model together with search and index capabilities.

- How to decide on a replication schema suitable for the application's needs. Replication allows you to distribute the analysis load across multiple nodes in the graph data cluster.

- What the advantages of a native graph database are. Native graph DBMSs are preferable to non-native ones because they map the model (the way in which we represent the data) one-to-one with the underlying data engine. Such a match allows better performance.

References

[Angles and Gutierrez, 2017] Angles, Renzo, and Claudio Gutierrez. "An Introduction to Graph Data Management." arXiv, December 29, 2017. https://arxiv.org/pdf/1801.00036.pdf.

[Bahga and Madisetti, 2016] Bahga, Arshdeep and Madisetti, Vijay K. *Big Data Science & Analytics: A Hands-on Approach.* VPT, 2016.

[Corbo et al., 2017] Corbo, Jacomo, Carlo Giovine, and Chris Wigley. "Applying Analytics in Financial Institutions' Fight Against Fraud." McKinsey & Company, April 2017. http://mng.bz/xGZq.

[Cormen et al., 2009] Cormen, Thomas H., Charles E. Leiserson, Ronald L. Rivest, and Clifford Stein. *Introduction to Algorithms.* 3rd ed. Boston, MA: MIT Press, 2009.

[Coyle, 2016] Coyle, Peadar. "Interview with a Data Scientist: Greg Linden." October 12, 2016. http://mng.bz/l2Zz.

[Domo, 2020] Domo. "Data Never Sleeps 8.0." 2020. https://www.domo.com/learn/data-never-sleeps-8.

[Eagle, Quinn and Clauset, 2009] Eagle, Nathan, John A. Quinn, and Aaron Clauset. "Methodologies for Continuous Cellular Tower Data Analysis." *Proceedings of the 7th International Conference on Pervasive Computing* (2009): 342–353.

[Fowler and Sadalage, 2012] Fowler, Martin, and Pramod J. Sadalage. *NoSQL Distilled: A Brief Guide to the Emerging World of Polyglot Persistence.* Upper Saddle River, NJ: Addison-Wesley Professional, 2012.

[Gatner, 2017] Gartner. "Master Data Management (MDM)." 2017. http://mng.bz/rmZE.

[Health Data Archiver, 2018] Health Data Archiver (2018). "Health Data Volumes Skyrocket, Legacy Data Archives on the Rise." August 3, 2018. http://mng.bz/dmWz.

[Johnson, 2013] Johnson, Ralph. "2.5 Quintillion Bytes of Data Created Every Day. How Does CPG & Retail Manage It?" IBM Consumer Products Industry blog, April 24, 2013.

[Jürgensen, 2016] Jürgensen, Knut. "Master Data Management (MDM): Help or Hindrance?" Redgate Hub, May 16, 2016. http://mng.bz/ZY9j.

[Laney, 2001] Laney, Douglas. "3D Data Management: Controlling Data Volume, Velocity, and Variety." META Group, February 6, 2001. http://mng.bz/BKzq.

[Marz and Warren, 2015] Marz, Nathan, and James Warren. *Big Data.* Shelter Island, NY: Manning, 2015.

[Nelson, 2016] Nelson, Patrick. "Just One Autonomous Car Will Use 4,000 GB of Data/Day." *Network World,* December 7, 2016. http://mng.bz/Paw2.

[Özsu, 2015] Özsu, M. Tamer. "An Overview of Graph Data Management and Analysis." ADC PhD School, June 4, 2015. http://hkbutube.lib.hkbu.edu.hk/st/display.php?bibno=b3789774.

[Özsu and Valduriez, 2011] Özsu, M. Tamer, and Patrick Valduriez. *Principles of Distributed Database Systems.* 3rd ed. New York: Springer, 2011.

[Parkin, 2018] Parkin, Simon. "The Never-Ending War on Fake Reviews." *The New Yorker,* May 31, 2018. http://mng.bz/1A5Z.

[Puget and Thomas, 2016] Puget, Jean Francois, and Rob Thomas. "A Practical Guide to Machine Learning: Understand, Differentiate, and Apply." IBM Community, August 16, 2016.

[Robinson et al., 2015] Robinson, Ian, Jim Webber, and Emil Eifrem. *Graph Databases.* 2nd ed. Sebastopol, CA: O'Reilly, 2015.

[Rund, 2017] Rund, Ben. "The Good, The Bad, and the Hype About Graph Databases for MDM." *TDWI,* March 14, 2017. http://mng.bz/VG9r.

[Shafer, 2017] Shafer, Tom. "The 42 V's of Big Data and Data Science." Elder Research, April 1, 2017. https://www.elderresearch.com/blog/42-v-of-big-data.

[Shannon, 2017] Shannon, Sarah. "Updated for 2018: The Five Vs of Big Data: How Can They Help Your Business?" XSI, February 15, 2017.

[Villedieu, n.d.] Villedieu, Jean. "GraphGist: Credit Card Fraud Detection." Neo4j. http://mng.bz/A1GE.

[Webber, 2011] Webber, Jim. "On Sharding Graph Databases." World Wide Webber, February 16, 2011.

[Webber, 2017] Webber, Jim. "The Motivation for Native Graph Databases." May 17, 2017. http://mng.bz/2z6N.

[Webber, 2018] Webber, Jim. "Not All Graph Databases Are Created Equal: Why You Need a Native Graph." *Database Trends and Applications,* March 7, 2018. http://mng.bz/RKwn.

[Wilder-James, 2012] Wilder-James, Edd. "What Is Big Data? An Introduction to the Big Data Landscape." https://www.oreilly.com/ideas/what-is-big-data.

[Woodie, 2016] Woodie, Alex. "Neo4j Pushes Graph DB Limits Past a Quadrillion Nodes." Datanami, April 26, 2016. http://mng.bz/Jvwp.

Graphs in machine learning applications

This chapter covers

- The role of graphs in the machine learning workflow
- How to store the training data and the resulting model properly
- Graph-based algorithms for machine learning
- Data analysis with graph visualization

In this chapter, we'll explore in more detail how graphs and machine learning can fit together, helping to deliver better services to end users, data analysts, and business-people. Chapters 1 and 2 introduced general concepts in machine learning, such as

- The different phases that compose a generic machine learning project (specifically, the six phases of the CRISP-DM model: business understanding, data understanding, data preparation, modeling, evaluation, and deployment)
- The importance of data quality and quantity to create a valuable and meaningful model that can provide accurate predictions
- How to handle a large amount of data (big data) by using a graph data model

Here, we will see how to harness the power of the graph model as a way of representing data that makes it easy to access and analyze, as well as how to use the "intelligence" of the machine learning algorithms based on graph theory. I would like to start this chapter with an image (figure 3.1) that represents the path of converting raw data, available from multiple sources, to something that is more than simple knowledge or insight: *wisdom*.

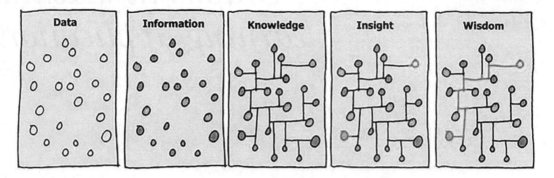

Figure 3.1   Illustration by David Somerville, based on the original by Hugh McLeod[1]

We are flooded by data. Data is *everywhere*. News, blog posts, emails, chats, and social media are only a few examples of the multiple data-generating sources that surround us. Furthermore, at the time of this writing, we are in the middle of the IoT explosion: today even my washing machine sends me data, reminding me that my pants are clean, and my car knows when I should stop driving and take a coffee break.

Data by itself is useless, though; on its own, it doesn't provide any value. To make sense of the data, we have to interact with it and organize it. This process produces information. Turning this information into knowledge, which reveals relationships between information items—a quality change—requires further effort. This transformation process connects the dots, causing previously unrelated information to acquire sense, significance, and logical semantics. From knowledge come insight and wisdom, which are not only relevant, but also provide guidance and can be converted to actions: producing better products, making users happier, reducing production costs, delivering better services, and more. This action is where the true value of data resides, at the end of a long transformation path—and machine learning provides the necessary intelligence for distilling value from it.

Figure 3.1 to some extent represents the learning path for the first part of this chapter:

1 Data and information are gathered from one source or several sources. This data is the training data, on top of which any learning will happen, and it is managed in the form of a graph (section 3.2).

---

[1] www.smrvl.com.

2 When the data is organized in the form of knowledge and represented by a proper graph, machine learning algorithms can extract and build insights and wisdom on top of it (section 3.3).

3 The prediction models that are created as the result of the training of a machine learning algorithm on the knowledge are stored back in the graph (section 3.4), making the wisdom inferred permanent and usable.

4 Finally, the visualization (section 3.5) shows the data in a way that the human brain can easily understand, making the derived knowledge, insights, and wisdom accessible.

This path follows the same mental model used in chapters 1 and 2 to highlight and organize the multiple ways in which graphs can be a valuable help in your machine learning project (figure 3.2).

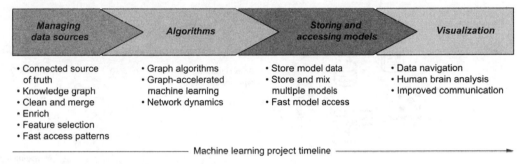

Figure 3.2 Mental model for graph-powered machine learning

We'll start from the beginning of this mental model and go in deep, showing some of the many techniques and approaches that use graph features to deliver a better machine learning project.

3.1 Graphs in the machine learning workflow

The CRISP-DM model described in chapter 1 [Wirth and Hipp, 2000] allows us to define a generic machine learning workflow that can be decomposed, for the purposes of our discussion, into the following macro steps:

1 Select the data sources, gather data, and prepare the data.
2 Train the model (the learning phase).
3 Provide predictions.

Some learning algorithms don't have a model.[2] The instance-based algorithms don't have a separate learning phase; they use the entries in the training dataset during the prediction phase. Although the graph approach can be a valid support even in these cases, we will not consider these algorithms in our analysis.

---

[2] See appendix A for details.

Furthermore, quite often, data needs to be visualized in multiple shapes to achieve the purpose of the analysis. Hence, visualization plays an important role as a final step that completes the machine learning workflow, allowing further investigation.

This workflow description matches the mental model in figure 3.2, which you will see throughout this chapter (and the book) to help you figure out where we are in each step. In such a workflow, it is important to look at the role of the graph from operational, task-based, and data-flow perspectives. Figure 3.3 illustrates how data flows from the data sources through the learning process to end users in the form of visualizations or predictions.

The process starts, as usual, from the data available. Different data sources will have different schemas, structure, and content. Generally, the data used in machine learning applications can be classified as big data. (We discussed working with big data in chapter 2.) This data must be organized and managed before the learning process

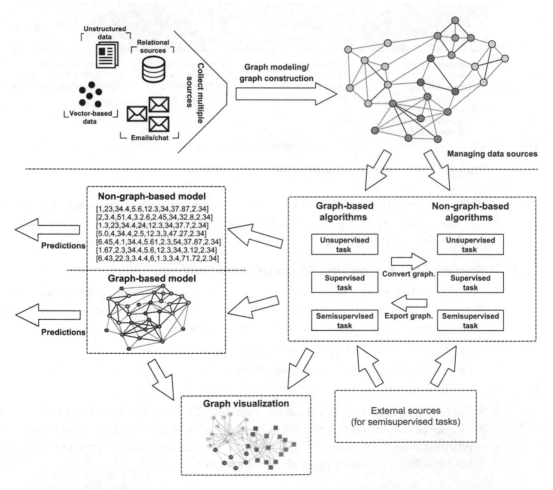

Figure 3.3   The role of graphs in the machine learning workflow

can begin. The graph model helps with data management by creating a connected and well-organized source of truth. The transformation from the original data shape to a graph could be done through multiple techniques that can be classified in two groups:

- *Graph modeling*—Data is converted to some graph representation by means of a modeling pattern. The information is the same, only in a different format, or the data is aggregated to make it more suitable to feed into the learning process.
- *Graph construction*—A new graph is created, starting from the data available. The resulting graph contains more information than before.

After this preparation, the data is stored in a well-structured format, ready for the next phase: the learning process. The graph representation of the data doesn't support only graph-based algorithms; it can feed multiple types of algorithms. Specifically, the graph representation is helpful for the following tasks:

- *Feature selection*—Querying a relational database or extracting a key from a value in a NoSQL database is a complex undertaking. A graph is easy to query and can merge data from multiple sources, so finding and extracting the list of variables to use for training is made simpler by the graph approach.
- *Data filtering*—The easy-to-navigate relationships among objects make it easy to filter out useless data before the training phase, which speeds the model-building process. We'll see an example in section 3.2.4, where we'll consider the recommendation scenario.
- *Data preparation*—Graphs make it easy to clean the data, removing spurious entries, and to merge data from multiple sources.
- *Data enrichment*—Extending the data with external sources of knowledge (such as semantic networks, ontologies, and taxonomies) or looping back the result of the modeling phase to build a bigger knowledge base is straightforward with a graph.
- *Data formatting*—It's easy to export the data in whichever format is necessary: vectors, documents, and so on.

In both scenarios (graph-based or non-graph-based algorithms), the result could be a model that is well suited to a graph representation; in that case, it can be stored back in the graph or stored in a binary or proprietary format.

Whenever the predictive model allows it, storing the model back in the graph gives you the opportunity to perform predictions as queries (more or less complex) on the graph. Moreover, the graph provides access to the same model from different perspectives and for different scopes. Recommendations, described in section 3.2.4, are an example of the potential of this approach.

Finally, the graph model can be used to visualize the data in a graph format, which often represents a big advantage in terms of communication capabilities. Graphs are whiteboard friendly, so the visualizations can also improve communication between business owners and data scientists in the early stages of a machine learning project.

Not all the phases and steps described here are mandatory; depending on the needs of the machine learning workflow, only some might be helpful or necessary. Later sections present a range of concrete example scenarios. For each scenario presented, the role of the graph is clearly illustrated.

3.2 Managing data sources

As we've seen, graphs are extremely useful for encoding information, and data in graph format is increasingly plentiful. In many areas of machine learning—including natural language processing, computer vision, and recommendations—graphs are used to model local relationships between isolated data items (users, items, events, and so on) and to construct global structures from local information [Zhao and Silva, 2016]. Representing data as graphs is often a necessary step (and at other times only a desirable one) in dealing with problems arising from applications in machine learning or data mining. In particular, it becomes crucial when we want to apply graph-based learning methods to the datasets. Figure 3.4 highlights the role of graphs related to the management of data sources in machine learning projects.

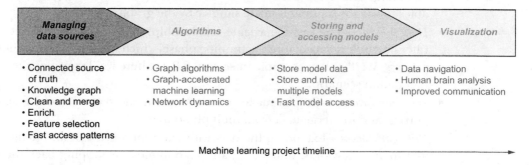

Figure 3.4 **Managing data sources in the mental model**

The transformation from structured or unstructured data to a graph representation can be performed in a lossless manner, but this lossless representation is not always necessary (or desirable) for the purpose of the learning algorithm. Sometimes, a better model is an aggregated view of the data. If you are modeling a phone call between two people, for example, you can decide to have a relationship between the two entities (the caller and the receiver) for each call, or you can have a single relationship that aggregates all the calls. You can construct a graph from the input dataset in two ways:

- By designing a graph model that represents the data
- By using some convenient graph formation criteria

In the first case, the graph model is an alternative representation of the same information available in the dataset itself or in multiple datasets. The nodes and the relationships in the graph are a mere representation (aggregated or not) of the data available in the original sources. Furthermore, in this case the graph acts as a connected data source that merges data coming from multiple heterogeneous sources, operating as the single trusted source of truth at the end of the process. There are multiple methodologies, techniques, and best practices for applying this model shift and representing data in a graph format, and we will discuss some of them here, considering multiple scenarios. Other data model patterns are presented in the rest of the book.

In the second scenario—using some convenient graph formation criteria—the data items are stored in the graph (generally as nodes), and a graph is created by means of some edge construction mechanism. Suppose that in your graph, each node represents some text, such as a sentence or an entire document. These entries are *isolated entries*. There are no relationships among the nodes unless they are explicitly connected (such as via a citation in a paper). In machine learning, text is generally represented as a vector, with each entry containing the weight of a word or a feature in the text. Edges can be created (constructed) by using the similarity or dissimilarity value between the vectors. A new graph is created starting from unrelated information. In such a case, the resulting graph embeds more information than the original datasets. This additional information is made up of several ingredients, the most important of which is the structural or topological information of the data relationships.

The result of both processes is a graph that represents the input data and that becomes the training dataset for the relevant machine learning algorithms. In some cases, these algorithms are themselves graph algorithms, so they require a graph representation of the data; in other cases, the graph is a better way of accessing the same data. The examples and scenarios described here represent both cases.

Figure 3.5 shows the required steps in the process of converting data to its graph representation (or creating it as a graph).

Let's take a closer look at each step:

1 *Identify the data sources.* Identify the data available for algorithm training purposes, as well as the sources from which such data can be extracted. This step corresponds to the second phase in a machine learning project, after the goals are defined (the data preparation phase of the CRISP-DM data model).

2 *Analyze the data available.* Analyze each data source available, and evaluate the content, in terms of quality and quantity. To achieve good results from the training phase, it's imperative to have a large amount of good-quality data.

3 *Design the graph data model.* This step is twofold. According to the specific analytics requirements, you must

    a Identify the meaningful information to be extracted from the data sources.

    b Design a specific graph model, considering the data available, access patterns, and extensibility.

4 *Define the data flow.* Design the architecture of the ingestion process (known as the *ETL process*) that extracts, transforms, and loads the data from the multiple sources into the graph database, using the schema designed.

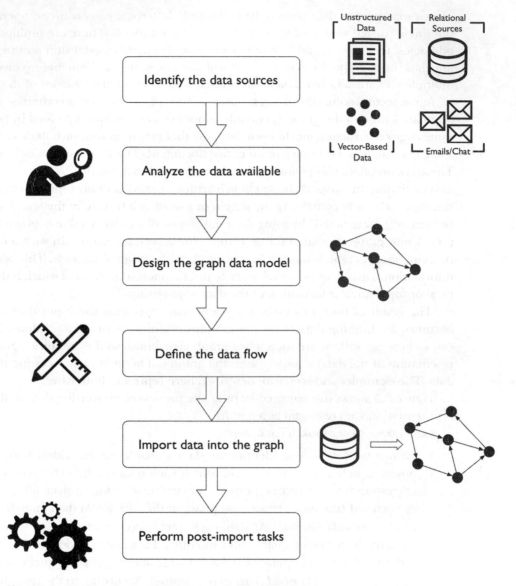

Figure 3.5   Process of converting data to a graph representation

5 *Import data into the graph.* Start the ETL process defined in step 4. Generally, steps 3, 4, and 5 are iterative until you arrive at the right model and the right ETL process.

6 *Perform postimport tasks.* Before you start the analysis, the data in the graph might require some preprocessing. These tasks include

  a *Data cleaning*—Remove or correct incomplete or incorrect data.

b *Data enrichment*—Extend the existing data sources with external sources of knowledge or with knowledge extracted from the data itself. The latter case falls under graph creation.

c *Data merging*—Because the data comes from multiple sources, related elements in the dataset can be merged in a single element or can be connected through new relationships.

Steps 5 and 6 can be inverted or mixed. In some cases, the data may pass through a process of cleaning before the ingestion happens. In any case, at the end of those six steps, the data is ready for the next phase, which involves the learning process.

The new representation of the data provides several advantages that we'll investigate here through the lens of multiple scenarios and multiple models. You'll be seeing some of these scenarios for the first time, but others were introduced in chapters 1 and 2, and will be extended further throughout the book. For each scenario presented, I describe the context and purpose—key aspects of defining the right model and understanding the value of the graph approach to storing and managing data and of graphs as input for the next steps in the analysis.

Starting with part 2, the book describes in detail the techniques for representing different datasets by using a graph model. This chapter highlights, through the example scenarios, the primary advantages of using a graph to manage the data available for training the prediction model.

3.2.1 Monitor a subject

Suppose again that you are a police officer. You would like to attempt to track a suspect and predict their future movements by using cellular tower data collected from the continuous monitoring signals every phone sends to (or receives from) all towers it can reach. Using graph models and graph clustering algorithms, it is possible to structure cellular tower data to represent a subject's positions and movements in a simple, clear manner. Then you can create a predictive model.[3]

The goal in this scenario is to monitor a subject and create a predictive model that identifies location clusters relevant to the subject's life and that is able to predict and anticipate subsequent movements according to the subject's current position and last movements [Eagle, Quinn, and Clauset, 2009]. The data in this scenario is cellular tower data generated by the interactions between the subject's phone and the cellular towers, as represented in figure 3.6.

For the purpose of such an analysis, data can be collected from the towers or from the phones belonging to the monitored subjects. The data from the cellular towers is easy to obtain with the necessary permissions, but it requires a lot of cleaning (removing the irrelevant numbers) and merging (data from multiple cellular towers). Gathering

---

[3] This scenario was introduced in chapter 2 for different purposes. Here, it is extended and split in the multiple tasks composing our mental model. Let me apologize for the small (but necessary) repetition.

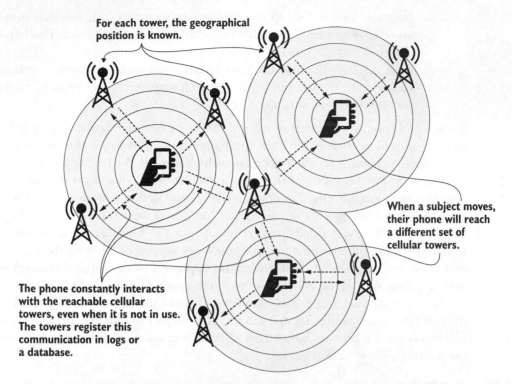

For each tower, the geographical position is known.

When a subject moves, their phone will reach a different set of cellular towers.

The phone constantly interacts with the reachable cellular towers, even when it is not in use. The towers register this communication in logs or a database.

Figure 3.6   Phones communicating with cellular towers

data from the phones requires hacking, which is not always possible, but this data is clean and already merged. In their paper, Eagle, Quinn, and Clauset consider this second data source, and we do the same here, but the results and the considerations are the same regardless of the source of the data.

Let's suppose that the phones will provide data in the format shown in table 3.1.

Table 3.1   Examples of the data provided by a single phone with the four towers (identified by ID) reached at each timestamp

Phone identifier	Timestamp	Cellular tower 1	Cellular tower 2	Cellular tower 3	Cellular tower 4
562d6873b0fe	1530713007	eca5b35d	f7106f86	1d00f5fb	665332d8
562d6873b0fe	1530716500	f7106f86	1d00f5fb	2a434006	eca5b35d
562d6873b0fe	1530799402	f7106f86	eca5b35d	2a434006	1d00f5fb
562d6873b0fe	1531317805	1d00f5fb	665332d8	f7106f86	eca5b35d
562d6873b0fe	1533391403	2a434006	665332d8	eca5b35d	1d00f5fb

For the sake of simplicity, this table represents the data provided by a single phone. (The phone identifier is always the same.) The phone records the four towers with the strongest signals at 30-second intervals.

The analysis requires us to identify locations in which the monitored subject spends time. The cellular tower data available on the phone cannot provide this information by itself, because it contains only the identifiers of the four towers with the highest signal strengths. But starting from such data, it is possible to identify key locations by passing through a graph representation of the data and a graph algorithm. Therefore, this data can be modeled as a graph that represents a cellular tower network (CTN). As you'll recall from chapter 2, each node in this graph is a unique cellular tower; edges exist between any two nodes that co-occur in the same record, and each edge is assigned a weight according to the total amount of time that pair of nodes co-occurred in a record, across all records. A CTN is generated for the subject that shows every tower logged by their phone during the monitoring period. The result looks like figure 3.7.

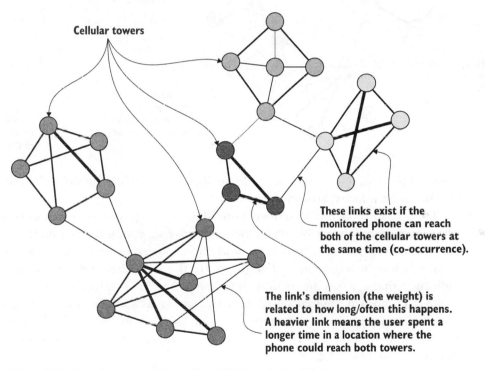

Figure 3.7   A graph representation of the CTN for a single subject

A graph clustering algorithm is applied to this graph to identify the main locations where the subject spent a significant amount of time (at the office, at home, at the supermarket, at church, and so on). The result of the analysis looks like figure 3.8, in which multiple clusters are identified and isolated.

This scenario shows how well adapted a graph model is to representing the data for the specific purposes of this analysis. By performing a graph-based analysis using the community detection algorithm, we can easily identify areas where the subject

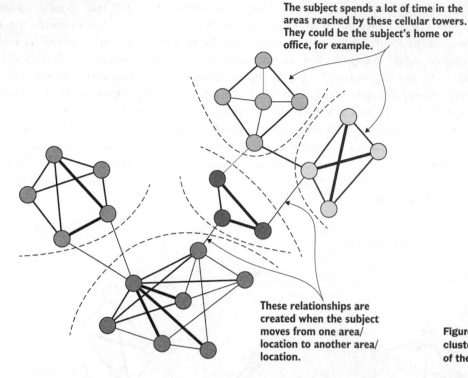

The subject spends a lot of time in the areas reached by these cellular towers. They could be the subject's home or office, for example.

These relationships are created when the subject moves from one area/ location to another area/ location.

Figure 3.8   A clustered view of the CTN

spends a lot of time—a task that would be difficult, if not impossible, with other representations or analysis methods.

The graph modeling described here illustrates a graph construction technique. The resulting graph can be generalized as a *co-occurrence graph*. The nodes represent entities (in this case, cellular towers), and the relationships represent the fact that two entities belong to a common set or group. (In the CTN, the set is the row in the table indicating that at a specific point in time, the phone can reach two towers.) This technique is a powerful one that's used in many algorithms and machine learning applications as a data-preprocessing step before analysis. Quite often, this type of graph construction technique is used in applications related to text analysis; we'll see an example in section 3.3.2.

3.2.2   *Detect a fraud*

Suppose again that you would like to create a fraud detection platform for banks that reveals the point of origin of a credit card theft. A graph representation of the transactions can help you identify, even visually, the location of the theft.[4]

---

[4] For the same reasons as in the previous example, there is a bit of repetition from chapter 2. In this chapter, the scenario is described in more detail.

In this scenario, the data available is the credit card transactions, with details about the date (timestamp), the amount, the merchant, and whether the transaction is disputed or undisputed. When a person's credit card details have been stolen, real operations are mixed with illegal or fraudulent operations in their transaction history. The goal of the analysis is to identify the point where the fraud started—the shop where the theft occurred. The transactions at that shop will be real, but any transactions that have taken place afterward may be fraudulent. The data available looks like table 3.2.

Table 3.2 A subset of user transactions

User identifier	Timestamp	Amount	Merchant	Validity
User A	01/02/2018	$250	Hilton Barcelona	Undisputed
User A	02/02/2018	$220	AT&T	Undisputed
User A	12/03/2018	$15	Burger King New York	Undisputed
User A	14/03/2018	$100	Whole Foods	*Disputed*
User B	12/04/2018	$20	AT&T	Undisputed
User B	13/04/2018	$20	Hard Rock Cafe	Undisputed
User B	14/04/2018	$8	Burger King New York	Undisputed
User B	20/04/2018	$8	Starbucks	*Disputed*
User C	03/05/2018	$15	Whole Foods	Disputed
User C	05/05/2018	$15	Burger King New York	Undisputed
User C	12/05/2018	$15	Starbucks	*Disputed*

Our aim is to identify some common pattern that reveals the point at which users start disputing their transactions, which will help us to locate the establishment where the card details were stolen. This analysis can be performed by using a graph representation of the transactions. The data in table 3.2 can be modeled in a transaction graph, as shown in figure 3.9.

As described in chapter 2, by starting from this representation of the transactions and using graph queries, we can determine that the theft occurred at Burger King. (The steps taken to arrive at this conclusion are described in section 2.2.2 and will not be repeated here.)

The graph of the transactions allows us to easily identify where the card thief operates. In this case, the analysis is performed on the graph as it appears after the ETL phase; no other intermediate transformation is required. This data representation expresses the information in such a way that it is possible to quickly recognize behavioral patterns in a long list of transactions and spot where the issue is.

Transaction graphs like the one shown in figure 3.9 can represent any kind of event that involves two entities. Generally, these graphs are used for modeling monetary

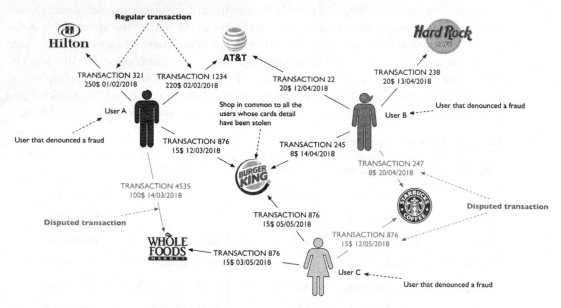

Figure 3.9   A transaction graph for credit card fraud detection

transactions in an unaggregated way, which means that every single operation can be related to a specific portion of the graph. For the majority of cases, in the resulting graph each transaction is represented in one of the following two ways:

- As a *directed edge* between the two entities involved in the transaction. If User A makes a purchase at Shop B, this event is translated into a directed edge that starts with User A and terminates at Shop B. In this case, all the relevant details about the purchase, such as the date and amount, are stored as properties of the edge (figure 3.10 (a)).
- As a *node* that contains all the relevant information about the event and is connected via edges to the related nodes. In the case of the purchase, the transaction itself is modeled as a node; then it is connected to the source and destination of the purchase (figure 3.10 (b)).

The first approach is generally used when the amount of information related to the event is small or when a simpler model is preferable for the purpose of the analysis. The second approach is generally preferred when the event itself contains valuable information that could be connected to other information items or when the event involves more than two items.

Transaction graphs are quite common in fraud detection analysis and all machine learning projects in which each event contains relevant information that would be lost if the events were aggregated.

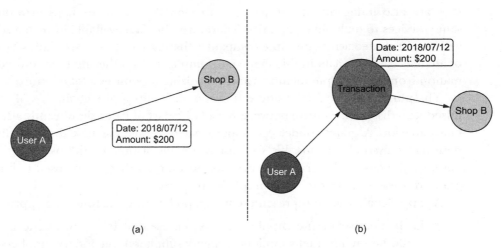

(a)   (b)

Figure 3.10   Transaction modeling examples

3.2.3   *Identify risks in a supply chain*

Suppose that you have to implement a risk management system that identifies or predicts possible risks in a supply chain. A *supply chain network* (SCN) is a common way to represent supply chain elements and their interactions in a graph. Such a representation, together with proper graph analysis algorithms, makes it easy and fast to spot issues throughout the chain.

This scenario has become more and more relevant in recent years, for multiple reasons, including the following:

- With the development of the global economy, any supply chain can have a global dimension, so the problems that supply chain management faces are becoming more complex.
- Customers located at the end of the chain are becoming more interested in the origins of the products they buy.

Managing the disruption risk and making the chain more transparent are mandatory tasks in any supply chain. Supply chains are inherently fragile and face a variety of threats, from natural disasters and attacks to contamination of raw products, delivery delays, and labor shortages [Kleindorfer and Saad, 2005]. Furthermore, because the parts of the chain are complex and interrelated, the normal operation of one member—and the efficient operation of the chain as a whole—often relies on the normal operation of other components. The members of a supply chain include suppliers, manufacturers, distributors, customers, and so on. All members are dependent on one another and cooperate through material, information, and financial flows, but they are also independent entities operating on their own, perhaps providing the same services to multiple companies. Therefore, the data available in such a scenario will be distributed across multiple companies that have different structures. Any kind of analysis based on data in this shape is a complex task; gathering the required information from the multiple members and organizing it requires a lot of effort.

The purpose of the analysis here is to spot elements in the chain that, if compromised, can disrupt the entire network (or a large part of it) or significantly affect normal behavior. A graph model can support such an analysis task through different network analysis algorithms. We will discuss details of the algorithms in section 3.3; here, we'll focus on the graph construction techniques that can be used to build the graph representation from the multiple sources available.

A supply chain can be represented in a graph by using the following approach:

- Each member of the supply chain is represented by a node. The members could be raw-product suppliers (primary suppliers), secondary suppliers, intermediate distributors, transformation processes, organizational units in a big company, final retailers, and so on. The granularity of the graph is related to the risk evaluation required.
- Each relation in the graph represents a dependency between two members of the chain. The relationships could include transport from a supplier to an intermediate distributor, a dependency between two processing steps, the delivery to the final retailer, and so on.
- To each node, it is possible to relate some temporal data that could store historic as well as forecasting information.

The network structure might evolve over time as well. The graph model can be designed to keep track of the changes, but that design would make it too complicated for the purpose of this example. Our example graph model is shown in figure 3.11.

This model represents an important method for gathering data and organizing it in an organic and homogeneous way, and it provides a suitable representation for the type of analysis that risk management requires. The algorithms that allow us to perform the analysis to reveal high-risk elements in the chain are discussed in section 3.3.1.

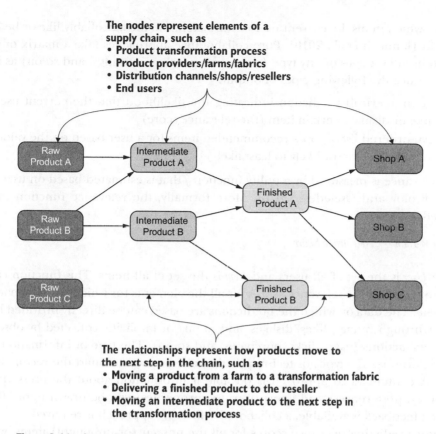

**The nodes represent elements of a
supply chain, such as**
- **Product transformation process**
- **Product providers/farms/fabrics**
- **Distribution channels/shops/resellers**
- **End users**

**The relationships represent how products move to
the next step in the chain, such as**
- **Moving a product from a farm to a transformation fabric**
- **Delivering a finished product to the reseller**
- **Moving an intermediate product to the next step in
  the transformation process**

Figure 3.11   A supply chain network

3.2.4   Recommend items

Suppose that you would like to recommend items to users in an e-commerce
shop, using the data you have about previous interactions (clicks, purchases, ratings, and so on). Graphs can help you store the User-Item dataset in a way that
speeds access to it, and storing the predictive models in the graph not only facilitates the predictions, but also allows you to merge multiple models smoothly.

One of the most common use cases for graphs in machine learning is recommendations. I wrote the first recommendation engine ever built on top of Neo4j in 2012.
That's how my career with graphs started, and it's why this specific topic is close to my
heart. Throughout this book, using multiple examples, we will discover the great
advantages of using graphs for building multimodel recommendation engines, but
here, we'll start with a simple example by considering the most basic implementation.

It is possible to use multiple approaches to provide recommendations. In this specific example, the approach selected is based on a technique called *collaborative filtering*. The main idea of collaborative approaches to recommendations is to exploit
information about the past behavior or opinions of an existing user community to

predict which items the current user of the system will most probably like or be interested in [Jannach et al., 2010]. Pure collaborative approaches take a matrix of given user-item interactions of any type (views, past purchases, ratings, and so on) as input and produce the following types of output:

- A (numerical) prediction indicating the likelihood that the current user will like or dislike a certain item (the relevance score)
- An ordered list of top *n* recommended items for a user based on the value predicted (from most likely to least likely)

The relevance is measured by a utility function *f* that is estimated based on user feedback [Frolov and Oseledets, 2016]. More formally, the relevance function can be defined as

f: User × Item → Relevance Score

where *User* is the set of all users and *Item* is the set of all items. This function can be used to compute the relevance scores for all the elements for which no information is available. The data on which the predictions are based can be directly provided by the users (through ratings, likes/dislikes, and so on) or implicitly collected by observing the users' actions (page clicks, purchases, and so on). The type of information available determines the types of techniques that can be used to build the recommendations. A content-based approach is possible if information about the users (profile attributes, preferences) and items (intrinsic properties) can be drawn upon. If only implicit feedback is available, a collaborative filtering approach is required.

After predicting relevance scores for all the unseen (or unbought) items, we can rank them and show the top *n* items to the user, performing the recommendation. As usual, we start our discussion from the data available. The data source in this case looks like table 3.3 (in which 1 is a low rating and 5 means that the user has a high opinion of the item).

Table 3.3   An example User-Item dataset represented in a matrix

User	Item 1	Item 2	Item 3	Item 4	Item 5
Bob	-	3	-	4	?
User 2	3	5	-	-	5
User 3	-	-	4	4	-
User 4	2	-	4	-	3
User 5	-	3	-	5	4
User 6	-	-	5	4	-
User 7	5	4	-	-	5
User 8	-	-	3	4	5

This table is a classic User-Item matrix containing the interactions (in this case, the ratings) between the users and the items. The cells with the symbol - mean that the user has not bought or rated that item. In an e-commerce scenario like the one we are considering, there could be a large number of users and items, so the resulting table could be quite sparse; each user will buy only a small subset of the available items, so the resulting matrix will have a lot of empty cells. In our example table, the unseen or unbought element that we would like to predict interest in is item 5 for user Bob.

Starting from the data available (in the shape described) and from the basic idea of collaborative filtering, multiple ways of implementing this prediction exist. For the purpose of this scenario, in this part of the book we will consider the *item-based* algorithms. The main idea of item-based algorithms is to compute predictions by using the similarity between items. Therefore, we will consider the table column by column, with each column describing a vector of elements (called the *rating vector*) where the - symbol is replaced by a 0 value. Let's examine our User-Item dataset and make a prediction for Bob for item 5. First, we compare all the rating vectors of the other items and look for items that are similar to item 5. Now the idea of item-based recommendation is to look at Bob's ratings for these similar items. The item-based algorithm computes a weighted average of these other ratings and uses this average to predict a rating for item 5 for user Bob.

To compute the similarity between items, we must define a *similarity measure. Cosine similarity* is the standard metric in item-based recommendation approaches: it determines the similarity between two vectors by calculating the cosine of the angle between them [Jannach et al., 2010]. In machine learning applications, this measure is often used to compare two text documents, which are represented as vectors of terms; we will use it frequently in this book.

The formula to compute the cosine of the angle between the two vectors and, therefore, the similarity between two items a and b, is as follows:

$$sim(\vec{a}, \vec{b}) = \cos(\vec{a}, \vec{b}) = \frac{\vec{a} \cdot \vec{b}}{|\vec{a}| \times |\vec{b}|}$$

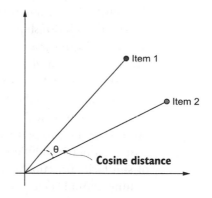

The · symbol indicates the dot product of the two vectors. $|\vec{a}|$ is the Euclidian length of the vector, which is defined as the square root of the dot product of the vector with itself.

Figure 3.12 shows a representation of cosine distance in 2D space.

To further explain the formula, let's consider the cosine similarity of item 5, described by the rating vector [0, 5, 0, 3, 4, 0, 5, 5], and item 1, described by the vector [0, 3, 0, 2, 0, 0, 5, 0]. It is calculated as follows:

Figure 3.12   Cosine distance representation in 2D space

$$sim(\overrightarrow{I5}, \overrightarrow{I1}) = \frac{0 \times 0 + 5 \times 3 + 0 \times 0 + 3 \times 2 + 4 \times 0 + 0 \times 0 + 5 \times 5 + 5 \times 0}{\sqrt{5^2 + 3^2 + 4^2 + 5^2 + 5^2} \times \sqrt{3^2 + 2^2 + 5^2}}$$

The numerator is the dot product between the two vectors, computed from the sum of the products of the corresponding entries of the two sequences of numbers. The denominator is the product of the Euclidian lengths of the two vectors. The *Euclidian distance* is the distance between two points in the multidimensional space of the vectors. Figure 3.13 illustrates the concept in 2D space.

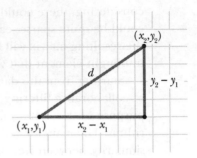

The formula is as follows:

$$|x,y| = \sqrt{(x_1 - y_1)^2 + (x_2 - y_2)^2}$$

Figure 3.13   Euclidian distance in 2D space

The *Euclidian length* is the Euclidian distance of the vector from the origin of the space (the vector [0,0,0,0,0,0,0,0], in our case):

$$|x| = \sqrt{x_1^2 + x_2^2}$$

The similarity values range between 0 and 1, with 1 indicating the strongest similarity. Consider now that we have to compute this similarity for each pair of items in the database, so if we have 1 million products, we need to compute 1M × 1M similarity values. We can reduce this number by half because similarity is commutative—$cos(a,b)$ = $cos(b,a)$—but we still have a lot of computations to make. In this case, a graph can be a valuable helper to speed the machine learning algorithm for the recommendations. The User-Item dataset can be converted easily to a graph like the one in figure 3.14.

In this graph representation, all the users are on the left, and all the items are on the right. The relationships go only from nodes in one subset to nodes in the other subset; no relationships occur between nodes of the same set. This figure is an example of a *bipartite graph*, or *bigraph*. More formally, a *bigraph* is a special type of graph whose vertices (nodes) can be divided into two disjoint and independent sets *U* and *V* such that every edge connects a vertex in *U* to one in *V*, or vice versa. Vertex sets *U* and *V* are usually called the *parts* of the graph [Diestel, 2017].

How can a bipartite graph representation reduce the number of similarity computations we have to perform? To understand this concept, it is necessary to understand cosine similarity a little better (although the principle can be extended to a wider set of similarity functions). The cosine similarity metric measures the angle between two *n*-dimensional vectors, so the two vectors have a cosine similarity equal to 0 when they are *orthogonal* (perpendicular). In the context of our example, this happens when there are no overlapping users between two items (users that rate both the items). In such cases, the numerator of the fraction will be 0. We can compute the distance

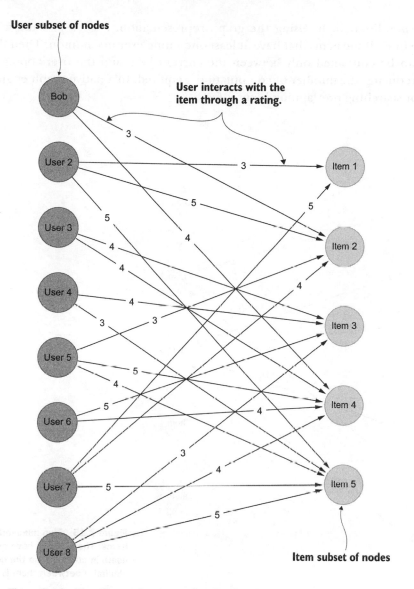

User subset of nodes

**User interacts with the
item through a rating.**

Item subset of nodes

Figure 3.14 Bipartite graph representing the User-Item dataset

between item 2, described by the vector [3, 5, 0, 0, 3, 0, 4, 0], and item 3, described by the vector [0, 0, 4, 4, 0, 5, 0, 3], as follows:

$$sim(\overrightarrow{I2}, \overrightarrow{I3}) = \frac{3 \times 0 + 5 \times 0 + 0 \times 4 + 0 \times 4 + 3 \times 0 + 0 \times 5 + 4 \times 0 + 0 \times 3}{\sqrt{3^2 + 5^2 + 3^2 + 4^2} \times \sqrt{4^2 + 4^2 + 5^2 + 3^2}}$$

In this case, the similarity value will be 0 (figure 3.15). In a sparse User-Item dataset, the probability of orthogonality is quite high, so the number of useless computations is correspondingly high. Using the graph representation, it is easy to use a simple query to find all the items that have at least one rating user in common. Then the similarity can be computed only between the current item and the overlapping items, greatly reducing the number of computations required. In a native graph engine, the query for searching overlapping items is fast.

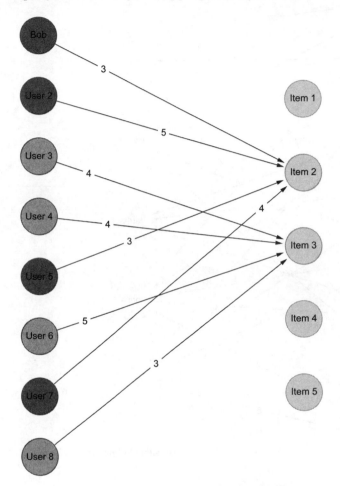

Figure 3.15   Two nonoverlapping items. These items have no rating users in common, so the cosine similarity between them is 0.

Another approach is to separate the bipartite graph into clusters and compute the distance only between the items belonging to the same cluster.

In the scenario presented in this section, the graph model helps to improve performance by reducing the amount of time required to compute the similarities between the items and, therefore, the recommendations. In section 3.4, we will see how, starting from this graph model, it is possible to store the results of similarity computations to perform fast recommendations. Furthermore, cosine similarity will be used as a technique for graph construction.

3.3   *Algorithms*

Section 3.2 described the role of the graph model in representing the training data that is used for the learning phase. Such a representation of the source of truth has multiple advantages, as described previously, whether the learning algorithm is graph-based or not.

This section describes, again using multiple scenarios, some machine learning techniques that use graph algorithms to achieve the project's goals. We'll consider two approaches:

- The graph algorithm as the *main* learning algorithm
- The graph algorithm as a *facilitator* in a more complex algorithm pipeline

Figure 3.16 highlights the role of graph-based algorithms in machine learning projects.

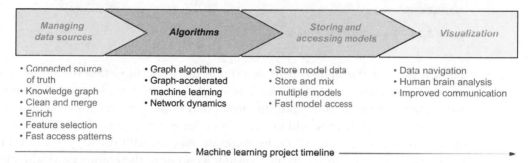

Figure 3.16   Algorithms in the mental model

In the rest of the book, an entire catalog of algorithms is described in detail with implementation examples. In this chapter, the purpose is to highlight the role of graph algorithms for delivering predictions to the end user. These techniques, by contrast with the traditional methods, provide alternative and novel ways to solve the challenging problems posed by machine learning use cases. The focus here (and in the rest of the book) is on showing how to use these techniques in real-world applications, but we will also take into account the design of the methods introduced that are complementary or helpful in terms of performance and computational complexity.

3.3.1   *Identify risks in a supply chain*

Supply chain risk management aims primarily at determining the susceptibility of the chain to disruptions, also known as *supply chain vulnerability* [Kleindorfer and Saad, 2005]. Evaluating the vulnerability of supply chain ecosystems is challenging because it cannot be observed or measured directly. The failure or overloading of a single node can lead to cascading failures spreading across the whole network. As a result, serious damage will occur within the supply chain system. The analysis of vulnerability, therefore, must take into account the entire network, evaluating the effect of a disruption of each node. This approach requires identifying the nodes that, more than others, represent critical elements in the network. If the supply chain is represented as a network, as in figure 3.17, several graph algorithms can be applied to identify nodes that expose it to greater vulnerability.

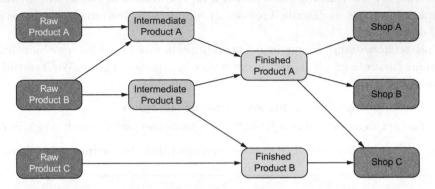

Figure 3.17   A supply chain network

The purpose of the analysis is to determine the most important or central nodes in the network. This type of analysis will reveal the supply chain's nodes of interest—the most likely targets of attack and the nodes that require the most protection, because any disruption of them would gravely affect the entire supply chain and its ability to operate normally. In figure 3.17, for example, an issue with the supply of Raw Product B (the disruption could be on the provider's end or in the connection) will affect the entire chain because it is on the paths to all the shops.

Importance has many possible definitions; consequently, many centrality measures could be used for the network. We will consider two of them, not only because they are useful for the specific scenario of the supply chain, but also because they are powerful techniques used in multiple examples later in the book:

- *PageRank*—This algorithm works by counting the number and quality of edges to a node to arrive at a rough estimate of the node's importance. The basic idea implemented by the PageRank model, invented by the founders of Google for their search engine, is that of voting or recommendation. When a node is connected to another node by an edge, it is basically casting a vote for that node. The more votes a node receives, the more important it is—but the importance of the "voters" matters too. Hence, the *score* associated with a node is computed based on the votes that are cast for it and the scores of the nodes casting those votes.
- *Betweenness centrality*—This algorithm measures the importance of a node by considering how often it lies on the shortest paths between other nodes. It applies to a wide range of problems in network theory. In a supply chain network, for example, a node with higher betweenness centrality will have more control of the network because more goods will pass through that node.

Figure 3.18 illustrates these two algorithms.

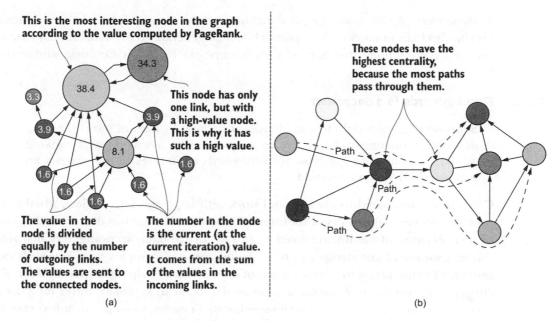

Figure 3.18   PageRank (a) and betweenness centrality (b) examples

In the supply chain vulnerability use case, both algorithms can be used to determine the most interesting nodes in the supply chain network, but from two different perspectives:

- *Betweenness centrality* allows us to determine which nodes may have considerable influence within the supply chain by virtue of their control of the products passing through them. The nodes with highest centrality are also the ones whose removal from the supply chain network will most disrupt the products' flow, because they lie on the largest number of paths taken by the products. Suppose that in the chain, a single company is the only provider of a basic component of all the products in the supply chain, or that one company operates as the sole distributor of a particular product. In both cases, the greatest number of paths for that component or product pass through them, and any serious disruption of these nodes would affect the entire supply chain.

- *PageRank* allows us to identify nodes that, according to the relative importance of the nodes they are connected to, have a high value in the network. In this case, disrupting an important node might affect only a small portion of the network, but the disruption could still be significant. Suppose that in the chain, a transformation process converts a product to a form suitable only for one of the biggest end customers of the supply chain. In this case, not many paths pass through the process, so the node's betweenness centrality is quite low, but the value of the node is high because disrupting it would affect an important element in the chain.

As these examples illustrate, graph algorithms provide a powerful analysis mechanism for supply chain networks. This approach can be generalized for many similar scenarios, such as communication networks, social networks, biological networks, and terrorist networks.

3.3.2   *Find keywords in a document*

> Suppose that you would like to identify automatically a set of terms that best describe a document or an entire corpus. Using a graph-based ranking model, you can find the most relevant words or phrases in the text via an unsupervised learning method.

Companies often need to manage and work with large amounts of data, whether to provide services to end users or for internal processes. Most of this data takes the form of text. Because of the unstructured nature of textual data, accessing and analyzing this vast source of knowledge can be a challenging and complex task. Keywords can provide effective access to a large corpus of documents by helping to identify the main concepts. Keyword extraction can also be used to build an automatic index for a document collection, to construct domain-specific dictionaries, or to perform text classification or summarization tasks [Negro et al., 2017].

Multiple techniques, some of them simple and others more complex, can be used to extract a list of keywords from a corpus. The simplest possible approach is to use a relative-frequency criterion (identifying the terms that occur most frequently) to select the important keywords in a document—but this method lacks sophistication and typically leads to poor results. Another approach involves using supervised learning methods, wherein a system is trained to recognize keywords in a text based on lexical and syntactic features—but a lot of labeled data (text with the related keywords extracted manually) is required to train a model accurate enough to produce good results.

Graphs can be your secret weapon for solving a complex problem like this one, providing a mechanism to extract keywords or sentences from the text in an unsupervised manner by using a graph representation of the data and a graph algorithm like PageRank. *TextRank* [Mihalcea and Tarau, 2004] is a graph-based ranking model that can be used for this kind of text processing.

In this case, we need to build a graph that represents the text and interconnects words or other text entities with meaningful relations. Depending on the purpose, the text units extracted—keywords, phrases, or entire sentences for summarization—can be added as nodes in the graph. Similarly, the final scope defines the types of relations that are used to connect the nodes (lexical or semantic relations, contextual overlap, and so on). Regardless of the type and characteristics of the elements added to the graph, the application of TextRank to natural language texts consists of the following steps [Mihalcea and Tarau, 2004]:

1 Identify text units relevant to the task at hand, and add them to the graph as nodes.

2 Identify relations that connect the text units. The edges between nodes can be directed or undirected and weighted or unweighted.

3 Iterate the graph-based ranking algorithm until convergence or until the maximum number of iterations is reached.

4 Sort the nodes based on their final scores, use these scores for ranking/selection decisions, and eventually merge two or more text units in a single (phrase) keyword.

The nodes, therefore, are sequences of one or more lexical units extracted from text, and they are the elements that will be ranked. Any relation that can be defined between two lexical units is a potentially useful connection (edge) that can be added between the nodes. For keyword extraction, one of the most effective methods of identifying relationships is co-occurrence. In this case, two nodes are connected if both occur within a window of a maximum of N words (an N-gram), with N typically being between 2 and 10. This case is another example (maybe one of the most common) of using a co-occurrence graph; figure 3.19 shows an example of the result. Additionally, it is possible to use syntactic filters to select only lexical units of certain parts of speech (only nouns, verbs, and/or adjectives, for example).

When the graph has been constructed, the TextRank algorithm can be run on it to identify the most important nodes. Each node in the graph is initially assigned a value of 1, and the algorithm runs until it converges below a given threshold (usually for 20 to 30 iterations, at a threshold of 0.0001). After a final score has been determined for each node, the nodes are sorted in reverse order by score, and postprocessing is performed on the top T nodes (typically between 5 and 20). During this postprocessing, words that appear one after the other in the text and are both relevant are merged into a single keyword.

The accuracy achieved by this unsupervised graph-based algorithm matches that of any supervised algorithm [Mihalcea and Tarau, 2004]. This result indicates that with a graph approach, it's possible to avoid the considerable effort supervised algorithms require to provide prelabeled data for a task such as the one described here.

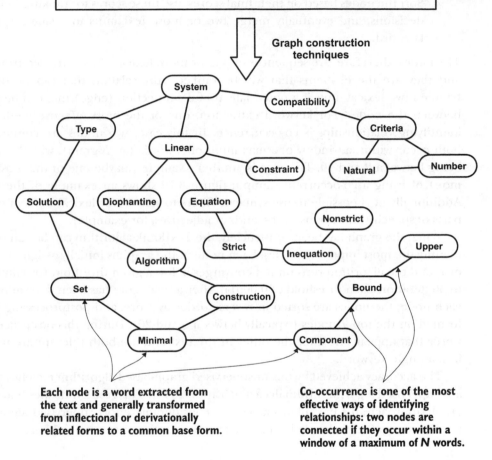

Compatibility of systems of linear constraints over the set of natural numbers. Criteria of compatibility of a system of linear Diophantine equations, strict inequations, and nonstrict inequations are considered. Upper bounds for components of a minimal set of solutions and algorithms of construction of minimal generating sets of solutions for all types of systems are given.

These criteria and the corresponding algorithms for constructing a minimal supporting set of solutions can be used in solving all the considered types of systems and systems of mixed types.

Graph construction techniques

Each node is a word extracted from the text and generally transformed from inflectional or derivationally related forms to a common base form.

Co-occurrence is one of the most effective ways of identifying relationships: two nodes are connected if they occur within a window of a maximum of *N* words.

Figure 3.19   A co-occurrence graph created by TextRank

3.3.3   *Monitor a subject*

Let's continue our discussion of how to monitor a subject's movements by using cellular tower data. Earlier in this chapter, we discussed how to convert the data distributed across multiple towers or multiple phones and stored in a tabular format to a homogeneous graph called a CTN (shown again here in figure 3.20). As explained in chapter 2, the nodes in the graph that have the highest total edge weight correspond to the towers that are most often visible to the subject's phone [Eagle, Quinn, and Clauset, 2009].

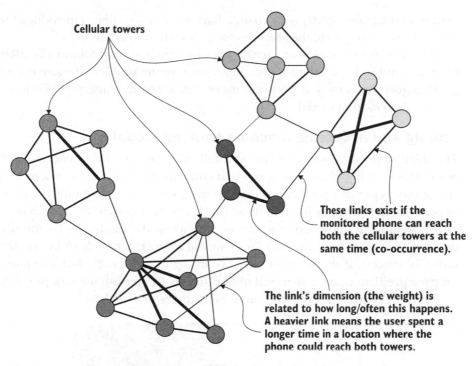

Cellular towers

These links exist if the monitored phone can reach both the cellular towers at the same time (co-occurrence).

The link's dimension (the weight) is related to how long/often this happens. A heavier link means the user spent a longer time in a location where the phone could reach both towers.

Figure 3.20   A graph representation of the CTN for a single subject

The graph construction described earlier in this chapter was a preliminary task for using graph clustering algorithms that allow us to identify groups of towers. The logic here is that a group of nodes connected to one another by heavily weighted edges and to other nodes by less heavily weighted edges should correspond to a location where the monitored subject spends a significant amount of time. *Graph clustering* is an unsupervised learning method that aims to group the nodes of the graph in clusters, taking into consideration the edge structure of the graph in such a way that there should be many edges within each cluster and relatively few between the clusters [Schaeffer, 2007]. Multiple techniques and algorithms exist for this purpose and are discussed extensively in the rest of the book.

When the graph is organized into multiple subgraphs that identify locations, the next step is using this information to build a predictive model that is able to indicate where the subject is likely to go next, based on their current position. The clusters of towers identified previously can be incorporated as states of a *dynamic model*.[5] Given a sequence of locations visited by a subject, the algorithm learns patterns in the subject's behavior and is able to calculate the probability that the subject will move to different locations in the future. The algorithm used for the modeling here [Eagle,

---

[5] A *dynamic model* is used to represent or describe systems whose state changes over time.

Quinn, and Clauset, 2009] is a dynamic Bayesian network that is introduced together with a simpler approach, the Markov chain, in section 3.4.2.

Whereas in the previous scenario, applying the graph algorithm (TextRank) was the main and only necessary action, here, because the problem is more complex, the graph algorithm is used as part of a more articulated learning pipeline to create an advanced prediction model.

3.4   *Storing and accessing machine learning models*

The third step in the workflow involves delivering predictions to end users. The output of the learning phase is a model that contains the result of the inference process and allows us to make predictions about unseen instances. The model has to be stored in permanent storage or in memory so that it can be accessed whenever a new prediction is required. The speed at which we can access the model affects the prediction performance. This time aspect is fundamental to the machine learning project's definition of success. If the accuracy of the resulting model is high, but it requires a long time for prediction, the system will not be able to accomplish the task properly.

Figure 3.21 summarizes how graphs contributes to this phase.

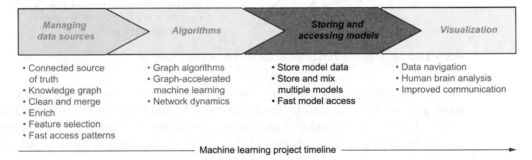

Figure 3.21   Storing and accessing models in the mental model

Consider the recommendation scenario for an e-commerce site. The user is looking for something but does not have a specific idea about what product to buy, so they start their navigation with a text search and then click here and there in the results list, navigating through the several options. At this point, the system starts recommending items to the user according to the navigation path and the clicks. All this is done in a matter of moments: with a decent network, the user navigates quickly, moving from one page to the next every 5 to 10 seconds or less. Therefore, if the recommendation process requires 10 or more seconds, it is useless.

This example shows the importance of having a system that is able to provide predictions quickly. In this sense, providing fast access to the model is a key aspect of success, and again, graphs can play an important role. This section explores, through some explanatory scenarios, the use of graphs for storing prediction models and providing fast access to them.

3.4.1   *Recommend items*

The item-based (or user-based) approach to collaborative filtering produces as a result of the learning phase an Item-Item matrix that contains the similarity between each pair of items in the User-Item dataset. The resulting matrix looks like table 3.4.

Table 3.4   Similarity matrix

	Item 1	Item 2	Item 3	Item 4	Item 5
Item 1	1	0.26	0.84	0	0.25
Item 2	0.26	1	0	0.62	0.25
Item 3	0.84	0	1	0.37	0.66
Item 4	0	0.62	0.37	1	0.57
Item 5	0.25	0.25	0.66	0.57	1

Having determined the similarities between the items, we can predict a rating for Bob for item 5 by calculating a weighted sum of Bob's ratings for the items that are similar to item 5. Formally, we can predict the rating of user u for a product p as follows [Jannach et al., 2010]:

$$pred(u,p) = \frac{\sum_{i \in ratedItems(u)} sim(i,p) \times r_{u,i}}{\sum_{i \in ratedItems(u)} sim(i,p)}$$

In this formula, the numerator contains the sum of the multiplication of the similarity value of each product that Bob rated to the target product and his rating of that product. The denominator contains the sum of all the similarity values of the items rated by Bob to the target product.

Let's consider only the line of the User-Item dataset shown in table 3.5 (technically, a slice of the User-Item matrix).

Table 3.5   User-Item slice for user Bob

User	Item 1	Item 2	Item 3	Item 4	Item 5
Bob	-	3	-	4	?

The preceding formula will appear as follows:

$$pred(\text{Bob,item 5}) = \frac{0.25 \times 3 + 0.57 \times 4}{0.25 + 0.57} = 3.69$$

The Item-Item similarity matrix from table 3.4 can be stored in the graph easily. Starting from the bipartite graph created for storing the User-Item matrix, storing this matrix is a matter of adding new relationships that connect items to other items (so the graph will not be bipartite anymore). The weight of the relationship is the value of the similarity, between 0 (in this case, no relationship is stored) and 1. The resulting graph looks like figure 3.22.

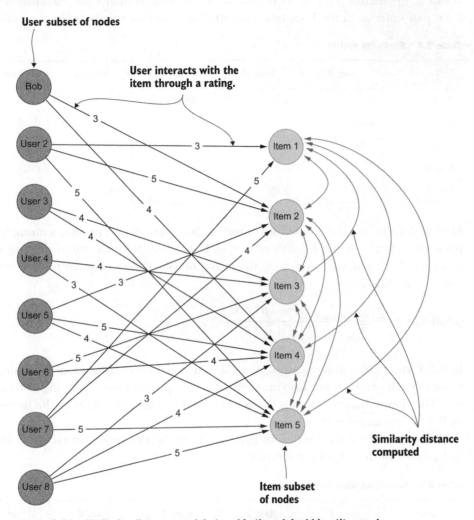

Figure 3.22   Similarity distance model stored in the original bipartite graph

In this figure, to reduce the number of arcs connecting the nodes, bidirectional relationships between items are represented; in reality, they are two different relationships. Additionally, because the number of relationships is $N \times N$, it could be quite difficult, in terms of both reading and writing, to store all the relationships. The typical approach is to store only the top K relationships for each node. When all the similarities are computed for each other item, they are sorted in descending order, from the most similar to the least similar, and only the first K are stored, because during the computation of the prediction, only the top K will be used. When the data is stored in this way, computing the topmost interesting item for a user is a matter of a few hops in the graph. According to the formula, all the items the target user rated are considered (in our case, items 2 and 4 are connected to the user Bob), and then for each of them, the similarity to the target item (item 5) is taken. The information for computing the prediction is local to the user, so making the prediction using the graph model presented is fast. There is no need for long data lookups.

Furthermore, it is possible to store more types of relationships and navigate them at the same time during the prediction to provide combined predictions based on multiple similarity measures. These predictions could be based on approaches other than pure collaborative filtering. We will discuss other techniques for computing similarity or distance (the same concept from a different point of view) in part 3 of the book.

3.4.2 *Monitoring a subject*

In the subject-monitoring scenario, after the identification of clusters of towers that represent locations where the subject spends significant amounts of time, the algorithm continues by learning patterns in the subject's behavior. Then we can use dynamic models, such as a dynamic Bayesian network, to build a predictive model for subject location.

A *Bayesian network* is a directed graph in which each node is annotated with quantitative probability information (such as 50% or 0.5, 70% or 0.7). The Bayesian network (aka *probabilistic graphical model* or *belief network*) represents a mix of probability theory and graph theory in which dependencies between variables are expressed graphically. The graph not only helps the user understand which variables affect which other ones, but also enables efficient computing of marginal and conditional probabilities that may be required for inference and learning. The full specification is as follows [Russell and Norvig, 2009]:

> *Each node corresponds to a random variable. These variables may be observable quantities, latent variables, unknown parameters, or hypotheses.*

> *Edges represent conditional dependencies. If there is an edge from node X to node Y, X is said to be a parent of Y. The graph has no directed cycles (and hence is a directed acyclic graph, or DAG). Nodes that are not connected (where there is no path between the variables in the Bayesian network) represent variables that are conditionally independent.*

> *Each node X_i has a conditional probability distribution $P(X_i, Parents(X_i))$ that quantifies the effect of the parents on the node. In other words, each node is associated with a probability function that takes (as input) a particular set of values for the node's parent variables and gives (as output) the probability, or probability distribution, if applicable, of the variable represented by the node.*

To make this discussion clearer, consider a simple example [Russell and Norvig, 2009]:

You have a new burglar alarm installed at home. It is fairly reliable at detecting a burglary, but also responds on occasion to minor earthquakes. . . . You also have two neighbors, John and Mary, who have promised to call you at work when they hear the alarm. John nearly always calls when he hears the alarm, but sometimes confuses the telephone ringing with the alarm and calls then, too. Mary, on the other hand, likes rather loud music and often misses the alarm altogether. Given the evidence of who has or has not called, we would like to estimate the probability of a burglary.

The related Bayesian network for this example appears in figure 3.23. Burglaries and earthquakes have a direct effect on the probability that the alarm will go off, as illustrated by the directed edges that connect the Burglary and Earthquake nodes at the top to the Alarm node. At the bottom, you can see that whether John or Mary calls depends only on the alarm (denoted by the edges connecting Alarm to the JohnCalls and MaryCalls nodes). They do not perceive the burglaries directly or notice minor earthquakes, and they do not confer before calling.

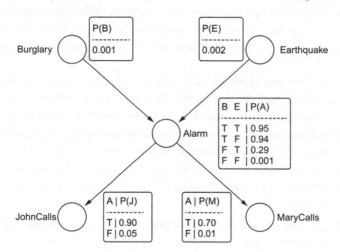

Figure 3.23   A typical Bayesian network, showing both the topology and the conditional probability tables

In figure 3.23, the tables near each node are the conditional distributions, represented as conditional probability tables (CPTs). A *conditional distribution* is a probability distribution for a subpopulation. Each row in a CPT contains the conditional probability of each node value, given the possible combinations of values for the parent nodes. $P(B)$ represents the probability of a burglary happening, for example, and $P(E)$ represents the probability of an earthquake happening. These distributions are simple because they don't depend on any other event. $P(J)$, the probability that John will call, and $P(M)$, the probability that Mary will call, depend on the alarm. The CPT for JohnCalls says that if the alarm is going off, the probability that John will call is 90%, whereas the probability of him calling when the alarm is not going off (recall that John can confuse the phone ringing with an alarm) is 5%. A little more complex is the CPT for the Alarm node, which depends on the Burglary and Earthquake nodes. Here, $P(A)$ (the probability that the alarm will go off) is 95% when a burglary and an earthquake happen at the same time, but it is 94% in the case of a burglary that does not coincide with an earthquake and 29% in the case of an earthquake with no burglary. A false alarm is rare, with a probability of 0.1%.

A *dynamic Bayesian network* (DBN) is a special type of Bayesian network that relates variables over adjacent time steps. Returning to our subject-monitoring scenario, the simplest version of a DBN that can be used for performing a location prediction is a *Markov chain*. The example shown in figure 3.24 is a pure graph, a special case of the more general graph representation of a Bayesian network. Nodes in this case represent the status (in our case, the subject's location) at point t, and the weights of the relationships represent the probability of a status transition at time $t + 1$.

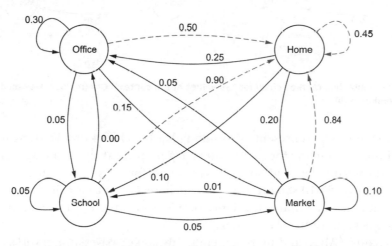

Figure 3.24   A simple Markov chain. (The most probable movement is shown in red.)

In the graph in figure 3.24, if the subject is at Home at time t, it is most likely that they will stay at home (45%). The probability that they will move to the Office is 25%; there is a 20% likelihood that they will instead go to the Market and a 10% probability that they will go to the School (perhaps to drop off the kids). This example is the representation of a model built from the observations. Starting from this model, computing the probability of a location t-step-ahead is a path navigation among nodes in which each node can appear more times.

This approach can be extended further. Eagle, Quinn, and Clauset [2009] noticed that patterns of movement for people in practice depend on the time of day and day of the week (Saturday night versus Monday morning, for example). Therefore, they created an extended model based on a *contextual Markov chain* (CMC), in which the probability of the subject being in a location is also dependent on the hour of the day and the day of the week (which represent the context). The CMC is not described in detail here, but figure 3.25 shows the basic ideas behind it.

The context is created considering the time of day, defined as "morning," "afternoon," "evening," or "night," and the day of the week, split into "weekday" or "weekend."

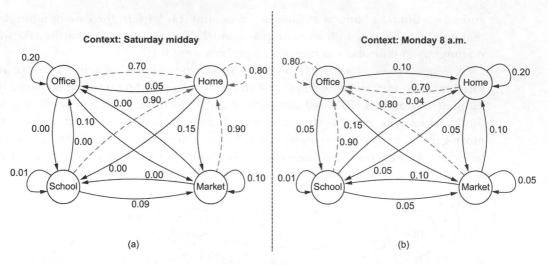

Figure 3.25   A simple contextual Markov chain for two values of the context: C = {midday, weekend} (a), and C = {morning, weekday} (b)

The graphs in figure 3.25 represent the resulting Markov chains after learning the maximum likelihood parameters for each context. Figure 3.25(a) shows the Markov chain for a midday during the weekend, so there is no school for the kids, and there is no work at the office. Figure 3.25(b) shows the Markov chain related to a morning on a weekday. Such graphs allow us to compute, through a simple query on the graph, a prediction of where the subject is most likely to go next.

Markov chains, CMCs, and more generally (dynamic) Bayesian networks are prediction models that work for a lot of use cases. The subject-monitoring scenario is used to illustrate here, but such models are actively used in many kinds of user modeling and especially in web analysis to predict user intentions.

3.5   *Visualization*

One of the main goals of machine learning is to make sense of data and deliver some sort of predictive capability to the end user (although as described at the beginning of this chapter, data analysis in general aims at extracting knowledge, insights, and finally wisdom from raw data sources, and prediction represents a small portion of possible uses). In this learning path, data visualization plays a key role because it allows us to access and analyze data from a different perspective. In our mental map of the machine learning workflow (figure 3.26), visualization is presented at the end of the process, because visualizing data after initial processing has been performed is much better than visualizing raw data, but data visualization can happen at any point in the workflow.

In this context, again, the graph approach plays a fundamental role. A growing trend in data analysis is to make sense of linked data as networks. Rather than looking solely at attributes of the data, network analysts also focus on the connections and

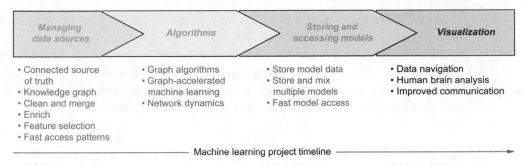

Figure 3.26 Visualization in the mental model

resulting structures in the data. If graphs are a helpful way of organizing data to better understand and analyze the relationships contained within that data, visualizations help expose that organization, further simplifying understanding. Combining the two methods helps data scientists to make sense of the data they have. Furthermore, successful visualizations are deceptive in their simplicity, offering the viewer new insights and understanding at a glance.

Why does visualizing data, specifically in the form of a graph, make it easier to analyze? There are several reasons:

- Humans are naturally visual creatures. Our eyes are our most powerful sensory receptors, and presenting data through information visualizations makes the most of our perceptual abilities [Perer, 2010].
- Many datasets today are too large to be inspected without computational tools that facilitate processing and interaction. Data visualizations combine the power of computers and the power of the human mind, capitalizing on our pattern-recognition abilities to enable efficient and sophisticated interpretation of the data. If we can see the data in the form of a graph, it's easier to spot patterns, outliers, and gaps [Krebs, 2016; Perer, 2010].
- The graph model exposes relationships that may be hidden in other views of the same data (such as tables and documents) and helps us pick out the important details [Lanum, 2016].

On the other hand, choosing an effective visualization can be a challenge, because different forms have different strengths and weaknesses [Perer, 2010]:

Not all information visualizations highlight the patterns, gaps, and outliers important to analysts' tasks, and furthermore, not all information visualizations "force us to notice what we never expected to see" [Tukey, 1977].

Moreover, visualizing big data requires significant effort in terms of filtering, organizing, and displaying it on a screen. But despite all these challenges, the graph view remains appealing to researchers in a broad range of areas.

Some good examples of using graph representations to reveal insights into human behavior appear in the work of social network analyst Valdis Krebs. An interesting aspect of Krebs's work is that he is able to take data from any kind of source (old documents, newspapers, databases, or web pages); convert it to a graph representation; perform some network analysis; and then visualize the results with his own software, called InFlow. Then he analyzes the graph and comes up with some conclusions. One example, which we saw in chapter 1, is his analysis of political-book purchases on Amazon.com from the two US presidential elections before 2003 (figure 3.27).

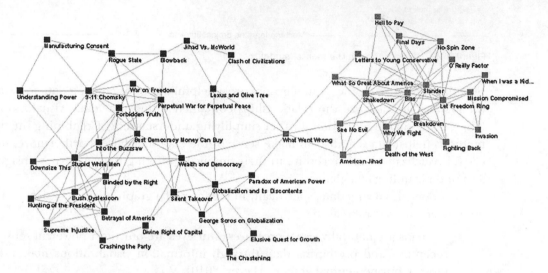

Figure 3.27   The political-book networks from the two US presidential elections before 2003 [Krebs, 2016]

Amazon provides summary purchase data that can be used to create a co-occurrence network (a type of graph we saw earlier in some of our example scenarios). Two books are connected when a customer buys both books. The more customers who purchase both items, the stronger the association between them is and the higher on the "customers who bought this item also bought" list the associated item appears. Consequently, by using Amazon data, it is possible to generate a network that provides significant insights into customers' preferences and purchasing behavior. As Krebs puts it, "With a little data mining and some data visualization, we can get great insights into the habits and choices of Amazon's customers—that is, we can come to understand groups of people without knowing about their individual choices."

In figure 3.27, it is possible to recognize two distinct political clusters: a red one (gray, in the print book) designating those who read right-leaning books and a blue one (black, in the print book) designating those who read left-leaning books. Only one book holds the red and blue clusters together; ironically, that book is named *What Went Wrong*. This graph visualization provides strong evidence of how polarized US citizens were during the political election in 2008. But this "evidence" is not so evident to a machine learning algorithm, because it requires a lot of contextual information that it's much easier for a human brain to supply: the political orientation of the book or the book's author, the circumstances of the ongoing political election, and so on.

3.6   *Leftover: Deep learning and graph neural networks*

Machine learning is a broad and constantly growing field. It is so huge that none of the books available covers the full spectrum of tasks and possibilities that such practices could accomplish. This book is not an exception. A lot of topics have been intentionally left out of our discussion. Among the others, one deserves at least to be mentioned because at the time of writing, it is shining in research and even in applications: *deep learning*. Let me introduce it a little bit to give you a high-level understanding of what it is, how it fits into the machine learning panorama, and how it can be applied to graphs.

As we have seen so far, and as we will discuss across the entire book, the performance (in terms of accuracy) of machine learning algorithms depends heavily on the quality of the data and the way in which it is represented. Each piece of information included in the representation and used during the training and the prediction is defined as a *feature*. Examples of features are a list of the items bought by a user, the places where a subject has spent some time, and the tokens in a text. The machine learning process takes these features and will infer a model capable of mapping this input with potential output. In the case of the recommendations, the process takes the items bought or rated by users and tries to predict what they could be interested in. In the case of subject monitoring, considering the previous locations, the algorithm predicts where a subject will be in the next hours or days. This book explains how to use graph data models to represent these features and how to simplify or improve the mapping.

Unfortunately, for many tasks, it is not so simple to identify features to be extracted for training a model. Suppose that you need to write an algorithm to recognize a face in a picture. A person has a pair of eyes, hair (not all of them) of some color, a nose, a mouth, and so on. A face is simple to describe in words, but how can we describe what an eye looks like in terms of pixels?

One possible solution to this representation problem is to use machine learning to discover not only the mapping from representation to output, but also the representation itself. This approach is known as *representation learning* [Goodfellow et al., 2016]. The resulting representations often result in much better performance compared with hand-picked features. Moreover, because the machine is capable of learning representations from simpler data (only the images or a bunch of text, for example), it can adapt to new tasks rapidly with reduced human effort. What requires minutes or days for a machine could require decades of research for humans.

Deep learning approaches the problem of representation learning by introducing representations that are expressed in terms of other, simpler representations [Goodfellow et al., 2016]. In deep learning, the machine builds multiple levels of increasing complexity over the underlying simpler concepts. The concept of an image of a person can be represented by combining corners and contours, which are in turn defined in terms of edges. Figure 3.28 describes the differences between classic machine learning and the subarea of deep learning.

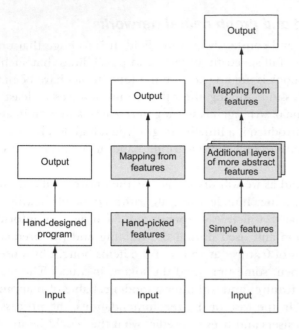

Figure 3.28   Differences between the rule-based approach, classical machine learning, and deep learning (inspired by Goodfellow et al., 2016)

In the preceding examples, we mentioned images, text, and so on. These data types are defined as Euclidean because they can be represented in a multidimensional space. What if we want to use such an approach on a graph, perhaps to recognize whether a node in a social network is a bot or to predict the formation of a link (and, hence, a correlation) between two nodes representing diseases? Figure 3.29 shows the representation of images and text in a Euclidean space versus the graph that cannot be represented easily in such a multidimensional space. (At bottom left in the figure, TF-IDF stands for *term frequency-inverse document frequency*.)

Graphs, with multiple node types and different types of relationships, are far from being a Euclidean space. This task is where graph neural networks (GNNs) comes in.

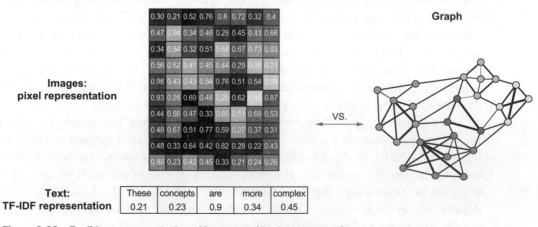

Figure 3.29   Euclidean representation of images and text versus graphs

GNNs are deep learning–based methods that operate on a graph domain to perform complex tasks such as node classification (the bot example), link prediction (the disease example), and so on. Due to its convincing performance, GNN has become a widely applied graph analysis method.

Figure 3.30 shows a generic encoding function that is capable of converting nodes (or relationships) in d-dimensional vectors. This function is generally used as an embedding technique. When the graph elements have been migrated in a Euclidean space, we can use classical machine learning techniques for images and text. The quality of this representation learning affects the quality and accuracy of the subsequent tasks.

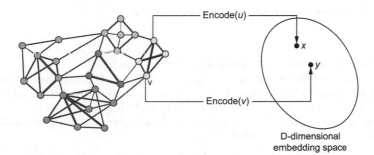

D-dimensional embedding space

Figure 3.30 A generic encoder example

GNNs are capable of generating representations of nodes that depend on the structure of the graph as well as on any feature information we have. These features could be nodes' properties, relationship types, and relationship properties. That's why GNNs could drive the final tasks to better results. These embeddings represent the input for tasks such as node classification, link prediction, and graph classification.

These concepts are more complex and require broader understanding of both machine learning (in particular, deep learning) and graphs, which is why I preferred to keep these topics out of this book. New techniques, such as deep learning and GNNs, don't invalidate what is presented in this book; they are built on the principles presented in these pages that represent the ground truth. I definitely think that the concepts presented here give the reader a mental model for understanding more recent approaches, allowing them to evaluate when to use each type.

Summary

This chapter presented a comprehensive array of use cases for graphs in machine learning projects. In this chapter, you learned

- How to use graphs and a graph model to manage data. Designing a proper graph model allows multiple data sources to be merged in a single connected and well-organized source of truth. This approach is useful not only because it creates a single knowledge base—the *knowledge graph*—that can be shared among multiple projects, but also because it can organize the data in a way that suits the kind of analysis to be performed.

- How to process data by using graph algorithms. Graph algorithms support a wide spectrum of analysis and can be used in isolation or as part of a more complex and articulated analytics pipeline.
- How to design a graph that stores the prediction model resulting from training to simplify and speed access during the prediction phase.
- How to visualize data in the form of graphs. Data visualization is a crucial aspect of predictive analysis. A graph can be a pattern for modeling the data so that it can be visualized by an analyst in an efficient and effective way; the human brain can do the rest.
- What deep learning and graph neural networks are.

References

[Diestel, 2017] Diestel, Reinhard. *Graph Theory.* 5th ed. New York: Springer, 2017.

[Eagle, Quinn, and Clauset, 2009] Eagle, Nathan, John A. Quinn, and Aaron Clauset. "Methodologies for Continuous Cellular Tower Data Analysis." Proceedings of the 7th International Conference on Pervasive Computing (2009): 342–353.

[Frolov and Oseledets, 2016] Frolov, Evgeny, and Ivan Oseledets. "Tensor Methods and Recommendation Engines." GroundAI, March 18, 2016.

[Goodfellow et al., 2016] Goodfellow, Ian, Yoshua Bengio, and Aaron Courville. *Deep Learning.* The MIT Press. 2016.

[Jannach et al., 2010] Jannach, Dietmar, Markus Zanker, Alexander Felfernig, and Gerhard Friedrich. *Recommender Systems: An Introduction.* Cambridge, UK: Cambridge University Press, 2010.

[Kleindorfer and Saad, 2005] Kleindorfer, Paul R., and Germaine H. Saad. "Managing Disruption Risks in Supply Chains." Production and Operation Management 14:1 (2005): 53–68.

[Krebs, 2016] Krebs, Valdis. Political Choices. T N T: The Network Thinkers, January 2016. http://www.thenetworkthinkers.com.

[Lanum, 2016] Lanum, Corey L. *Visualizing Graph Data.* Shelter Island, NY: Manning, 2016.

[Mihalcea and Tarau, 2004] Mihalcea, Rada, and Paul Tarau. "TextRank: Bringing Order into Text." Proceedings of the 2004 Conference on Empirical Methods in Natural Language Processing (2004): 404–411.

[Negro et al., 2017] Negro, Alessandro, Vlasta Kus, Miro Marchi, and Christophe Willemsen. "Efficient Unsupervised Keywords Extraction Using Graphs." GraphAware, October 3, 2017. http://mng.bz/w0Z7.

[Perer, 2010] Perer, Adam. "Finding Beautiful Insights in the Chaos of Social Network Visualizations." In *Beautiful Visualization,* edited by Julie Steele and Noah Iliinsky. Sebastopol, CA: O'Reilly, 2010. 157–173.

[Russel and Norvig, 2009] Russell, Stuart J., and Peter Norvig. *Artificial Intelligence: A Modern Approach.* 3rd ed. Upper Saddle River, NJ: Pearson, 2009.

[Schaeffer, 2007] Schaeffer, Satu Elisa. "Survey: Graph Clustering." Computer Science Review 1:1 (2007): 27–64.

[Tukey, 1977] Tukey, John W. *Exploratory Data Analysis.* Reading, MA: Addison-Wesley, 1977.

[Wirth and Hipp, 2000] Wirth, R., and J. Hipp. "CRISP-DM: Towards a Standard Process Model for Data Mining." Proceedings of the Fourth International Conference on the Practical Application of Knowledge Discovery and Data Mining (2000): 29–39.

[Zhao and Silva, 2016] Zhao, Liang, and Thiago Christiano Silva. *Machine Learning in Complex Networks.* New York: Springer, 2016.

Part 2

Recommendations

Representation is one of the most complex and compelling tasks in machine learning and computer science in general. Pedro Domingos, a computer science professor at the University of Washington, published an article [Domingos, 2012] in which he decomposed machine learning into three main components: representation, evaluation, and optimization. Representation specifically affects three core aspects of a machine learning project's life cycle:

- The formal language (or schema) in which a training dataset is expressed before it is passed as input to the learning process
- The way in which the result of the learning process—the *predictive model*—is stored
- How, during the prediction phase, the training data and the prediction model are accessed during forecasting

All these aspects are influenced by the learning algorithm used to infer the generalization from the observed examples in the training dataset, and they affect the overall performance in terms of forecast accuracy and training and prediction performance (speed).

Starting with the second part, this book focuses on *data modeling*: the formal structures used to represent the training dataset and the inferred model (the result of the learning process) so that a computer program (the learning agent[1]) can process and access it to provide forecasting or analysis to end users. Hence, two different models are taken into account:

---

[1] As defined in chapter 1, an agent is considered to be learning if, after making observations about the world, it is able to improve its performance on future tasks.

- The *descriptive model* is a simplified representation of reality (the training dataset) created to serve a specific learning purpose. The simplification is based on some assumptions about what is and is not relevant for the specific purpose at hand or sometimes on constraints on the information available.
- The *predictive model* is a formula for estimating the unknown value of interest: the target. Such a formula could be mathematical, a query on a data structure (a database or a graph, for example), a logical statement such as a rule, or any combination of these. It represents, in an efficient format, the result of the learning process on the training dataset, and it is accessed to perform the actual prediction.

The rest of the book illustrates graph-based techniques for data modeling that serve both purposes. In some cases (when the learning algorithm is a graph algorithm), the decision to use graphs as a data model is a necessary one. In other cases, the graph approach represents a better option than using a table or other alternatives.

Chapters 2 and 3 presented some modeling examples at a high level, such as using cellular tower networks for monitoring subjects, co-occurrence graphs for finding keywords, and bipartite graphs for representing a User-Item dataset in a recommendation engine. Those examples showed the advantages of a graph approach for modeling purposes in those specific scenarios. In this second part of the book. we'll go into more depth. By using three different macro goals—recommendations, fraud analytics, and text mining—the chapters in this part and the next parts present in greater detail a selection of modeling techniques and best practices for representing the training dataset, predictive models, and access patterns. Nonetheless, the focus remains on graph modeling techniques and the predictive algorithms. The main purpose is to provide you with the mental tools to represent the inputs or outputs of predictive techniques as graphs, showing the intrinsic value of the graph approach. Example scenarios are presented, and whenever possible and appropriate, the design techniques are projected—with the necessary extensions and considerations—into other scenarios where they are relevant.

From now until the end of the book, the chapters are also practical. Real datasets, pieces of code, and queries are introduced and discussed in detail. For each example scenario, datasets are selected, models are designed and ingested, and a predictive model is created and accessed to get forecasts. For queries, we will use one of the standard graph query languages, Cypher (https://www.opencypher.org). This SQL-like language began life as a proprietary query mechanism specifically for Neo4j databases, but since 2015, it has been an open standard. Several other companies (such as SAP HANA and Databricks) and projects (such as Apache Spark and RedisGraph) have since adopted it as a query language for graph databases.

No previous knowledge about the Cypher language is required for this part, and throughout the book, all the queries are described and commented in detail. If you're interested in learning more about it, I recommend taking a look at the official documentation and a few books that describe the topic in great detail [Robinson et al.,

2015, and Vukotic et al., 2014]. Furthermore, so that you can better understand the content of this part and the next parts, I recommend that you install and configure Neo4j and run the queries. This gives you the opportunity to learn a new query language, play with graphs, and fix the concepts presented here better in your mind. Appendix B provides a quick intro to Neo4j and Cypher, and explains why Neo4j is used in this book as a reference graph database. An installation guide is available there and on the Neo4j developer site (https://neo4j.com/docs/operations-manual). The queries and the code examples were tested with the version 4.x, the latest available at the time of writing.

The chapters of this part focus on data modeling as applied to recommendation engines. Because this topic is a common graph-related machine learning topic, several techniques are introduced in great detail.

The term *recommender system* (RS) refers to all software tools and techniques that, by using the knowledge they can gather about the users and items in question, suggest items that are likely to be of interest to a particular user [Ricci et al., 2015]. The suggestions can be related to various decision-making processes, such as what products to buy, which music to listen to, or which films to watch. In this context, *item* is the general term used to identify what the system recommends to users. An RS normally focuses on a specific type or class of items, such as books to buy, news articles to read, or hotels to book. The overall design and the techniques used to generate the recommendations are customized to provide useful and relevant suggestions for that specific type of item. Sometimes, it is possible to use information gathered from a class of items to provide recommendations on other types of items. Someone who buys suits might also be interested in business books or expensive phones, for example.

Although the main purpose of RSs is to help companies to sell more items, they also have a lot of advantages from the user's perspective. Users are continually overwhelmed by choice: what news to read, products to buy, shows to watch, and so on. The set of items offered by different providers is growing quickly, and users can no longer sift through all of them. In this sense, recommendation engines provide a customized experience, helping people find what they are looking for or what could be of interest to them more quickly. The result is that users' satisfaction will be higher because they get relevant results in a short amount of time.

More and more service providers are exploiting this set of tools and techniques [Ricci et al., 2015], for reasons including the following:

- *Increasing the number of items sold*—Helping a provider sell more items than it would without offering any kind of recommendation is probably the most important function of an RS. This goal is achieved because the recommended items are likely to suit the user's needs and wants. With the plethora of items (news articles, books, watches, or whatever) available in most contexts, users are often flooded by so much information that they cannot find what they are looking for, and the result is that they don't conclude their sessions with a concrete action. The RS represents in this sense a valid help in refining user needs and expectations.

- *Selling more diverse items*—Another important function that an RS can accomplish is allowing the user to select items that might be hard to find without a precise recommendation. In a tourism RS, for example, the service provider may want to promote the places that could be of interest to a particular user in the area, not only the most popular ones. By providing customized suggestions, the provider dramatically reduces the risk of advertising places that are not likely to suit that user's taste. By suggesting or advertising less popular (in the sense of less-known) places to users, the RS can improve the quality of their overall experience in the area and allow new places to be discovered and become popular.

- *Increasing user satisfaction*—A properly designed RS improves the user's experience with the application. How many times, while navigating an online bookstore like Amazon, have you looked at the recommendations and thought, "Wow, that book definitely looks interesting"? If the user finds the recommendations interesting, relevant, and gently suggested by a well-designed frontend, they will enjoy using the system. The killer combination of effective, accurate recommendations and a usable interface will increase the user's subjective evaluation of the system, and most likely, they will come back again. Hence, this approach increases system use, data available for the model building, the quality of the recommendations, and user satisfaction.

- *Increasing user loyalty*—Websites and other customer-centric applications appreciate and encourage loyalty by recognizing returning customers and treating them as valued visitors. Tracking returning users is a common requirement for RSs (with some exceptions) because the algorithms use the information acquired from users during previous interactions, such as their ratings of items, for making recommendations in the course of the user's next visit. Consequently, the more often a user interacts with the site or application, the more refined the user's model becomes; the representation of their preferences develops, and the effectiveness of the recommender's output is increased.

- *Getting a better understanding of what the user wants*—Another important side effect of a properly implemented RS is that it creates a model for the user's preferences, which are collected explicitly or predicted by the system itself. The service provider can reuse the resulting new knowledge for other goals, such as improving the management of the item's stock or production. In the travel domain, destination management organizations can decide to advertise a specific region to new customer sectors or use a particular type of promotional message derived by analyzing the data collected by the RS (transactions of the users).

These aspects must be taken into account during the design of an RS because they affect not only the way in which the system gathers, stores, and processes data, but also the way in which it is used for the predictions. For some of the reasons listed here, if not all, a graph representation of the data and graph-based analysis can play an important role by simplifying data management, mining, communication, and delivery. These aspects are highlighted throughout this part.

It is worth noting that we are talking about personalized recommendations. In other words, every user receives a different list of recommendations depending on their tastes, which are inferred based on previous interactions or information gathered by different methods [Jannach et al., 2010]. The provisioning of personalized recommendations requires the system to know something (or a lot of things) about each user and each item. Hence, the RS must develop and maintain a user model (or user profile) containing, for example, data on the user's preferences, as well as an item model (or item profile) containing information on the item's features or other details.

The creation of user and item models is central to every recommender system. The way in which this information is gathered, modeled, and exploited, however, depends on the particular recommendation technique and the related learning algorithms. According to the type of information used to build the models and the approach used to forecast user interests and provide predictions, different types of recommender systems can be implemented.

This part explores four main recommendation techniques. These techniques are only a sample of the solutions available, but I selected them because they cover a wide spectrum of opportunities and modeling examples. The four approaches are

- *Content-based recommendations* (chapter 4)—The recommendation engine uses item descriptions (manually created or automatically extracted) and user profiles that assign importance to different characteristics. It learns to find items that are similar in content to the ones that the user liked (interacted with) in the past. A typical example is a news recommender that compares the articles the user read previously with the most recent ones available to find items that are similar in terms of content.

- *Collaborative filtering* (chapter 5)—The basic idea behind collaborative recommendations is that if users had the same interests in the past—bought similar books or watched similar movies, for example—they will have the same behavior in the future. The most famous example of this approach is Amazon's recommender system, which uses user-item interaction history to provide users recommendations.

- *Session-based recommendations* (chapter 6)—The recommendation engine makes predictions based on session data, such as session clicks and descriptions of clicked items. A session-based approach is useful when user profiles and details of past activities are not available. It uses information about current user interactions and matches it with other users' previous interactions. An example is a travel site that provides details on hotels, villas, and apartments; users generally don't log in until the end of the process, when it's time to book. In such cases, no history about the user is available.

- *Context-aware recommendations* (chapter 7)—The recommendation engine generates relevant recommendations by adapting them to the specific context of the user [Adomavicius et al., 2011]. Contextual information could include location, time, or company (who the user is with). Many mobile applications use contextual information (location, weather, time, and so on) to refine the recommendations provided to users.

This list is not exhaustive and not the only classifications available. From some perspectives, session-based and context-aware recommendations might be considered subcategories of collaborative filtering, depending on the type of algorithms used to implement them. This list, however, reflects the way in which the approaches will be described in this book.

Each approach has advantages and disadvantages. Hybrid recommendation systems combine approaches to overcome such issues and provide better recommendations to users. Hybrid recommendation approaches are also discussed in chapter 7.

References

[Domingos, 2012] Domingos, Pedro. "A Few Useful Things to Know About Machine Learning." *Communications of the ACM* 55:10 (2012): 78–87. doi: http://dx.doi.org/10.1145/2347736.2347755

Cypher Query Language Reference, Version 9. http://mng.bz/zGza.

[Robinson et al., 2015], Robinson, Ian, Jim Webber, and Emil Eifrem. *Graph Databases*. 2nd ed. Sebastopol, CA: O'Reilly, 2015.

[Vukotic et al., 2014] Vukotic, Aleksa, Dominic Fox, Jonas Partner, Nicki Watt, and Tareq Abedrabbo. *Neo4j in Action*. Shelter Island, NY: Manning, 2014.

[Ricci et al., 2015] Ricci, Lior Rokach, and Bracha Shapira. *Recommender Systems Handbook*. 2nd ed. New York: Springer, 2015.

[Jannach et al., 2010] Jannach, Dietmar, Markus Zanker, Alexander Felfernig, and Gerhard Friedrich. *Recommender Systems: An Introduction*. Cambridge, UK: Cambridge University Press, 2010. doi: http://dx.doi.org/10.1017/CBO9780511763113

[Adomavicius et al., 2011] Adomavicius, Gediminas, Bamshad Mobasher, Francesco Ricci, and Alexander Tuzhilin. "Context-Aware Recommender Systems." *AI Magazine* 32:3 (2011): 67–80, 2011. DOI: https://doi.org/10.1609/aimag.v32i3.2364

Content-based recommendations
4

This chapter covers

- Designing proper graph models for a content-based recommendation engine
- Importing existing (nongraph) datasets into the designed graph models
- Implementing working content-based recommendation engines

Suppose you would like to build a movie recommender system for your local video rental store. Old-fashioned Blockbuster-style rental shops have largely been put out of business by new streaming platforms such as Netflix (http://mng.bz/0rBx), but some still exist here and there. There's one in my town. Back when I was at university (a long time ago), I used to go there with my brother every Sunday to rent some action movies. (Keep this preference in mind; it will be useful later!) The important fact here is that this scenario inherently has a lot in common with more-complex online recommender systems, including the following:

- *A small user community*—The number of users or customers is quite small. Most recommendation engines, as we'll discuss later, require a lot of active users (in terms of number of interactions, such as views, clicks, or buys) to be effective.
- *A limited set of well-curated items*—Each item (in this case, a movie) can have a lot of associated details. For movies, these details might include plot description, keywords, genres, and actors. These details are not always available in other scenarios, such as one in which the item has only an identifier.
- *Knowledge of user preferences*—The owner or shop assistant knows the preferences of almost all the customers, even if they've rented only a few movies or games.

Before we move on to discuss technicalities and algorithms, take a moment to think about the brick-and-mortar shop. Think about the owner or clerks and what they do to succeed. They make an effort to get to know their customers by analyzing their previous rental habits and remembering conversations with them. They try to create a profile for each customer, containing details on their tastes (horror and action movies rather than romcoms), habits (renting generally on the weekend or during the week), item preferences (movies rather than video games), and so on. They collect information over time to build up this profile and use the mental models they create to welcome each customer in an effective way, suggesting something that could be of interest to them, or perhaps sending them a message when a tempting new movie becomes available in the shop.

Now consider a virtual shop assistant that welcomes a site's users, suggesting movies or games to rent or sending them an email when something new that might be of interest comes into stock. The conditions described earlier preclude some approaches to recommendations because they require more data. In the case we're considering (both the real and the simplified virtual shop), a valuable solution is a *content-based recommender system (CBRS)*. CBRSs rely on item and user descriptions (content) to build item representations (or item profiles) and user profiles to suggest items similar to those a target user liked in the past. (These types of recommender systems are also known as *semantic-aware CBRSs*.) This approach allows the system to provide recommendations even when the amount of data available is quite small (that is, a limited number of users, items, or interactions).

The basic process of producing content-based recommendations consists of matching the attributes of the target user profile, in which preferences and interests are modeled, with the attributes of the items to find items similar to what the user liked in the past. The result is a relevance score that predicts the target user's level of interest in those items. Usually, attributes for describing an item are features extracted from metadata associated with that item or textual features somehow related to the item—descriptions, comments, keywords, and so on. These content-rich items contain a great deal of information by themselves that can be used for making comparisons or inferring a user's interests based on the list of items they've interacted with. For these reasons, CBRSs don't require a lot of data to be effective.

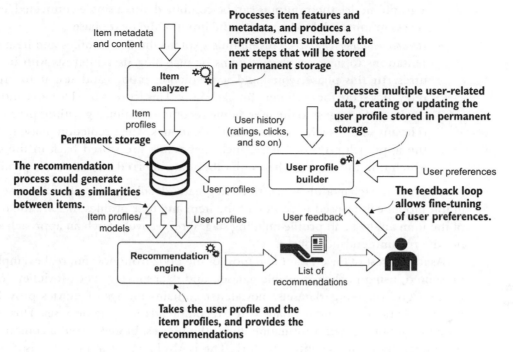

Figure 4.1 High-level architecture of a CBRS

Figure 4.1 shows the high-level architecture of a CBRS, one of many possible architectures and the one used in this section.

This figure decomposes the recommendation process into three main components:

- *Item analyzer*—The main purpose of this component is to analyze items, extract or identify relevant features, and represent the items in a form suitable for the next processing steps. It takes as input the item content (such as the contents of a book or a product description) and meta information (such as a book's author, the actors in a movie, or movie genres) from one or more information sources and converts them to an item model that is used later to provide recommendations. In the approach described here, this conversion produces graph models, which can be of different types. This graph representation is used to feed the recommendation process.

- *User profile builder*—This process collects data representative of user preferences and infers user profiles. This information set may include explicit user preferences gathered by asking users about their interests or implicit feedback collected by observing and storing user behavior. The result is a model—specifically, a graph model—that represents user interest in some item, item feature, or both. In the architecture shown in figure 4.1, the item profiles (created during the item analysis stage) and user profiles (created during this stage) converge in the same database. Moreover, because both processes return a graph model, their outputs can be combined into a single connected, easy-to-access graph model to be used as the input of the next phase.

- *Recommendation engine*—This module exploits the user profiles and item representations to suggest relevant items by matching user interests with item features. In this phase, you build a prediction model and use it to create a relevancy score for each item for each user. This score is used to rank and order the items to suggest to the user. Some recommendation algorithms precompute relevant values, such as item similarities, to make the prediction phase faster. In the approach proposed here, such new values are stored back in the graph, which is in this way enriched with other data inferred from the item profiles.

In section 4.1, each module is described in greater detail. Specifically, I describe how a graph model can be used to represent the item and user profiles that are the outputs of the item analysis and profile-building stages, respectively. Such an approach simplifies the recommendation phase.

As in the rest of the chapter and most of the book from now on, real examples are presented, using publicly available datasets and data sources. The MovieLens dataset (https://grouplens.org/datasets/movielens) contains ratings of movies provided by real users and is a standard dataset for recommendation engine tests. This dataset doesn't contain a lot of information about the movies, however, and a content-based recommender requires content to work. This is why in our examples, it is used in combination with data available from the Internet Movie Database (IMDb),[2] such as plot descriptions, keywords, genres, actors, directors, and writers.

4.1   *Representing item features*

In the content-based approach to recommendation, an item can be represented by a set of features. *Features* (also called *properties* or *attributes*) are important or relevant characteristics of that item. In simple cases, such characteristics are easy to discover, extract, or gather. In the movie recommendation example, each movie can be described by using

- Genres or categories (horror, action, cartoon, drama, and so on)
- Plot description
- Actors
- Tags or keywords manually (or automatically) assigned to the movie
- Year of production
- Director
- Writer(s)
- Producer(s)

---

[2] IMDb (https://www.imdb.com) is an online database of information related to films, television programs, home videos, video games, and internet streams, including details on the cast and production crew, plot summaries, trivia, and fan reviews and ratings.

Consider the information presented in table 4.1 (source: IMDb).

Table 4.1 Examples of movie-related data

Title	Genre	Director	Writers	Actors
Pulp Fiction	Action, Crime, Thriller	Quentin Tarantino	Quentin Tarantino, Roger Avary	John Travolta, Samuel Jackson, Bruce Willis, Uma Thurman
The Punisher (2004)	Action, Adventure, Crime, Drama, Thriller	Jonathan Hensleigh	Jonathan Hensleigh, Michael France	Thomas Jane, John Travolta, Samantha Mathis
Kill Bill: Volume 1	Action, Crime, Thriller	Quentin Tarantino	Quentin Tarantino, Uma Thurman	Uma Thurman, Lucy Liu, Vivica A. Fox

Such features are defined generally as *meta information* because they are not actually the content of the item. Unfortunately, there are classes of items for which it is not so easy to find or identify features, such as document collections, email messages, news articles, and images.

Text-based items do not tend to have readily available sets of features. Nonetheless, their content can be represented by identifying a set of features that describe them. A common approach is the identification of words that characterize the topic. Different techniques exist for accomplishing this task, some of which are described in section 12.4.2; the result is a list of features (keywords, tags, relevant words) that describe the content of the item. These features can be used to represent a text-based item in exactly the same way as the meta information here, so the approach described from now on can be applied when meta information features are easily accessible or when features have to be extracted from content. Extracting tags or features from images is out of the scope of this book, but when those features have been extracted, the approach is exactly the same as that discussed in this section.

Although representing such a list of features in a graph—more precisely, a *property graph*[3]—is straightforward, you should take into account some modeling best practices while designing the item model. Consider, as a simplistic example, the graph model in figure 4.2 of the movies in table 4.1 with their related features.

In this figure, the simplest possible representation of the item is used, with the related list of attributes. For each item, a single node is created, and the features are modeled as properties of the node. Listing 4.1 shows the Cypher queries used to create the three movies. (Run the queries one at a time). Please refer to appendix B for

---

[3] The property graph, introduced in chapter 2, organizes data as nodes, relationships, and properties (data stored on the nodes or relationships).

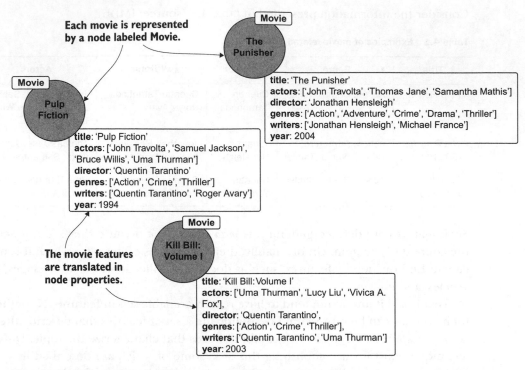

Each movie is represented by a node labeled Movie.

Movie
The Punisher

title: 'The Punisher'
actors: ['John Travolta', 'Thomas Jane', 'Samantha Mathis']
director: 'Jonathan Hensleigh'
genres: ['Action', 'Adventure', 'Crime', 'Drama', 'Thriller']
writers: ['Jonathan Hensleigh', 'Michael France']
year: 2004

Movie
Pulp Fiction

title: 'Pulp Fiction'
actors: ['John Travolta', 'Samuel Jackson', 'Bruce Willis', 'Uma Thurman']
director: 'Quentin Tarantino'
genres: ['Action', 'Crime', 'Thriller']
writers: ['Quentin Tarantino', 'Roger Avary']
year: 1994

Movie
Kill Bill: Volume I

The movie features are translated in node properties.

title: 'Kill Bill: Volume I'
actors: ['Uma Thurman', 'Lucy Liu', 'Vivica A. Fox'],
director: 'Quentin Tarantino',
genres: ['Action', 'Crime', 'Thriller'],
writers: ['Quentin Tarantino', 'Uma Thurman']
year: 2003

Figure 4.2 **Basic graph-based item representation**

basic information on Neo4j, guidance on the installation, and a quick intro to Cypher. You'll learn the rest throughout the book.

Listing 4.1 Queries to create a basic model for movie representation

Each CREATE statement creates a new node with Movie as the label.

The curly braces define the list of key/value properties of the node, beginning with title.

```
CREATE (p:Movie {
    title: 'Pulp Fiction',
    actors: ['John Travolta', 'Samuel Jackson', 'Bruce Willis', 'Uma Thurman'],
    director: 'Quentin Tarantino',
    genres: ['Action', 'Crime', 'Thriller'],
    writers: ['Quentin Tarantino', 'Roger Avary'],
    year: 1994
})

CREATE (t:Movie {
    title: 'The Punisher',
    actors: ['Thomas Jane', 'John Travolta', 'Samantha Mathis'],
    director: 'Jonathan Hensleigh',
    genres: ['Action', 'Adventure', 'Crime', 'Drama', 'Thriller'],
    writers: ['Jonathan Hensleigh', 'Michael France'],
    year: 2004
})
```

Properties can be of different types: strings, arrays, integers, doubles, and so on.

The parentheses define the boundaries of the created node instance.

```
CREATE (k:Movie {
    title: 'Kill Bill: Volume 1',
    actors: ['Uma Thurman', 'Lucy Liu', 'Vivica A. Fox'],
    director: 'Quentin Tarantino',
    genres: ['Action', 'Crime', 'Thriller'],
    writers: ['Quentin Tarantino', 'Uma Thurman'],
    year: 2003
})
```

In the Cypher queries, CREATE allows you to create a new node (or relationship). The parentheses define the boundaries of the created node instances, which in these cases are identified by p, t, and k, and a specific label, Movie, is assigned to each new node. The label specifies the type of a node or the role the node is playing in the graph. Using labels is not mandatory, but it is a common and useful practice for organizing nodes in a graph (and is more performant than assigning a type property to each node). Labels are a bit like tables in an old-fashioned relational database, identifying classes of nodes, but in a property graph database, there are no constraints on the list of attributes (as there are for columns in the relational model). Each node, regardless of the label assigned to it, can contain any set of properties or even no properties. Furthermore, a node can have multiple labels. These two features of the property graph database—no constraints on the list of attributes and multiple labels—make the resulting model quite flexible. Finally, a set of comma-separated properties is specified inside the curly braces.

The single-node design approach has the advantage of a one-to-one mapping between the node and the item with all the relevant attributes. With an effective index configuration, retrieving movies by feature values is fast. The Cypher query to retrieve all the movies directed by Quentin Tarantino, for example, looks like the following listing.

> **Listing 4.2 Query to search for all the movies directed by Quentin Tarantino**

The MATCH clause defines the graph pattern to match: a node with the label Movie in this case.

```
MATCH (m:Movie)
WHERE m.director = 'Quentin Tarantino'
RETURN m
```

The WHERE clause defines the filter conditions.

The RETURN clause specifies the list of elements to return.

In this query, the MATCH clause is used to define the graph pattern to match. Here, we are looking for all the Movie nodes. The WHERE clause is part of MATCH and adds constraints—filters—to it, as in relational SQL. In this example, the query is filtering by the director's name. The RETURN clause specifies what to return. Figure 4.3 shows the result of running this query from the Neo4j browser.

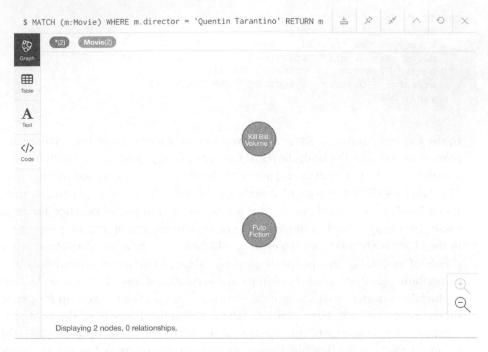

Figure 4.3   Query results from the Neo4j browser for the simple model

The simple model has multiple drawbacks, including the following:

- *Data duplication*—In each property, data is duplicated. The director name, for example, is duplicated in all the movies with the same director, and the same is true for authors, genres, and so on. Data duplication is an issue in terms of the disk space required by the database and data consistency (how can we know whether "Q. Tarantino" is the same as "Quentin Tarantino"?), and it makes change difficult.

- *Error proneness*—Particularly during data ingestion, this simple model is subject to issues such as misspelled values and property names. These errors are difficult to identify if the data is isolated in each node.

- *Difficult to extend/enrich*—If, during the life of the model, an extension is required, such as grouping genres to improve search capabilities or provide semantic analysis, these features are hard to provide.

- *Navigation complexity*—Any access or search is based on value comparison or, worse, string comparison. Such a model doesn't use the real power of graphs, which enable efficient navigation of relationships and nodes.

To better understand why such a model is poor in terms of navigation and access patterns, suppose that you wanted to query for "Actors who worked together in the same movie." Such a query can be written as shown in listing 4.3.

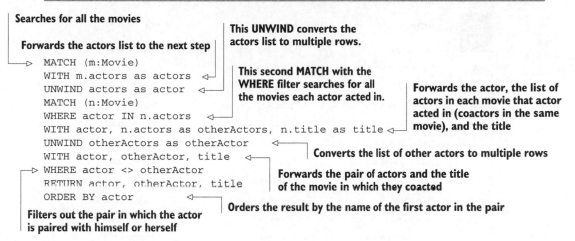

Listing 4.3 Query to find the actors who worked together (simple model)

This query works as follows:

1. The first MATCH searches for all the movies.

2. WITH is used to forward the results to the next step. The first one forwards only the actors list.

3. With UNWIND, you can transform any list back to individual rows. The list of actors in each movie is converted to a sequence of actors.

4. For each actor, the next MATCH with the WHERE condition finds all the movies they acted in.

5. The second WITH forwards the actor considered in this iteration, the list of actors in each movie they acted in, and the movie title.

6. The second UNWIND transforms the list of other actors and forwards the actor-other actor pair along with the title of the film they acted in together.

7. The last WHERE filters out pairs in which the actor is paired with their own self.

8. The query returns the names in each pair and the title of the movie in which both acted.

9. The results are sorted, with the clause ORDER BY, by the name of the first actor in the pair.

In such a query, all the comparisons are based on string matches, so if there is a misspelling or a different format ("U. Thurman" instead of "Uma Thurman", for example), the results will be incorrect or incomplete. Figure 4.4 shows the result of running this query on the graph database we created.

A more advanced model for representing items, which is even more useful and powerful for these specific purposes, exposes recurring properties as nodes. In this model, each entity, such as an actor, a director, or a genre, has its own representation—its own node. The relationships among such entities are represented by edges

```
$ MATCH (m:Movie) WITH m.actors as actors UNWIND ...
```

actor	otherActor	title
"Bruce Willis"	"John Travolta"	"Pulp Fiction"
"Bruce Willis"	"Samuel L. Jackson"	"Pulp Fiction"
"Bruce Willis"	"Uma Thurman"	"Pulp Fiction"
"John Travolta"	"Samuel L. Jackson"	"Pulp Fiction"
"John Travolta"	"Bruce Willis"	"Pulp Fiction"
"John Travolta"	"Uma Thurman"	"Pulp Fiction"
"John Travolta"	"Thomas Jane"	"The Punisher"
"John Travolta"	"Samantha Mathis"	"The Punisher"
"Lucy Liu"	"Uma Thurman"	"Kill Bill: Volume 1"
"Lucy Liu"	"Vivica A. Fox"	"Kill Bill: Volume 1"
"Samantha Mathis"	"Thomas Jane"	"The Punisher"
"Samantha Mathis"	"John Travolta"	"The Punisher"
"Samuel L. Jackson"	"John Travolta"	"Pulp Fiction"
"Samuel L. Jackson"	"Bruce Willis"	"Pulp Fiction"
"Samuel L. Jackson"	"Uma Thurman"	"Pulp Fiction"
"Thomas Jane"	"John Travolta"	"The Punisher"
"Thomas Jane"	"Samantha Mathis"	"The Punisher"
"Uma Thurman"	"John Travolta"	"Pulp Fiction"
"Uma Thurman"	"Samuel L. Jackson"	"Pulp Fiction"
"Uma Thurman"	"Bruce Willis"	"Pulp Fiction"
"Uma Thurman"	"Lucy Liu"	"Kill Bill: Volume 1"
"Uma Thurman"	"Vivica A. Fox"	"Kill Bill: Volume 1"
"Vivica A. Fox"	"Uma Thurman"	"Kill Bill: Volume 1"
"Vivica A. Fox"	"Lucy Liu"	"Kill Bill: Volume 1"

Started streaming 24 records after 10 ms and completed after 10 ms.

Figure 4.4   Results from the query with the sample database we created

in the graph. The edge can also contain some properties to further characterize the relationship. Figure 4.5 shows what the new model looks like for the movie scenario.

New nodes appear in the advanced model to represent each feature value, and the feature types are specified by labels such as Genre, Actor, Director, and Writer. Some nodes can have multiple labels, because they can have multiple roles in the same or different movies. Each node has some properties that describe it, such as name for actors and directors and genre for genres. Now the movies have only the title property because this property is specific to the item itself; there's no reason to extract it

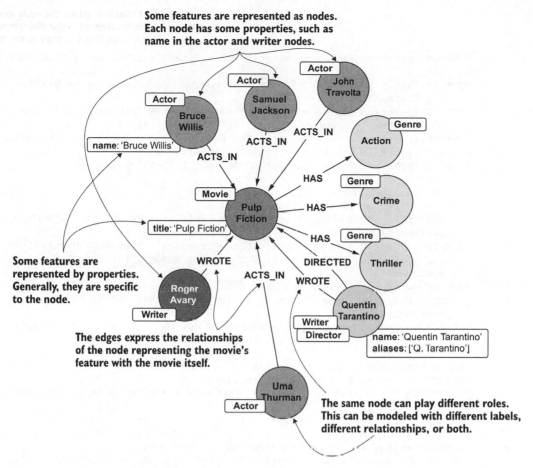

Figure 4.5 Advanced graph-based item representation

and represent it as a separate node. The queries to create this new graph model for the movie example are shown in the following listing.[4]

Listing 4.4 Queries to create an advanced model for movie representation

Each of these statements creates a unique constraint in the database.

```
CREATE CONSTRAINT ON (a:Movie) ASSERT a.title IS UNIQUE;
CREATE CONSTRAINT ON (a:Genre) ASSERT a.genre IS UNIQUE;
CREATE CONSTRAINT ON (a:Person) ASSERT a.name IS UNIQUE;

CREATE (pulp:Movie {title: 'Pulp Fiction'})
FOREACH (director IN ['Quentin Tarantino']
```

Each CREATE creates the movie with only the title as a property.

FOREACH loops over a list and executes the MERGE for each element.

---

[4] Please tidy your database with MATCH (n) DETACH DELETE n.

MERGE first checks whether the node already
exists, using the uniqueness of the director name
in this case; if not, it creates the node.

```
| MERGE (p:Person {name: director}) SET p:Director MERGE (p)-[:DIRECTED]->
➥ (pulp))
FOREACH (actor IN ['John Travolta', 'Samuel L. Jackson', 'Bruce Willis',
➥ 'Uma Thurman']
| MERGE (p:Person {name: actor}) SET p:Actor MERGE (p)-[:ACTS_IN]->(pulp))
FOREACH (writer IN ['Quentin Tarantino', 'Roger Avary']
| MERGE (p:Person {name: writer}) SET p:Writer MERGE (p)-[:WROTE]->(pulp))
FOREACH (genre IN ['Action', 'Crime', 'Thriller']
| MERGE (g:Genre {genre: genre}) MERGE (pulp)-[:HAS]->(g))

CREATE (punisher:Movie {title: 'The Punisher'})
FOREACH (director IN ['Jonathan Hensleigh']
| MERGE (p:Person {name: director}) SET p:Director MERGE (p)-[:DIRECTED]->
➥ (punisher))
FOREACH (actor IN ['Thomas Jane', 'John Travolta', 'Samantha Mathis']
| MERGE (p:Person {name: actor}) SET p:Actor MERGE (p)-[:ACTS_IN]->
➥ (punisher))
FOREACH (writer IN ['Jonathan Hensleigh', 'Michael France']
| MERGE (p:Person {name: writer}) SET p:Writer MERGE (p)-[:WROTE]->
➥ (punisher))
FOREACH (genre IN ['Action', 'Adventure', 'Crime', 'Drama', 'Thriller']
| MERGE (g:Genre {genre: genre}) MERGE (punisher)-[:HAS]->(g))

CREATE (bill:Movie {title: 'Kill Bill: Volume 1'})
FOREACH (director IN ['Quentin Tarantino']
| MERGE (p:Person {name: director}) SET p:Director MERGE (p)-[:DIRECTED]->
➥ (bill))
FOREACH (actor IN ['Uma Thurman', 'Lucy Liu', 'Vivica A. Fox']
| MERGE (p:Person {name: actor}) SET p:Actor MERGE (p)-[:ACTS_IN]->(bill))
FOREACH (writer IN ['Quentin Tarantino', 'Uma Thurman']
| MERGE (p:Person {name: writer}) SET p:Writer MERGE (p)-[:WROTE]->(bill))
FOREACH (genre IN ['Action', 'Crime', 'Thriller']
| MERGE (g:Genre {genre: genre}) MERGE (bill)-[:HAS]->(g))
```

Although graph databases are generally referred to as schemaless, in Neo4j it is possible to define some constraints in the database. In this case, the first three queries create three constraints on the uniqueness of the `title` in a `Movie`, the value of a `Genre`, and the name of a `Person`, respectively, which will prevent, for example, having the same person (actor, director, or writer) appear several times in the database. As described previously, in the new model the idea is to have a single entity represented by a single node in the database. The constraints help enforce this modeling decision.

After the constraint creation, the `CREATE` clause (repeated three times, once for each movie in the example) works as before to create each new `Movie` with the `title` as a property. Then the `FOREACH` clauses loop over directors, actors, writers, and genres, respectively, and for each element, they search for a node to connect to the `Movie` node, creating a new node if necessary. In the case of actors, writers, and directors, a generic node with the label `Person` is created by means of a `MERGE` clause. `MERGE` ensures that the supplied pattern exists in the graph, either by reusing existing nodes and relationships that match the supplied predicates or by creating new nodes and relationships. The SET clause in this case assigns a new specific label to the node, depending on needs. The MERGE in the FOREACH checks for (and creates if necessary) the relationship between the Person and the Movie. A similar approach is used for genres. The overall result is shown in figure 4.6.

Modeling pro tip

You can use multiple labels for the same node. In this case, this approach is both useful and necessary because, in the model, we would like to have each person represented uniquely regardless of the role they play in the movie (actor, writer, or director). For this reason, we opt for MERGE instead of CREATE and use a common label for all of them. At the same time, the graph model assigns a specific label for each role the person has. After it is assigned, a label becomes assigned to the node, so it will be easier and more performant to run queries such as "Find me all the producers who . . ."

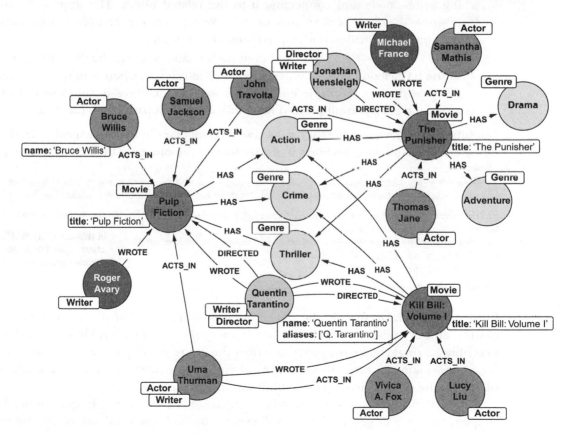

Figure 4.6 Advanced graph-based item representation for the three movies

The new descriptive model not only solves all the issues described earlier, but also provides multiple advantages:

- *No data duplication*—Mapping each relevant entity (person, genre, and so on) to a specific node prevents data duplication. The same entity can play different roles and have different relationships. (Uma Thurman is not only an actress in *Kill Bill: Volume I*, but also one of the writers.) Moreover, for each item a list of alternative forms or aliases can be stored (`"Q. Tarantino"`, `"Director Tarantino"`, `"Quentin Tarantino"`). This approach helps with searches and prevents the same concept from being represented in multiple nodes.
- *Error tolerance*—Preventing data duplication guarantees better tolerance to errors in the values. Unlike in the previous model, in which a misspelled value is hard to spot because it is distributed among all the nodes as a property, here the information is centralized in isolated and nonreplicated entities, making errors easy to identify.
- *Easy to extend/enrich*—Entities can be grouped by using a common label or creating a new node and connecting it to the related nodes. This approach can improve the query performance or style. We can connect multiple genres, such as Crime and Thriller, under a common Drama node.
- *Easy to navigate*—Each node and even each relationship can be the entry point of the navigation (actors, genres, directors, and so on), whereas in the previous schema, the only available entry points were the features in the nodes. This approach enables multiple and more efficient access patterns to the data.

Consider again the query for "Actors who worked together in the same movie." In the new model, constructing this query is much easier, as you can see in the following listing.

Listing 4.5   Query to find all the actors who worked together (advanced model)

```
MATCH (actor:Actor)-[:ACTS_IN]->(movie:Movie)<-[:ACTS_IN]-(otherActor:Actor)
WHERE actor <> otherActor
RETURN actor.name as actor, otherActor.name as otherActor,
movie.title as title
ORDER BY actor
```

In this case, the MATCH clause specifies a more complex graph pattern.

The identity pair is removed.

Listing 4.5 produces exactly the same result as listing 4.4, but it's much simpler, clearer, and even faster—evidently a better use of the MATCH clause. Here, instead of describing a single node, the query describes the entire graph pattern we are looking for; we're looking for two actors who worked on the same movie, movie, and the WHERE filters out the original actor. The result is shown in figure 4.7.

It is worth noting that there is no string comparison. Furthermore, the query is much simpler, and on a bigger database, it will execute faster. If you recall our discussion of the native graph database (section 2.3.4) and how Neo4j implements adjacency-free

```
$ MATCH (a:Actor)-[:ACTS_IN]->(m)<-[:ACTS_IN]-(o:Actor) WHERE a <> o RETURN a.name as...
```

actor	otherActor	title
"Bruce Willis"	"John Travolta"	"Pulp Fiction"
"Bruce Willis"	"Samuel L. Jackson"	"Pulp Fiction"
"Bruce Willis"	"Uma Thurman"	"Pulp Fiction"
"John Travolta"	"Samuel L. Jackson"	"Pulp Fiction"
"John Travolta"	"Bruce Willis"	"Pulp Fiction"
"John Travolta"	"Uma Thurman"	"Pulp Fiction"
"John Travolta"	"Thomas Jane"	"The Punisher"
"John Travolta"	"Samantha Mathis"	"The Punisher"
"Lucy Liu"	"Uma Thurman"	"Kill Bill: Volume 1"
"Lucy Liu"	"Vivica A. Fox"	"Kill Bill: Volume 1"
"Samantha Mathis"	"John Travolta"	"The Punisher"
"Samantha Mathis"	"Thomas Jane"	"The Punisher"
"Samuel L. Jackson"	"John Travolta"	"Pulp Fiction"
"Samuel L. Jackson"	"Bruce Willis"	"Pulp Fiction"
"Samuel L. Jackson"	"Uma Thurman"	"Pulp Fiction"
"Thomas Jane"	"John Travolta"	"The Punisher"

Started streaming 24 records after 6 ms and completed after 6 ms.

Figure 4.7   Results from listing 4.5 with the sample database created

indexes for node relationships (appendix B), it will be much faster than the index lookups on strings that are necessary in listing 4.3.

We've designed our final graph-based model for representing items. In a real machine learning project, the next step would be creating the database, importing data from one or more sources. As stated at the beginning of this section, the MovieLens dataset was selected as a testing dataset. You can download the dataset from GroupLens (https://grouplens.org/datasets/movielens). The code repository contains the instructions and the procedures to download in the right directories and set the code to run properly. Depending on how long you're willing to wait to see a first graph database, you can choose a suitable dataset size. (If you're impatient, choose the smallest.) The dataset contains only a little information about each movie, such as the title and a list of genres, but it also contains a reference to IMDb, where it is possible to access all sorts of details about the movie: plot, directors, actors, writers, and so on. This data is exactly what we need.

Listings 4.6 and 4.7 contain the Python code necessary for reading the data from the MovieLens dataset, storing the first nodes in the graph, and then enriching them by using the information available on IMDb. (You should tidy your database, but doing so is not mandatory.)

Listing 4.6   Importing basic movie information from MovieLens

```
def import_movies(self, file):
    with open(file, 'r+') as in_file:
        reader = csv.reader(in_file, delimiter=',')
```

Reads the values from a CSV file (movies.csv)

Begins a new transaction, which will allow the atomicity (all in or all out) of the operations on the database

Starts a new session connecting to Neo4j

Creates constraints to guarantee the uniqueness of people and genres. The function executeNoException wraps the exception generated if the constraint already exists.

Creates the movie and the genres (the MERGE prevents creating the same genre multiple times) and connects them

Pro tip: To avoid a huge commit at the end, this check ensures that the commit to the database happens for every 1,000 lines processed.

```python
        next(reader, None)
        with self._driver.session() as session:
            self.executeNoException(session,
                "CREATE CONSTRAINT ON (a:Movie) ASSERT a.movieId IS UNIQUE; ")
            self.executeNoException(session,
                "CREATE CONSTRAINT ON (a:Genre) ASSERT a.genre IS UNIQUE; ")

            tx = session.begin_transaction()

            i = 0;
            j = 0;
            for row in reader:
                try:
                    if row:
                        movie_id = strip(row[0])
                        title = strip(row[1])
                        genres = strip(row[2])
                        query = """
                            CREATE (movie:Movie {movieId: $movieId,
                            ➥ title: $title})
                            with movie
                            UNWIND $genres as genre
                            MERGE (g:Genre {genre: genre})
                            MERGE (movie)-[:HAS]->(g)
                        """
                        tx.run(query, {"movieId": movie_id, "title": title,
                        ➥ "genres": genres.split("|")})
                        i += 1
                        j += 1

                        if i == 1000:
                        tx.commit()
                        print(j, "lines processed")
                        i = 0
                        tx = session.begin_transaction()
                except Exception as e:
                    print(e, row, reader.line_num)
            tx.commit()
            print(j, "lines processed")
```

Listing 4.7   Enriching the database with details available on IMDb

```python
def import_movie_details(self, file):
    with open(file, 'r+') as in_file:
        reader = csv.reader(in_file, delimiter=',')
        next(reader, None)
        with self._driver.session() as session:
            self.executeNoException(session, "CREATE CONSTRAINT ON (a:Person)
            ➥ ASSERT a.name IS UNIQUE;")
            tx = session.begin_transaction()
            i = 0;
            j = 0;
            for row in reader:
                try:
```

Creates a new constraint to make people unique

```
                                    if row:
                                        movie_id = strip(row[0])
```
Gets movie details
from IMDb
```
                                        imdb_id = strip(row[1])
                                        movie = self._ia.get_movie(imdb_id)
                                        self.process_movie_info(movie_info=movie, tx=tx,
                                        ➡ movie_id=movie_id)          ◄─┐
                                        i += 1                          │   Processes information from
                                        j += 1                          │   IMDb and stores it in the graph
```

```
                                    if i == 10:
                                        tx.commit()
                                        print(j, "lines processed")
                                        i = 0
                                        tx = session.begin_transaction()
```
Same as listing 4.4   `                  except Exception as e:`
except that the   `                      print(e, row, reader.line_num)`
movie already   `              tx.commit()`
exists   `              print(j, "lines processed")`

```
  def process_movie_info(self, movie_info, tx, movie_id):
└─➡   query = """
          MATCH (movie:Movie {movieId: $movieId})
          SET movie.plot = $plot
          FOREACH (director IN $directors | MERGE (d:Person {name: director})
          ➡ SET d:Director MERGE (d)-[:DIRECTED]->(movie))
          FOREACH (actor IN $actors | MERGE (d:Person {name: actor}) SET
          ➡ d:Actor MERGE (d)-[:ACTS_IN]->(movie))
          FOREACH (producer IN $producers | MERGE (d:Person {name: producer})
          ➡ SET d:Producer MERGE (d)-[:PRODUCED]->(movie))
          FOREACH (writer IN $writers | MERGE (d:Person {name: writer}) SET
          ➡ d:Writer MERGE (d)-[:WROTE]->(movie))
          FOREACH (genre IN $genres | MERGE (g:Genre {genre: genre}) MERGE
          ➡ (movie)-[:HAS]->(g))
      """
      directors = []
      for director in movie_info['directors']:
          if 'name' in director.data:
              directors.append(director['name'])

      genres = ''
      if 'genres' in movie_info:
          genres = movie_info['genres']

      actors = []
      for actor in movie_info['cast']:
          if 'name' in actor.data:
              actors.append(actor['name'])

      writers = []
      for writer in movie_info['writers']:
          if 'name' in writer.data:
              writers.append(writer['name'])

      producers = []
      for producer in movie_info['producers']:
```

```
          producers.append(producer['name'])

  plot = ''
  if 'plot outline' in movie_info:
      plot = movie_info['plot outline']
```
> Takes the plot value from the movie info to create a plot property on the node

```
  tx.run(query, {"movieId": movie_id, "directors": directors,
      "genres": genres, "actors": actors, "plot": plot,
              "writers": writers, "producers": producers})
```

This code is oversimplified, and it takes ages to complete because accessing and parsing IMDb pages require time. In the book's code repository, in addition to the complete implementation of the code, there is a parallel version of the function import_movie_details, in which multiple threads are created to download and process several IMDb pages at the same time. After it completes, the resulting graph has the structure described in figure 4.6.

EXERCISES

Play with the newly created database and write queries to do the following:

1 Search for pairs of actors who worked on the same movie.

   TIP Use listing 4.3 but add LIMIT 50 at the end of the query; otherwise, the query will produce a lot of results.

2 Count, for each actor, how many movies they acted in.
3 Get a movie (by movieId), and list all the features.

The items (movies, in this scenario) are properly modeled and stored in a real graph database. In section 4.2, we are going to model the users.

4.2   *User modeling*

In a CBRS, several methods exist for gathering and modeling user profiles. The selected design model will vary according to how the preferences are collected (implicitly or explicitly) and the type of filtering strategy or recommendation approach. A straightforward way to collect user preferences is to ask the user. The user might express interest in specific genres or keywords, or in particular actors or directors.

From a high-level perspective, the purpose of the user profile and the defined model is to help the recommendation engine assign a score to each item or item feature. The score helps rank the items suggested to the specific user, ordered from high to low. For this reason, recommender systems belong to the area of machine learning called *learning to rank*.

We can add preferences or interests to the model we are designing by adding nodes for users and connecting them to the features of interest. The resulting schema will look like figure 4.8.

The graph model defined for modeling user preferences extends the model previously described for the items, adding a new node for each user and connecting it to the features of interest to the user.

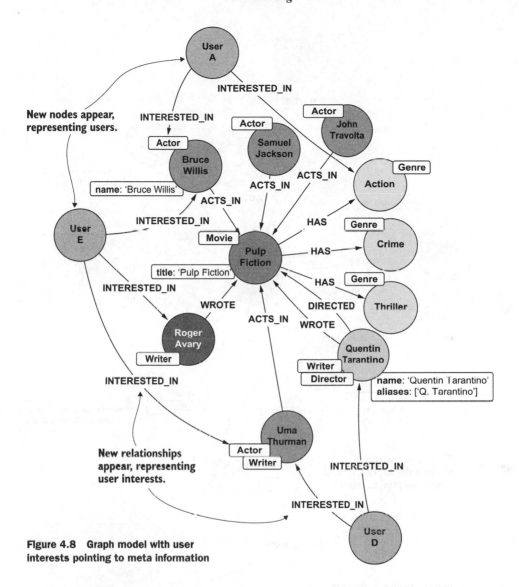

Figure 4.8 Graph model with user interests pointing to meta information

Alternatively, the system can explicitly ask the user to rate some items. The optimal approach is to select items that will help us understand, in the broadest sense, the user's tastes. The resulting graph model looks like figure 4.9.

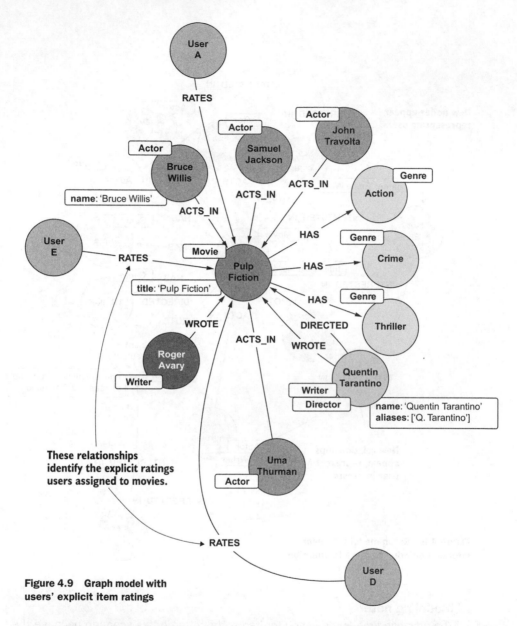

Figure 4.9   Graph model with users' explicit item ratings

In this case, the user nodes are connected to the movies. The ratings are stored on the edges as a property. These approaches are called *explicit* because the system asks the users to manifest their own tastes and preferences.

At the other end of the spectrum, another approach is to infer the users' interests, tastes, and preferences *implicitly* by considering the interactions each user has with items. If I buy soy milk, for example, it is highly probable that I'm interested in similar products, such as soy yogurt. Soy in this case is the relevant feature. Similarly, if a user watches the first episode of *The Lord of the Rings* trilogy, it is highly probable that they'll be interested in the other two episodes or in other movies of the same fantasy-action genre. The resulting model looks like figure 4.10. This model is the same as the one in figure 4.9; the only difference is that the system in figure 4.10 collects and stores data on user behavior to infer users' interests implicitly.

It's worth noting that when the system models relationships between users and items, regardless of whether information on users' interests is collected implicitly or

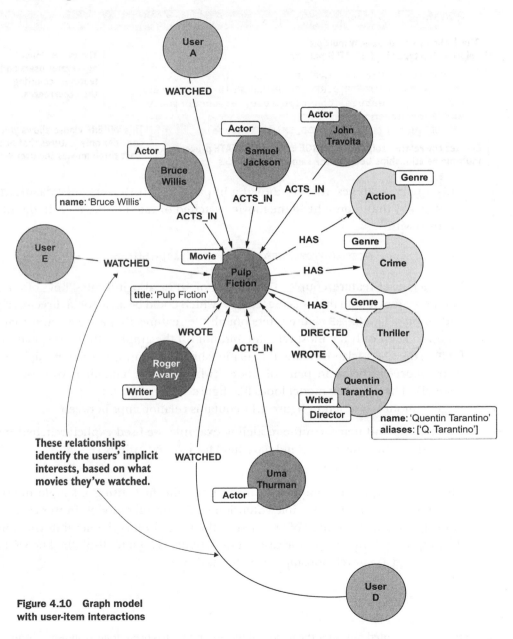

Figure 4.10 Graph model with user-item interactions

explicitly, it is possible to infer the users' interests in specific item features by using different approaches. Starting from the graph depicted in figures 4.9 and 4.10, the Cypher query in listing 4.8 computes new relationships between users and features and then *materializes* them (stores as new relationships to improve access performance) by creating new edges in the graph.

Listing 4.8   Query for computing relationships between users and item features[5]

The | allows you to specify multiple relationship types in the MATCH pattern.

The WITH clause aggregates users and features, counting the occurrences.

```
MATCH (user:User)-[:WATCHED|RATED]->(movie:Movie)-
  ➡ [:ACTS_IN|WROTE|DIRECTED|PRODUCED|HAS]-(feature)
WITH user, feature, count(feature) as occurrences
WHERE occurrences > 2
MERGE (user)-[:INTERESTED_IN]->(feature)
```

Creates the relationship. Using MERGE instead of CREATE prevents multiple relationships between the same pairs of nodes.

This WHERE clause allows you to consider only features that occur in at least three movies the user watched.

This query searches for all the graph patterns (`(u:User)-[:WATCHED|RATED]->`
`(m:Movie)`) that represent all the movies watched or rated by the user. It identifies the features with

```
(movie:Movie)-[:ACTS_IN|WROTE|DIRECTED|PRODUCED|HAS]-(feature)
```

For each user-feature couple, the output of `WITH` also indicates how often a user watched a movie with that specific feature (which could be an actor, a director, a genre, and so on). The `WHERE` clause filters out all the features that appear fewer than three times, to keep only the most relevant and not fill the graph with useless relationships. Finally, the `MERGE` clause creates the relationships, preventing storing multiple relationships between the same pairs of nodes (which would happen if you used `CREATE` instead). The resulting model looks like figure 4.11.

The model depicted in figure 4.11 contains relationships between

- Users and items. (In the modeling example, we used explicit watched relationships, but the same would have held for explicit ratings.)
- Users and features.

The second type was computed starting from the first, using a simple query. This example shows another possible extension of the starting model. In this case, instead of using an external source of knowledge, the model infers the new information from the graph itself. In this specific case, a graph query is used to distill the knowledge and convert it to a new relationship for better navigation.

---

[5] This query can be executed only after the import of the user rating has been done as shown in listing 4.9.

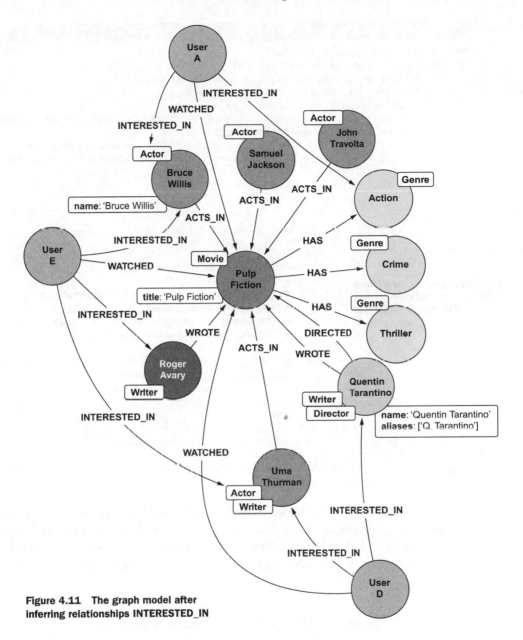

Figure 4.11 The graph model after inferring relationships INTERESTED_IN

The MovieLens dataset contains explicit user-item pairings based on the users' ratings. (The pairings are considered to be explicit because the users decided to rate the items.) In listing 4.9, the ratings are used to build a graph as modeled in figure 4.10, with the only difference being that WATCHED is replaced by RATED because it represents what the user explicitly rated. The function reads from a CSV file, creates users, and connects them to the movies they rated.

Listing 4.9   Importing user-item pairings from MovieLens

```
def import_user_item(self, file):
    with open(file, 'r+') as in_file:
        reader = csv.reader(in_file, delimiter=',')
        next(reader, None)
        with self._driver.session() as session:
            self.executeNoException(session, "CREATE CONSTRAINT ON (u:User)
            ➥ ASSERT u.userId IS UNIQUE")

            tx = session.begin_transaction()
            i = 0;
            for row in reader:
                try:
                    if row:
                        user_id = strip(row[0])
                        movie_id = strip(row[1])
                        rating = strip(row[2])
                        timestamp = strip(row[3])
                        query = """
                            MATCH (movie:Movie {movieId: $movieId})
                            MERGE (user:User {userId: $userId})
                            MERGE (user)-[:RATED {rating: $rating,
                            ➥ timestamp: $timestamp}]->(movie)
                        """
                        tx.run(query, {"movieId":movie_id, "userId": user_id,
                        ➥ "rating":rating, "timestamp": timestamp})
                        i += 1
                    if i == 1000:
                        tx.commit()
                        i = 0
                        tx = session.begin_transaction()
                except Exception as e:
                    print(e, row, reader.line_num)
            tx.commit()
```

> Creates a constraint to guarantee User uniqueness (pointing to the CREATE CONSTRAINT line)

> The query searches for a Movie by movieId and then creates the User if it does not exist and connects them. (pointing to the query line)

At this point, the graph model we've designed is capable of representing both items and users properly and also accommodating several variations or extensions, such as semantic analysis and implicit or explicit information. We've created and filled a real graph database, using data obtained by combining the MovieLens dataset and information from the IMDb.

EXERCISES

Play with the database and write queries to do the following:

1 Get a user (by userId), and list all the features that user is interested in.
2 Find pairs of users who have common interests.

Section 4.3 discusses how to use this model to deliver recommendations to the end users in the movie rental scenario we're considering.

4.3   Providing recommendations

During the recommendation phase, a CBRS uses user profiles to match users with the items that are most likely to be of interest to them. Depending on the information available and the models defined for both users and items, different algorithms or techniques can be used for this purpose. Starting from the models described previously, this section describes several techniques for predicting user interests and providing recommendations, presented in increasing order of complexity and accuracy.

The first approach is based on the model presented in figure 4.12, in which users are explicitly asked to indicate their interest in features or interest is inferred from user-item interactions.

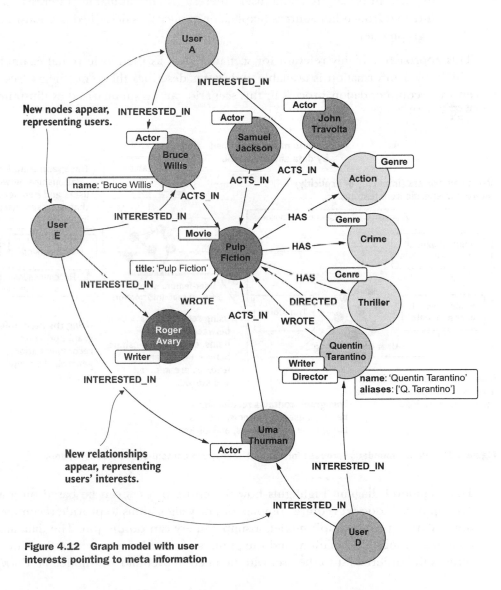

Figure 4.12   Graph model with user interests pointing to meta information

This approach is applicable when

- The *items* are represented by a list of *features* that are related to the items, such as tags, keywords, genres, and actors. Such features may be curated by users manually (tags) or professionals (keywords), or generated automatically through some extraction process.
- The *user profiles* are represented by connecting the users to features that are of interest to them. These connections are described in a binary form: *like* (in the graph, represented with an edge between the user and the feature) and *don't like/unknown* (represented by no edge between the user and the feature). When explicit information about user interests is not available, interests can be inferred from other sources (explicit or implicit), as described previously, using a graph query.

This approach is highly relevant for scenarios such as the movie rental example, in which meta information is available and better describes the items themselves. The entire recommendation process in this scenario can be summarized as illustrated in figure 4.13.

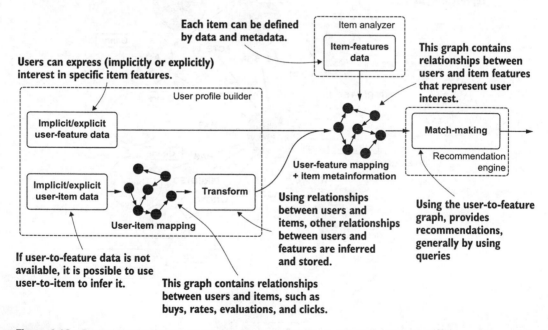

Figure 4.13   Recommendation process for the first scenario in content-based recommenders

This high-level diagram highlights how the entire process can be based on graphs. This approach doesn't require complex or fancy algorithms to provide recommendations. With a proper graph model, a simple query can do the job. The data already contains enough information, and the graph structure helps compute the score and returns the ordered list to the user with no need to prebuild any model: *the description and prediction models overlap.* This pure graph-based approach is simple but has a lot of advantages:

- *It produces good results.* The quality of the recommendations is quite high, considering the limited effort required by this method.
- *It's simple.* It doesn't require complex computations or complex code that reads and preprocesses the data before providing recommendations. If the data is modeled properly in the graph, as shown previously, it is possible to perform the queries and reply to users in real time.
- *It's extensible.* The graph can contain other information that can be useful for refining the results according to other data sources or contextual information. The queries can easily be changed to take new aspects into account.

The task of providing recommendations is accomplished by means of queries like the one in listing 4.10.

Listing 4.10 Query for providing recommendations to a user

Starting from a user, the **MATCH** clause
searches for all the movies that have
features of interest for that user.

The NOT exists() filters out all the movies
already WATCHED or RATED by the user.

```
MATCH (user:User)-[i:INTERESTED_IN]->(feature)-[]-(movie:Movie)
WHERE user.userId = "<user Id>" AND NOT exists((user)-[]->(movie))
RETURN movie.title, count(i) as occurrences
ORDER BY occurrences desc
```

Sorting in reverse order helps bring
to the top the movies shared more
with the selected user.

This query starts from the user (the WHERE clause specifies a userId as string), identifies all the features of interest to the user, and finds all the movies that contain them. For each movie, the query counts the overlapping features and orders the movies according to this value: the higher the number of overlapping features, the higher the likelihood is that the item might be of interest to the user.

This approach can be applied to the database we created earlier. The MovieLens dataset contains connections among users and items but no relationships between users and features of interest for the users; these features are not available in the dataset. We enriched the dataset by using IMDb as a source of knowledge for movie features, and by applying listing 4.8, it is possible to compute the missing relationships between users and item features. Use the code and the queries to play with the graph database and provide recommendations. It will not be fast, but it will work properly. Figure 4.14 shows the result of running listing 4.7 on the imported database. It's worth noting that user 598 in the example shown here had already rated *Shrek* and *Shrek 2.*

Later in this chapter and book, different techniques and methods for improving performance are described; here, the focus is on different graph modeling techniques and design options.

```
$ MATCH (user:User)-[i:INTERESTED_IN]->(feature)-[]-(movie:Movie)  WHERE user.userId = "598" …
```

movie.title	occurrences
"Shrek the Third (2007)"	15
"Shrek Forever After (a.k.a. Shrek: The Final Chapter) (2010)"	12
"Confessions of a Dangerous Mind (2002)"	10
"Monsters vs. Aliens (2009)"	9
"Batman: Mask of the Phantasm (1993)"	9
"Shrek the Halls (2007)"	9
"Puss in Boots (2011)"	9
"Osmosis Jones (2001)"	9
"Cloudy with a Chance of Meatballs 2 (2013)"	8
"Rubber (2010)"	8
"Tenchi Muy ! In Love (1996)"	8
"Agent Cody Banks (2003)"	8
"Sinbad: Legend of the Seven Seas (2003)"	8
"Summer Wars (Sam w zu) (2009)"	8
"Escaflowne: The Movie (Escaflowne) (2000)"	7
"Cinderella (1997)"	7
"Aelita: The Queen of Mars (Aelita) (1924)"	7
"Chronicles of Narnia: Prince Caspian, The (2008)"	7
"Dragonheart 2: A New Beginning (2000)"	7
"Nancy Drew (2007)"	7
"Green Hornet, The (2011)"	7
"The Book of Life (2014)"	7
"Ernest & C lestine (Ernest et C lestine) (2012)"	7
"Interstate 60 (2002)"	7

Started streaming 9343 records after 567 ms and completed after 586 ms, displaying first 1000 rows.

Figure 4.14   The result of running listing 4.10 on the imported MovieLens database

EXERCISE

Rewrite listing 4.10 to consider only movies of a specific genre or from a specific year.

TIP   Add a condition to the WHERE clause by using EXISTS.

This approach works well and is simple, but with a small amount of effort, it can be greatly improved. The second approach extends the previous one by considering two main aspects that can be improved:

- In the user profile, interest in an item feature is represented by a Boolean value. This value is *binary*, representing only the fact that the user is interested in the feature. It doesn't ascribe any weight to this relationship.
- Counting the overlapping features between user profiles and items is not enough. We need a function that computes the similarity or commonalities between user interests and items.

Regarding the first point, as is stated often in this book, models are representations of reality, and the reality is that we are modeling a user who is likely to be interested more in some features than others (likes action movies but loves movies with Jason Statham, for example). This information can improve the quality of the recommendations.

Regarding the second point, instead of counting the overlapping features, a better method of finding interesting items for a specific user consists of measuring the similarity between the user profile and the item's features—the closer, the better. This approach requires

- A *function* that measures the similarity
- A *common representation* for both items and user profiles so that the similarity is measurable

The selected function defines the required representation for items and user profiles. Different functions are available. One of the most accurate functions is *cosine similarity*, introduced in chapter 3:

$$sim(\vec{a}, \vec{b}) \ = \ \cos(\vec{a}, \vec{b}) = \frac{\vec{a} \cdot \vec{b}}{|\vec{a}| \times |\vec{b}|}$$

Like most of the common similarity functions, this function requires that each item and each user profile be projected into a common *vector space model (VSM)*, which means that each element has to be represented by a fixed-dimension vector. The entire recommendation process in this second scenario can be summarized by the high-level diagram in figure 4.15.

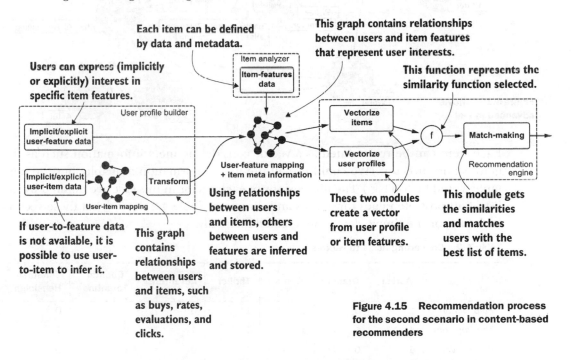

Figure 4.15 Recommendation process for the second scenario in content-based recommenders

Compared with the previous approach, in this case an intermediate step before the recommendation process projects the items, and user profiles are projected into the VSM. To describe this process of converting items and user profiles to their representations in the VSM, let's consider our movie recommendation scenario. Suppose that our movie dataset is as represented in figure 4.16.

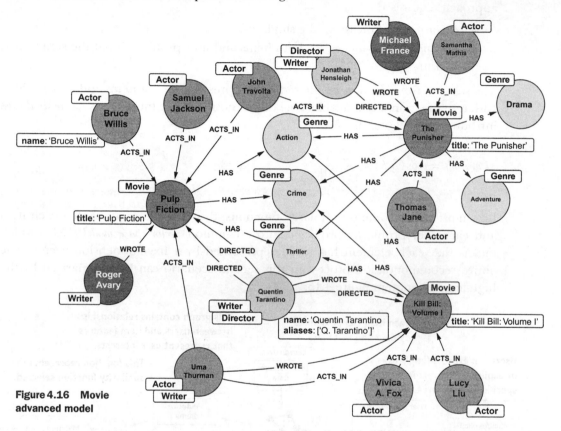

Figure 4.16   Movie advanced model

Each item can be represented as a vector considering meta information such as the genres and director. (We could use all the meta information available, but the next table would be too big.) The dimensions of each vector in this case are defined by the list of all possible values for genres and directors. Table 4.2 shows what these vectors look like for the simple dataset we created manually.

Table 4.2   Converting items to vectors

	Action	Drama	Crime	Thriller	Adventure	Quentin Tarantino	Jonathan Hensleigh
Pulp Fiction	1	0	1	1	0	1	0
The Punisher	1	1	1	1	1	0	1
Kill Bill: Vol I	1	0	1	1	0	1	0

These vectors are Boolean vectors because the values can be only 0, which means absence, and 1, which means presence. The vectors representing the three movies are

Vector(Pulp Fiction) = [1, 0, 1, 1, 0, 1, 0]

Vector(The Punisher) = [1, 1, 1, 1, 1, 0, 1]

Vector(Kill Bill:Volume 1) = [1, 0, 1, 1, 0, 1, 0]

These binary vectors can be extracted from the graph model in figure 4.16 through the following query.

Listing 4.11 Extracting Boolean vectors for movies

OPTIONAL MATCH allows us to consider all the features, even if they are not related to the movie selected.

Searches for the movie Pulp Fiction. Using STARTS WITH is preferable to an exact string comparison because the movies generally have the year in the title.

Searches for all the features that are Director or Genre, using the labels function to get the list of labels assigned to a node

```
MATCH (feature)
WHERE "Genre" in labels(feature) OR "Director" in labels(feature)
WITH feature
ORDER BY id(feature)
MATCH (movie:Movie)
WHERE movie.title STARTS WITH "Pulp Fiction"
OPTIONAL MATCH (movie)-[r:DIRECTED|HAS]-(feature)
RETURN CASE WHEN r IS null THEN 0 ELSE 1 END as Value,
CASE WHEN feature.genre IS null THEN feature.name ELSE feature.genre END as
Feature
```

This CASE clause returns the name of the director or the genre.

This CASE clause returns 0 if no relationship exists and 1 otherwise.

The query starts by looking for all the nodes that represent genres or directors, and it returns all of them ordered by node identifier. The order is important because in each vector, the specific genre or director must be represented in the same position. Then the query searches for a specific movie by title, and OPTIONAL MATCH checks whether the movie is connected to the feature. Unlike MATCH, which filters out the nonmatching elements, OPTIONAL MATCH returns null if the relationship doesn't exist. In the RETURN, the first CASE clause returns 0 if no relationship exists and 1 otherwise; the second returns the name of the director or the genre. Figure 4.17 shows the result of the query run against the database imported from MovieLens.

As is evident from the screenshot in figure 4.17, the real vectors are large because there are a lot of possible dimensions. Although this full representation is manageable by the implementation discussed here, chapter 5 introduces a better way to represent such long vectors.

```
$ MATCH (n) WHERE "Genre" in labels(n) OR "Director" i...
```

Value	Feature
0	"Adventure"
0	"Animation"
0	"Children"
1	"Comedy"
0	"Fantasy"
0	"Romance"
1	"Drama"
0	"Action"
1	"Crime"
1	"Thriller"
0	"Horror"
0	"Mystery"
0	"Sci-Fi"
0	"IMAX"
0	"Documentary"
0	"War"

Figure 4.17   Result of running listing 4.11 on the MovieLens dataset

Adding an index

Running this query on the MovieLens database can take a long time. The time is spent in the filter condition, `movie.title` STARTS WITH `"Pulp Fiction"`. Adding an index can greatly improve performance. Run the following command and then try the query again:

```
CREATE INDEX ON :Movie(title)
```

Much faster, isn't it?

It is possible to generalize this vector approach to all sorts of features, including those that have numerical values, such as the average ratings in our movie scenario.[6] In the vector representation, the related components hold the exact values of these features. In our example, the vector representations for the three movies become

---

[6] The average rating is not a valuable feature, but it will serve the purpose in our example.

$Vector(Pulp\ Fiction)\ =\ [1, 0, 1, 1, 0, 1, 0, 4]$

$Vector(The\ Punisher)\ =\ [1, 1, 1, 1, 1, 0, 1, 3.5]$

$Vector(Kill\ Bill:Volume\ 1)\ =\ [1, 0, 1, 1, 0, 1, 0, 3.9]$

The last element represents the average rating. It doesn't matter whether some components of the vectors are Boolean and others are real-valued or integer-valued [Ullman and Rajaraman, 2011]. It is still possible to compute the cosine distance between vectors, although if we do so, we should consider some appropriate scaling of the non-Boolean components so that they neither dominate the calculation nor are irrelevant. To do so, we multiply the values by a scaling factor:

$Vector(Pulp\ Fiction)\ =\ [1, 0, 1, 1, 0, 1, 0, 4\alpha]$

$Vector(The\ Punisher)\ =\ [1, 1, 1, 1, 1, 0, 13.5\alpha]$

$Vector(Kill\ Bill:Volume\ 1)\ =\ [1, 0, 1, 1, 0, 1, 0, 3.9\alpha]$

In this representation, if α is set to 1, the average rating will dominate the value of the similarity; if it is set to 0.5, the effect will be reduced by half. The scaling factor can be different for each numerical feature and depends on the weight assigned to that feature in the resulting similarity.

With the proper vector representation of the items in hand, we need to project the user profile into the same VSM, which means that we need to create vectors with the same components in the same order as in the item vectors that describe the user's preferences. As described in section 4.2.2, the information available in the content-based case regarding user preferences or tastes can be a user-item pair or a user-feature pair. Both pairs can be collected implicitly or explicitly. Because the vector space has the feature values as dimensions, the first step in the projection is to migrate the user-item matrix to the user-feature space (unless it is already available). Different techniques can be used for this conversion, including aggregating by counting the occurrences of each feature in a user's list of previously liked[7] items. This option works well for Boolean values; another option is to compute the average values for numerical features. In the movie scenario, each user profile can be represented as shown in table 4.3.

Table 4.3 User profiles represented in the same vector space as movies

	Action	Drama	Crime	Thriller	Adventure	Quentin Tarantino	Jonathan Hensleigh	Total
User A	3	1	4	5	1	3	1	9
User B	0	10	1	2	3	0	1	15
User C	1	0	3	1	0	1	0	5

---

[7] *Liked* here means any kind of interaction between user and item: watched, rated, and so on.

Each cell represents how many movies the user watched that have that specific feature. User A has watched three movies directed by Quentin Tarantino, for example, but User B hasn't watched any movies he directed. The table also contains a new column representing the total number of movies watched by each user; this value will be useful in the creation of the vectors to normalize the values.

These user-feature pairs with related counts are easy to obtain from the graph model we've been using so far for representing user-item interactions. To simplify the next steps, I recommend materializing these values by storing them properly in the graph itself. In a property graph database, the weight representing how much the user is interested in a specific item feature can be modeled with a property on the relationship between the user and the feature. Modifying listing 4.8, used earlier for inferring the relationship between users and features, it is possible to extract this information, create new relationships, and add these weights to the edges. The new query looks like the following listing.

> ### Listing 4.12 Query for extracting weighted relationships between users and features

```
MATCH (user:User)-[:WATCHED|RATED]->(m:Movie)-
➥ [:ACTS_IN|WROTE|DIRECTED|PRODUCED|HAS]-(feature)
WITH user, feature, count(feature) as occurrence
WHERE occurrence > 2
MERGE (user)-[r:INTERESTED_IN]->(feature)
SET r.weight = occurrence                    ◄
```
SET adds or modifies the weight property on the INTERESTED_IN relationship.

In this version, `occurrence` is stored as a property on the relationship `INTERESTED_IN`, whereas in listing 4.8, it was used only as a filter. Figure 4.18 shows the resulting model.

On their own, the numbers in the table could lead to incorrect computations of the similarities between the user profile vector and the item vector. They have to be normalized to better represent the real interest of a user in a specific feature. If a user has watched 50 movies and only 5 are dramas, for example, we might conclude that user is less interested in this genre than a user who watched 3 dramas in a total of 10 movies, even though the first user watched more total movies of this type.

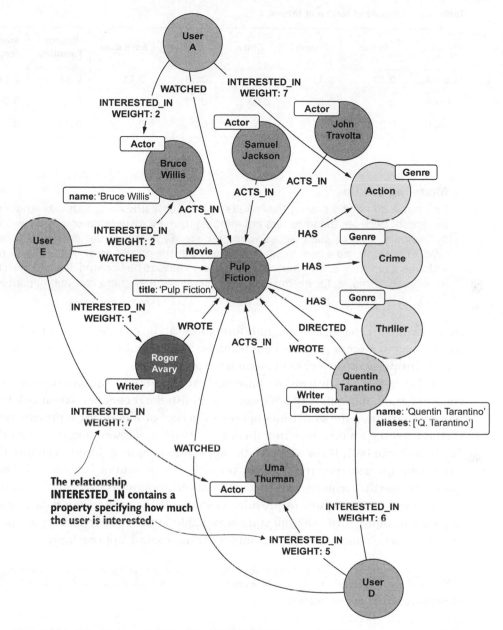

Figure 4.18 The graph model after inferring `INTERESTED_IN` relationships with the weights

If we *normalize* each value in table 4.3 with the total number of movies watched, we see that the first user has 0.1 interest in the drama genre, whereas the second has 0.6. Table 4.4 shows the normalized user profiles.

Table 4.4   Normalized version of table 4.3

	Action	Drama	Crime	Thriller	Adventure	Quentin Tarantino	Jonathan Hensleigh
User A	0.33	0.11	0.44	0.55	0.11	0.33	0.11
User B	0	0.66	0.06	0.13	0.2	0	0.06
User C	0.2	0	0.6	0.2	0	0.2	0

Modeling pro tip

I do not recommend storing the results of the normalization process as weights in the graph, because these results are affected by the total number of movies watched by the user. Storing such values would require us to recompute each weight every time a user watched a new movie. If we store only the counts as weights, when a user watches a new movie, only the affected features have to be updated. If a user watches an adventure movie, for example, only the count for that genre has to be updated.

In the explicit scenario, this weight information can be collected by asking the user to assign rates to a set of possible item features. The related values can be stored in the weight property on the edges between users and features.

At the end of this process, we have both items and user profiles represented in a common and comparable way. We can accomplish the recommendation task for each user by computing the similarities between the user profile vector representation and each not-yet-seen movie, ordering them from highest to lowest and returning the top N, where N can be 1, 10, or whatever the application requires. In this scenario, the recommendation task requires complex operations that cannot be accomplished by a query because they require complex computations, looping, transformation, and so on.

Listing 4.13 shows how to provide recommendations when the data is stored as depicted in figure 4.18. The full code is available in the code repository as ch04/recommendation/content_based_recommendation_second_approach.py.

Listing 4.13   Method to provide recommendations using the second approach

This function provides recommendations.

```
def recommendTo(self, userId, k):
    user_VSM = self.get_user_vector(userId)
    movies_VSM = self.get_movie_vectors(userId)
    top_k = self.compute_top_k (user_VSM, movies_VSM, k);
    return top_k

def compute_top_k(self, user, movies, k):    ◄
    dtype = [ ('movieId', 'U10'),('value', 'f4')]
    knn_values = np.array([], dtype=dtype)
    for other_movie in movies:
```

This function computes the similarities between the user profile vector and the movie vectors, and gets back the top *k* movies that best match the user profile.

```
        value = cosine_similarity([user], [movies[other_movie]])
        if value > 0:
            knn_values = np.concatenate((knn_values, np.array([[(other_movie,
              value)], dtype=dtype)))
    knn_values = np.sort(knn_values, kind='mergesort', order='value' )[::-1]
    return np.array_split(knn_values, [k])[0]
```

We use the cosine_similarity
function provided by scikit-learn.

```
def get_user_vector(self, user_id):
    query = """
```

This function
creates the user
profile; note how
it is provided with
a single query and
mapped with a
vector.

```
            MATCH p=(user:User)-[:WATCHED|RATED]->(movie)
            WHERE user.userId = $userId
            with count(p) as total
            MATCH (feature:Feature)
            WITH feature, total
            ORDER BY id(feature)
            MATCH (user:User)
            WHERE user.userId = {userId}
            OPTIONAL MATCH (user)-[r:INTERESTED_IN]-(feature)
            WITH CASE WHEN r IS null THEN 0 ELSE
    (r.weight*1.0f)/(total*1.0f) END as value
            RETURN collect(value) as vector
            """
    user_VSM = None
    with self._driver.session() as session:
        tx = session.begin_transaction()
        vector = tx.run(query, {"userId": user_id})
        user_VSM = vector.single()[0]
    print(len(user_VSM))
    return user_VSM;
```

The order is critical because it allows
us to have comparable vectors.

This function provides
the movie vectors.

```
def get_movie_vectors(self, user_id):
    list_of_moview_query = """
```

This query gets
only relevant not-
seen-yet movies
for the user, which
speeds the
process.

```
            MATCH (movie:Movie)-[r:DIRECTED|HAS]-(feature)<-
              [i:INTERESTED_IN]-(user:User {userId: $userId})
            WHERE NOT EXISTS((user)-[]->(movie)) AND EXISTS((user)-[]->
              (feature))
            WITH movie, count(i) as featuresCount
            WHERE featuresCount > 5
            RETURN movie.movieId as movieId
            """

    query = """
```

This query creates the movie vectors.

```
            MATCH (feature:Feature)
            WITH feature
            ORDER BY id(feature)
            MATCH (movie:Movie)
            WHERE movie.movieId = {movieId}
            OPTIONAL MATCH (movie)-[r:DIRECTED|HAS]-(feature)
            WITH CASE WHEN r IS null THEN 0 ELSE 1 END as value
            RETURN collect(value) as vector;
            """
    movies_VSM = {}
    with self._driver.session() as session:
        tx = session.begin_transaction()
```

```
        i = 0
        for movie in tx.run(list_of_moview_query, {"userId": user_id}):
            movie_id = movie["movieId"];
            vector = tx.run(query, {"movieId": movie_id})
            movies_VSM[movie_id] = vector.single()[0]
            i += 1
            if i % 100 == 0:
                print(i, "lines processed")
        print(i, "lines processed")
    print(len(movies_VSM))
    return movies_VSM
```

If you run this code for user 598 (the same user as in the previous scenario), you will see that the list of recommended movies is not that different from the results obtained in the previous case, but these new results should be better in terms of prediction accuracy. Thanks to the graph, it is possible to easily get movies that contain at least five features in common with the user profile.

Also be aware that this recommendation process takes a while to produce results. Don't be worried; the goal here is to show the concepts in the simplest way, and various optimization techniques are discussed later in the book. If you're interested, in the code repository you'll find an optimized version of this code that uses a different approach to vector creation and similarity computation.

EXERCISES

Considering the code in listing 4.13,

1 Rewrite the code to use a different similarity function, such as the Pearson correlation (https://libguides.library.kent.edu/SPSS/PearsonCorr), instead of cosine similarity.

TIP Search for a Python implementation, and replace the `cosine_similarity` function.

2 Look at the optimized implementation in the code repository, and figure out how the new vectors are created. How much faster is it now? Chapter 5 introduces the concept of sparse vectors.

The third approach we will consider for content-based recommendations can be described as "Recommend items that are similar to those the user liked in the past" [Jannach et al., 2010]. This approach works well in general and is the only option when it is possible to compute relevant similarities between items but difficult or not relevant to represent user profiles in the same way.

Consider our training dataset, as represented in figures 4.9 and figure 4.10. The user preferences are modeled by connecting users to items instead of users to items' meta information. This approach could be necessary when meta information for each item is not available, limited, or not relevant, so it is not possible (or necessary) to extract data on the users' interest in some features. Nonetheless, the content or content description related to each item is somehow available; otherwise, the content-based approach would not be applicable. Even when meta information is available, this third approach greatly outperforms the previous one in terms of recommendation accuracy. This technique, known as the *similarity-based retrieval* approach, is a valuable approach to cover for several reasons:

- It was introduced in chapter 3. Here, different item representations are used for computing similarities.
- Similarities are easy to store back in the graph as relationships between items. This example represents a perfect use case for graph modeling, and navigating similarity relationships provides for fast recommendations.
- It is one of the most common and powerful approaches to CBRSs.
- It is flexible and general enough to be used in many scenarios, regardless of the type of data/information available for each item.

The entire recommendation process in this scenario can be summarized by the high-level diagram in figure 4.19.

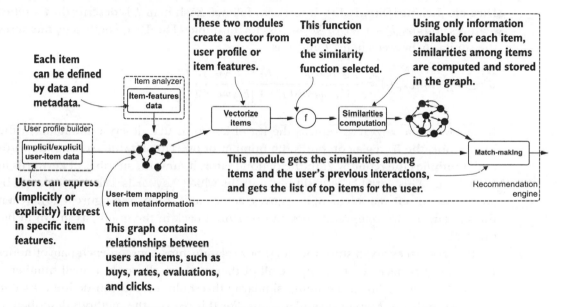

Figure 4.19 Recommendation process for the third approach in content-based recommenders

It's worth noting here, because this is the biggest difference with the collaborative filtering approach described in chapter 5, that the similarities between items are computed only by using the item-related data, whatever that is. The user-item interaction is used only during the recommendation phase.

According to figure 4.19, three key elements are necessary in this scenario:

- *User profile*—The user profile is represented by modeling the interactions the user has with items, such as rated, bought, or watched. In the graph, these interactions are represented as relationships between the user and the items.
- *Item representation/description*—To compute similarities between items, it is necessary to represent each item in a measurable way. How this is done depends on the function selected for measuring similarities.
- *Similarity function*—We need a function that, given two item representations, computes the similarity between them. We described applying the cosine similarity metric from chapter 3 to a simplified example of collaborative filtering. Here, different techniques are described in more detail, applied to content-based recommendations.

As in the second approach, the first two elements listed are strictly related because each similarity formula requires a specific item representation. Conversely, according to the data available for each item, some functions can be applied, and others cannot.

A typical similarity metric, which is suitable for multivalued characteristics, is the Dice coefficient [Dice, 1945]. It works as follows. Each item I_i is described by a set of features $features(I_i)$—a set of keywords, for example. The Dice coefficient measures the similarity between items I_i and I_j as

$$dice\_coefficient(I_i, I_j) = \frac{2 \times |keywords(I_i) \cap keywords(I_j)|}{|keywords(I_i)| + |keywords(I_j)|}$$

In this formula, `keywords` returns the list of keywords that describe the item. In the numerator, the formula computes the number of overlapping/intersecting keywords and multiplies the result by 2. In the denominator, it sums the number of keywords in each item. This formula is a simple one, in which `keywords` can be replaced by anything—in our movie example, genres, actors, and so on (see figure 4.20). When the similarities are computed, they can be stored back in the graph, as shown in figure 4.21.

It is not necessary to store the neighbor relationships between each pair of nodes (although it is necessary to compute all of them). Generally, only a small number is stored. You can define a minimum similarity threshold, or you can define a k value and keep only the k topmost similar items. For this reason, the methods described in this approach are known as *k-nearest neighbor (k-NN)* methods regardless of the similarity function selected.

The k-NN methods are used in a lot of machine learning tasks, from recommendations to classifications. They are flexible in terms of data types and can be applied to textual data as well as structured data. In the recommendations, k-NN methods have the advantage of being relatively simple to implement—even though we need to take into account the time required to compute the similarities (a problem that we will address in sections 6.3 and 9.2)—and adapt quickly to recent changes in the dataset.

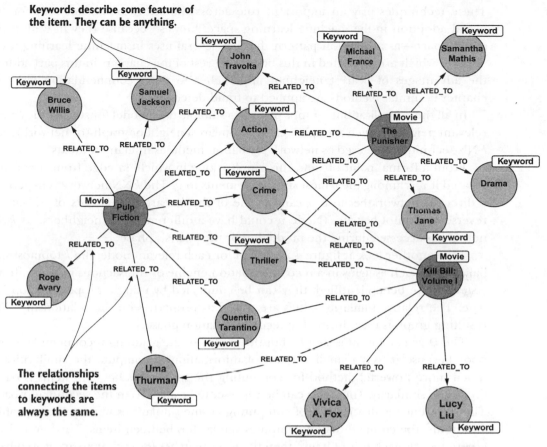

Keywords describe some feature of the item. They can be anything.

The relationships connecting the items to keywords are always the same.

Figure 4.20   The graph model for representing keywords

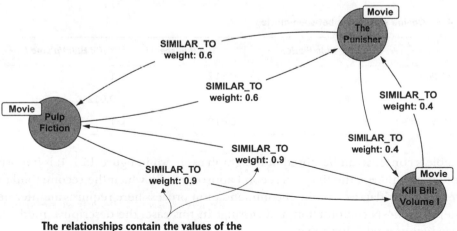

The relationships contain the values of the similarities computed among nodes. They are symmetric: the similarity between *A* and *B* is the same regardless of the order.

Figure 4.21   Storing similarities back in the graph

These techniques play an important role across the entire book, not only for the broad adoption in the machine learning space, but also because they fit well in the graph space—as a common pattern that has several uses in machine learning tasks, many of which are presented in this book. The rest of the chapters in this part address the advantages of nearest neighbor approaches to the recommendation tasks. In chapter 9, similar methods are applied to fraud detection.

In all these applications, graphs provide a suitable data model for storing the k most relevant neighbor. Such a graph is called a k-nearest neighbor graph (or network), and k-NN techniques are used as network formation methods in many contexts.

From a formal point of view, this graph is one in which an edge from v_i and v_j is created if v_j is among the k most similar elements to v_i. The k-NN network is in general a directed network because v_j can be one of the k-nearest neighbors of v_i, but the reverse could not be true. (Node v_j could have a different set of neighbors.) A k-NN network is accessed during the prediction or the analysis phase.

Take another look at figure 4.21. When for each relevant node, the k topmost similar nodes (such as items in a recommendation engine or transactions in an antifraud system) have been identified, they can be connected by using a proper relationship type. The relative similarity values are stored as properties on the relationship. The resulting graph is used during the recommendation phase.

The Dice coefficient is simple, but the quality of the resulting recommendations is poor because it uses a small amount of information to compute the similarities. A much more powerful method for computing the similarities between items is based on cosine similarity. The items can be represented exactly as in the second approach. The difference is that instead of computing cosine similarities between user profiles and items, the cosine function computes similarities between items. This similarity is computed for each pair of items; then the top k matches for each item are stored back in the graph as similarity relationships. Consider the similarities listed in table 4.5.

Table 4.5   Cosine similarities between movies

	Pulp Fiction	*The Punisher*	*Kill Bill: Volume I*
Pulp Fiction	1	0.612	1
The Punisher	0.612	1	0.612
Kill Bill: Volume I	1	0.612	1

The table's contents can be stored in the graph as shown in figure 4.21. It is important to note that unlike in the first and second approaches, in which the recommendation process uses the data as it is, the recommendation process here requires an intermediate step: this k-NN computation and storing. In this case, the descriptive model and the prediction model don't match.

Listing 4.14 shows a Python script for computing *k*-NN and storing this data back in the graph. It works on the graph database we imported from the MovieLens dataset.

Listing 4.14   Code for creating the *k*-NN network

```
def compute_and_store_similarity(self):            Overall function that performs
    movies_VSM = self.get_movie_vectors()          all the tasks for all the movies
    for movie in movies_VSM:
        knn = self.compute_knn(movie, movies_VSM.copy(), 10);
        self.store_knn(movie, knn)
                                        This function projects
def get_movie_vectors(self):            each movie in the VSM.
    list_of_moview_query = """
                MATCH (movie:Movie)
                RETURN movie.movieId as movieId
            """

    query = """
                MATCH (feature:Feature)
                WITH feature
                ORDER BY id(feature)
                MATCH (movie:Movie)
                WHERE movie.movieId = $movieId
                OPTIONAL MATCH (movie)-[r:DIRECTED|HAS]-(feature)
                WITH CASE WHEN r IS null THEN 0 ELSE 1 END as value
                RETURN collect(value) as vector;
            """
    movies_VSM = {}
    with self._driver.session() as session:
        tx = session.begin_transaction()

        i = 0
        for movie in tx.run(list_of_moview_query):
            movie_id = movie["movieId"];
            vector = tx.run(query, {"movieId": movie_id})
            movies_VSM[movie_id] = vector.single()[0]
            i += 1
            if i % 100 == 0:
                print(i, "lines processed")
        print(i, "lines processed")
    print(len(movies_VSM))
    return movies_VSM

                                          This function computes
def compute_knn(self, movie, movies, k):   the k-NN for each movie.
    dtype = [ ('movieId', 'U10'),('value', 'f4')]
    knn_values = np.array([], dtype=dtype)
    for other_movie in movies:
        if other_movie != movie:
            value = cosine_similarity([movies[movie]], [movies[other_movie]])
            if value > 0:
                knn_values = np.concatenate((knn_values,
                    np.array([(other_movie, value)], dtype=dtype)))
```

Here, it uses the cosine_similarity available in scikit.

```
    knn_values = np.sort(knn_values, kind='mergesort', order='value' )[::-1]
    return np.array_split(knn_values, k)[0]
```

This function stores the *k*-NN on the graph database.

```
def store_knn(self, movie, knn):
    with self._driver.session() as session:
        tx = session.begin_transaction()
        test = {a : b.item() for a,b in knn}
        clean_query = """MATCH (movie:Movie)-[s:SIMILAR_TO]-()
            WHERE movie.movieId = $movieId
            DELETE s
        """
        query = """
            MATCH (movie:Movie)
            WHERE movie.movieId = $movieId
            UNWIND keys($knn) as otherMovieId
            MATCH (other:Movie)
            WHERE other.movieId = otherMovieId
            MERGE (movie)-[:SIMILAR_TO {weight: $knn[otherMovieId]}]-(other)
        """
        tx.run(clean_query, {"movieId": movie})
        tx.run(query, {"movieId": movie, "knn": test})
        tx.commit()
```

Before storing the new similarity, deletes the old

This code may take a while to complete. Here, I am presenting the basic ideas; in sections 6.3 and 9.2, I discuss several optimization techniques for real projects. Moreover, I would like to mention that Neo4j provides a plugin for data science called Graph Data Science Library[8] (GDS), which contains many similarity algorithms. If you are using Neo4j, I recommend using this library. The preceding code is more generic and can be used in any circumstance.

EXERCISES

When the *k*-NN has been computed via the code in listing 4.14, write a query to do the following:

1   Get a movie (by `movieId`), and get the list of the 10 most similar items.
2   Search for the 10 most similar pairs of items.

The next step in the recommendation process for this third approach, as depicted in figure 4.19, consists of making the recommendations, which we do by drawing on the *k*-NN network and the user's implicit/explicit preferences for items. The goal is to predict those not-yet-seen/bought/clicked items that could be of interest to a user.

This task can be accomplished in different ways. In the simplest approach [Allan, 1998], the prediction for a not-yet-seen item *d* for a user *u* is based on a voting mechanism considering the *k* most similar items (in our scenario, movies) to the item *d*. Each of these similar items "expresses" a vote for *d* if the user *u* watched or rated it. If the current user liked 4 out of *k* = 5 of the items most similar to *d*, for example, the system may guess that the chance that the user will also like *d* is relatively high.

---

[8] https://neo4j.com/product/graph-data-science-library/.

Another, more-accurate approach is inspired by collaborative filtering, specifically by item-based collaborative filtering recommendations [Sarwar et al., 2001, and Deshpande and Karypis, 2004]. This approach involves predicting the interest of a user in a specific item by considering the sum of all the similarities of the target item to the other items the user interacted with before:

$$interest(u,p) = \sum_{i \in Items(u)} sim(i, p)$$

Here, *Items(u)* returns all the items the user has interacted with (liked, watched, bought, clicked). The returned value can be used to rank all the not-yet-seen items and return the top *k* to the user as recommendations. The following listing implements the final step: providing recommendations for this third scenario.

Listing 4.15 Code for getting a ranked list of items for the user

```
def recommendTo(self, user_id, k):
    dtype = [('movieId', 'U10'), ('value', 'f4')]        ⟵ This function provides the
    top_movies = np.array([], dtype=dtype)                  recommendations to the user.
    query = """                                           ⟵ This query returns the recommendations;
        MATCH (user:User)                                    it requires the model built previously.
        WHERE user.userId = $userId
        WITH user
        MATCH (targetMovie:Movie)
        WHERE NOT EXISTS((user)-[]->(targetMovie))
        WITH targetMovie, user
        MATCH (user:User)-[]->(movie:Movie)-[r:SIMILAR_TO]->(targetMovie)
        RETURN targetMovie.movieId as movieId, sum(r.weight)/count(r) as
    ➥ relevance
        order by relevance desc
        LIMIT %o
    """
    with self._driver.session() as session:
        tx = session.begin_transaction()
        for result in tx.run(query % (k), {"userId": user_id}):
            top_movies = np.concatenate((top_movies,
     np.array([(result["movieId"], result["relevance"])], dtype=dtype)))

    return top_movies
```

When you run this code, you'll notice that it is fast. When the model is created, providing recommendations takes only a few milliseconds.

Other approaches can also be used, but they are out of the scope of this chapter and this book. The main purpose here is to show how, when you've defined a proper model for items, users, and the interaction between them, you can use multiple approaches to provide recommendations without changing the base graph model defined.

EXERCISE
Rewrite the method that computes the similarity between items to use a different function from cosine similarity, such as the Jaccard index (http://mng.bz/qePA), Dice coefficient, or Euclidian distance (http://mng.bz/7jmm).

4.4 Advantages of the graph approach

In this chapter, we discussed how to create a CBRS by using graphs and graph models for storing different types of information that are useful as input and output for several steps of the recommendation process. Specifically, the main aspects and advantages of the graph-based approach to content-based recommendations are

- Meaningful information must be stored as unique node entities in the graph so that these entities can be shared across items and users.
- Converting user-item data to user-feature data is a trivial task when the meta information is available and is meaningful; you need a query to compute and materialize it.
- It is possible to extract several vector representations for both items and user profiles from the same graph model. The capability to extract several types of vectors easily improves the feature selection because it reduces the effort required to try different approaches.
- It is possible to store different similarity values computed with different functions and use them in combination.
- The code showed how easy it is to switch among different models or even combine them if they are described by a proper graph model.

The great advantage is the flexibility provided by the graph representation of the information, enabling the same data model to serve many use cases and scenarios with small adaptations. Furthermore, all the scenarios can coexist in the same database, which frees data scientists and data engineers from having to deal with multiple representations of the same information. These advantages are shared by all the recommendation methods described in the following chapters.

Summary

This chapter introduced you to graph-based data modeling techniques. In this first chapter on the topic, we focused on recommendation engines, exploring how to model data sources used for training, how to store the resulting model, and how to access it to make predictions.

In this chapter, you learned

- How to design a graph model for a user-item as well as a user-feature dataset
- How to import data from the original format into the graph model you've designed
- How to project user profile and item data and metadata into a vector space model

- How to compute similarities between user and item profiles and among pairs of items by using cosine similarity and other functions
- How to store item similarities in the graph model
- How to query the resulting model to perform predictions and recommendations
- How to design and implement a graph-powered recommendation engine from end to end, using different approaches of increasing complexity
- The role of k-NN and k-NN networks in machine learning in general and in graph-based machine learning

References

[Allan, 1998] Allan, James. "Topic Detection and Tracking Pilot Study Final Report." *Proceedings of the DARPA Broadcast News Transcription and Understanding Workshop* (1998): 194–218.

[Deshpande and Karypis, 2004] Deshpande, Mukund, and George Karypis. "Item-Based Top-*N* Recommendation Algorithms." *ACM Transactions on Information Systems* 22:1 (2004): 143–177. DOI: http://mng.bz/jB6x.

[Dice, 1945] Dice, Lee Raymond. "Measures of the Amount of Ecologic Association Between Species." *Ecology* 26:3 (1945): 297–302. DOI: http://mng.bz/9N8l. JSTOR 1932409.

[Jannach et al., 2010] Jannach, Dietmar, Markus Zanker, Alexander Felfernig, and Gerhard Friedrich. *Recommender Systems: An Introduction.* Cambridge, UK: Cambridge University Press, 2010. DOI: http://mng.bz/K4dK.

[Sarwar et al., 2001] Sarwar, Badrul, George Karypis, Joseph Konstan, and John Riedl. "Item-Based Collaborative Filtering Recommendation Algorithms." *Proceedings of the 10th International World Wide Web Conference* (2001): 285–295. http://mng.bz/Wrm0.

[Ullman and Rajaraman, 2011], Ullman, Jeffrey David, and Anand Rajaraman. *Mining of Massive Datasets.* New York: Cambridge University Press, 2011.

Collaborative filtering 5

This chapter covers

- Designing proper graph models for a collaborative filtering approach
- Importing existing (nongraph) datasets into the graph models designed
- Implementing working collaborative filtering recommendation engines

The content-based (also called content-filtering or cognitive) approach to recommendations described in chapter 4 creates profiles for users and items to characterize them. The profiles allow systems to match users with relevant items. The general principle of content-based methods is to identify the common characteristics of items that have received favorable feedback from a user (a positive rating, a purchase, a click) and then recommend to this user new items that share these characteristics. Content-based strategies require gathering information that might not be readily available, easy to collect, or directly relevant.

An alternative to content filtering relies only on past user behavior, such as previous transactions or item ratings, or the opinions of an existing user community to predict which items the users will most probably like or be interested in without requiring the creation of explicit profiles for both items and users based on item features. This approach is known as *collaborative filtering*, a term coined by the developers of Tapestry [Goldberg et al., 1992], the first recommender system. Collaborative filtering analyzes relationships between users and interdependencies among items to predict new user-item associations. Figure 5.1 represents a mental model for collaborative filtering recommenders considering input and output.

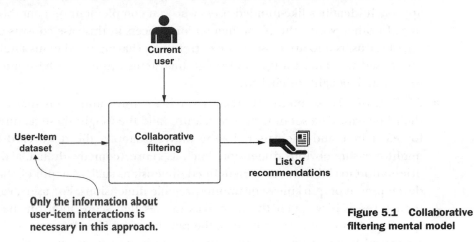

Figure 5.1   Collaborative filtering mental model

A major appeal of collaborative filtering is that it is domain free and doesn't require any detail about the items. It can be applied to a vast variety of use cases and scenarios, and it can address data aspects that are often elusive and difficult to profile by using content filtering.

Although it is generally more accurate than content-based techniques, collaborative filtering suffers from what is called the *cold-start problem* due to its inability to provide reasonable (in terms of accuracy) recommendations for new items and users or when limited interaction data is available. Nonetheless, mechanisms do exist that mitigate the effect of the cold-start problem by using different algorithms, such as the graph approach (discussed in section 5.5) or other sources of knowledge, such as social networks.

Collaborative filtering techniques are generally classified into two main approaches or areas:

- *Memory-based*—Memory-based supposes that if a user likes the movie *Saving Private Ryan*, they may like similar movies, such as war movies, Spielberg movies, and Tom Hanks movies [Koren et al., 2009]. To predict a particular user's rating for *Saving Private Ryan*, we would look for the movie's nearest neighbors that this user rated. Alternatively, the algorithm can look for similar users based on the set of films they watched and suggest something that the current user hasn't watched yet. In these methods, the User-Item dataset that is stored is used directly to predict ratings for items.

These methods are also referred to as *neighborhood methods* because they center on computing the relationships among items or users. The *item-oriented* approach predicts a user's preference for an item based on ratings of neighboring items by the same user. An item's neighbors are other items that tend to get similar ratings when rated by the same user. By contrast, the *user-oriented* approach identifies like-minded users who can complement one another's ratings. In other words, the recommendation process in this case consists of finding other users who are close to the current one (having rated items similarly or purchased the same things) and suggesting items those users have interacted with (rated, bought, or clicked).

- *Model-based*—These methods create models for users and items that describe their behavior via a set of factors or features and the weight these features have for each item and each user. In the movie example, the discovered factors might measure obvious dimensions such as genre (comedy, drama, action) or orientation to children; less well-defined dimensions such as depth of character development or quirkiness; or uninterpretable dimensions. For users, each factor expresses how much the user likes movies that score high on the corresponding factor. In these methods, the raw data (the User-Item dataset) is first processed offline, with the information on ratings or previous purchases used to create this predictive model. At run time, during the recommendation process, only the precomputed or learned model is required to make predictions. Latent factor models represent the most common approaches in this class. They try to explain the ratings by characterizing both items and users on, say, 20 to 100 factors inferred from the rating patterns. In a sense, such factors comprise a computerized alternative to the human-created features encountered in the content-based recommendation systems.

NOTE Although recent investigations show state-of-the-art model-based approaches as being superior to neighborhood ones at the task of predicting ratings [Koren, 2008, and Takács et al., 2007], an understanding is emerging that good prediction accuracy alone does not guarantee users an effective and satisfying experience [Herlocker et al., 2004].

As stated in the introduction to part 2, some of the main reasons why companies implement recommendation engines are to increase user satisfaction and loyalty, and to sell more diverse items. Moreover, recommending to a user a movie directed by their favorite director constitutes a novel recommendation if the user was not aware of that movie, but the user probably would have discovered that movie on their own [Ning et al., 2015].

This example shows another relevant factor that has been identified as playing an important role in users' appreciation of the recommender system: serendipity [Herlocker et al., 2004, and Sarwar et al., 2001]. Serendipity extends the concept of novelty by helping users find interesting items that they might not have discovered otherwise.

This aspect of recommendation increases user satisfaction and helps companies sell more diverse items.

This example illustrates the way in which model-based approaches excel at characterizing the preferences of a user with latent factors. In a movie recommender system, such methods may determine that a given user is a fan of movies that are both funny and romantic without having to define the notions *funny* and *romantic*. This system, therefore, would be able to recommend to the user a romantic comedy that may not have been known to them. In terms of prediction accuracy, this approach delivers the best result possible, but it may be difficult for the system to recommend a movie that does not quite fit this high-level genre (such as a funny parody of a horror movie).

Neighborhood approaches, on the other hand, capture local associations in the data. Consequently, it is possible for a movie recommender system based on this type of approach to recommend a movie quite different from the user's usual taste or to recommend a movie that is not well known (such as a repertoire film) if one of their closest (user) neighbors has given it a strong rating. This recommendation may not be a guaranteed success, as a romantic comedy might be, but it could help the user discover a new genre, or a new favorite actor or director. Neighborhood-based methods have numerous advantages, such as the following:

- *Simplicity*—Neighborhood-based methods are intuitive and relatively simple to implement. In their simplest form, only one parameter (the number of neighbors used in the prediction) requires tuning. Model-based approaches, on the other hand, generally use matrix factorization techniques that are implemented with optimization algorithms to find near-optimal solutions. These optimization techniques, such as stochastic gradient descent[1] (SGD) and alternating least squares[2] (ALS), have a lot of hyperparameters that must be tuned carefully to avoid falling into a local minimum.

- *Justifiability*—These methods provide concise and intuitive justification for the computed predictions. In item-based recommendations, the list of neighboring items, as well as the ratings given by the user to these items, can be presented to the user as justification for the recommendations. This explanation can help the user better understand the recommendation process and how the relevance is computed, increasing the user's trust in the recommender system (and the platform providing it). It could also serve as a basis for an interactive system in which users select the neighbors to whom greater importance should be given in the recommendations [Bell et al., 2007].

---

[1] Stochastic gradient descent is an optimization technique common in machine learning. It tries to minimize the objective function (specifically, a differentiable objective function) via an iterative method. It is called *stochastic* because samples are selected randomly (or shuffled) instead of as a single group (as in standard gradient descent) or in the order in which they appear in the training set. In collaborative filtering, it is used during matrix factorization.

[2] Alternating least squares is another optimization technique that has the advantage of being parallelized easily.

- *Efficiency*—One strong point of neighborhood-based systems is their time efficiency. By comparison with most model-based systems, they require fewer expensive training phases, which need to be carried out at frequent intervals in large commercial applications. These systems may require precomputing nearest neighbors in an offline step but are typically much cheaper than model training in a model-based approach. Furthermore, it is possible to identify a small portion of the model to be recomputed when new information is available. These features help provide near-instantaneous recommendations. Moreover, storing these nearest neighbors requires little memory, making such approaches scalable to applications with millions of users and items.

- *Stability*—Another useful property of recommender systems based on this approach is that they are little affected by the addition of users, items, and ratings, as is typically observed in large commercial applications. When item similarities have been computed, an item-based system can readily make recommendations to new users without being retrained. Moreover, when a few ratings have been entered for a new item, only the similarities between this item and the ones already in the system need to be computed.

- *Graph-based*—Another great advantage, related to the topic of this book, is that the origin dataset and the nearest neighbor model can be easily mapped in graph models. The resulting graph provides great advantages with regard to local navigation of data during model updating or forecasting, justifiability, and access efficiency. It also helps solve the cold-start problem, described in section 5.5.

For these reasons, this chapter focuses mainly on this class of collaborative filtering recommendation systems. But although neighborhood-based methods have gained popularity due to these advantages, they are known to suffer from the problem of limited coverage, which causes some items to never be recommended. Also, traditional methods in this category are known to be sensitive to sparseness of ratings and the cold-start problem when the system has only a few ratings or no ratings for new users and items. In section 5.5, I discuss techniques for mitigating or solving the cold-start problem. Finally, no single approach to recommendation engines can fit all cases, which is why hybrid approaches are generally used in production-ready recommendation engine systems. These methods are described in chapter 7.

5.1   *Collaborative filtering recommendations*

In this section, you are going to learn how to design graph models and the algorithms on top to implement a recommender system for an e-commerce site that uses a collaborative filtering approach to gently suggest to users items that could be of interest to them.

The site might sell many types of items, such as books, computers, watches, and clothing. The details about each item are not curated; some items have only a title, one or more pictures, and a small and useless description. Suppliers don't provide a lot of information, and due to the number of items and the number of suppliers, it's not practical to have an internal team take care of this task at scale.[3] On the site, users can buy items only if they are registered and logged in. Thanks to cookies, it is possible to log the users in automatically as soon as they reach the site. Little information is tracked about each user—only what's necessary for payments and shipping.

In this scenario, a content-based approach like the one described in chapter 4 is not applicable. Often, no data that is useful for creating profiles about users or items is available. Nonetheless, users' activity is tracked. Each user is logged in most of the time, and it is possible to collect and store a huge variety of interactions between users and items (purchases, clicks, searches, and ratings). Collaborative filtering approaches use this data to provide recommendations to users. The overall recommendation process, which takes advantage of graph models, can be summarized by the high-level schema in figure 5.2.

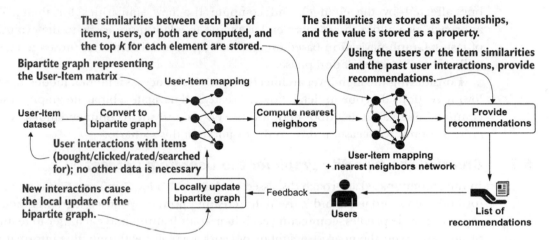

Figure 5.2 A graph-powered collaborative filtering recommender system

This figure shows the main elements and tasks of the collaborative filtering recommendation engine, which uses graphs as the data representation for both the User-Item dataset and the nearest neighbor network. Suppose that user John buys two books from the e-commerce site: technical books about machine learning and graphs. As the first step, the User-Item matrix is converted to a bipartite graph. In this case, John, represented by a node, will be connected to two nodes representing the two books purchased. The resulting graph is used as input for the creation of the nearest neighbors network by computing similarities between users, items, or both, depending on the algorithm used for recommendations. Hence, John is similar to users who are interested in graphs and machine learning and who bought the same set of books. The two books are also similar to others that have been purchased by the same set of

---

[3] You may face these types of issues in real projects. The problem of content curation is common on e-commerce sites, and I've seen it in a lot of the projects I've followed.

users, probably on the same topic. Then the top *k*-nearest neighbors for each element (users or items) are stored back in the original graph, which is enriched with these new relationships among users, items, or both. The similarity value is stored as a property of the relationship, assigning it a weight. The higher this weight value is, the more similar the users are by this relationship. Providing recommendations for users at this point is a matter of using their previous interactions and the nearest neighbors network. Such a task can be accomplished with a simple graph-matching query. Then the list of recommendations is provided to the user.

Further interactions can be looped back into the system to update the model. This task can use the locality provided by the graph model; new interactions will affect only a small portion of the nearest neighbor network. If a user watches a new movie, it will be easy to find the affected movies (all the movies that share at least one user with the one affected by the change) and compute the new similarities for them. This approach also allows the recommender engine to adapt more easily to the evolution of tastes. Graph navigation based on relationship traversal facilitates those updates as well as the recommendation phase.

Considering the high-level architecture, which also acts as a mental model, the following sections describe in detail how to create and navigate a bipartite graph, how to compute the nearest neighbor network, and how to provide recommendations. A concrete e-commerce dataset is used as the example in this scenario.

5.2   *Creating the bipartite graph for the User-Item dataset*

In the content-based approach discussed in chapter 4, a lot of information is available for both items and users and is useful for creating profiles. We used a graph model to represent these profiles, connecting each item to its features and each user to features of interest. Even the nearest neighbor network was built with only this information. The collaborative filtering approach, on the other hand, relies on data related to different kinds of interactions between users and items. Such information is generally referred to as a *User-Item dataset*. An example of such a dataset was described in chapter 3; here, the discussion is extended and refined. Figure 5.3 highlights the creation of a bipartite graph from a User-Item dataset in the recommendation process.

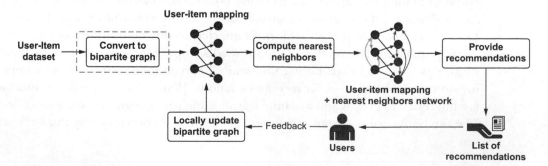

Figure 5.3   Bipartite graph creation in the recommendation process

Table 5.1 shows an example dataset. The items are books that different users have bought.

Table 5.1 Example User-Item dataset for the e-commerce scenario

	Fluent Python	Machine Learning: A Probabilistic Perspective	Graph Analysis and Visualization	Bayesian Reasoning	Fraud Analytics	Deep Learning
User A	1	1	1	1	1	1
User B	0	1	0	0	0	1
User C	1	0	0	0	0	0
User D	0	1	0	1	0	1

This table contains data on only one type of interaction: purchases. In different scenarios, including the e-commerce site, several types of interactions are available (views, clicks, ratings, and so on) and can be used in the recommendation process. *Multimodal* recommender systems [da Costa and Manzato, 2014] combine multiple interaction types to provide recommendations. One of the best approaches is to create an isolated recommender system for each interaction type and then combine the interactions in a hybrid recommender. Because the focus here is on data modeling and algorithms for collaborative filtering, we will focus on a single type, but the extension to more is straightforward and is discussed in section 7.2.

The User-Item dataset (which in real life will be much bigger than the sample shown here) represents the input of the recommendation process in the collaborative filter. This initial data is easy to obtain. Here are a few examples:

- Online merchants keep records of which customers bought which products and sometimes of whether they liked those products.
- Supermarket chains usually keep purchase records for their regular customers by using reward cards.

People's preferences for things, such as for certain products sold by a retailer, can be represented as graphs in recommendation networks [Newman, 2010] and used in recommender systems. The fundamental and most common representation of a recommendation network is a bipartite graph or bigraph. We looked at these graphs in chapter 3. Figure 5.4 shows a simple, generic bipartite graph in which the nodes are type U or V.

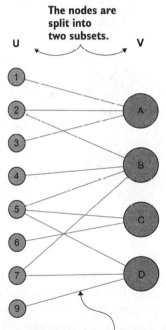

The nodes are split into two subsets.

Edges exist only between nodes belonging to two different sets. The relationships can be directed and weighted.

Figure 5.4 A generic bipartite graph

Let's apply this simple concept to our scenario and to recommendation systems that use a collaborative filtering approach. In recommendation networks, one vertex type represents products (or items in general), and the other type represents users. Edges connect users to the items they interact with (buy or like, for example). It is also possible to represent strengths or weights on the edges to indicate how often a person has bought an item or how much they like it [Newman, 2010].

Using this model, it is possible to convert the User-Item dataset in a bipartite graph. From our simple dataset for the e-commerce site in table 5.1, it is possible to create the graph in figure 5.5.

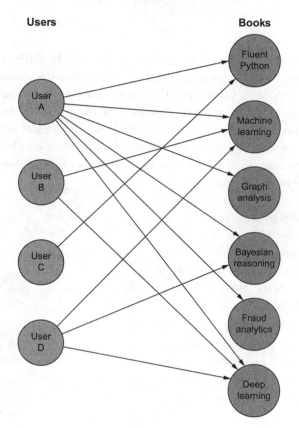

Figure 5.5   A bipartite graph representing table 5.1

Although a bipartite graph can represent an entire recommendation network, it is often convenient and useful to work with direct connections between vertices of only one type. From a bipartite graph, it is possible to infer connections between nodes of the same type, creating a one-mode projection. Two projections can be generated for each bipartite graph. The first projection connects the U nodes (users), and the second connects V nodes (books). Figure 5.6 shows the two projections computed from the bipartite graph in figure 5.5.

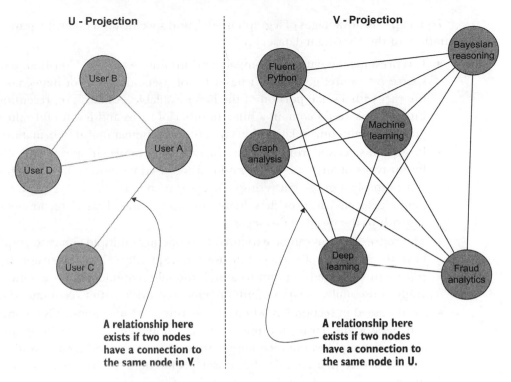

U - Projection

V - Projection

A relationship here exists if two nodes have a connection to the same node in V.

A relationship here exists if two nodes have a connection to the same node in U.

Figure 5.6   The two possible projections of the graph in figure 5.5

The projections of the bipartite graph show the relationships among users who made the same purchases, even only one, and relationships between books that were purchased by the same users, even only one. This one-mode projection is often useful and widely employed, but its construction hides a lot of information from the original bipartite graph, so in a sense it is less powerful in terms of representation. In the case of items and users, it doesn't show how many users purchased both of the two items. To solve this problem, it is possible to add a property to the relationships whose value captures this information, making such projection weighted. This projection is a co-occurrence network (described in chapter 3) whose source is the bipartite graph. In a User-Item matrix, two items are connected in the V-mode projection if they co-occur in at least one user's preferences.

The projections—weighted and unweighted—of a bipartite graph represent data in a way that allows us to perform some analysis more easily than with the original format. Therefore, projections are commonly used in recommendation systems [Grujić, 2008]. Often, graph clustering analysis (discussed in part 3) is performed on these networks to reveal groups of items that are generally purchased together or, in the other projection, to identify customer segments based on preferences for some specific set of items. Projections are also powerful visualization techniques that can reveal patterns that are difficult to discover or identify in the original format.

To recap, the advantages of a graph model, and specifically a bipartite graph representation, of the User-Item dataset are

- It represents the data in a compact and intuitive way. The User-Item dataset is sparse by nature; generally, it has a lot of users and a lot of items, and users interact with a small portion of the items available. A matrix representing such interactions would contain a huge number of zeros and few useful values. The graph contains only relationships that represent meaningful information.

- Projections derived from the bipartite graph are information rich and allow different types of analyses, both graphical (after visualization) and via algorithms (an example is graph clustering). Analyses such as customer segmentation and item clustering can provide valuable support to the classical recommendation algorithms discussed in this section.

- The representation can be extended by modeling multiple bipartite graphs that have the same set of vertices but use different edges. This extension helps us represent data used as input to a multimodal recommendation engine. These engines use multiple types of interactions to provide better recommendations.

- As discussed in section 5.3, when the nearest neighbor network is computed, it can be stored, sharing the user and item nodes of the bipartite graph. This approach simplifies the recommendation phase by providing access to a single data structure that contains both user preferences and the nearest neighbors network.

Now that you understand the graph model describing the User-Item dataset, let's get practical and create a real database. The following listing, which is similar to the one used for the content-based scenario, imports data from the Retail Rocket[4] dataset (https://retailrocket.net), converting the User-Item matrix to a bipartite graph.

Listing 5.1 Code for importing User-Item dataset

```
def import_user_item(self, file):
    with open(file, 'r+') as in_file:
        reader = csv.reader(in_file, delimiter=',')
        next(reader, None)
        with self._driver.session() as session:
            self.executeNoException(session, "CREATE CONSTRAINT ON (u:User)
            ➥ ASSERT u.userId IS UNIQUE")
            self.executeNoException(session, "CREATE CONSTRAINT ON (u:Item)
            ➥ ASSERT u.itemId IS UNIQUE")

            tx = session.begin_transaction()
            i = 0
            j = 0
            query = """
                MERGE (item:Item {itemId: $itemId})
```

Creates the constraints to prevent duplicates. Each user and item must be unique.

The query uses MERGE to create users or items when they don't exist. The CREATE for the PURCHASES relationship stores one relationship for each purchase.

---

[4] The data is available through Kaggle at http://mng.bz/8W8P.

```
        MERGE (user:User {userId: $userId})
        CREATE (user)-[:PURCHASES{ timestamp: $timestamp}]->(item)
"""
for row in reader:
    try:
        if row:
            timestamp = strip(row[0])
            user_id = strip(row[1])
            event_type = strip(row[2])
            item_id = strip(row[3])
```

The dataset has multiple event types (view, add to cart, and so on). We consider here only completed transactions or actual purchases.

```
            if event_type == "transaction":
                tx.run(query, {"itemId":item_id, "userId":
                    user_id,  "timestamp": timestamp})
                i += 1
                j += 1
                if i == 1000:
                    tx.commit()
                    print(j, "lines processed")
                    i = 0
                    tx = session.begin_transaction()
    except Exception as e:
        print(e, row, reader.line_num)
tx.commit()
print(j, "lines processed")
```

At the end of the import, which should take a few seconds, it is possible to run the following query and visualize a portion of the graph:

```
MATCH p=()-[r:PURCHASES]->() RETURN p LIMIT 25
```

The graph created from the bipartite model represents the entry point of the next phase, as described in the mental model of the process in figure 5.2. Section 5.3 describes how to compute and store the nearest neighbor network.

EXERCISES

With the newly created database, run queries to do the following:

- Find the best sellers (the items with the highest number of purchases).
- Find the best buyers (the users with the highest number of purchases).
- Find recurrent buys (items purchased more than one time by the same user).

5.3 Computing the nearest neighbor network

The next task in the recommendation process is computing similarities between elements—users or items or both—and constructing the nearest neighbor network. Figure 5.7 highlights the creation of the nearest neighbor network as enrichment of the bipartite graph in the recommendation process.

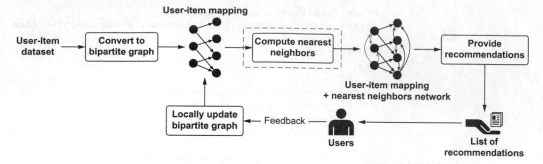

Figure 5.7   **Computing the nearest neighbor network in the recommendation process**

As described earlier, there are two possible approaches to memory-based recommendation for collaborative filtering:

- *Item-based*—The similarities are computed between items based on the users who interact with them (rating, buying, clicking, and so on).
- *User-based*—The similarities are computed between users based on the list of items they interact with.

It is important to note that unlike in the content-based case, with the neighborhood methods, the information used for computing the similarities is related only to the interactions available in the User-Item dataset. Each item and each user can be identified only by an ID (or a node without any relevant properties different from the identifier). This approach has the advantage that the model can be created with no details available for items and users. Nonetheless, the procedure for the similarity computation is the same as that for the content-based approach:

1. Identify/select a similarity function that allows you to compute distances between homogeneous elements in the graph (among users or items, for example).
2. Represent each element in a way that's suitable for the selected similarity function.
3. Compute similarities, and store them in the graph.

The graph model, with its great flexibility, allows us to easily extract various representations for either users or items when the function is chosen. For the sake of simplicity and because it is the best suited to our example scenario, we'll again use the cosine similarity.[5] The difference is in how to extract the vectors in the vector space model (VSM) required for the computation. Consider a simple bipartite graph that models a reduced version of a bigger User-Item dataset, as shown in figure 5.8.

---

[5] By this point, you should be familiar with the formula, which is always the same as in all the use cases described previously, so I won't repeat it here. If you need a refresher, see section 4.2.3.

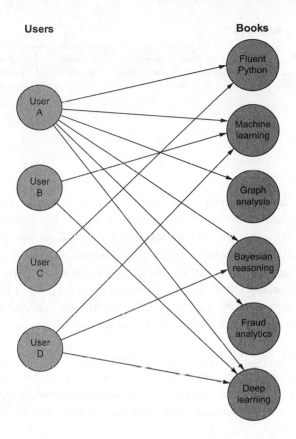

Users

Books

Figure 5.8 A bipartite graph representing a scaled-down User-Item dataset

Depending on the similarity we have to compute—among users or among items—it is possible to extract two vector representations from this graph. The vector creation process in this scenario is essentially the same as in the content-based approach. In that case, a vector is created for each item, considering the set of available features possibly describing it. In this case, for each item we consider the set of users who are interested in it, taking into account the items the users liked in the past. The following tables show how this task is accomplished. Depending on the similarity we have to compute—among users or among items—it is possible to extract two vector representations from this graph. The vector creation process in this scenario is essentially the same as in the content-based approach. In that case, a vector is created for each item, considering the set of available features possibly describing it. In this case, for each item we consider the set of users who are interested in it, taking into account the items the users liked in the past. Tables 5.2 and 5.3 show how this task is accomplished.

Table 5.2   User vectors table from the graph in figure 5.8

	Fluent Python	Machine Learning: A Probabilistic Perspective	Graph Analysis and Visualization	Bayesian Reasoning	Fraud Analytics	Deep Learning
User A	1	1	1	1	1	1
User B	0	1	0	0	0	1
User C	1	0	0	0	0	0
User D	0	1	0	1	0	1

In table 5.2, each row is a user, and each column represents an item (a book). The column order during vector creation must always be the same; otherwise, two vectors cannot be compared. In this example, the vectors are binary or Boolean: we are not considering the *value* of the relationships between users and items, only the fact that they exist. Such a value could model the rating the user assigned to a book, the number of times the user clicked a product, and so on, and it is represented as a property of the relationship in the graph model. Migrating to a nonbinary representation requires replacing the 1 with the actual value of the weight of the relationship between the user and the item.

In section 4.1, we saw that it is possible to mix binary values with real (integer, float, and double) values in the same vector construction. This approach is useful when we would like to create a vector for each item that represents more relationship types, as in the multimodal recommendation. This case is not considered here for the sake of simplicity.

From table 5.2, we can extract the following compressed representation of the users in the VSM:

Vector(User A) = [1, 1, 1, 1, 1, 1]

Vector(User B) = [0, 1, 0, 0, 0, 1]

Vector(User C) = [1, 0, 0, 0, 0, 0]

Vector(User D) = [0, 1, 0, 1, 0, 1]

Table 5.3 shows the item vectors.

Table 5.3   Item vectors table

	User A	User B	User C	User D
Fluent Python	1	0	1	0
Machine Learning: A Probabilistic Perspective	1	1	0	1
Graph Analysis and Visualization	1	0	0	0

Table 5.3 Item vectors table *(continued)*

	User A	User B	User C	User D
Bayesian Reasoning	1	0	0	1
Fraud Analytics	1	0	0	0
Deep Learning	1	1	0	1

This table takes the same approach to items. In this case, each row is an item, and each column represents a different user. The column order is important here, too. The resulting vector representation looks like this:

Vector(Fluent Python) = [1, 0, 1, 0]

Vector(Machine Learning) = [1, 1, 0, 1]

Vector(Graph Analysis) = [1, 0, 0, 0]

Vector(Bayesian Reasoning) = [1, 0, 0, 1]

Vector(Fraud Analytics) = [1, 0, 0, 0]

Vector(Deep Learning) = [1, 1, 0, 1]

Those vectors, in both cases, can be extracted easily from the graph database by using a query. This example shows again that graphs not only are an appropriate data representation model for keeping complex data in a format that is easy to access and navigate, but also offer the flexibility to export data in a format that can suit different learning processes. A similar model can feed both a content-based approach and a neighborhood approach, and these approaches can even coexist in the same graph. And we are only beginning to uncover the power of graphs!

Before we examine the vector query itself, let's take a quick look at some considerations that can help you obtain a significant boost in the way that data is extracted and processed. Representing vectors in a memory-efficient way and accessing their values efficiently are important machine learning tasks. The best approach to vector representation varies according to the nature of the vector and how it will be used. In the content-based scenario, vector creation for items relies on a small number of possible vector dimensions. The sparseness or denseness of a vector's data is the most important consideration. Figure 5.9 shows examples of each type of vector.

If you recall our discussion of vector creation for movies based on predefined features, the number of possible features was relatively limited. Considering all possible actors and directors together with all genres and so on, the number of features will be no more than 10,000 or 20,000. The same is true of using text to create the vectors. In that case, the size of the vector is defined by the language vocabulary or the number of words in the language that are used. Although the number of nonzero values is small compared with the vector's dimensionality, overall, the vector is small.

Dense vector

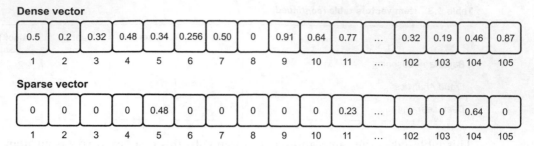

Sparse vector

0	0	0	0	0.48	0	0	0	0	0	0.23	...	0	0	0.64	0
1	2	3	4	5	6	7	8	9	10	11	...	102	103	104	105

Figure 5.9   Example of dense and sparse vectors (with random values)

A vector with relatively many nonzero values in relationship to its size is called *dense*. Such a vector can be represented by an implementation that stores values in an array of doubles or floats. Vector indices correspond directly to array indices. A dense vector's advantage is speed: being array-backed, it's quick to access and update any of its values.

At the other end of the spectrum, a typical e-commerce site contains more than 1 million items and (ideally for them) a number of users of the same order of magnitude. Each user, even one who has a compulsive e-shopping disorder (as I do for books) can buy only a small portion of the overall possible items. On the other side of the coin, each item—even a best seller—is purchased by a relatively small number of users, so the total number of nonzero values in the respective vectors will always be small. This type of vector, in which the total percentage of nonzero values is small, is called a *sparse vector*. Representing sparse vectors with an array is not only a waste of memory, but also makes any computation expensive.

It is possible to represent a sparse vector in different ways to optimize memory and simplify manipulation. In Java, some of the most common methods are available in Apache Mahout,[6] a distributed linear algebra framework used for creating scalable performant machine learning applications. For the similarity computation, I use a different representation for sparse vectors that still uses an array of floats or doubles as the basic data structure. The structure of my preferred implementation of a sparse vector is described in figure 5.10.

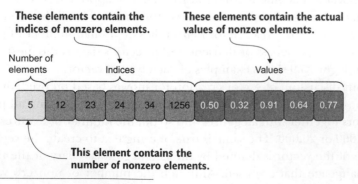

Figure 5.10   A sparse vector representation

[6] See, for example, http://mng.bz/EVjJ or http://mng.bz/N8jD.

Figure 5.10 shows how a sparse vector can be represented in a compact format. The first element contains the number of nonzero values in the original array. We will define it as N. The second part, which starts from position 1 (remember that the vector indexing starts at 0) and ends at position N, contains the indices of the nonzero values. The last part, which starts at $N + 1$ and continues to the end of the vector, contains the actual values.

Such a representation has the advantage that with a single small array, it is possible to represent a long and complex sparse vector. This array requires minimal memory and can be stored easily as a property of nodes. This advantage is a big one when you have to process a lot of data. My personal Java implementation is available in the code repository in the ch05/java directory.

To keep this chapter aligned with the rest, listing 5.2 contains the representation of a sparse vector in Python. In this programming language, a sparse vector can be represented as a dictionary in which the key is the position of the element in the vector, and the value is the effective element value. In this case, the number of nonzero elements is the size of the dictionary, making the representation simple enough. The relative code can be found in the code repository in the util/sparse_vector.py file.

Listing 5.2   Sparse vector implementation in Python

```
def convert_sparse_vector(numbers):        ◁———  Function that creates a dict
    vector_dict = {}                              (sparse vector) from a vector
    for k, c in enumerate(numbers):        ◁———
        if c:                                     Loops through the vector, taking
            vector_dict[k] = c                    the position and the value
    return vector_dict

if __name__ == '__main__':
    print(convert_sparse_vector([1, 0, 0, 1, 0, 0]))  #{0: 1, 3: 1}
    print(convert_sparse_vector([1, 1, 0, 0, 0, 0]))  #{0: 1, 1: 1}
    print(convert_sparse_vector([1, 1, 0, 0, 0, 1]))  #{0: 1, 1: 1, 5: 1}
```

Checks that the value is not null or 0 ——▷ (annotation pointing to `if c:`)

There is no real threshold you should consider for using a sparse rather than a dense vector. Generally, I prefer using sparse vectors because they optimize similarity computation. In most of the examples from now on in this book, we will use sparse vectors.

Now we have all the elements required for extracting the user and item vectors and computing similarities between them. The queries for extracting the nonzero elements of each vector for users and items are shown in the next two listings.

NOTE In these queries, we are using the node ID as an index, but any integer or long value could work. We could use any numeric ID identifying the items, for example, such as `itemId`.

Listing 5.3   Query for extracting a sparse vector for a user

```
MATCH (u:User {userId: "121688"})-[:PURCHASES]->(i:Item)
return id(i) as index, 1 as value
order by index
```

Listing 5.4   Query for extracting a sparse vector for an item

```
MATCH (i:Item {itemId: "37029"})<-[:PURCHASES]-(u:User)
RETURN id(u) as index, 1 as value
ORDER BY index
```

In the MATCH clauses, the relationship PURCHASES is used to find all the items a user purchased or all the users who bought an item. The RETURN clause extracts the non-zero elements of the resulting vector. Because no value indicates the weight of the relationship, a binary approach is used, so by default, 1 is assigned to each value.

EXERCISE

Change the preceding queries to use itemId and userId instead of the node ID.

> **HINT**   Consider that the queries are stored as strings even though they are integers, and remember that we need a numeric value for the index.

The next step is computing and storing the similarities. For each user or item, we have to do the following:

1 Compute the similarities with all the other elements (homogeneously: each user with other users and each item with other items).
2 Order the similarities in a descending order.
3 Keep only the top k, where the value of k is predefined. Alternatively, fix a threshold or minimum similarity value, and keep only the similarities above it.
4 Store the top k similar elements in the graph as new relationships between users or items.

Figure 5.11 explodes the "Compute nearest neighbor" block of the recommendation process, summarizing the preceding sequence of steps.

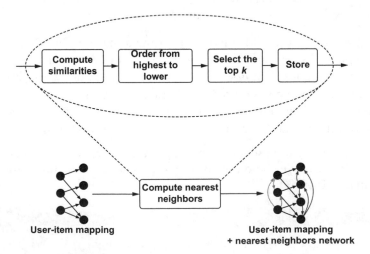

User-item mapping

User-item mapping + nearest neighbors network

Figure 5.11   Detail on computing nearest neighbor

The following listing shows the Python implementation for this task, using a sparse vector representation. The code is available in the ch05/recommendation/collaborative_filtering/recommender.py file.

Listing 5.5 Similarity computation

Setting some variables for user-based similarity: the labels of the nodes and the attribute with the element id. The variables for the items are in the code repository.

Query to extract the user purchases as a vector. The first element in each row returned is the itemId; the second is fixed to 1 because we are interested only in the purchase event, not in a rate or how many times the user bought the item. See listing 5.3.

```python
label = "User"
property = "userId"
sparse_vector_query = """
    MATCH (u:User {userId: $id})-[:PURCHASES]->(i:Item)
    return id(i) as index, 1.0 as value
    order by index
"""

def compute_and_store_KNN(self, size: int) -> None:
    print("fetching vectors")
    vectors = self.get_vectors()
    print(f"computing KNN for {len(vectors)} vectors")
    for i, (key, vector) in enumerate(vectors.items()):
        # index only vectors
        vector = sorted(vector.keys())
        knn = FixedHeap(size)
        for (other_key, other_vector) in vectors.items():
            if key != other_key:
                # index only vectors
                other_vector = sorted(other_vector.keys())
                score = cosine_similarity(vector, other_vector)
                if score > 0:
                    knn.push(score, {"secondNode": other_key, "similarity":
                        score})
        self.store_KNN(key, knn.items())
        if (i % 1000 == 0) and i > 0:
            print(f"{i} vectors processed...")
    print("KNN computation done")

def get_vectors(self) -> Dict:
    with self._driver.session() as session:
        tx = session.begin_transaction()
        ids = self.get_elements(tx)
        vectors = {id_: self.get_sparse_vector(tx, id_) for id_ in ids}
    return vectors

def get_elements(self, tx) -> List[str]:
    query = f"MATCH (u: {self.label}) RETURN u.{self.property} as id"
    result = tx.run(query).value()
    return result

def get_sparse_vector(self, tx: Transaction, current_id: str) -> Dict[int,
        float]:
    params = {"id": current_id}
```

Entry-point function to compute and store the similarities for all users. Changing the variables, you'll get the same result for the items.

Loops over the dictionary with the sparse vectors for all the users, computes all the similarities, keeps only the *k* highest values for each node, and calls the function to store the *k*-NN

Function that creates a dictionary in which the key is the userId and the value is the user's sparse vector

Function that returns the list of elements' (Users or Items) IDs by querying the database

Function that returns for the specified user (or item) the related sparse vector by querying to the graph database

```
        result = tx.run(self.sparse_vector_query, params)
        return dict(result.values())
```

Function that stores the *k*-NN in the database

```
    def store_KNN(self, key: str, sims: List[Dict]) -> None:
        deleteQuery = f"""
            MATCH (n: self.label )-[s:SIMILARITY]->()
            WHERE n. self.property  = $id
            DELETE s"""
```

Query to delete all the similarities of the node

Query to store in one shot all the similarities

```
        query = f"""
            MATCH (n: self.label )
            WHERE n. self.property  = $id
            UNWIND $sims as sim
            MATCH (o: self.label )
            WHERE o. self.property  = sim.secondNode
            CREATE (n)-[s:SIMILARITY {{ value: toFloat(sim.similarity) }}]->
            (o)"""

        with self._driver.session() as session:
            tx = session.begin_transaction()
            params = {
                "id": key,
                "sims": sims}
            tx.run(deleteQuery, params)
            tx.run(query, params)
            tx.commit()
```

As is evident from the preceding code, the similarity computation requires $N \times N$ computations to be performed, where N is $|U|$ or $|V|$. This operation may take a while when N is big.

Figure 5.12 shows what the resulting graph model looks like when the relationships are stored in the graph. Because the graph is small, the k value is set to 2.

The graph in figure 5.12 is not a bipartite graph anymore, because there now exist relationships among elements in the same partition. But we can have multiple subgraphs of the same graph by considering only a subset of nodes and relationships, so the graph can be split into three highly relevant subgraphs:

- The subgraph with both U and I (U represents all the users, and I represents all the items) as nodes and only the PURCHASES relationships is the bipartite graph we had before.
- The subgraph with U as nodes and SIMILARITY as the relationship is the nearest neighbor network for U (the k-NN for U).
- The subgraph with I as nodes and SIMILARITY as the relationship is the nearest neighbor network for I (the k-NN for I).

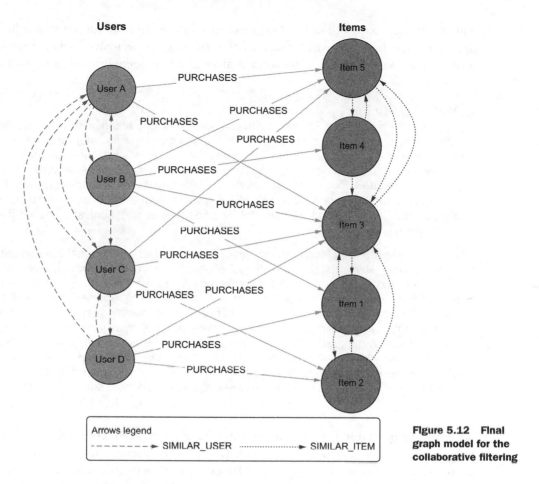

Figure 5.12   Final graph model for the collaborative filtering

In section 5.4, these graphs are used as input for the last task, providing recommendations, but it is important to notice that these graphs already contain a lot of information. The process distills new knowledge from the bipartite graph and stores it back in a way that can serve various purposes in addition to recommendations:

- *Clustering items*—By applying some graph clustering algorithms on the items' nearest neighbor network, it is possible to recognize (for example) groups of products that are generally bought together or movies that are watched by the same group of users.
- *Segmenting users*—The same clustering algorithms can be applied on the users' nearest neighbor network, and the result will be a group (*segment*) of users who generally buy the same products or see the same movies.
- *Finding similar products*—The items' nearest neighbor network itself is useful. If a user is looking at a specific product, by querying the graph it is possible to show a list of similar products based on the SIMILARITY relationship, and this operation will be fast.

The graph approach not only allows us to mix information by storing it in a flexible data structure, but also provides various opportunities for us to access data, reveal patterns, extract knowledge, and perform analysis in a homogeneous data environment.

Modeling pro tip

This section and the equivalent one in chapter 4 describe techniques for converting different types of data to graphs. Such techniques are generally referred to as *graph construction techniques*. In the content-based case, the data is defined by metadata and contents, such as actors, genres, and even the plots of movies, whereas in the collaborative filtering case, the data is the User-Item matrix. In both cases, a similarity function and a proper data conversion to a vector space model allow us to create a graph that imparts greater knowledge and has greater communication power than the original version of the data.

In many areas of machine learning, graphs are used to model local relationships between data elements and to build global structures from local information [Silva and Zhao, 2016]. Building graphs is sometimes necessary for dealing with problems arising from applications in machine learning or data mining, and at other times, it's helpful for managing data. It's important to note that the transformation from the original data to a graph data representation can always be performed in a lossless manner. The opposite is not always true. For these reasons, the techniques and use cases described here represent concrete examples of how to perform these graph conversions; these examples may be of use not only in the scenarios described, but also in a lot of real use cases. Play with the data you have, and try to convert it to a graph.

So far, we've been using cosine similarity as a basic function for computing similarities. Other metrics have been proposed—such as adjusted cosine similarity, Spearman's rank correlation coefficient, mean squared difference, and the Pearson coefficient—and are commonly used as alternatives to this function. Specifically, the Pearson coefficient outperforms other measures for user-based recommendations [Herlocker et al., 1999], whereas cosine similarity is the best for item-based recommendations.

In this part of the book, the focus is on data modeling, so cosine similarity is the reference function. Later in the book, other solutions are described when their use is appropriate.

EXERCISES

Query the graph obtained by running the code that computes similarity to find the following:

- Given an item, the list of similar items
- Given a user, the list of similar users
- The highest value of similarity (search the database to understand why)

5.4 Providing recommendations

The final task of the recommendation process is to provide a list of suggestions to users whenever this list is necessary or valuable. Figure 5.13 highlights the recommendations provision of the recommendation process.

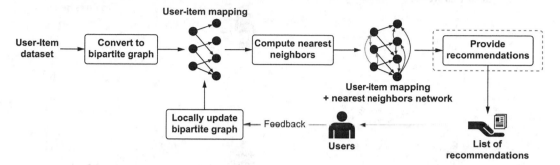

Figure 5.13 Last step in the recommendation process

In our scenario, while the user is navigating the e-commerce site, in some boxes we would like to provide recommendations that are customized for that user. At a high level, the recommendation process produces the following types of output:

- *Relevance scores*—Numerical predictions indicating the degree to which the current user likes or dislikes a certain item.
- *Recommendations*—A list of *N* recommended items. Such a top-*N* list should not, of course, contain items that the current user has already bought unless the purchases can be recurring purchases.

In the neighborhood approach to collaborative filtering, the first output—relevance scores—can be produced by looking at the user's nearest neighbors (the user-based approach) network or the item's nearest neighbors (the item-based approach) network. Let's take a closer look at these two approaches.

The basic idea in the user-based approach is that given the current user as input, the bipartite graph representing the interaction database, and the nearest neighbors network, for every product p that the user has not seen or bought, a prediction is computed based on the ratings for p made by the peer users (the users in that user's nearest neighbors network). Consider the diagram in figure 5.14.

Alessandro bought the four products on the left. The idea of the user-based approach is to find similar users who also bought those products and then find other products they bought that Alessandro hasn't bought yet. The underlying assumptions of such methods [Jannach, et al., 2010] are

- If two users had similar tastes in the past, they will have similar tastes in the future.
- Users' preferences remain stable and consistent over time.

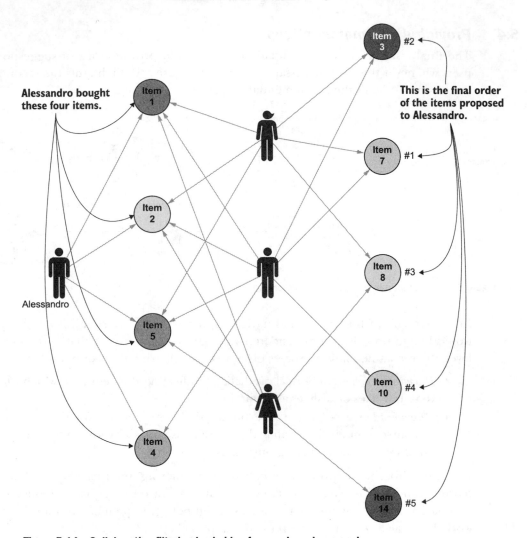

Figure 5.14   Collaborative filtering basic idea for user-based approach

Some methods mitigate such assumptions, but they are out of the scope of the scenario we are considering.

Let's convert the idea expressed in words and images to a formula that computers can understand. Two cases can occur. In one case, the interactions between users and items (clicks, purchases, and views) contain no weight. This case is called the *binary* or *Boolean* model. In the second case, there is a weight to the interactions (such as ratings). The formula for this case is

$$pred(a,p) = \frac{\sum_{b \in KNN(a)} sim(a,b)}{\sum_{b \in KNN(a)} sim(a,b)} \times r_{b,p}$$

This formula predicts the ratings that the user a would assign to the item p. $KNN(a)$ represents the k-nearest neighbors of the user a, and $r_{b,p}$ represents the rating assigned by the user b to the product p. This rating can be 0 if user b doesn't rate item p. Some variations of this formula exist, but they are out of the scope of this chapter.

The Boolean case is a little trickier, because in the literature, no single method is recognized as the best approach. The following formula [Sarwar et al., 2000] seems to me to be one of the most reasonable and is widely applied on e-commerce sites:

$$score(a,p) = \frac{1}{|KNN(a)|} \times \sum_{b \in KNN(a)} r_{b,p}$$

Here, $r_{b,p}$ will be 1 if the user b purchased the product p and 0 otherwise, so the sum will return how many of the nearest neighbors of a bought the product p. This value is normalized with the number of nearest neighbors for a (the value of $|KNN(a)|$).

The following listing contains an example implementation in Python that uses the nearest neighbor network created previously. The code is available in the ch05/recommendation/collaborative_filtering/recommender.py file.

Listing 5.6 Providing recommendations through a user-based approach

```
score_query = """                                              ◁──   Query for scoring items
    MATCH (user:User)-[:SIMILARITY]->(otherUser:User)               based on similarity
    WHERE user.userId = $userId                                     among users
    WITH otherUser, count(otherUser) as size
    MATCH (otherUser)-[r:PURCHASES]->(target:Target)
    WHERE target.itemId = $itemId
    return (+1.0/size)*count(r) as score
"""


def get_recommendations(self, user_id: str, size: int) -> List[int]:    ◁──
    not_seen_yet_items = self.get_not_seen_yet_items(user_id)
    recommendations = FixedHeap(size)                           Function that provides
    for item in not_seen_yet_items:                             the recommendations
        score = self.get_score(user_id, item)
        recommendations.push(score, item)
    return recommendations.items()


def get_not_seen_yet_items(self, user_id: str) -> List[int]:    ◁──   Function that
    query = """                                                       provides the list
        MATCH (user:User {userId:$userId})                            of not-yet-seen
        WITH user                                                     (in this case, not-
        MATCH (item:Item)                                             yet-bought)
        WHERE NOT EXISTS((user)-[:PURCHASES]->(item))                 items
        return item.itemId
    """
    with self._driver.session() as session:
        tx = session.begin_transaction()
        params = {"userId": user_id}
        result = tx.run(query, params).value()
    return result
```

```
def get_score(self, user_id: str, item_id: str) -> float:
    with self._driver.session() as session:
        tx = session.begin_transaction()
        params = {"userId": user_id, "itemId": item_id}
        result = tx.run(self.score_query, params)
        result = result.value() + [0.0]
    return result[0]
```

Function that predicts the score of an item for a user by using a simple query. The query has been specified in the variable.

Although user-based approaches have been applied successfully in different domains, some serious challenges remain when it comes to large e-commerce sites, where it is necessary to handle millions of users and millions of catalog items. In particular, due to the necessity of scanning a vast number of potential neighbors, it is practically impossible to compute predictions in real time, even using a graph approach. Large-scale e-commerce sites, therefore, often use different techniques. Item-based recommendations are among these techniques because they allow for the computation of recommendations in real time even for a large rating matrix [Sarwar et al., 2001].

The main idea of item-based algorithms is to compute predictions by using the similarity between items, not users. Let's examine a concrete example to make this idea clearer. Consider the graph database in figure 5.15, and suppose that we need to make a prediction of user Alessandro's rating for Item 5.

First, we compare the rating vectors of the other items and look for items that have ratings similar to Item 5 (that is, are similar to Item 5). In the example, we see that the ratings for Item 5 [3, 5, 4, 1, 0] are similar to the ratings for Item 1 [3, 4, 3, 1, 5] (two are the same, two are off by 1, and the 0 occurs because Alessandro did not rate Item

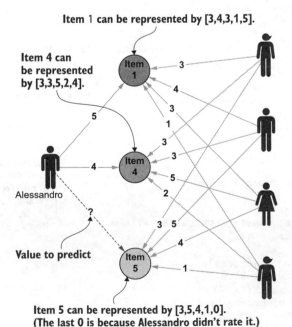

Item 1 can be represented by [3,4,3,1,5].

Item 4 can be represented by [3,3,5,2,4].

Alessandro

Value to predict

Item 5 can be represented by [3,5,4,1,0]. (The last 0 is because Alessandro didn't rate it.)

Figure 5.15 Collaborative filtering basic idea for item-based approach

5), and there is a partial similarity with Item 4 [3, 3, 5, 2, 4] (one is the same, and three are off by 1). The idea of item-based recommendations is to look at Alessandro's ratings for these similar items. He gave a 5 to Item 1 and a 4 to Item 4. An item-based algorithm computes a weighted average of these other ratings and predicts a rating for Item 5 somewhere between 4 and 5.

Again, to convert these words to a concrete formula to feed to a computer program, we need to consider both use cases: with an explicit rating and with a simple Boolean value that says whether the user interacted with the item (purchasing it, clicking it, and so on). In the case of Boolean values, the goal is not to predict a rating (as in 0–5, for example) but to predict the extent to which Item 5 will be of interest to Alessandro in a range from 0 to 1 (0 = not of interest, 1 = most likely of interest).

If the original User-Item dataset contains rating values, the formula to predict the rating for a not-yet-seen product in the dataset [Sarwar et al., 2001] is

$$pred(a,p) = \frac{\sum_{q \in ratedItem(a)} (sim(p,q) \times r_{a,q} \times |KNN(q) \cap \{p\}|)}{\sum_{q \in ratedItem(a)} (sim(p,q) \times |KNN(q) \cap \{p\}|)}$$

This formula can be rewritten in different forms according to how you decide to navigate the data. In our case,

- $q \in ratedItem(a)$ considers all the products rated by user a.
- For each q, it multiplies three values:
  - The similarity between q and the target product p.
  - The rating assigned by the user to q.
  - $|KNN(q) \cap \{p\}|$, which is 1 if p is in the set of nearest neighbors of q and 0 otherwise. It is possible to consider only the nearest neighbors of q and not all the similarities.
- The denominator normalizes the value to not exceed the max value of the rating.

Consider the data in figure 5.15. The similarities among all the three items are

- Item 1–Item 4: 0.943
- Item 1–Item 5: 0.759
- Item 4–Item 5: 0.811

Because there are only three items, we consider all the similarities in the nearest neighbor; hence, for us $|KNN(q) \cap \{p\}|$ is always 1. The user Alessandro rated Item 1 with 5 stars and Item 4 with 4 stars. The formula for predicting Alessandro's interest/stars for Item 5 is

$$pred(a,p) = \frac{0.759 \times 5 + 0.811 \times 4}{0.759 + 0.811} = \frac{7.039}{1.57} = 4.48$$

As with the user-based approach, for the Boolean case there is no accepted standard approach for computing the scores, so I'll present one of my favorites [Deshpande and Karypis, 2004]:

$$score(a,p) = \sum_{q \in ratedItem(a)} (sim(p,q) \times |KNN(q) \cap \{p\}|)$$

In this case, we have no ratings, so the formula is simpler. Furthermore, it doesn't return a prediction, but a generic score. Such a score can be normalized in different ways to facilitate comparisons.

The following listing presents an example implementation of the item-based version of the neighborhood approach. The code is available in the ch05/recommendation/collaborative_filtering/recommender.py file.

> **Listing 5.7 Providing recommendations by using a item-based approach**

The only required change from listing 5.6 is the score_query parameter. Here, the value is computed by considering the similarities among the previous user's purchases and the target items.

```
score_query = """
    MATCH (user:User)-[:PURCHASES]->(item:Item)-[r:SIMILARITY]->(target:Item)
    WHERE user.userId = $userId AND target.itemId = $itemId
    return sum(r.value) as score
"""

def get_recommendations(self, user_id: str, size: int) -> List[int]:

[… See Listing 5.6 …]
```

EXERCISE

Run the code in the preceding listing (which is available in the book's code repository), changing the users and observing how the list of recommendations changes. Then use a query to check the graph database and see whether the suggested items are in line with previous items bought by a user.

5.5 *Dealing with the cold-start problem*

Before I close this chapter on collaborative filtering, it is important to discuss a problem that affects collaborative filtering recommender systems: data sparsity. In real-world e-commerce applications, User-Item matrices tend to be sparse, as customers typically have bought (or have provided ratings for) only a small fraction of the products in the catalog. The problem is even worse for new users or new items that have had no or few interactions. This problem is referred to as the cold-start problem, and it further illustrates the importance of addressing the issue of data sparsity.

In general, the challenge related to the cold-start problem is to compute good predictions when relatively little information is available. One straightforward option for dealing with this problem is to exploit additional information about the users, such as gender, age, education, interests, or any other available data that can help classify a user. Other approaches exist, such as creating hybrid recommender systems that merge multiple approaches in a single prediction mechanism (chapter 7).

These approaches are no longer purely collaborative, and new questions arise as to how to acquire the additional information and combine the different classifiers. Nevertheless, to reach the critical mass of users needed in a collaborative approach, such techniques might be helpful in the ramp-up phase of a newly installed recommendation service.

Among the various approaches proposed over the years, a graph-based approach [Huang et al., 2004] explores transitive associations (similarities) among consumers through past transactions and feedback. The main idea of this approach is to exploit the supposed transitivity of customer tastes when they share items. Users' preferences are represented by the items and their interactions with the items.

The following example illustrates the idea of exploring transitive associations in recommender systems. Suppose that we have a simple User-Item dataset like the one in table 5.4.

Table 5.4   A sample User-Item dataset

	Item 1	Item 2	Item 3	Item 4
User 1	0	1	0	1
User 2	0	1	1	1
User 3	1	0	1	0

At this point in the book, you should be able to easily represent this table as a bipartite graph. The result should look like figure 5.16.

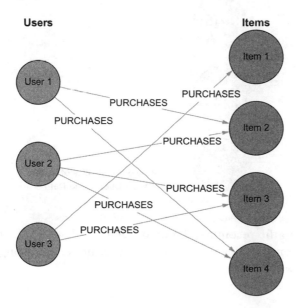

Figure 5.16   Graph representation of the User-Item dataset in table 5.4

The proposed method uses this representation method to solve the data sparsity problem. Moreover, a weight can be assigned to each edge, such as the value of its corresponding rating.

Suppose that the recommender system needs to recommend items for User 1. When we use a standard collaborative filtering approach, User 2 will be considered to be a peer of User 1 because both users bought Item 2 and Item 4. Item 3 will be recommended to User 1 because that user's nearest neighbor, User 2, also bought or liked it. No strong similarity can be found between User 1 and User 3.

In the transitive associations method, the recommendation approach can be easily implemented in a graph-based model by computing the associations between item nodes and user nodes. The recommendations are determined by determining paths between users and items. Standard collaborative filtering approaches, including both the user-based and item-based approaches, consider only paths with length equal to 3. (As a reminder, the path length is computed by considering the edges in the path.)

Consider our small example. In the bipartite graph in figure 5.16, the association between User 1 and Item 3 is determined by all paths of length 3 connecting User 1 and Item 3. It is easy to see from the diagram that two paths connect User 1 and Item 3: User 1–Item 2–User 2–Item 3 and User 1–Item 4–User 2–Item 3. Figure 5.17 highlights all paths of length 3 in the graph from figure 5.16.

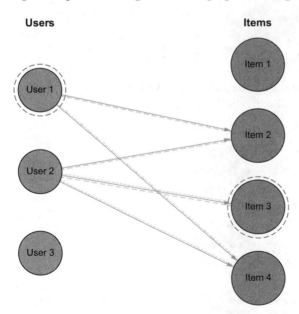

Figure 5.17   Paths of length 3 between User 1 and Item 3

This strong association leads to the recommendation of Item 3 to User 1. The higher the number of unique paths connecting an item node to a user node, the stronger the association is between those two nodes.

Because the number of such paths of length 3 is small in sparse rating databases, the idea is to also consider longer paths—the so-called *indirect associations*—to compute recommendations. Extending the preceding approach to explore and incorporate transitive associations is straightforward in a graph-based model.

By considering paths whose length exceeds 3, the model can explore transitive associations. Two paths of length 5 connect User 1 and Item 1, for example: User 1–Item 2–User 2–Item 3–User 3–Item 1 and User 1–item 4–User 2–Item 3–User 3–Item 1. Figure 5.18 highlights all paths of length 5 in the graph from figure 5.16.

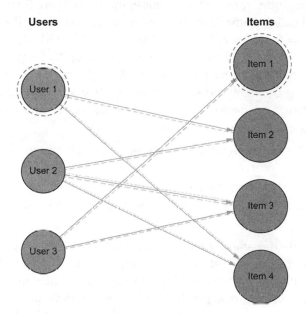

Figure 5.18   Paths of length 5 between User 1 and Item 1

Thus, Item 1 could be recommended to User 1 when transitive associations are taken into consideration in the recommendation.

Even with this approach, it is necessary to define a scoring mechanism to order the recommendations list. In this case, recommendations are made based on the associations computed for pairs of user nodes and item nodes. Given a user node *User t* and an item node *Item j*, the association between them, *score(User t, Item j)*, is defined as the sum of the weights of all distinctive paths connecting *User t* and *Item j*.

In this formula, only paths whose length is less than or equal to the maximum defined length *M* will be considered. The limit *M* is a parameter that the designer of the recommender system can control. It is worth noting that *M* has to be an odd number because transitive associations are represented in a bipartite graph.

$$score(user, item) = \sum_{p \in pathsBetween(user,\ item,\ M)} \alpha^{length(p)}$$

In this formula, *pathsBetween(user,item,M)* returns all the paths between *user* and *item* of length *x* where $x \leq M$. The weight of the path is computed as α^x, where α is a constant between 0 and 1, ensuring that longer paths have lesser impact.

The particular value for α can be determined by the system designer based on the characteristics of the underlying application domain. In applications in which transitive associations can be a strong predictor of consumer interests, α should take a value close to 1, whereas in applications where transitive associations tend to convey little information, α should take a value close to 0.

Let's illustrate this computation by using the example shown in figure 5.16. When *M* is set to 3 (as in standard collaborative filtering), *score(User 1, Item 3)* = $0.5^3 + 0.5^3$ = 0.25, and *score(User 1, Item 1)* = 0. When *M* is 5, *score(User 1, Item 3)* = $0.5^3 + 0.5^3$ = 0.25, and *score(User 1, Item 1)* = $0.5^5 + 0.5^5$ = 0.0625. For consumer User 1, the preceding score computation is repeated for all items in the dataset. As in the previous cases, the items are sorted in decreasing order by this score. Then the first *k* items (excluding the items that User 1 purchased in the past) of this sorted list are recommended to User 1. This approach requires our attention for different reasons:

- It generates high-quality recommendations even when a small amount of information is available.
- It uses the same User-Item dataset used so far in this chapter.
- It is purely graph-based, and it uses the same bipartite graph model discussed in our examples.

Moreover, a comparison with the standard user-based and item-based algorithms shows that the quality of the recommendations can be significantly improved by the proposed technique based on indirect relationships, in particular when the ratings matrix is sparse. Also, for new users, the algorithm leads to measurable performance increases compared with standard collaborative filtering techniques. When the rating matrix reaches a certain density, however, the quality of recommendations can decrease compared with standard algorithms.

The approach described in this section uses path-based similarity to compute the recommendations. Other graph-based approaches use more sophisticated graph algorithms.

5.6   *Advantages of the graph approach*

This chapter focuses on the creation of a collaborative filtering recommendation engine using graphs and graph models. In particular, it explores the neighborhood approach, which is well suited to a graph representation and graph-based navigation of the data. The main aspects and advantages of the graph-based approach to collaborative filtering recommendation engines implemented with neighborhood methods are as follows:

- The User-Item dataset can easily be represented as a bipartite graph, in which the weight of each user-item pair is represented as an optional property of the relationship.

- The bipartite graph representation of the User-Item dataset not only has the advantage of allowing us to store only relevant information—avoiding wasting memory by storing useless zeros, as in the matrix representation—but also of speeding access during model creation by focusing only on the potentially relevant neighbors.

- It is possible to extract several vector representations for both items and users from the same graph model.

- The resulting model, consisting of similarities among users or items or both, can be naturally represented as new relationships that connect users and items. The resulting new graphs are the nearest neighbor (*k*-NN) networks.

- The algorithm, based on similarity computation, for creating the *k*-NN networks represents one of the most powerful and most widely adopted techniques for graph construction. The resulting networks not only are easy to navigate during the recommendation process, but also contain new knowledge distilled from the existing User-Item dataset that can be used for analyzing the data from other perspectives, such as item clustering, customer segmentation, and so on.

- A widely adopted technique for solving the data sparsity issue and the cold-start problem is based on graph representation, navigation, and processing. Graph navigation methods (like the pathfinding example described earlier) and graph algorithms (such as PageRank) are applied to fill some gaps and create a denser representation of the User-Item dataset.

- Even in this scenario, it is possible to mix multiple recommendation algorithms in a single graph and combine the power of multiple approaches to providing recommendations.

Summary

This chapter continued our discussion of data modeling and, specifically, recommendations by introducing one of the most common techniques for implementing recommendation engines: the collaborative filtering approach.

In this chapter, you learned

- How to model a User-Item dataset in the form of a bipartite graph and how to project it into the two related graphs
- How to compute similarities among users and items by using only the information related to the user-item interactions, instead of static information about the users and items
- How to store such similarities in a *k*-NN model

- How to use such similarities to provide a recommendation list to the user via both a user-based and an item-based approach and considering binary and non-binary values

- What the advantages of having a sparse vector are, when to use it, and how to implement it

- How to use graph-based techniques to solve the data sparsity problem and in particular the cold-start problem

References

[Bell et al., 2007] Bell, Yehuda Koren, and Chris Volinsky. "Modeling Relationships at Multiple Scales to Improve Accuracy of Large Recommender Systems." *Proceedings of the 13th ACM SIGKDD International Conference on Knowledge Discovery and Data Mining* (2007): 95-104.

[Börner, 2010] Börner, Katy. *Atlas of Science: Visualizing What We Know.* Cambridge, MA: MIT Press, 2010.

[da Costa and Manzato, 2014] da Costa, Arthur F., and Marcelo Garcia Manzato. "Multimodal Interactions in Recommender Systems: An Ensembling Approach." *Proceedings of the Brazilian Conference on Intelligent Systems* (2014): 67-72.

[Deshpande and Karypis, 2004] Deshpande, Mukund, and George Karypis. "Item-Based Top-N Recommendation Algorithms." *ACM Transactions on Information Systems* 22:1 (2004): 143-177. DOI: http://dx.doi.org/10.1145/963770.963776.

[Diestel, 2008] Diestel, Reinhard. *Graph Theory (Graduate Texts in Mathematics).* 5th ed. Berlin: Springer, 2008.

[Go et al., 2007] Go, Kwang-Il Goh, Michael E. Cusick, David Valle, Barton Childs, Marc Vidal, and Albert-László Barabási. "The Human Disease Network." *PNAS* 104:21 (2007): 8685-8690. DOI: https://doi.org/10.1073/pnas.0701361104.

[Goldberg et al., 1992] Goldberg, David, David Nichols, Brian M. Oki, and Douglas Terry. "Using Collaborative Filtering to Weave an Information Tapestry." *Communications of the ACM* 35:12 (1992): 61-70. DOI: http://doi.acm.org/10.1145/138859.138867.

[Grujić, 2008] Grujić, Jelena. "Movies Recommendation Networks as Bipartite Graphs." *Proceedings of the 8th International Conference on Computational Science, Part II* (2008): 576-583.

[Herlocker et al., 1999] Herlocker, Joseph A. Konstan, Al Borchers, and John Riedl. "An Algorithmic Framework for Performing Collaborative Filtering. *Proceedings of the 22nd Annual International ACM SIGIR Conference on Research and Development in Information Retrieval* (1999): 230-237. DOI: http://dx.doi.org/10.1145/312624.312682.

[Herlocker et al., 2004] Herlocker, Joseph A. Konstan, Loren G. Terveen, and John T. Riedl. "Evaluating Collaborative Filtering Recommender Systems." *ACM Transactions on Information Systems* 22:1 (2004): 5-53. DOI: http://dx.doi.org/10.1145/963770.963772.

[Huang et al., 2004] Huang, Zan, Hsinchun Chen, and Daniel Zeng. "Applying Associative Retrieval Techniques to Alleviate the Sparsity Problem in Collaborative Filtering." *ACM Transactions on Information Systems* 22:1 (2004): 116-142. DOI: http://dx.doi.org/10.1145/963770.963775.

[Jannach, et al., 2010] Jannach, Dietmar, Markus Zanker, Alexander Felfernig, and Gerhard Friedrich. *Recommender Systems: An Introduction.* Cambridge, UK: Cambridge University Press, 2010. DOI: http://dx.doi.org/10.1017/CBO9780511763113.

[Koren, 2008] Koren, Yehuda. "Factorization Meets the Neighborhood: A Multifaceted Collaborative Filtering Model." *Proceedings of the 14th ACM SIGKDD International Conference on Knowledge Discovery and Data Mining* (2008): 426-434. DOI: https://doi.org/10.1145/1401890.1401944.

[Koren et al., 2009] Koren, Yehuda, Robert Bell, and Chris Volinsky. "Matrix Factorization Techniques for Recommender Systems." *Computer* 42:8 (2009): 30-37. DOI: http://dx.doi.org/10.1109/MC.2009.263.

[Newman, 2010] Newman, Mark. *Networks: An Introduction*. Oxford, UK: Oxford University Press, 2010.

[Ning et al., 2015] Ning, Xia, Christian Desrosiers, and George Karypis. "A Comprehensive Survey of Neighborhood-Based Recommendation Methods." In *Recommender Systems Handbook*, edited by Francesco Ricci, Lior Rockach, and Bracha Shapira, 37-76. New York: Springer, 2015. 37-76. 2015. DOI: https://doi.org/10.1007/978-1-4899-7637-6.

[Sarwar et al., 2000] Sarwar, Badrul, George Karypis, Joseph Konstan, and John Riedl. "Analysis of Recommendation Algorithms for E-commerce." *Proceedings of the 2nd ACM Conference on Electronic Commerce* (2000): 158-167. DOI= http://dx.doi.org/10.1145/352871.352887.

[Sarwar et al., 2001] Sarwar, Badrul, George Karypis, Joseph Konstan, and John Riedl. "Item-Based Collaborative Filtering Recommendation Algorithms." *Proceedings of the 10th International World Wide Web Conference* (2001) 285-295. DOI: https://doi.org/10.1145/371920.372071.

[Silva and Zhao, 2016] Silva, Thiago C., and Liang Zhao. *Machine Learning in Complex Networks*. New York: Springer, 2016.

[Takács et al., 2007] Takács, Gábor, István Pilászy, Bottyán Németh, and Domonkos Tikk. "Major Components of the Gravity Recommendation System." *SIGKDD Explorations Newsletter* 9:2 (2007): 80-83. DOI: https://doi.org/10.1145/1345448.1345466.

Session-based recommendations

This chapter covers

- Implementing recommendation systems by using session data
- Designing graph models for session-based recommendation engines
- Importing existing datasets into the graph models

Chapters 4 and 5 introduced two of the most common approaches to implementing recommendation engines: content-based and collaborative filtering. The advantages of each approach were highlighted, but several drawbacks also emerged during the discussion. Notably, these techniques require information about users that is not always available. This chapter covers another approach to recommendations that is useful when it is difficult or impossible to get access to user interaction history or other details about the users. In such cases, applying the classic approaches would not produce good results.

6.1   *The session-based approach*

Suppose that you would like to build a recommendation engine for an online travel site. The site offers lodging reservations but doesn't require login or registration in the early stages of the process. Using a session-based recommendation engine, it is possible to deliver recommendations even in cases like this one, in which little about the user is known.

This scenario is common on websites that book accommodations. On this type of website, as well as in many other real-life recommendation scenarios, users generally don't log in or even register—until the end of the selection process. Only after they've selected their accommodations do users log in or register to complete the reservation.

Conventional recommendation approaches rely on user profiles created from purchase history, explicit ratings, or other past interactions, such as views and comments. They use these long-term preference models to determine the items to be presented to the user. More specifically, content-based approaches recommend items based on their similarity to those present in the user's profile, whereas collaborative filtering approaches make predictions based on the choices of users who have similar profiles. In both cases, informative user profiles are assumed to be available.

In many recommendation scenarios, however, like the one described here, such long-term user models are not available for a large fraction of the users because they are first-time visitors or are not logged in. In these circumstances, the users are largely anonymous, so the recommender systems we've looked at so far cannot deliver accurate results. Although other methods of user identification are available, such as cookies and fingerprinting techniques, the applicability of these methods is limited because of their relatively low reliability and privacy concerns [Tuan and Phuong, 2017]. In addition, the creation of an informative profile requires the user to have had sufficient interactions with the system in the past.

Nevertheless, providing effective recommendations that will be capable of capturing the current user's interests and needs is the key to delivering a high-quality service, increasing user satisfaction, and getting users to come back again. Therefore, suitable recommendations have to be determined based on other types of information. Although the data available is not in the classic format, all is not lost; it is possible to use the user's most recent interactions with the site or application as a basis for recommendations. In this case, interactions between an anonymous, unique user and the system can be organized into *sessions*. Recommendation techniques that rely solely on the user's actions in an ongoing session and that adapt their recommendations to the user's actions are called *session-based recommendation approaches* [Quadrana et al., 2018]. Figure 6.1 describes the key elements of a session-based recommendation engine and their relationships.

A *session* is a chunk of interactions that take place within a given time frame. It may span a single day, several days, weeks, or even months. A session usually has a time-limited goal, such as finding a restaurant for dinner tonight, listening to music of a certain style or mood, or looking for a location for one's next holiday. Figure 6.2 shows how a user searching for a holiday location changes their mind until finding the right place.

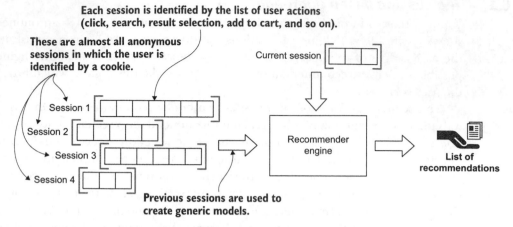

Figure 6.1   Session-based recommendation mental model

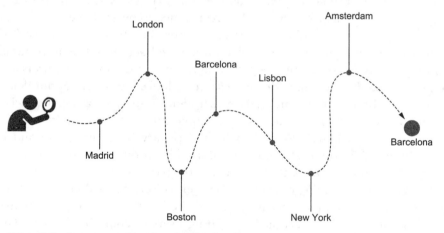

Figure 6.2   A user searching for a holiday location

Based on the information available from the user session, the recommender system should create a model for the user and make predictions. Session data has many important characteristics:

- Session clicks and navigation are sequential by nature. The order of clicks as well as the navigational path may contain information about user intent.
- Viewed items often have metadata such as names, categories, and descriptions, that provides information about the user's tastes and what they are looking for.
- Sessions are limited in time and scope. A session has a specific goal and generally ends when that goal is accomplished: rent a hotel for a business trip, find a restaurant for a romantic date, and so on. The session has intrinsic informational power related to a specific item, such as the hotel or restaurant that's eventually booked.

When their use is practical and makes sense, session-based recommendation engines can deliver high-quality recommendations that predict the final goal of the user with high accuracy, shortening the navigational path and the time required to satisfy the user's specific needs.

Problem solved, right? We can easily provide recommendations even when the user is anonymous. Awesome!

Unfortunately, the situation is not that simple. The problem of working with sessions is that it is not always easy to recognize when a session starts and ends (when the task has been accomplished or the session is not relevant anymore). Think about your own experiences. How many times have you started thinking about where you might go on your next vacation during a work break? You start looking at hotels in one of the locations you're dreaming about; then you have to get back to work. You might come back to the task days or even weeks later, maybe with a different idea of where you'd like to go. For a system, understanding when a session can be considered closed or not relevant anymore is a hard task. Luckily, some domain-specific best practices can be applied to identify the end of a search session, such as considering the days of inactivity or the successful booking of a hotel.

This chapter's example scenario illustrates some methods for implementing a session-based recommendation engine. Such methods help you deal with situations in which user-item interaction data is not available.

In the literature, sequential recommendation problems (and, hence, session-based recommendations) are typically implemented as the task of predicting the next user action. From an algorithmic perspective, early prediction approaches were based on sequential pattern mining techniques. Later, more sophisticated methods based on Markov models were proposed and successfully applied to the problem. Most recently, the use of deep learning approaches based on artificial neural networks has been explored as another solution. Recurrent neural networks (RNNs),[1] which are capable of learning models from sequentially ordered data, are a natural choice for this problem, and significant advances in the prediction accuracy of such algorithms have been reported in recent literature [Devooght and Bersini, 2017; Hidasi and Karatzoglou, 2018; Hidasi et al., 2016 a, b; Tan et al., 2016].

Some results presented by Ludewig and Jannach [2018] and in previous work [Verstrepen and Goethals, 2014; Jannach and Ludewig, 2017 a; Kamehkhosh et al., 2017] show that computationally and conceptually, nearest neighbor–based approaches often lead to predictions that are as accurate as, or even better than, those of current techniques based on deep learning models. Different nearest neighbor schemes exist, and all of them fit well with a graph-based approach to data modeling and recommendations.

---

[1] RNNs are distributed real-valued hidden state models with nonlinear dynamics. At each time step, the hidden state of the RNN is computed from the current input in the sequence and the hidden state from the previous step. Then the hidden state is used to predict the probability of the next items in the sequence. The recurrent feedback mechanism memorizes the influence of each past data sample in the hidden state of the RNN, overcoming the fundamental limitation of Markov chains. Therefore, RNNs are well suited to modeling the complex dynamics in user action sequences [Quadrana et al., 2017].

For these reasons, this section focuses on such methods. Figure 6.3 depicts the recommendation process for this scenario.

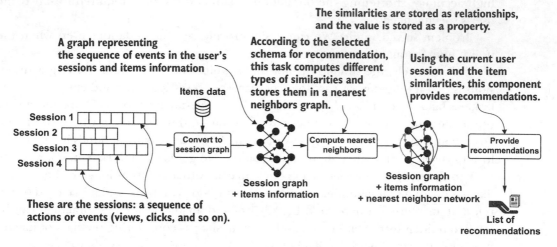

Figure 6.3   A graph-powered session-based recommender system diagram

Section 6.2 describes how to model session data in the form of a graph. Section 6.3 illustrates various techniques for building predictive models and providing recommendations.

6.2   The events chain and the session graph

Session data can be modeled in several ways, according to the type of learning algorithm and the nature of the data available. First, consider some of the desired properties of a session-based recommendation engine [Tuan and Phuong, 2017], related to the way in which the training data is modeled:

- The data representation should be able to model sequential patterns in streams of clicks. One of the most popular methods, and one of the selected approaches in our scenario, is item-to-item k-NN. This method makes recommendations based on item co-occurrences but ignores the order of clicks. To solve this problem partially, we can introduce a time decay or a relevance window to consider only a small portion of a longer sequence of events.

- The method should provide a simple way to represent and combine item IDs with metadata. Usually, an item is associated with features of different types. A product may have an ID, a name, and a description, for example, and it generally belongs to one or more categories (sometimes organized in category hierarchies). It would be more convenient to have a general way to represent different feature types and jointly model their interactions, taking into account relationships and dependencies among them.

- User interests and goals evolve during the navigation. Step by step, the user focuses on a more specific goal; their idea gets clearer with each click. Thus, an item clicked at the beginning of the selection process is less relevant than one clicked later. Time has to be modeled properly to assign more value to more recent items than to older ones.

The graph model in figure 6.4 represents the session data, taking into account the required properties.

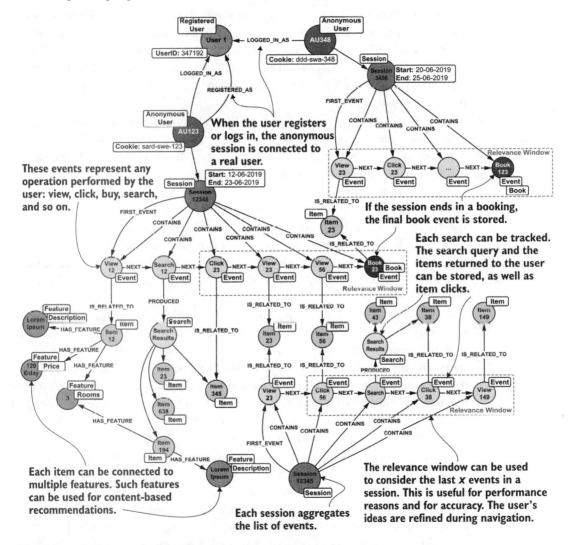

Figure 6.4   A session graph for the session-based recommendation schema

This model satisfies all the requirements and supports different types of recommendation algorithms. Let's describe it in more detail:

- The main entities (nodes) in the model are sessions, users, items, and clicks. These elements represent the steps of the entire navigation path.
- Users can be split into two categories: anonymous users and registered/logged-in users. Both types of users can be connected to a session, even at the same time, because an anonymous user has to log in or register to complete a booking or purchase. The relationship between the anonymous user and the related registered user is tracked, so it is possible to keep track of all the items a user clicked in their history. Such information is useful for a more traditional collaborative filtering approach on a simple User-Item dataset. This information could be relevant for sending custom emails or other types of marketing activities (such as an offline marketing campaign).
- The session is the click aggregator. All the clicks happen in a specific session to which they are connected. Each session belongs to a user. Sessions can have some contextual information, such as a start time, end time, location, and device. Such contextual information can be relevant for improving the quality of the recommendations.
- *Item* is a wide concept, representing several elements of interest, such as pages, products, search items, and search queries. Each item holds some properties that describe some specific features. As in the content-based approach, some properties are modeled as nodes and then are connected to the items; others (those specific to an item, such as ID) are modeled as properties of the item node.
- A click connects a session to an item. It also contains some information, such as time and location. The click stream defines a path and contains terrifically valuable information. It represents not only a navigational path, but also a mental path. During navigation, the user refines the search, clarifying their goals and applying some filters. This information is valuable and has to be modeled effectively. In the model depicted in figure 6.4, the navigation is stored by using the NEXT relationship, which connects each click with the next one. For performance reasons, a connection with the session is also stored.
- The user refines their thoughts and goals during the navigation; the first click is less relevant than the last one. For that reason, it is important to model (at least conceptually) a relevance decay in the model. Different options exist for taking time into account during learning and prediction. Consider two of them:
  - *Time decay*—A lower weight is assigned to older clicks. If the last click is weighted at (has a relevance of) 1.0, a click two hours ago might have a relevance of 0.8 or 0.5. Different decay functions—such as linear ad exponential—can be defined, depending on how fast the algorithm should forget about past events.

- *Relevance window*—One or more sliding windows that include only the last N (with N configurable) clicks limit the amount of data considered during model training or prediction.

- A session can last for a long time and contain a lot of clicks. A threshold, specified in terms of time or number of clicks, can be defined to consider only the relevant clicks and throw away the others. This approach helps reduce the size of the database, ensuring that only relevant information is stored and guaranteeing high performance over time.

- A final piece of relevant information is how the session ends up—whether it concludes with a purchase or a leave. This information is modeled in the graph representation by marking the last item with a specific label, `AddToCartItem`. The final decision not only represents valuable information, because it allows us to recognize a successful session, but also, some approaches compute only the distance between each item and items with the label `AddToCartItem`.

It is worth noting that the model defined here is not only useful for the purpose of session-based recommendation, but also represents a way of modeling any sequential events to facilitate further analysis.

Now that we've defined the graph for modeling the events chain, let's consider a real example, which we'll import by using the schema defined for our graph database. The dataset we'll use is provided in the context of the ACM RecSys 2015 Challenge[2] and contains recorded click sequences (item views and purchases) for six months. The dataset consists of two files:

- *yoochoose-clicks.dat*—Click events. Each record/line in the file has the following fields:
  - *Session ID*—The ID of the session. One session may have one or many clicks.
  - *Timestamp*—The time when the click occurred.
  - *Item ID*—The unique identifier of the item.
  - *Category*—The category of the item.
- *yoochoose-buys.dat*—Buy events. Each record/line in the file has the following fields:
  - *Session ID*—The ID of the session. One session may have one or many buying events.
  - *Timestamp*—The time when the buy occurred.
  - *Item ID*—The unique identifier of the item.
  - *Price*—The price of the item.
  - *Quantity*—How many units of this item were bought.

The session ID in yoochoose-buys.dat will always exist in the yoochoose-clicks.dat file; the records with the same session ID together form the sequence of click events of a

---

[2] https://recsys.acm.org/recsys15/challenge.

certain user during the session. The session could be short (a few minutes) or long (a few hours), and it could have one click or hundreds of clicks. Everything depends on the activity of the user. The following listing shows the code that creates the session data according to the model designed so far.

Listing 6.1   Importing session data from yoochoose file

```
def import_session_data(self, file):                         Creates constraints to
    with self._driver.session() as session:          guarantee the uniqueness of
        self.executeNoException(session,                   the sessions and items
"CREATE CONSTRAINT ON (s:Session) ASSERT s.sessionId IS UNIQUE")
        self.executeNoException(session,
"CREATE CONSTRAINT ON (i:Item) ASSERT i.itemId IS UNIQUE")
        query = """
            MERGE (session:Session {sessionId: $sessionId})
            MERGE (item:Item {itemId: $itemId, category: $category})
            CREATE (click:Click {timestamp: $timestamp})
            CREATE (session)-[:CONTAINS]->(click)         Checks for the existence of
            CREATE (click)-[:IS_RELATED_TO]->(item)        the session and the item;
        """                                                otherwise, creates them
        dtype = {"sessionID": np.int64, "itemID": np.int64, "category":
            np.object}
        j = 0;                                       Defines the types for the imported
        for chunk in pd.read_csv(file,               CSV file (helpful in Pandas to
                        header=0,                    prevent issues with typecasting)
                        dtype=dtype,
                        names=['sessionID', 'timestamp', 'itemID',
                            'category'],
                        parse_dates=['timestamp'],
                        chunksize=10**6):         Reads the CSV file and
            df = chunk                            commits in chunks of 10 ^ 6
            tx = session.begin_transaction()      rows to speed the process
            i = 0;
            for row in df.itertuples():
                try:
                    timestamp = row.timestamp
                    session_id = row.sessionID
                    category = strip(row.category)
                    item_id = row.itemID
                    tx.run(query, {"sessionId": session_id, "itemId": item_id,
                        "timestamp": str(timestamp), "category": category})
                    i += 1
                    j += 1
                    if i == 10000:
                        tx.commit()
                        print(j, "lines processed")
                        i = 0
                        tx = session.begin_transaction()
                except Exception as e:
                    print(e, row)
            tx.commit()
            print(j, "lines processed")
        print(j, "lines processed")
```

Left margin annotations:

- Creates the click and all the relationships among the item, click, and session
- Loops over the rows and runs the queries, passing the parameters to create new clicks for each session

Each line in the CSV file contains a click of a specific item. The MERGE clauses allow us to create the session and the item only once; then the click node connects the session to the item. The following listing adds information on buys to the existing sessions that ended with a purchase.

Listing 6.2　Importing buys data from yoochoose file

```
def import_buys_data(self, file):
    with self._driver.session() as session:
query = """
        MATCH (session:Session {sessionId: $sessionId})
        MATCH (item:Item {itemId: $itemId})
        CREATE (buy:Buy:Click {timestamp: $timestamp})
        CREATE (session)-[:CONTAINS]->(buy)
        CREATE (buy)-[:IS_RELATED_TO]->(item)
    """
        dtype = {"sessionID": np.int64, "itemID": np.int64, "price":
        np.float, "quantity": np.int}
        j = 0;
        for chunk in pd.read_csv(file,
                        header=0,
                        dtype=dtype,
                        names=['sessionID', 'timestamp', 'itemID',
                        'price', 'quantity'],
                        parse_dates=['timestamp'],
                        chunksize=10**6):
            df = chunk
            tx = session.begin_transaction()
            i = 0;
            for row in df.itertuples():
                try:
                    timestamp = row.timestamp
                    session_id = row.sessionID
                    item_id = row.itemID
                    tx.run(query, {"sessionId": session_id, "itemId":
                    item_id, "timestamp": str(timestamp)})
                    i += 1
                    j += 1
                    if i == 10000:
                        tx.commit()
                        print(j, "lines processed")
                        i = 0
                        tx = session.begin_transaction()
                except Exception as e:
                    print(e, row)
            tx.commit()
            print(j, "lines processed")
        print(j, "lines processed")
```

Creates the buy (a special type of click) and all the relationships among the item, buy, and session

Searches for the session and the item

Defines the types for the imported CSV file (helpful in Pandas to prevent issues with typecasting)

Reads the CSV file in chunks of 10 ^ 6 rows to speed the process

Loops over the rows and runs the queries, passing the parameters to create new clicks for each session

---

This code, though correct, is slow. It's simple to understand and linear, which is why it's preferred here, but it can run for hours. In the code repository for this chapter, you will find a different version that's much more performant but also more complex.

Regardless of which version you run, the result will be the same. The following query allows you to visualize the result of the import, considering a single session (the one with ID 140837).

Listing 6.3   Query to show the subgraph related to a specific session

```
MATCH p=(s:Session {sessionId: 140837})-[:CONTAINS]->(c)
MATCH q=(c)-[:IS_RELATED_TO]->(item:Item)
return p,q
```

EXERCISES

Play with the new database, and write queries to find the following:

- The 10 most-clicked items
- The 10 most-purchased items (did they match?)
- The longest session (did it contain a purchase?)

6.3   *Providing recommendations*

The model designed in section 6.2 is flexible enough to serve different recommendation approaches. As described in the introduction to this chapter, session-based recommendation engines are useful in a lot of scenarios. This topic is widely investigated, and a great variety of solutions have been proposed to provide the best recommendations possible.

A first natural approach consists of using a collaborative filtering method, specifically, the *k*-nearest neighbor approach, by using session-item data in place of the user-item matrix. Nevertheless, due to the sequential nature of the events in the chain, some researchers have proposed the use of RNNs or convolutional neural networks (CNNs)[3] to reveal sequential patterns in sessions and use them to provide recommendations [Jannach and Ludewig, 2017 a; Quadrana et al., 2018; Tuan and Phuong, 2017]. Compared with the collaborative filtering approach, which fundamentally ignores the actual sequence of actions, RNNs and CNNs consider the overall navigation path and can model sequential patterns of session clicks. Although it has been proved that such methods can deliver high-quality recommendations, they are quite complex to implement and require a lot of data to be properly trained. Moreover, if properly implemented. The *k*-NN approach can outperform deep learning methods in both efficiency and quality [Jannach and Ludewig, 2017 a; Ludewig and Jannach, 2018].

For these reasons, in this section we'll consider different *k*-NN approaches to the problem of suggesting a top-*N* list of items in session-based recommendation engines. Over the years, multiple implementations have been proposed for such a task. The

---

[3] CNNs are neural networks specialized for processing data that has a known gridlike topology, such as a User-Item matrix or time-series data that can be modeled as a one-dimensional matrix. The name *convolutional* derives from the mathematical linear operation, convolution, used in the neural network in place of the general matrix multiplication in at least one of their layers [Goodfellow et al., 2016].

most relevant for our scenario and the purpose of this section [Ludewig and Jannach, 2018] are

- *Item-based k-NN (Item-KNN)*—This method, introduced by Hidasi et al. [2016 a], considers only the last element in a given session (the current one) and recommends those items that are most similar to it in terms of their co-occurrence in other sessions. If the user is currently looking at a villa in Bilbao, the system will suggest other villas that appear frequently in other sessions when the user was looking at the same villa in Bilbao.
- *Session-based k-NN (SKNN)*—This method, instead of considering only the last event in the current session, compares the entire current session (or a significant part of it, considering only the latest *N* clicks) with the past sessions in the training data to determine the items to be recommended [Bonnin and Jannach, 2014; Hariri et al., 2012; Lerche et al., 2016]. If a user viewed villas in Bilbao, Barcelona, and Madrid, the algorithm would search for similar sessions (similar because they contain more or less the same entries) and compute the scores of items to suggest by considering how many similar sessions contain the target item.

The second approach is a bit more complex to implement than the first, of course, but its accuracy is comparable with that of more complex implementations such as RNNs and CNNs while requiring less data for training the model. Even the item-based approach can provide valuable features, however, so the following sections consider both approaches.

6.3.1 *Item-based k-NN*

Suppose that you're browsing for shoes. Would it be useful if the system showed you shoes similar to the ones you're currently looking at, based on what other users were looking at before and after they reached the same pair of shoes as you? The item-based *k*-NN approach uses session data to compute similarities between pairs of items. The overall approach is the same as in the case of item-based collaborative filtering; the only difference is that instead of a User-Item matrix, the session-item data is used. As in the classic approach, the first step is representing the item in a vector space model (VSM) in which each element corresponds to a session and is set to 1 if the item appeared in the session. The similarity of two items can be determined by using the cosine similarity measure, for example, and the number of neighbors *k* is implicitly defined by the desired recommendation list length. The overall process is depicted in figure 6.5.

Conceptually, the method implements a form of "Customers who bought . . . also bought." The use of the cosine similarity metric makes the method less susceptible to popularity bias. Although item-to-item approaches are comparably simple, they are commonly used in practice and sometimes considered to represent a strong baseline [Davidson et al., 2010; Linden et al., 2003]. It's worth noting that item metadata

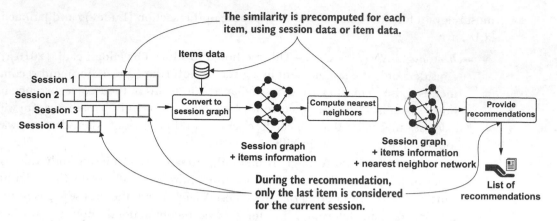

Figure 6.5 Session-based recommendation schema using Item-KNN

information can be used in this case, even in combination with session data, to compute similarities between items. This technique is useful when you have a new item without any history.

In terms of the implementation, all similarity values can be precomputed and sorted in the training process to ensure fast responses at recommendation time. Updates are required on a time basis (every x hours) or on a session volume basis (every x new session clicks).

Consider an example with trivial data, and follow the process step by step. Suppose that we have the five sessions described in table 6.1.

Table 6.1 Session examples

Session #	Session content (ordered list of item IDs)
1	[Item 12, Item 23, Item 7, Item 562, Item 346, Item 85]
2	[Item 23, Item 65, Item 12, Item 3, Item 9, Item 248]
3	[Item 248, Item 12, Item 7, Item 9, Item 346]
4	[Item 85, Item 65, Item 248, Item 12, Item 346, Item 9]
5	[Item 346, Item 7, Item 9, Item 3, Item 12]

The goal is to suggest something to the user in session 5. The current item is 12. The first step consists of computing the distance between this item and all the not-yet-seen items. Table 6.2 (the VSM representation) is useful for easily extracting the vector representations of the items, as we saw in chapter 5.

Table 6.2 Sessions of table 6.1 represented in VSM

Session #	3	7	9	12	23	65	85	248	346	562
1	0	1	0	1	1	0	1	0	1	1
2	1	0	1	1	1	1	0	1	0	0
3	0	1	1	1	0	0	0	1	1	0
4	0	0	1	1	0	1	1	1	1	0
5	1	1	1	1	0	0	0	0	1	0

It is important to notice that the click order is lost. The following piece of code does all the necessary computations for you. Using it is easier than doing the computations manually, and it introduces `sklearn`,[4] which is a powerful machine learning library.

Listing 6.4 Computing similarity between item 12 and all the not-yet-seen items

```
from sklearn.metrics.pairwise import cosine_similarity

#Vector representation of the items
item3 = [0,1,0,0,1]
item7 = [1,0,1,0,1]
item9 = [0,1,1,1,1]
item12 = [1,1,1,1,1]
item23 = [1,1,0,0,0]
item65 = [0,1,0,1,0]
item85 = [1,0,0,1,0]
item248 = [0,1,1,1,0]
item346 = [1,0,1,1,1]
item562 = [1,0,0,0,0]

# Compute and print relevant similarities
print(cosine_similarity([item12], [item23])) # 0.63245553
print(cosine_similarity([item12], [item65])) # 0.63245553
print(cosine_similarity([item12], [item85])) # 0.63245553
print(cosine_similarity([item12], [item248])) # 0.77459667
print(cosine_similarity([item12], [item562])) # 0.4472136
```

In this case, the most similar item is item 248. Other items have the same similarity score or even higher, such as items 9 and 346, but in our recommendation policy, we decided to avoid showing items that the user has already seen.

Now that the process is clear, let's move from the trivial example to our real database. We will split the process into two parts. The first part will precompute similarity among items and store the top *k*-nearest neighbors, and the second will provide recommendations. Listing 6.5 shows the code for similarity precomputation.

---

[4] https://scikit-learn.org.

Listing 6.5   Extracting item vectors from graph; computing and storing similarities

```python
def compute_and_store_similarity(self):
    items_VSM = self.get_item_vectors()
    for item in items_VSM:
        knn = self.compute_knn(item, items_VSM.copy(), 20);
        self.store_knn(item, knn)

def get_item_vectors(self):
    list_of_items_query = """
                MATCH (item:Item)
                RETURN item.itemId as itemId
        """

    query = """
                MATCH (item:Item)<-[:IS_RELATED_TO]-(click:Click)<-
                [:CONTAINS]-(session:Session)
                WHERE item.itemId = $itemId
                WITH session
                ORDER BY id(session)
                RETURN collect(distinct id(session)) as vector;
        """
    items_VSM_sparse = {}
    with self._driver.session() as session:
        i = 0
        for item in session.run(list_of_items_query):
            item_id = item["itemId"];
            vector = session.run(query, {"itemId": item_id})
            items_VSM_sparse[item_id] = vector.single()[0]
            i += 1
            if i % 100 == 0:
                print(i, "rows processed")
        print(i, " rows processed")
    return items_VSM_sparse

def compute_knn(self, item, items, k):
    dtype = [ ('itemId', 'U10'),('value', 'f4')]
    knn_values = np.array([], dtype=dtype)
    for other_item in items:
        if other_item != item:
            value = cosine_similarity(items[item], items[other_item])
            if value > 0:
                knn_values = np.concatenate((knn_values,
                    np.array([(other_item, value)], dtype=dtype)))
    knn_values = np.sort(knn_values, kind='mergesort', order='value' )[::-1]
    return np.split(knn_values, [k])[0]

def store_knn(self, item, knn):
    with self._driver.session() as session:
        tx = session.begin_transaction()
        knnMap = {a : b.item() for a,b in knn}
        clean_query = """
            MATCH (item:Item)-[s:SIMILAR_TO]->()
            WHERE item.itemId = $itemId
            DELETE s
```

Annotations:
- Entry point that processes all the items
- Searches for items and creates the vectors for each
- Query that gets the list of items
- Query that extracts the vector for each item based on sessions it belongs to
- Entry point that processes all the items
- For each item, computes the top *k*-nearest neighbors among all the other items
- Computes the cosine similarity between two sparse vectors
- Sorts the neighbor based on similarity value
- Stores the model (the *k*-NN)
- Cleans up the old model for the node

```
"""
query = """
    MATCH (item:Item)
    WHERE item.itemId = $itemId
    UNWIND keys($knn) as otherItemId
    MATCH (other:Item)
    WHERE other.itemId = otherItemId
    MERGE (item)-[:SIMILAR_TO {weight: $knn[otherItemId]}]->(other)
"""
tx.run(clean_query, {"itemId": item})
tx.run(query, {"itemId": item, "knn": knnMap})
tx.commit()
```

Stores the new model as the relationship **SIMILAR_TO** between the current item and the top *k* similar items

Notice that this code is similar to the code we used for item-based recommendation in the collaborative filtering approach. Such code has to be executed periodically to keep the similarity values up to date.

Before moving on, I would like to mention an issue you may encounter. Although it's formally correct, the code in the preceding listing will take a while (a long while, actually) to complete. This problem is common in working with nearest neighbors in general. So far, we've been working with small datasets, so it hasn't been an issue, but as I promised you at the beginning, this book aims to be a concrete book that helps you solve real machine learning problems, not trivial examples. Computing nearest neighbors requires you to compute $N \times N$ similarities, and when you have a lot of items, this process can take a long time. Moreover, considering that occasionally you also have to update the nearest neighbor network to keep it aligned with the latest clicks by the user, the preceding code is not useful in production-ready projects.

You can use different techniques to solve this problem. If your goal is to compute the similarity of every pair, there is nothing you can do to reduce the work, although parallel processing can reduce the elapsed time. You can use analytics engines for large-scale data processing, such as Apache Spark[5] or Apache Flink.[6]

Another approach is to consider only an approximate version of the *k*-nearest neighbors. Often, we want only the most similar pairs or all pairs that are above some lower bound in similarity. In that case, we can focus our attention only on pairs that are likely to be similar without investigating every pair. Different algorithms exist for computing approximate versions of *k*-NN. One of those algorithms, illustrated in figure 6.6, is called *locality-sensitive hashing (LSH)* or *near-neighbor search* [Ullman and Rajaraman, 2011].

One general approach to LSH is to hash items several times, in such a way that similar items are more likely to be hashed to the same bucket than dissimilar items are. Then we consider any pair that hashed to the same bucket on any occasion to be a candidate pair, and we check only the candidate pairs for similarity. The hope is that most of the dissimilar pairs will never hash to the same bucket and therefore will never

---

[5] https://spark.apache.org.
[6] https://flink.apache.org.

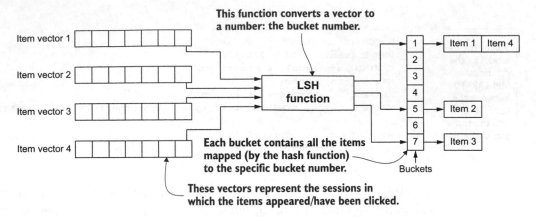

Figure 6.6   The mental model explaining LSH

be checked. Those dissimilar pairs that do hash to the same bucket are false positives; we hope that these pairs will be only a small fraction of all pairs. We also hope that most of the truly similar pairs will hash to the same bucket at least once. Those that do not are false negatives, and we hope that they will be a small fraction of the truly similar pairs. An implementation that uses this technique is available in the code repository as an advanced version of listing 6.5.

When the *k*-NN for each item has been precomputed, the recommendation process is a trivial query such as the following.

Listing 6.6   Query for providing recommendations by using the Item KNN approach

```
MATCH (i:Item)-[r:SIMILAR_TO]->(oi:Item)
WHERE i.itemId = $itemId
RETURN oi.itemId as itemId, r.weight as score
ORDER BY score desc
LIMIT %s
```

This query takes 1 ms to complete on my laptop because everything is precomputed, and navigating the graph of similarities is fast.

EXERCISES

In the database, do the following:

- Find the 10 closest items.
- The results of the preceding query will show that a lot of them have similarity values close to 1 or even higher due to approximation. Navigate that portion of the graph to see why.
- Search for the best seller items and their neighbors. Are they also best sellers?

Through the queries, you will notice how simple it is to navigate the graph. Try to get more insights from the graph yourself.

6.3.2 Session-based *k*-NN

The key differentiator of the session-based approach, compared with the previous one, is that the similarity is computed among sessions instead of among items. Such similarities, stored in the graph as *k*-NN, are used to score the items and return recommendations to the user. The overall approach is described in figure 6.7.

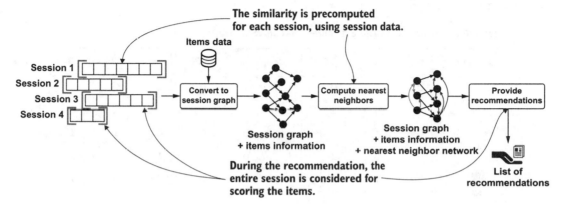

Figure 6.7   Session-based recommendation schema using SKNN

In this case metadata, such as a title, description, or list of features, is not relevant for the algorithm selected. Another interesting aspect of this approach is the fact that it doesn't require a lot of information to be effective. In more detail, given a session *s*, the recommendation process is structured in the following way:

1. Compute the *k* most similar past sessions (neighbors) by applying a suitable session similarity measure, such as the Jaccard index or cosine similarity on binary vectors over the item space [Bonnin and Jannach, 2014]. According to Quadrana [2017], the binary cosine similarity measure leads to the best results. Moreover, as Jannach and Ludewig [2017 a] show, using *k* = 500 as the number of neighbors to consider leads to good performance results for many datasets.

2. Given the current session *s*, its neighbors *k*, and the similarity values, compute the score for each item, order them, and return the top *N*.

It is possible to use different formulas as scoring functions. One function that leads to good results [Bonnin and Jannach, 2014] is

$$score(i,s) = \sum_{n \in KNN(s)} sim(s,n) \times 1_n(i)$$

where

- *KNN(s)* is the *k*-nearest neighbors network for *s*.
- *sim(s,n)* represents the cosine similarity between the sessions *s* and *n*.

- $1_n(i)$ is a function that returns 1 if the session n contains the target item i and 0 otherwise. (This function allows us to consider only the sessions that contain the target items, filtering out the others.)

To understand the formula and the overall process, consider again our sample sessions from table 6.1 and their VSM representation, shown again for your convenience in table 6.3.

Table 6.3   Sessions of table 6.1 represented in VSM

Session #	3	7	9	12	23	65	85	248	346	562
1	0	1	0	1	1	0	1	0	1	1
2	1	0	1	1	1	1	0	1	0	0
3	0	1	1	1	0	0	0	1	1	0
4	0	0	1	1	0	1	1	1	1	0
5	1	1	1	1	0	0	0	0	1	0

In this case, we are interested in the session vectors, which we can extract by reading line by line. In the following listing, we compute the distances between session 5 (our target) and all the other sessions.

Listing 6.7   Computing similarity between item 12 and all the not-yet-seen items

```
from sklearn.metrics.pairwise import cosine_similarity

session1 = [0,1,0,1,1,0,1,0,1,1]
session2 = [1,0,1,1,1,1,0,1,0,0]
session3 = [0,1,1,1,0,0,0,1,1,0]
session4 = [0,0,1,1,0,1,1,1,1,0]
session5 = [1,1,1,1,0,0,0,0,1,0]

print(cosine_similarity([session5], [session1]))  #0.54772256
print(cosine_similarity([session5], [session2]))  #0.54772256
print(cosine_similarity([session5], [session3]))  #0.8
print(cosine_similarity([session5], [session4]))  #0.54772256
```

Now we can compute the scores for all the not-yet-seen items as follows:

$$score(\text{item } 23, \text{session } 5) = 0.547 \times 0 + 0.547 \times 1 + 0.8 \times 1 + 0.547 \times 1 = 1.894$$

$$score(\text{item } 65, \text{session } 5) = 0.547 \times 1 + 0.547 \times 1 + 0.8 \times 0 + 0.547 \times 0 = 1.094$$

$$score(\text{item } 85, \text{session } 5) = 0.547 \times 0 + 0.547 \times 1 + 0.8 \times 0 + 0.547 \times 1 = 1.094$$

$$score(\text{item } 248, \text{session } 5) = 0.547 \times 0 + 0.547 \times 1 + 0.8 \times 1 + 0.547 \times 1 = 1.894$$

$$score(\text{item } 562, \text{session } 5) = 0.547 \times 1 + 0.547 \times 0 + 0.8 \times 0 + 0.547 \times 0 = 0.547$$

In this case, the highest score is achieved by items 23 and 248.

During the recommendation phase, time constraints mean that determining the similarity of the current session with millions of past sessions and then computing the score for each not-yet-seen item is not practical. A variety of approaches can be implemented to optimize and speed this process, and many of them could use the graph model. We will consider two approaches here.

FIRST OPTIMIZATION

This technique provides optimization by using the graph model in the following ways:

- *k-NN precomputation*—It is possible, as in the previous case, to precompute (and keep updated) the *k*-nearest neighbors stored as relationships among the sessions. A background process can update these relationships according to some criteria, such as time or volume.
- *Postfiltering*—For each item, we already have a relationship with all the sessions in which the item appears. These relationships can be used to filter out all the sessions in the *k*-NN(s) that don't contain the item.

Considering the graph model designed for this scenario, shown in figure 6.4, the following listing shows how to precompute the similarities among all the sessions.

Listing 6.8 Computing and storing in graph the k-NN for each session

```python
def compute_and_store_similarity(self):          ◁──┐  Entry-point function that
    sessions_VSM = self.get_session_vectors()         │  computes and stores the k-NN
    for session in sessions_VSM:                      │  model for all the sessions
        knn = self.compute_knn(session, sessions_VSM.copy(), 20);
        self.store_knn(session, knn)

def compute_knn(self, session, sessions, k):    ◁──┐  Function that computes
    dtype = [ ('itemId', 'U10'),('value', 'f4')]     │  the similarities
    knn_values = np.array([], dtype=dtype)
    for other_session in sessions:
        if other_session != session:
            value = cosine_similarity(sessions[session],
            ⇨ sessions[other_session])
            if value > 0:
                knn_values = np.concatenate((knn_values,
                ⇨ np.array([(other_session, value)], dtype=dtype)))
    knn_values = np.sort(knn_values, kind='mergesort', order='value' )[::-1]
    return np.split(knn_values, [k])[0]           │  Searches for the session and
                                                  │  creates the related vector for
def get_session_vectors(self):            ◁───────┘  each based on items clicked
    list_of_sessions_query = """
            MATCH (session:Session)
            RETURN session.sessionId as sessionId
        """

    query = """
            MATCH (item:Item)<-[:IS_RELATED_TO]-(click:Click)<-
            ⇨ [:CONTAINS]-(session:Session)
            WHERE session.sessionId = $sessionId
            WITH item
```

```
                        ORDER BY id(item)
                        RETURN collect(distinct id(item)) as vector;
                    """
        sessions_VSM_sparse = {}
        with self._driver.session() as session:
            i = 0
            for result in session.run(list_of_sessions_query):
                session_id = result["sessionId"];
                vector = session.run(query, {"sessionId": session_id})
                sessions_VSM_sparse[session_id] = vector.single()[0]
                i += 1
                if i % 100 == 0:
                    print(i, "rows processed")
                    break
            print(i, " rows processed")
        print(len(sessions_VSM_sparse))
        return sessions_VSM_sparse


    def store_knn(self, session_id, knn):
        with self._driver.session() as session:
            tx = session.begin_transaction()
            knnMap = {a : b.item() for a,b in knn}
            clean_query = """
                MATCH (session:Session)-[s:SIMILAR_TO]->()
                WHERE session.sessionId = $sessionId
                DELETE s
            """
            query = """
                MATCH (session:Session)
                WHERE session.sessionId = $sessionId
                UNWIND keys($knn) as otherSessionId
                MATCH (other:Session)
                WHERE other.sessionId = toInt(otherSessionId)
                MERGE (session)-[:SIMILAR_TO {weight: $knn[otherSessionId]}]->
                    (other)
            """
            tx.run(clean_query, {"sessionId": session_id})
            tx.run(query, {"sessionId": session_id, "knn": knnMap})
            tx.commit()
```

> **Query that cleans up the existing model for the current session**

> **Query that creates the new model**

The postfiltering, which will help us consider only the sessions in *k*-NN that contain the current item, can be implemented by using the following query.

Listing 6.9   Query for implementing postfiltering

```
MATCH (target:Session)-[r:SIMILAR_TO]->(otherSession:Session)-[:CONTAINS]->
    (:Click)-[:IS_RELATED_TO]->(item:Item)
WHERE target.sessionId = 12547 AND item.itemId = 214828987
RETURN DISTINCT otherSession.sessionId
```

Starting from this query, it is possible to generalize it so that we can generate the list of recommendations using the score function defined.

Listing 6.10 Recommendation process using this optimization

```
def recommend_to(self, session_id, k):
    top_items = []
    query = """
        MATCH (target:Session)-[r:SIMILAR_TO]->(d:Session)-[:CONTAINS]->
        ➥ (:Click)-[:IS_RELATED_TO]->(item:Item)
        WHERE target.sessionId = $sessionId
        WITH DISTINCT item.itemId as itemId, r
        RETURN itemId, sum(r.weight) as score
        ORDER BY score desc
        LIMIT %s
    """
    with self._driver.session() as session:
        tx = session.begin_transaction()
        for result in tx.run(query % (k), {"sessionId": session_id}):
            top_items.append((result["itemId"], result["score"]))

    top_items.sort(key=lambda x: -x[1])
    return top_items
```

So far, so good, but if you run the whole process with the sample dataset, it will take a while and require a lot of memory to compute the k-NN. After it is computed, the recommendation process requires only a few milliseconds. As usual, in the code repository you'll find an advanced version, which uses a Python library called Annoy[7] (Approximate Nearest Neighbors Oh Yeah) as an alternative to LSH. But for our dataset, which contains 850,000 sessions, it still takes a long time to complete.

To solve these issues, I'm going to propose a second optimization that takes advantage of the graph way of storing the data.

SECOND OPTIMIZATION

This technique optimizes the process in the following way:

- *k-NN elements sampling*—From the set of possible neighbors, a subsample of M sessions is extracted by choosing them randomly or using a heuristic. One of the most effective heuristics consists in focusing on the most recent sessions, if such information is available; focusing on recent trends (sessions) has proved to be effective for recommendations in e-commerce [Jannach and Ludewig, 2017 b] and led to even better results than when all past sessions were taken into account. From the set of M sessions, the k-nearest neighbors of the current session s are extracted: the k-NN(s).

- *Score computation prefiltering*—The set of recommendable items R is extracted, considering only items that appear in one of the sessions in the k-NN(s). Finally, the algorithm computes the scores for the items in R by using the formula described previously.

---

[7] https://github.com/spotify/annoy.

The k-NN(s) are highly variable because new sessions are created continuously. Therefore, the k-NN(s) for each session are not stored as relationships in the graph (they are computed in real time), but the graph is used during sampling and prefiltering. The second optimization allows operations such as similarity computations and the final predictions to be done efficiently. In the experiments reported by Jannach and Ludewig [2017 a], it was sufficient to consider, for example, only the 1,000 most recent sessions from several million existing ones and still obtain high-quality results.

6.4   Advantages of the graph approach

In this chapter, we've discussed how to create a session-based recommendation engine that uses a nearest neighbor approach. The proposed solutions are well suited to a graph representation of the data, which provides the right indexing structure for speeding the recommendation process. Moreover, the different optimizations can use a graph approach to optimize computation and accuracy. Specifically, the main aspects and advantages of the graph-based approach to session-based recommendation engines implemented using nearest neighbor methods are

- The events chain, such as the order of clicks in a session, is easily represented in a graph model.
- Graphs make it easy to access the events in order and focus on the more recent events, discarding or discounting older events and sessions, simplifying implementation of the deletion policy.
- The graph provides the necessary flexibility to add item metadata that is relevant for some algorithms, such as CNNs [Tuan and Phuong, 2017].
- During the recommendation process, specifically for the algorithms described in this chapter, graphs provide a natural indexing structure that enables us to access the relevant information faster. In non-graph-based approaches, it is often necessary to create indexing and other caching data structures to speed the recommendation process. Graphs provide all the data access patterns required by the algorithm, reducing the need for other tools.

Summary

This chapter presented session-based recommendation engines. The various data models show how the flexibility of graphs enables them to satisfy many needs in terms of training data and model storage. In this chapter, you learned

- How to implement a recommendation engine when the users are largely anonymous, using a session-based approach
- How to model the training data and the models for the session-based approach
- How to use different approaches for providing recommendations by using session data
- How to optimize the k-NN computation by using different techniques, such as LSH

References

[Bonnin and Jannach, 2014] Bonnin, Geoffray, and Dietmar Jannach. "Automated Generation of Music Playlists: Survey and Experiments." *ACM Computing Surveys* 47:2 (2014): Article 26.

[Davidson et al., 2010] Davidson, James, Benjamin Liebald, Junning Liu, Palash Nandy, Taylor Van Vleet, Ullas Gargi, Sujoy Gupta, Yu He, Mike Lambert, Blake Livingston, and Dasarathi Sampath. "The YouTube Video Recommendation System." *Proceedings of the 4th ACM Conference on Recommender Systems* (2010): 293–296.

[Devooght and Bersini, 2017] Devooght, Robin, and Hugues Bersini. "Long and Short-Term Recommendations with Recurrent Neural Networks." *Proceedings of the 25th Conference on User Modeling, Adaptation and Personalization* (2017): 13–21.

[Goodfellow et al., 2016] Goodfellow, Ian, Yoshua Bengio, and Aaron Courville. 2016. *Deep Learning*. The MIT Press.

[Hariri et al., 2012] Hariri, Negar, Bamshad Mobasher, and Robin Burke. "Context-Aware Music Recommendation Based on Latent Topic Sequential Patterns." *Proceedings of the 6th ACM Conference on Recommender Systems* (2012): 131–138.

[Hidasi and Karatzoglou, 2018] Hidasi, Balázs, and Alexandros Karatzoglou. "Recurrent Neural Networks with Top-k Gains for Session-Based Recommendations." *Proceedings of the 27th ACM International Conference on Information and Knowledge Management* (2018): 843–852.

[Hidasi et al., 2016 a] Hidasi, Balázs, Alexandros Karatzoglou, Linas Baltrunas, and Domonkos Tikk. "Session-Based Recommendations with Recurrent Neural Networks." *Proceedings of the 4th International Conference on Learning Representations* (2016).

[Hidasi et al., 2016 b] Hidasi, Balázs, Massimo Quadrana, Alexandros Karatzoglou, and Domonkos Tikk. "Parallel Recurrent Neural Network Architectures for Feature-Rich Session-Based Recommendations." *Proceedings of the 10th ACM Conference on Recommender Systems* (2016): 241–248.

[Jannach and Ludewig, 2017 a] Jannach, Dietmar, and Malte Ludewig. "When Recurrent Neural Networks Meet the Neighborhood for Session-Based Recommendation." *Proceedings of the 11th ACM Conference on Recommender Systems* (2017): 306–310.

[Jannach and Ludewig, 2017 b] Jannach, Dietmar, and Malte Ludewig. "Determining Characteristics of Successful Recommendations from Log Data: A Case Study." *Proceedings of the Symposium on Applied Computing* (2017): 1643–1648.

[Kamehkhosh et al., 2017] Kamehkhosh, Iman, Dietmar Jannach, and Malte Ludewig. "A Comparison of Frequent Pattern Techniques and a Deep Learning Method for Session-Based Recommendation." *Proceedings of the 1st Workshop on Temporal Reasoning in Recommender Systems* (2017): 50–56.

[Lerche et al., 2016] Lerche, Lukas, Dietmar Jannach, and Malte Ludewig. "On the Value of Reminders Within E-Commerce Recommendations." *Proceedings of the 24th Conference on User Modeling, Adaptation and Personalization* (2016): 27–35.

[Linden et al., 2003] Linden, Greg, Brent Smith, and Jeremy York. "Amazon.com Recommendations: Item-to-Item Collaborative Filtering." *IEEE Internet Computing* 7:1 (2003): 76–80.

[Ludewig and Jannach, 2018] Ludewig, Malte, and Dietmar Jannach. "Evaluation of Session-Based Recommendation Algorithms." arXiv preprint arXiv:1803.09587 (2018).

[Quadrana, 2017] Quadrana, Massimo. "Algorithms for Sequence-Aware Recommender Systems." PhD dissertation, Politecnico di Milano (2017).

[Quadrana et al., 2017] Quadrana, Massimo, Alexandros Karatzoglou, Balázs Hidasi, and Paolo Cremonesi. "Personalizing Session-Based Recommendations with Hierarchical Recurrent Neural Networks." *Proceedings of the 11th ACM Conference on Recommender Systems* (2017): 130–137.

[Quadrana et al., 2018] Quadrana, Massimo, Paolo Cremonesi, and Dietmar Jannach. "Sequence-Aware Recommender Systems." *ACM Computing Surveys* 51:4 (2018): Article 66.

[Tan et al., 2016] Tan, Yong Kiam, Xinxing Xu, and Yong Liu. "Improved Recurrent Neural Networks for Session-Based Recommendations." *Proceedings of the 1st Workshop on Deep Learning for Recommender Systems* (2016): 17–22.

[Tuan and Phuong, 2017] Tuan, Trinh Xuan, and Tu Minh Phuong. "3D Convolutional Networks for Session-Based Recommendation with Content Features." *Proceedings of the 11th ACM Conference on Recommender Systems* (2017): 138–146.

[Ullman and Rajaraman, 2011] Ullman, Jeffrey David, and Anand Rajaraman. *Mining of Massive Datasets*. Cambridge, UK: Cambridge University Press, 2011.

[Verstrepen and Goethals, 2014] Verstrepen, Koen, and Bart Goethals. "Unifying Nearest Neighbors Collaborative Filtering." *Proceedings of the 8th ACM Conference on Recommender Systems* (2014): 177–184.

Context-aware and
hybrid recommendations

This chapter covers

- Implementing a recommendation engine that takes into account the user's context
- Designing graph models for context-aware recommendation engines
- Importing existing datasets into the graph models
- Combining multiple recommendation approaches

This chapter introduces into the recommendation scenario another variable that the previous approaches ignored: *context*. The specific conditions in which the user expresses a desire, preference, or need have a strong influence on their behavior and expectations. Different techniques exist to consider the user's context during the recommendation process. We'll cover the main ones in this chapter.

Furthermore, to complete our overview of recommendation engine models and algorithms, we'll see how it's possible to use a hybrid approach that combines the different types of systems presented so far. Such an approach will enable us to create a unique and powerful recommendation ecosystem capable of overcoming all the issues, limitations, and drawbacks of each individual recommendation method.

7.1   *The context-based approach*

Suppose that you would like to implement a mobile application that provides recommendations about movies to watch at the cinema; we'll call it Reco4.me. By using context-aware techniques, you'll be able to take into account environmental information during the recommendation process, suggesting, for example, movies playing at cinemas close to the user's current location.

Let's further refine the scenario with a concrete example. Suppose that you're in London, and you would like to find a movie to watch at a nearby cinema. You take out your phone, open the Reco4.me app, and hope for some good recommendations. What kinds of recommendations do you expect? You want to know about movies that are currently playing in cinemas close to where you are. Ideally, you would also like to have recommendations that suit your preferences. I don't know about you, but for me, the context changes my preferences. When I'm alone at home, I love to watch action or fantasy movies. When I'm with my kids, I prefer to watch cartoons or family movies. When I'm with my wife, "we" prefer to watch chick flicks or romcoms. The app should take into account this environmental information and provide accurate recommendations that suit the user's current context.

This example shows how essential it can be to consider context in a recommender system, because it may have a subtle but powerful influence on user behaviors and needs. Considering the context, therefore, can dramatically affect the quality of the recommendations, converting what might be a good tip in some circumstances to a useless suggestion in others. This situation is true not only in scenarios like the one described here, but also in many others. Think about how you use an e-commerce site such as Amazon, for example. You might use it to buy a book for yourself, a gift for your fiancé, or a toy for your kids. You have a single account, but your behavior and your preferences are driven by the specific needs you have while you are navigating the site. So although it could be useful to see recommendations of books that might be of interest to you while you are looking for a skateboard for your son, it would be more effective to get suggestions that suit your current needs, based on previous gifts you've bought for your kids.

Traditional recommender systems, such as those based on the content-based and collaborative filtering approaches discussed in chapters 4 and 5, tend to use fairly simple user models. User-based collaborative filtering models users simply as vectors of item ratings, for example. As additional observations are made about users' preferences, the user models are extended, and the full collection of user preferences is used to generate recommendations or make predictions. This approach, therefore, ignores the notion of "situated actions" [Suchman, 1987]—the fact that users interact with the system within a particular context or specific scope, and that preferences for items within one context may be different from those in another context. In many application domains, a context-independent representation may lose predictive power because potentially useful information from multiple contexts is aggregated.

More formally, interactions between users and items exhibit a multifaceted nature. User preferences typically are not fixed and may change with respect to a specific situation. Going back to the example of the Reco4.me app, a simplified schema of the possible contextual information is depicted in figure 7.1.

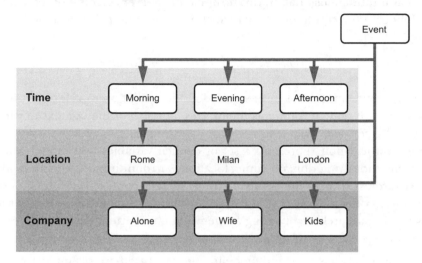

Figure 7.1　Contextual information for the app Reco4.me

This example is a small subset of the types of contextual information that could be considered. Context might include the season of the year or day of the week, the type of electronic device the user is using, the user's mood—almost anything [Bazire and Brézillon, 2005; Doerfel et al., 2016]. It's worth mentioning too that the contextual information is defined by what the system knows or can guess about the specific conditions in which an action or interaction occurs.

In content-based and collaborative filtering approaches, the recommendation problem is defined as a prediction problem in which, given a user profile (defined in different ways) and a target item, the recommender system's task is to predict that user's rating of or interest in that item, reflecting the degree of user preference for the item. Specifically, a recommender system tries to estimate a rating function:

f: User × Item → ratings

Such a function maps user-item pairs to an ordered set of score values. Note that f can be viewed as a general-purpose utility (or preference) measure for user-item pairs. The ratings for all user-item pairs are not known and therefore must be inferred, which is why we talk about *prediction*. When an initial set of ratings has been collected, implicitly or explicitly, a recommender system tries to estimate the rating values for items that have not yet been rated by the users. From now on, we'll refer to these traditional recommender systems as *two-dimensional* (2D) because they consider only the Users and Items dimensions as input in the recommendation process.

By contrast, *context-aware* recommender systems try to incorporate or use additional environmental evidence (beyond information about users and items) to estimate user preferences for unseen items. When such contextual evidence can be incorporated as part of the input to the recommender system, the rating function can be viewed as multidimensional. In this formula, *Context* represents a set of factors that further delineate the conditions under which the user-item pair is assigned a particular rating:

$$f: \text{User} \times \text{Item} \times Contex_1 \times Contex_2 \times \ldots \times Contex_n \rightarrow \text{ratings}$$

The underlying assumption of this extended model is that user preferences for items are a function not only of the items themselves, but also of the context in which the items are being considered.

Context information represents a set of explicit variables that model contextual factors in the underlying domain (time, location, surroundings, device, occasion, and so on). Regardless of how the context is represented, context-aware recommenders must be able to obtain contextual information that corresponds to the user's activity (such as making a purchase or rating an item). Such information, in a context-aware recommender system, has a twofold purpose:

- It is part of the learning and modeling process (used, for example, for discovering rules, segmenting users, or building regression models).
- For a given target user and target item, the system must be able to identify the values of specific contextual variables as part of the user's ongoing interaction with the system. This information is used to ensure that the right recommendation is delivered, considering the context.

Contextual information can be obtained in many ways, either explicitly or implicitly. Explicit contextual information may be obtained from users themselves or from sensors designed to measure specific physical or environmental information [Frolov and Oseledets, 2016]. In some cases, however, contextual information must be derived or inferred from other observed data. Here some examples:

- *Explicit*—The application may ask a person who's looking for a restaurant recommendation to specify whether they're going on a date or going out with co-workers for a business dinner.
- *Explicit/implicit*—If the restaurant recommender is a mobile app, additional contextual information can be obtained through the device's GPS and other sensors about the location, time, and weather conditions.
- *Implicit*—An e-commerce system may attempt, using previously learned models of user behavior, to distinguish (for example) whether the user is likely to be purchasing a gift for their spouse or a work-related book.

Approaches to implicitly infer contextual information typically require building predictive models from historical data [Palmisano et al., 2008].

Figure 7.2 shows the mental model of a context-aware recommendation engine. The user's events—input of the system—are contextualized and converted to a graph; then the process of building a model and providing recommendations can start.

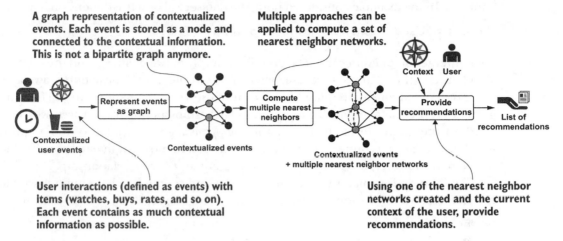

A graph representation of contextualized events. Each event is stored as a node and connected to the contextual information. This is not a bipartite graph anymore.

Multiple approaches can be applied to compute a set of nearest neighbor networks.

User interactions (defined as events) with items (watches, buys, rates, and so on). Each event contains as much contextual information as possible.

Using one of the nearest neighbor networks created and the current context of the user, provide recommendations.

Figure 7.2   A graph-powered context-aware recommender system

7.1.1   Representing contextual information

In content-based and collaborative filtering approaches, the user-item interactions—buy, click, view, rate, watch, and so on—are represented as a 2D matrix, which we've defined as the User x Item (U x I) dataset. Such a matrix can easily be represented as a bipartite graph, in which one set of vertices represents the users and the other set represents the items. The interaction is modeled via a relationship between the user (the subject of the event) and the item (the object of the event).

In context-aware recommendation systems, each interaction event brings more information with it. It is described not only by the user and the item, but also by all the environmental information that contextualizes the situated action. If a user is watching a movie at home with their kids in the evening, the contextual information is composed of

- *Time*—Evening, weekday
- *Company*—Kids
- *Location*—Home

This example is only a subset of the relevant information that can describe the event "watch." Other information could include the device being used, the mood of the users, the ages of the viewers, or the occasion (date night, party, or kids' bedtime movie). Some variables may be discrete (contextual information with defined sets of values, such as device and location), and others are continuous (numerical values such as age). In the latter case, it's generally preferable to discretize the variables somehow. In the case of age, you might have buckets—such as 0–5, 6–14, 15–21, 22–50, and over 50—depending on the specific requirements of the recommendation engine.

The resulting dataset, which represents the input for the recommendation process, can no longer be represented as a simple 2D matrix. It requires an *N*-dimensional matrix, in which two dimensions are the users and the items, and the others represent contexts. In the example considered here, the dataset will be a five-dimensional matrix:

$$\text{dataset} = \text{User} \times \text{Item} \times \text{Location} \times \text{Company} \times \text{Time}$$

Each interaction or event cannot be described simply by two elements and the relationship between them. In the best case, when all the contextual information is available, three other elements are required, so we cannot use a simple relationship in a bipartite graph to represent an event. To represent relationships among five vertices, we would need a hypergraph. In mathematics, a *hypergraph* is a generalization of the graph in which one edge can connect any number of vertices. In most graph databases (including Neo4j), however, it is not possible to represent an *n*-vertex relationship.

The solution is to materialize events as nodes and connect each event node with all the elements, or dimensions, that describe the event. The result will look like figure 7.3.

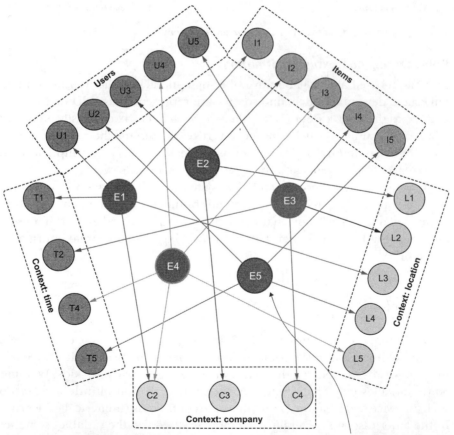

Figure 7.3   An *n*-partite graph representing contextual information about events

Each event E1, E2, and so on is connected to specific contextual information (not necessarily one for each class).

The new graph representation is a 6-partite graph because we have users, items, location information, time information, and company information plus the events. This graph represents the input for the next steps in the recommendation process depicted in figure 7.2.

Passing from a 2D representation to an *n*-dimensional representation ($n = 5$ in our case) makes data sparsity an even bigger concern. It will be hard to find a lot of events that happen for multiple users under exactly the same circumstances. This problem is exacerbated when we have detailed contextual information (higher values of n), but it can be mitigated by introducing hierarchies in the contextual information. Figure 7.4

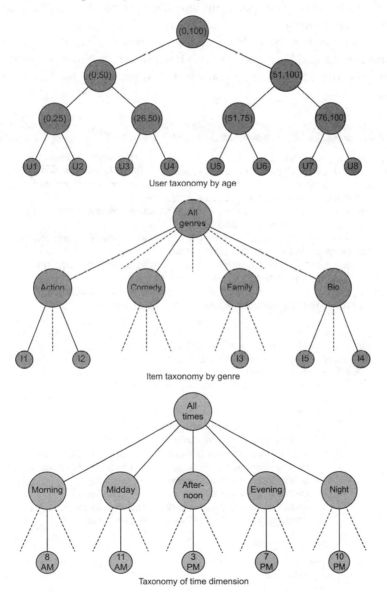

User taxonomy by age

Item taxonomy by genre

Taxonomy of time dimension

Figure 7.4 Taxonomies of users, items, and times

shows some examples of possible hierarchies—represented in the form of a graph—considering some of the contextual information for our specific scenario. These hierarchies are defined as taxonomies.

These taxonomies will be used during the recommendation phase to solve the sparsity problem and enable us to provide recommendations even when we don't have much information about the current user's specific context.

In this section, we will use the DePaulMovie dataset[1] [Zheng et al., 2015], which contains data collected from surveys conducted with students. It contains data from 97 users about 79 movies, rated in different contexts (time, location, and companion). Such a dataset matches our needs perfectly, and it's often used to perform comparisons of context-aware recommender systems [Ilarri et al., 2018].

To begin, let's import the data from the DePaulMovie dataset selected for this example. Please run the code using a fresh database; you can clean it up[2] or decide to use a different one and keep the one you created in previous chapters for further experimentation.

Listing 7.1 Importing data from the DePaulMovie dataset

```
def import_event_data(self, file):              ◁──┐ Entry point for importing
    with self._driver.session() as session:        │ the data from the CSV file
        self.executeNoException(session, "CREATE CONSTRAINT ON (u:User)
        ➥ ASSERT u.userId IS UNIQUE") #B
        self.executeNoException(session, "CREATE CONSTRAINT ON (i:Item)
        ➥ ASSERT i.itemId IS UNIQUE") #B
        self.executeNoException(session, "CREATE CONSTRAINT ON (t:Time)
        ➥ ASSERT t.value IS UNIQUE") #B
        self.executeNoException(session, "CREATE CONSTRAINT ON
        ➥ (l:Location) ASSERT l.value IS UNIQUE")
        self.executeNoException(session, "CREATE CONSTRAINT ON
        ➥ (c:Companion) ASSERT c.value IS UNIQUE")

        j = 0;
        with open(file, 'r+') as in_file:
            reader = csv.reader(in_file, delimiter=',')
            next(reader, None)
            tx = session.begin_transaction()
            i = 0;
            query = """
                    MERGE (user:User {userId: $userId})
                    MERGE (time:Time {value: $time})
                    MERGE (location:Location {value: $location})
                    MERGE (companion:Companion {value: $companion})
                    MERGE (item:Item {itemId: $itemId})
                    CREATE (event:Event {rating:$rating})
                    CREATE (event)-[:EVENT_USER]->(user)
                    CREATE (event)-[:EVENT_ITEM]->(item)
```

Queries that create the constraints in the database to prevent duplicates and speed access → (points to the CREATE CONSTRAINT queries)

Query which in one shot creates the events and connects them to the related dimensions → (points to the query block)

---

[1] http://mng.bz/D1jE.

[2] To clean the existing database, you could run MATCH (n) DETACH DELETE n, but it could take longer. Another option is to stop the database and purge the data directory.

```
              CREATE (event)-[:EVENT_LOCATION]->(location)
              CREATE (event)-[:EVENT_COMPANION]->(companion)
              CREATE (event)-[:EVENT_TIME]->(time)
          """

    for row in reader:
        try:
            if row:
                user_id = row[0]
                item_id = strip(row[1])
                rating = strip(row[2])
                time = strip(row[3])
                location = strip(row[4])
                companion = strip(row[5])
                tx.run(query, {"userId": user_id, "time": time,
                ➡ "location": location, "companion": companion,
                ➡ "itemId": item_id, "rating": rating})
                i += 1
                j += 1
                if i == 1000:
                    tx.commit()
                    print(j, "lines processed")
                    i = 0
                    tx = session.begin_transaction()
        except Exception as e:
            print(e, row)
    tx.commit()
    print(j, "lines processed")
print(j, "lines processed")
```

In the complete version in the code repository, you'll notice that I've also imported some information about the movies. This information will be useful for getting a sense of the results and also for the following exercises.

EXERCISES

After you've imported the data, play with the graph database. Here are some things to try:

- Look for the most frequent contextual information—the most frequent time for watching a movie, for example.
- Look for the most active users, and check the variability of their contextual information.
- Try adding some taxonomies to see whether the results of the preceding queries change.
- Search for movies or genres that are commonly watched during the week and those that are more often watched on the weekend.

7.1.2 Providing recommendations

Classical recommender systems provide recommendations by using limited knowledge of user preferences (that is, user preferences for some subset of the items), and the input data for these systems is typically based on records of the form `<user, item, rating>`. As described in previous chapters, the recommendation processes generally use the U x I matrix to create a model and provide recommendations based only on user interaction and preferences.

By contrast, context-aware recommender systems typically deal with data records of the form `<user, item, context1, context2, …, rating>`, in which each record includes not only how much a given user liked a specific item, but also contextual information about the conditions in which the user interacted with the item (`context1 = Saturday`, `context2 = wife`, and so on). This "rich" information is used to create the model. Furthermore, information about the user's current context can be used in various stages of the recommendation process, leading to several approaches to context-aware recommender systems. From an algorithmic perspective, the vast majority of the context-aware recommendation approaches do the following things:

- Take as input the contextualized (extended) User × Item dataset in the form $U \times I \times C_1 \times C_2 \times … \times C_n$, where C_i is an additional contextual dimension.
- Produce a list of contextual recommendations $i_1, i_2, i_3, …$ for each user u, based on the current context of the user.

Based on how the contextual information, the current user, and the current item are used during the recommendation process, context-aware recommendation systems can take one of the three forms shown in figure 7.5.

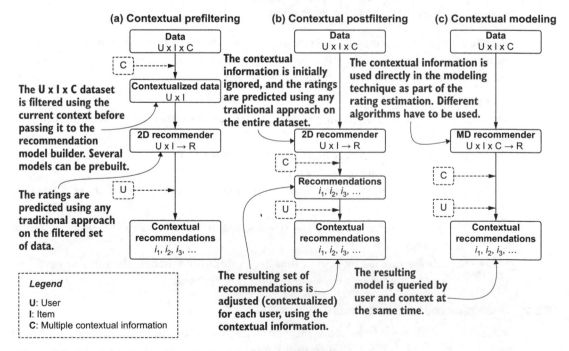

Figure 7.5   The three forms of a context-aware recommender system

The three types of context-aware recommendation system are [Ilarri et al., 2018]

- *Contextual prefiltering (or contextualization of recommendation input)*—In this paradigm, information about the current context c is used only for selecting the relevant set of data, and ratings are predicted by using any traditional 2D recommender system on the selected data. For efficiency, several models must be precomputed, considering the most probable combinations of contexts.
- *Contextual postfiltering (or contextualization of recommendation output)*—In this paradigm, contextual information is initially ignored, and the ratings are predicted by using any traditional 2D recommender system on the entire dataset. Then the resulting set of recommendations is adjusted (contextualized) for each user, using the contextual information. Only one model is built, so it's easier to manage, and the contextual information is used only during the recommendation phase.
- *Contextual modeling (or contextualization of the recommendation function)*—In this paradigm, contextual information is used directly in the modeling technique as part of model building.

The following sections describe the three paradigms in more detail, highlighting the role of the graph approach for each (especially the first two).

CONTEXTUAL PREFILTERING

As shown in figure 7.6, the contextual prefiltering approach uses contextual information to select the most relevant User × Item matrices and create models from them; then it generates recommendations through the inferred models.

When the User × Item datasets are extracted, any of the numerous traditional recommendation techniques proposed in the literature (such as the approaches discussed in chapters 4 and 5) can be used to build the model and provide recommendations. This technique represents one of the biggest advantages of the first approach to context-aware recommendation engines.

Note that the prefiltering approach is related to the task of building multiple

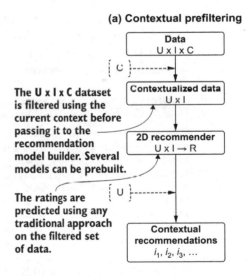

(a) Contextual prefiltering

The U x I x C dataset is filtered using the current context before passing it to the recommendation model builder. Several models can be prebuilt.

The ratings are predicted using any traditional approach on the filtered set of data.

Figure 7.6   Contextual prefiltering

local models in machine learning and data mining based on the most relevant combination of contextual information. Rather than building the global rating estimation model using all the available ratings, the prefiltering approach builds (prebuilds in the real scenario) a local rating estimation model that uses only the ratings pertaining to the user-specified criteria for the recommendation (such as Saturday or weekday).

In this approach, the context *c* essentially serves as a filter for selecting relevant rating data. Here's an example of a contextual data filter for a movie recommender system: if a person wants to see a movie on Saturday, only the Saturday rating data is used to recommend movies. Extracting the relevant dataset, building the model, and providing the recommendations require time, of course, especially if the dataset is big. For this reason, multiple versions are precomputed, using the most relevant combinations of contextual information.

In the graph approach, considering the model depicted in figure 7.3, performing such prefiltering consists in selecting the relevant events by running a query like the following.

Listing 7.2   Filtering events based on relevant contextual information

```
MATCH (event:Event)-[:EVENT_ITEM]->(item:Item)
MATCH (event)-[:EVENT_USER]->(user:User)
MATCH (event)-[:EVENT_TIME]->(time:Time)
MATCH (event)-[:EVENT_LOCATION]->(location:Location)
MATCH (event)-[:EVENT_COMPANION]->(companion:Companion)
WHERE time.value = "Weekday"
AND location.value = "Home"
AND companion.value = "Alone"
RETURN user.userId, item.itemId, event.rating
```

In this query, we are considering only the events that happen during a weekday alone at home. The output is a slice of our multidimensional matrix. If we instead want to get a User × Item matrix for the context <Weekend, Cinema, Partner>, the query would look like the following.

Listing 7.3   Filtering events based on different contextual information

```
MATCH (event:Event)-[:EVENT_ITEM]->(item:Item)
MATCH (event)-[:EVENT_USER]->(user:User)
MATCH (event)-[:EVENT_TIME]->(time:Time)
MATCH (event)-[:EVENT_LOCATION]->(location:Location)
MATCH (event)-[:EVENT_COMPANION]->(companion:Companion)
WHERE time.value = "Weekend"
AND location.value = "Cinema"
AND companion.value = "Partner"
RETURN user.userId, item.itemId, event.rating
```

The resulting matrices will be different.

It is not necessary to specify all the contextual information, of course. Some of the dimensions can be ignored. We could have a context <Cinema, Partner> in which the time dimension would be irrelevant, for example. The query in this case would look like the following.

Listing 7.4 Filtering events by considering only two items of contextual information

```
MATCH (event:Event)-[:EVENT_ITEM]->(item:Item)
MATCH (event)-[:EVENT_USER]->(user:User)
MATCH (event)-[:EVENT_LOCATION]->(location:Location)
MATCH (event)-[:EVENT_COMPANION]->(companion:Companion)
WHERE location.value = "Cinema"
AND companion.value = "Partner"
RETURN user.userId, item.itemId, event.rating
```

The graph model is highly flexible. As mentioned previously, after the data is filtered, any classic method can be applied to build the model and provide recommendations. Suppose that we would like to use the collaborative approach—specifically, the nearest neighbor approach. We have to compute similarities among items, users, or both. The resulting similarities can be stored as simple relationships between items and/or users, but the information about the prefiltering condition would be lost. A property can be added to the relationships to keep track of the sources used for computing them, but it's difficult to query; also, most important, this approach doesn't use the graph capabilities to speed navigation through nodes and relationships.

The best modeling choice in this case is to materialize the similarities by using nodes and connect them to the relevant contextual information used for computing them: the prefiltering conditions. The resulting graph model would look like figure 7.7.

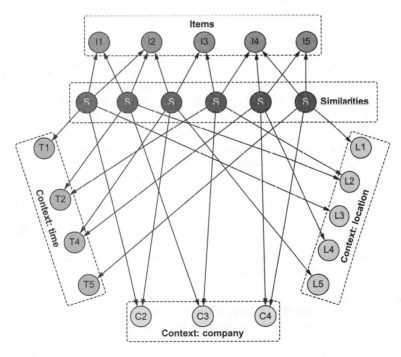

Figure 7.7 Graph model with the similarity nodes after the computation

This model is easy to navigate during the recommendation process. We can assign an ID to each set of contextual information to make querying easier; this ID isn't mandatory, but it's helpful because it allows faster and simpler access. We can get the k-NN for a specific context by using a query like the following.[3]

Listing 7.5   Query to get the k-NN given specific contextual information

```
MATCH p=(n:Similarity)-->(i)
WHERE n.contextId = 1          ◁——————    Assigning IDs to specific sets of contextual
RETURN p                                   information allows us to query by context ID.
limit 50
```

The following listing allows you to create such a graph model.

Listing 7.6   Code for computing and storing similarities in the prefiltering approach

Entry point for computing similarities in prefiltering. The context parameter specifies the contextual information. This function has to be run multiple times for multiple combinations of contextual information.

Computes the similarities. The cosine function is the same one used many times in chapters 4, 5, and 6.

```
  ┌▷ def compute_and_store_similarity(self, contexts):
         for context in contexts:
             items_VSM = self.get_item_vectors(context)
             for item in items_VSM:
                 knn = self.compute_knn(item, items_VSM.copy(), 20);      ◁——
                 self.store_knn(item, knn, context)


     def get_item_vectors(self, context):       ◁——
         list_of_items_query = """
                 MATCH (item:Item)
                 RETURN item.itemId as itemId
             """
         context_info = context[1].copy()
         match_query = """
                 MATCH (event:Event)-[:EVENT_ITEM]->(item:Item)
                 MATCH (event)-[:EVENT_USER]->(user:User)
             """
         where_query = """
                 WHERE item.itemId = $itemId
             """
         if "location" in context_info:          ◁——
             match_query += "MATCH (event)-[:EVENT_LOCATION]->(location:Location) "
             where_query += "AND location.value = $location "

         if "time" in context_info:
             match_query += "MATCH (event)-[:EVENT_TIME]->(time:Time) "
             where_query += "AND time.value = $time "
```

Prefilters the dataset, considering the relevant contextual information, and returns the usual item list with related sparse vectors

if statements that change the query according to the contextual information

---

[3] The query can be run after the code finishes creating the k-NN. Here, the purpose is to show how to query the model.

```
        if "companion" in context_info:
            match_query += "MATCH (event)-[:EVENT_COMPANION]->
            ➥ (companion:Companion) "
            where_query += "AND companion.value = $companion "

    return_query = """
                WITH user.userId as userId, event.rating as rating
                ORDER BY id(user)
                RETURN collect(distinct userId) as vector
            """

    query = match_query + where_query + return_query
    items_VSM_sparse = {}
    with self._driver.session() as session:
        i = 0
        for item in session.run(list_of_items_query):
            item_id = item["itemId"];
            context_info["itemId"] = item_id
            vector = session.run(query, context_info)
            items_VSM_sparse[item_id] = vector.single()[0]
            i += 1
            if i % 100 == 0:
                print(i, "rows processed")
        print(i, "rows processed")
    print(len(items_VSM_sparse))
    return items_VSM_sparse

def store_knn(self, item, knn, context):
    context_id = context[0]
    params = context[1].copy()
    with self._driver.session() as session:
        tx = session.begin_transaction()
        knnMap = {a: b for a, b in knn}
        clean_query = """
            MATCH (s:Similarity)-[:RELATED_TO_SOURCE_ITEM]->(item:Item)
            WHERE item.itemId = $itemId AND s.contextId = $contextId
            DETACH DELETE s
        """
        query = """
            MATCH (item:Item)
            WHERE item.itemId = $itemId
            UNWIND keys($knn) as otherItemId
            MATCH (other:Item)
            WHERE other.itemId = otherItemId
            CREATE (similarity:Similarity {weight: $knn[otherItemId],
            ➥ contextId: $contextId})
            MERGE (item)<-[:RELATED_TO_SOURCE_ITEM]-(similarity)
            MERGE (other)<-[:RELATED_TO_DEST_ITEM ]-(similarity)
        """
        if "location" in params:
            query += "WITH similarity MATCH (location:Location
            ➥ {value: $location}) "
            query += "MERGE (location)<-[:RELATED_TO]-(similarity) "
```

Query that cleans up the previous stored model

Query that creates the new similarity nodes and connects them to the related items and contextual information

if statements that modify the query according to the filter conditions

```
    if "time" in params:
        query += "WITH similarity MATCH (time:Time {value: $time}) "
        query += "MERGE (time)<-[:RELATED_TO]-(similarity) "

    if "companion" in params:
        query += "WITH similarity MATCH (companion:Companion
    ➥ {value: $companion}) "
        query += "MERGE (companion)<-[:RELATED_TO]-(similarity) "

    tx.run(clean_query, {"itemId": item, "contextId": context_id})
    params["itemId"] = item
    params["contextId"] = context_id
    params["knn"] = knnMap
    tx.run(query, params)
    tx.commit()

def compute_knn(self, item, items, k):
    knn_values = []
    for other_item in items:
        if other_item != item:
            value = cosine_similarity(items[item], items[other_item])
            if value > 0:
                knn_values.append((other_item, value))
    knn_values.sort(key=lambda x: -x[1])
    return knn_values[:k]
```

As mentioned previously, the exact context can be too narrow. Consider, for example, the context of watching a movie with your partner in a cinema on Saturday—or, more formally, *c* = <Partner, Cinema, Saturday>. Using this exact context as a data-filtering query may be problematic, because there may not be enough data available for accurate rating prediction. To address this issue, Adomavicius and Tuzhilin [2005] suggest generalizing the filtering conditions by aggregating narrower context details, which may not be significant. These generalizations are the taxonomies we discussed earlier, some examples of which were shown in figure 7.4. So, for example, Saturday can become Weekend, whereas Monday to Friday are considered to be Weekdays. It's easy not only to represent such hierarchies or aggregations in a graph, but also to query them. Using broader concepts while filtering data can deliver better results.

When considering the prefiltering approach, it's important to determine whether the local (specific to some contextual information) model it generates outperforms the global model of the traditional 2D technique, which ignores all the information associated with the contextual dimensions. It may be better to use contextual prefiltering to recommend movies to watch in a movie theater on the weekend but use the traditional 2D technique (ignoring the contextual information) to recommend movies to watch at home on demand. The trade-off during the calculation of an unknown rating in this case is between the following:

- Using more specific (in the sense of narrower contextual information) but relevant data (the prefiltering)
- Using all the data available (the traditional 2D recommendation)

No simple rule helps us choose between these two calculations; which approach will be more successful depends on many factors, such as the type of contextual information, the application domain, the user behaviors, and the amount and sparsity of data available. For that reason, the prefiltering recommendation method may outperform traditional 2D recommendation techniques in some contexts but not in others. Based on this observation, Adomavicius and Tuzhilin [2005] propose combining contextual prefilters with the traditional 2D technique when no filtering is done.

CONTEXTUAL POSTFILTERING

As shown in figure 7.8, the contextual postfiltering approach ignores contextual information during model generation.

Furthermore, the ranked list of all candidate items is computed regardless of the context. The postfiltering approach uses contextual information in a later phase to adjust the obtained recommendation list for each user. The adjustment to the top N items can be performed in two ways:

- Filtering out recommendations that are irrelevant in a given context
- Adjusting the ranking of recommendations in the list

In our movie recommendation application Reco4.me, if the user watches only comedies on the weekend, the recommendation system could filter out all noncomedies in the recommendation list for weekend viewing or penalize them by reducing their ratings.

Which method is preferable will depend on the application. Panniello et al. [2009] per-

(b) Contextual postfiltering

The contextual information is initially ignored, and the ratings are predicted using any traditional approach on the entire dataset.

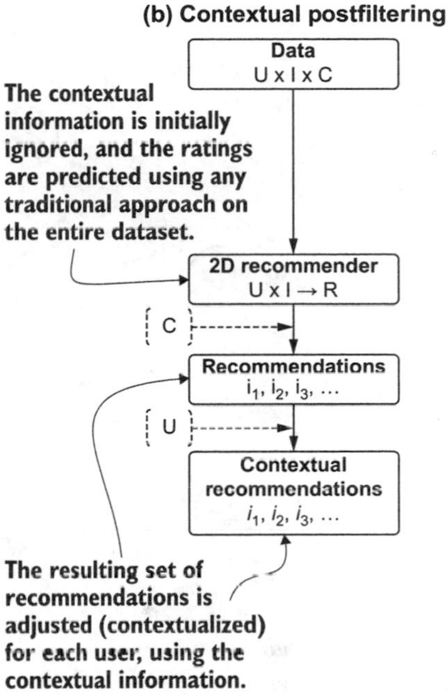

Figure 7.8 Contextual postfiltering

formed an experimental comparison of the exact (that is, nongeneralized) prefiltering method with postfiltering methods they called Weight and Filter, using several real-world e-commerce datasets. Their results showed that the Weight postfiltering method outperformed the exact prefiltering approach, which in turn outperformed the Filter method. Depending on your application, however, your results may vary.

The methods for filtering or adjusting rankings can be classified as *heuristic-based* or *model-based*. Heuristic postfiltering approaches focus on finding common item characteristics (attributes) for a given user in a given context (such as preferred actors to watch on Saturday in a cinema) and then uses these attributes to adjust the recommendations. This method requires storing metadata about each item and searching for common patterns in user preferences.

In the graph model, representing item metadata is straightforward, and multiple modeling techniques have been presented in previous chapters (specifically for the content-based approach). Mixing such models with the User × Item × Contexts graph representation is a simple exercise; figure 7.9 presents a possible result.

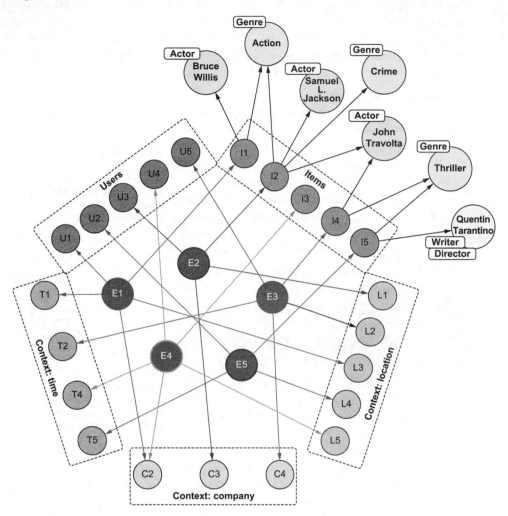

Figure 7.9   An *n*-partite graph representing contextual information of events plus the item attributes

The DePaulMovie dataset contains references to IMDb IDs for each movie, so we can reuse the code we implemented in chapter 4 to get and add information from IMDb. The code is presented in the file import_depaulmovie.py in the repository for this chapter.

After the import, queries like the following can be used to compute commonalities based on contextual information for users. Note that the queries shown here focus on a specific user to prove the concept. The queries consider only two contexts of all the possible combinations: <Cinema, Partner> and <Home, Alone>. We'll start with the <Cinema, Partner> context (listing 7.7).

Listing 7.7 Query for getting user profile for the context `<Cinema, Partner>`

```
MATCH (user:User)<-[:EVENT_USER]-(event:Event)
MATCH (event)-[:EVENT_ITEM]->(item:Item)-[]-(feature:Feature)
MATCH (event)-[:EVENT_LOCATION]->(location:Location)
MATCH (event)-[:EVENT_COMPANION]->(companion:Companion)
WHERE user.userId = "1032"
AND location.value = "Cinema"
AND companion.value = "Partner"
RETURN CASE 'Genre' IN labels(feature)
    WHEN true THEN feature.genre
    ELSE feature.name END AS feature, count(event) as occurrence
ORDER BY occurrence desc
```

The results of listing 7.7 are shown in figure 7.10.

feature	occurrence
"Comedy"	4
"Romance"	4
"Drama"	4
"Action"	4
"Adventure"	3
"Roland Emmerich"	3
"Dan Brown"	3
"Tom Hanks"	2
"Al Jean"	2
"Mike Scully"	2
"Matt Groening"	2

Figure 7.10 Results of listing 7.7

From the results, it is clear that when this user is watching a movie at the cinema with their partner, the user prefers comedies, romances, dramas, and action movies. The preferred actors/directors follow the same logic. Now let's take a look at the `<Home, Alone>` context (listing 7.8).

Listing 7.8   Query for getting user preferences/profile for the context `<Home, Alone>`

```
MATCH (user:User)<-[:EVENT_USER]-(event:Event)
MATCH (event)-[:EVENT_ITEM]->(item:Item)-[]-(feature:Feature)
MATCH (event)-[:EVENT_LOCATION]->(location:Location)
MATCH (event)-[:EVENT_COMPANION]->(companion:Companion)
WHERE user.userId = "1032"
AND location.value = "Home"
AND companion.value = "Alone"
RETURN CASE 'Genre' IN labels(feature)
    WHEN true THEN feature.genre
    ELSE feature.name END AS feature, count(event) as occurrence
ORDER BY occurrence desc
```

The results of this query are shown in figure 7.11.

feature	occurrence
"Comedy"	12
"Adventure"	9
"Action"	9
"Sci-Fi"	6
"Crime"	6
"Drama"	6
"Jonah Hill"	5
"Thriller"	5
"Animation"	4
"Family"	4
"Fantasy"	4
"Steve Carell"	4
"Andrew Stanton"	4
"Judd Apatow"	4
"Romance"	4
"Michael Bay"	3

Figure 7.11   Results of listing 7.8

Is this user the same one as before? The results here are different, showing the extent to which the context plays a role in the user's preferences. Results obtained in this way can be used to postfilter or fine-tune the results of a traditional collaborative filtering approach. Preferences based on context can be precomputed and stored back in our graph model. The result will look like figure 7.12.

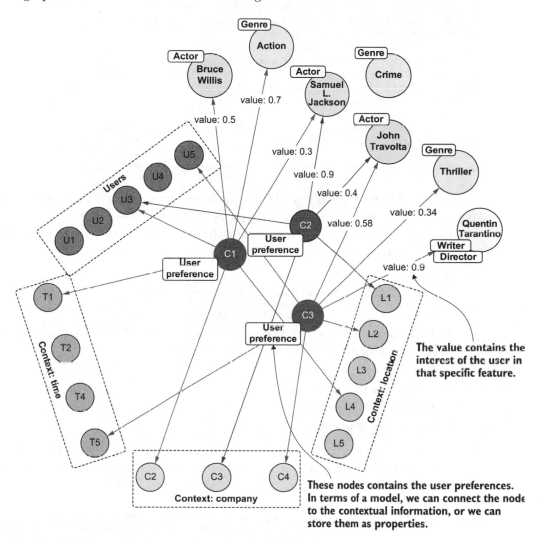

Figure 7.12   Graph model for the contextualized user preferences

The types of nodes and relationships presented in the model in figure 7.12 can be created by running queries like the following.

Listing 7.9   Query for creating user preferences

```
MERGE (userPreference:UserPreference {userId: "1032", location:"Home",
➥ companion: "Alone"})
WITH userPreference
MATCH (user:User)<-[:EVENT_USER]-(event:Event)
MATCH (event)-[:EVENT_LOCATION]->(location:Location)
MATCH (event)-[:EVENT_COMPANION]->(companion:Companion)
WHERE user.userId = userPreference.userId
AND location.value = userPreference.location
AND companion.value = userPreference.companion
WITH userPreference, user, collect(distinct event) as events
MERGE (userPreference)<-[:HAS_PREFERENCE]-(user)
WITH userPreference, events, size(events) as size
UNWIND events as event
MATCH (event)-[:EVENT_ITEM]->(item:Item)-[]-(feature:Feature)
WITH feature, userPreference, 1.0f*count(event)/(1.0f*size) as
➥ preferenceValue
MERGE (userPreference)-[:RELATED_TO {value: preferenceValue}]->(feature)
```

It worth noting that this query uses properties to represent the contextual information of the user preferences. This example is a slight deviation from the model design
shown in figure 7.12, but it's a valid option. In the following exercises, you are invited
to create an equivalent query that matches the model perfectly.

EXERCISES

Using listing 7.9 as the basis, create the following queries:

- The same query for a different context
- An equivalent query that uses relationships to contextual information instead
  of using properties for specifying the context
- A query for actors only
- A query for directors only
- A query for writers only
- A query for genres only

During the recommendation process, we can use this information about user preferences to determine how to adjust the results obtained in the first approach. The query
to get this information is simple, as you can see in listing 7.10.

Listing 7.10   Query for getting the boosting factors for the features

```
MATCH (user:User)-[:HAS_PREFERENCE]->(userPreference:UserPreference)-
➥ [r:RELATED_TO]->(feature:Feature)
WHERE user.userId = "1032"
AND userPreference.location = "Home"
AND userPreference.companion = "Alone"
RETURN CASE 'Genre' IN labels(feature)
    WHEN true THEN feature.genre
    ELSE feature.name END AS feature, r.value
```

This query returns values we can use as boosting factors after the first generic recommendation list has been obtained in one of the classic approaches. The alternative to the heuristic approach to postfiltering is the model-based approach. Here, we build predictive models that calculate the probability that the user will choose a certain type of item in a given context (the likelihood of choosing movies of a certain genre when alone and at home, for example) and then use this probability to adjust the recommendations. The algorithms for computing probability are beyond the scope of this chapter, but when they are computed, they can be stored in the graph model exactly as shown in figure 7.12.

It is important to note that, as was the case with contextual prefiltering, the greatest advantage of the contextual postfiltering approach is that it allows the use of any traditional recommendation technique.

CONTEXTUAL MODELING

The third type of context-aware recommendation system is based on contextual modeling. This approach, illustrated in figure 7.13, uses contextual information directly during model creation, giving rise to truly multidimensional recommendation functions that represent either predictive models (such as decision trees and regressions) or heuristic calculations that incorporate contextual information in addition to the user and item data.

In the past few years, a large number of recommendation algorithms based on a variety of heuristics as well as predictive modeling techniques have been developed. Some of these techniques can be considered to be extensions of the 2D to the multidimensional recommendation settings. Frolov and Oseledets [2016] show how to represent the User × Item × Contexts dataset as a multidimensional matrix, or tensor.[4] Such a tensor can be represented as

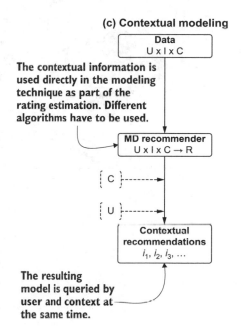

Figure 7.13 Contextual modeling

shown in figure 7.14, with each event representing an element, and the contexts, users, and items representing the dimensions. In such a representation, some operations on tensors, such as slicing, are easy to do with simple queries.

Other researchers have addressed the task of contextual modeling with a purely graph-based approach, considering context-aware recommendation as a searching problem to find interesting items for a user given a so-called context graph [Wu et al., 2015].

---

[4] A *matrix* is a 2D grid of numbers. A *tensor* is a generalization of the concept of matrix that can have any number of dimensions: 0 (a single number), 1 (a vector), 2 (a traditional matrix), 3 (a cube of numbers), or more. These higher-dimensional structures are difficult to visualize. The dimension of a tensor is known as its *rank* (aka *order* or *degree*).

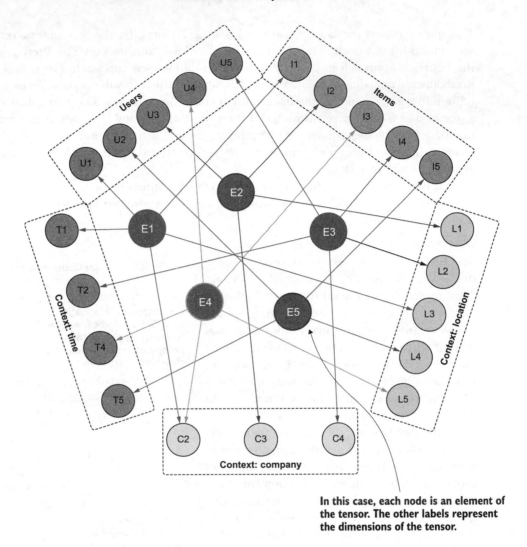

In this case, each node is an element of the tensor. The other labels represent the dimensions of the tensor.

Figure 7.14   Tensor representation in a graph model (as a multipartite graph)

The previously suggested method for creating the graph would not work in this case because the model design is different. Instead, the graph is created as follows. Given a context graph $G = \{V, E\}$, the vertices and the edges are defined so that

- The vertex set V is divided into several distinct sets, such as a set of users U, a set of items I, a set of attributes A, and a set of contexts C. C represents the combination of contextual information in a node. <Home, Alone, Weekday> is a node, for example. Nodes A represent the static features or attributes of users or items—information that does not change for different ratings, unlike the contextual information.

- The edge set E consists of the existing connections of the Cartesian product: V × V. Edges with diverse types have distinct semantics. U × A connects users and their attributes (user interests), U × I connects users with the items they have interacted with (the old User × Item dataset), and U × C connects users and contexts. The submatrix U × U, which stores social network information, may exist or not.

The context graph G can be represented as an adjacent matrix in which all submatrices are configured as symmetric (UI^T is the transport matrix of UI, for example), as shown in table 7.1.

Table 7.1 An adjacent matrix representation of contextual user-item interactions

	Users	Items	Contexts	Attributes
Users	UU	UI	UC	UA
Items	UI^T	0	IC	IA
Contexts	UC^T	IC^T	0	0
Attributes	UA^T	IA^T	0	0

The resulting graph is shown in figure 7.15.

Avoiding too many details, a random walk approach (specifically, the Personalized PageRank or PageRank with restart algorithm) is used to compute the relevance of the nodes in the graph. The recommendation process uses these relevance scores to estimate the likelihood that an unseen item *i* will be accessed by a user *u*. For a detailed description, see Wu et al. [2015].

PROS AND CONS

Each of the three techniques discussed for context-based recommendation has advantages and disadvantages:

- Prefiltering
  - *Pros*—This method is not only easy to implement, but also allows you to use any of the traditional recommendation techniques. It can deliver quite accurate results if relevant data for the user's current context is available.
  - *Cons*—The data-sparsity problem is common here because it's highly probable that for some contexts, there won't be enough data available for accurate recommendations. Moreover, to be performant, this approach requires you to prebuild a high number of models and keep them all updated.
- Postfiltering
  - *Pros*—This method is even easier to implement: you use a traditional technique (such as collaborative filtering) to generate the recommendations and then apply the filter to the result.

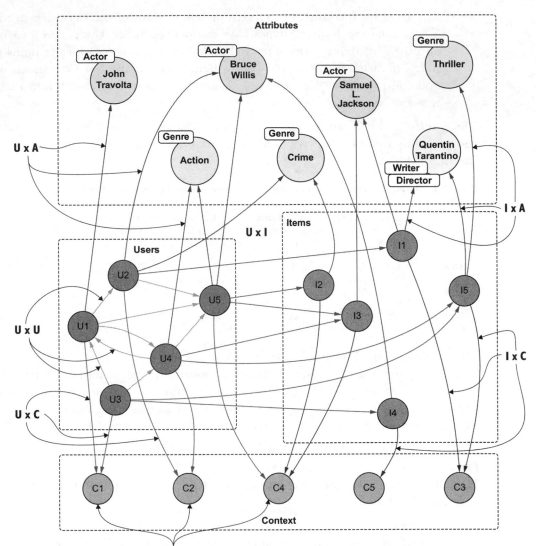

In this case, the context node represents a combination of contextual information, such as: <Cinema, Alone, Weekday>.

Figure 7.15   Representation of a context graph

– *Cons*—The postfiltering filters out or reduces the ratings for elements that are not relevant to the user's current context. Prediction accuracy is almost independent from context and mostly aligned with the traditional methods. Data sparsity is a problem here too, as it is for the traditional methods; it may be that all the resulting elements are irrelevant to the current context.

- Contextual modeling
  - *Pros*—The methods in this category are the most recent and tend to be the most accurate. The main disadvantage of the previous approach is that context is not integrated tightly into the recommendation algorithm, preventing you from taking full advantage of the relationships among the various user-item combinations and contextual values. Contextual modeling takes context into account from the beginning, enabling the creation of precise models that can be queried by using user, item, and contextual information.
  - *Cons*—Most of the methods available for contextual modeling are complex to implement, and a lot of computational power is required to create and update the model.

The choice of technique depends on weighing these pros and cons. More specifically, the choice depends on the type and quantity of data available, the frequency of new data, and how closely the model should be aligned with the current data.

7.1.3 Advantages of the graph approach

In this section, we've discussed different approaches to creating a context-aware recommendation engine: prefiltering, postfiltering, and contextual modeling. All the methods and algorithms presented here can use the graph representation of the User × Item × Contexts dataset, which simplifies accessing and navigating this complex data. Specifically, the main aspects and advantages of the graph-based approach to context-aware recommendation systems are

- The User × Item × Contexts multidimensional matrix, which represents the input of any such system, can be represented by a graph materializing the interaction event. This data model speeds the filtering phase and prevents the data-sparsity problem, which can be problematic in this scenario.
- A proper graph model can store the multimodel results of contextual prefiltering. Specifically, in the case of the nearest neighbor approach to prefiltering, which results in different sets of similarities among the items or users, graphs can store the results of multiple models by materializing the similarity nodes.
- During the recommendation phase, graph access patterns simplify the selection of relevant data based on the current user and the current context.
- In the contextual modeling approach, graphs provide a suitable method for storing tensors, simplifying some operations. Additionally, some specific approaches not only use a graph representation of the data (the context graph described earlier), but also use graph algorithms such as random walk and PageRank for building models and then providing recommendations.

7.2   *Hybrid recommendation engines*

The recommendation approaches discussed in this book exploit different sources of information and follow different paradigms to make recommendations. Although they produce results that are considered to be personalized based on the assumed interests of their recipients, they perform with varying degrees of success in different application domains. Collaborative filtering exploits a specific type of information (item ratings) from a user model to derive recommendations, whereas content-based approaches rely on product features and textual descriptions as well as on user profiles. Session-based approaches use the clickstreams of anonymous users, whereas context-aware methods use contextual information together with item ratings to fine-tune the recommendations according to the current needs of the user.

Each of these approaches has its pros and cons (highlighted in detail in this chapter and previous chapters), including the ability to handle the data-sparsity and cold-start problems, and the amount of effort required for content or context acquisition and processing.

Figure 7.16 sketches a recommendation system as a black box that transforms input data into a ranked list of items as output. Potential inputs, based on the approaches discussed here, include user models and contextual information as well as session data and item data; other inputs, required by other recommendation models, could be included as well. None of the basic approaches is able to fully exploit all these inputs, however. Consequently, building hybrid systems that combine the strengths of different algorithms and models to overcome some of the aforementioned shortcomings and problems has become the target of recent research.

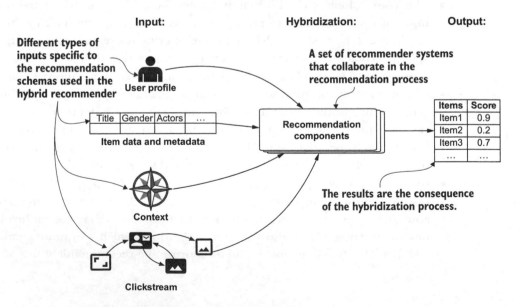

Figure 7.16   Hybrid recommendation system as a black box

Hybrid recommender systems are technical implementations that combine multiple algorithms or recommendation components. Burke's [2002] taxonomy distinguishes among seven hybridization strategies. From a more general perspective, the seven variants can be abstracted into three base designs:

- *Monolithic*—This hybridization design incorporates aspects of several recommendation strategies in one algorithm implementation. Several recommenders contribute virtually because the hybrid uses additional input data that is specific to another recommendation algorithm, or the input data is augmented by one technique and factually exploited by another. Feature combination and feature augmentation strategies can be assigned to this category. *Feature combination* uses a diverse range of input data. It can combine collaborative features, such as a user's likes and dislikes, with content features of catalog items. *Feature augmentation* applies complex transformation steps. The output of a contributing recommender system augments the feature space of the actual recommender by preprocessing its knowledge sources. See figure 7.17 a.

- *Parallelized*—This approach requires at least two separate recommender implementations, which are subsequently combined (see figure 7.17 b). Parallelized hybrid recommender systems operate independently of one another and produce separate recommendation lists. In a subsequent hybridization step, their output is combined into a final set of recommendations. Following Burke's taxonomy, the weighted, mixed, and switching strategies require recommendation components to work in parallel.

- *Pipelined*—In this case, several recommender systems are joined in a pipeline architecture (see figure 7.17 c). The output of one recommender becomes part of the input of the subsequent one. Optionally, the subsequent recommender components may use parts of the original input data, too. The cascade and meta-level hybrids, as defined by Burke, are examples of such architectures.

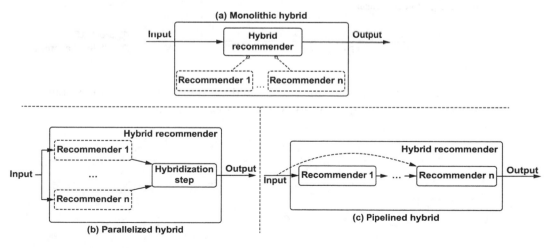

Figure 7.17 Hybridization design techniques

In this chapter, we will focus on the parallelized hybridization technique, which allows multiple recommender systems to operate in parallel, each using its own input and producing its own output model. The resulting models have to be stored somewhere so that they can be accessed and mixed or merged easily during the recommendation phase. In this context, graphs provide

- A suitable representation for storing in a single, homogeneous, and connected data source all the different sets of information required by each recommender
- A model for storing the results of the training process so that they can be queried easily in parallel and then merged according to the hybridization strategy

7.2.1 *Multiple models, single graph*

Let's take a closer look at the parallelized hybrid approach (figure 7.18). Suppose that you have two types of recommender systems to be hybridized: one content-based, like the ones described in chapter 4, and one collaborative, like those described in chapter 5. This scenario is a common one: it's often useful to merge these types of recommender systems because each can solve the issues of the other. The content-based approach mitigates the cold-start problem that occurs when data is missing, such as in the case of a new user, item, or new platform, whereas the collaborative filtering approach provides more accurate results and also works without information or metadata about users and items.

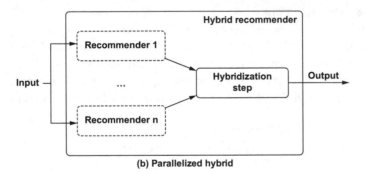

Figure 7.18
Parallelized approach

The graph used as input for the parallelized hybrid recommendation system that uses these two types of recommenders as input looks like figure 7.19.

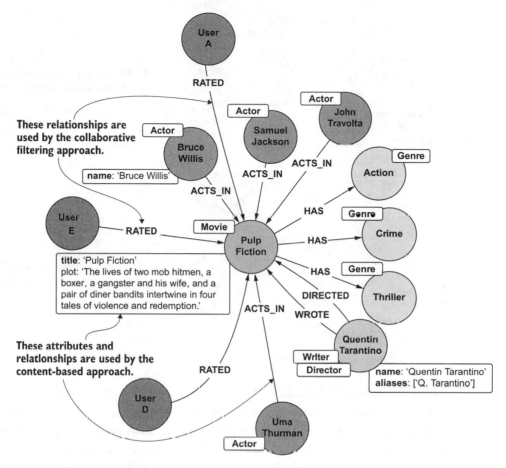

Figure 7.19 Example graph model that combines collaborative filtering and content-based approaches

In this case, it is important to note how the rated connection is used by both recommender systems in different ways. In the collaborative-filtering approach, it is used for creating the User-Item dataset; in the content-based approach, it is used for accessing the features of interest for the user. When the models are computed, they can be stored back in the graph, as depicted in figure 7.20.

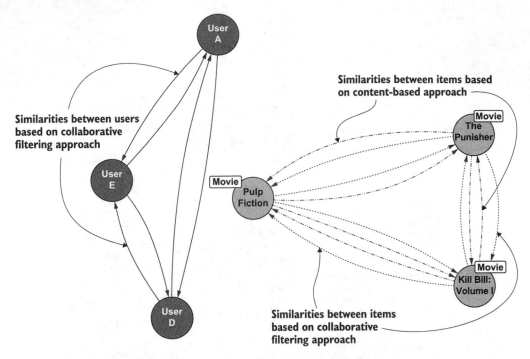

Figure 7.20   Mixing multiple recommendation models in the same graph

7.2.2   *Providing recommendations*

Now that we've built the models and stored them in the graph, we can combine their outputs to obtain a unique list (or sometimes multiple lists) of items to recommend to the user. As described earlier, parallelized hybridization designs employ several recommenders side by side and use a specific hybridization mechanism to aggregate their outputs. The hybridization mechanism defines the strategy to provide recommendations to the user. According to Burke's [2002] classification, three main strategies can be applied: mixed, weighted, and switching. Additional combination strategies for multiple recommendation lists, such as majority voting schemes, may also be applicable.

MIXED

The *mixed* hybridization strategy combines the results of different recommender systems at the level of the user interface. Results from different techniques are presented together; therefore, the recommendation result for user *u* is a set of lists of items.

The top-scoring items for each recommender are displayed to the user next to one another, generally specifying to the user the criteria for each item. Sometimes in the mixed approach, some type of conflict resolution is necessary to prevent too many overlaps in the multiple lists.

WEIGHTED

A *weighted* hybridization strategy combines the recommendations of two or more recommender systems by computing weighted sums of their scores. Figure 7.21 is a graphical model showing how it works.

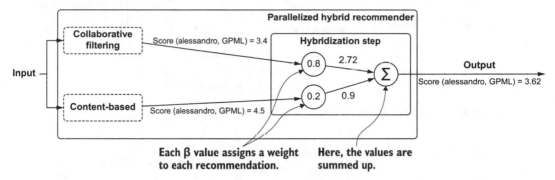

Figure 7.21 Weighted method explained with graphical model

Thus, given n different recommendation functions $score_k(u, i)$ with associated relative weights β_k, the final score will be computed according to the formula

$$score_{weighted}(u,i) = \sum_{k=1}^{n} b_k \times score_k(u,i)$$

where n is the number of recommenders whose outputs have to be mixed. Furthermore, the item scores need to be restricted to the same range for all recommenders, and the sum of all β_k must be 1. This technique is straightforward and thus is a popular strategy for combining the predictive power of different recommendation techniques in a weighted manner.

It is worth noting that the value of β_k can be dynamic, changing over the life of the recommendation system, privileging (for example) the content-based approach over collaborative filtering in the early stages when not enough information is available for the latter to be effective and then gradually giving it more weight when more data has been gathered. Moreover, the values can be dynamic per user, assigning a higher value of β_k to the content-based recommendations until the system has acquired enough data for the collaborative filtering approach to be effective. Different techniques can be applied to evaluate how to set and then evolve the values of the weights.

SWITCHING

Switching hybrids require an oracle that decides which recommender should be used in a specific situation, depending on the user profile and/or the quality of recommendation results. Figure 7.22 is a graphical model describing how it works.

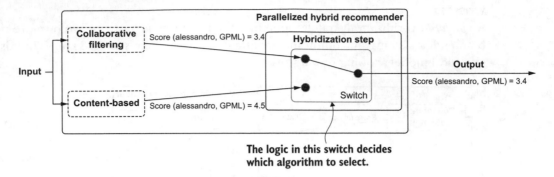

Figure 7.22   Switching method explained by a graphical model

Such an evaluation could be carried out as follows,

$$score_{switching}(u,i) = score_k(u,i)$$

where k is determined by the switching condition. To overcome the cold-start problem, a content-based and collaborative switching hybrid could initially make content-based recommendations until enough rating data is available. When the collaborative filtering component can deliver recommendations with sufficient confidence, the recommendation strategy could be switched. In an extreme case, dynamic weight adjustment could be implemented as a switching hybrid. The weights of all but one dynamically selected recommender are set to 0, and the output of the single remaining recommender is assigned a weight of 1.

7.2.3   *Advantages of the graph approach*

In this section, we've discussed how to create a hybrid recommendation engine, focusing on parallelized hybridization approaches: mixed, weighted, and switching. All the methods presented here can take advantage of a graph representation of the data, both for training and in the resulting models. The main aspects and advantages of the graph-based approach to hybrid methods are

- Various sets of information can coexist in the same data structure, making it easier to meet the data management needs of a hybrid recommender.
- The independent models resulting from each recommender can be stored together and then accessed easily during the recommendation phase.

Summary

This chapter presented the latest advanced techniques for implementing recommendation engines using contextual information and showed how to combine different approaches for greater effect. The various data models illustrate the usefulness and flexibility of graphs for satisfying different requirements in terms of training data and model storage. In this chapter, you learned

- How to improve the quality of the recommendations by embedding contextual information in the model and the related graph model
- How to use the graph to feed the context-aware design approaches: pre-/ postfiltering and contextual modeling
- How to combine multiple algorithms in a single recommendation engine
- How to mix different training datasets and models in a single big graph

References

[Adomavicius and Tuzhilin, 2005] Adomavicius, Gediminus, and Alexander Tuzhilin. "Toward the Next Generation of Recommender Systems: A Survey of the State-of-the-Art and Possible Extensions." *IEEE Transactions on Knowledge and Data Engineering* 17(6): 734–749.

[Bazire and Brézillon, 2005] Bazire, Mary, and Patrick Brézillon. "Understanding Context Before Using It." *Proceedings of the 5th International and Interdisciplinary Conference on Modeling and Using Context* (2005): 29–40.

[Burke, 2002] Burke, Robin. "Hybrid Recommender Systems: Survey and Experiments." *User Modeling and User-Adapted Interaction* 12:4 (2002): 331–370.

[Doerfel et al., 2016] Doerfel, Stephan, Robert Jäschke, and Gerd Stumme. "The Role of Cores in Recommender Benchmarking for Social Bookmarking Systems." *ACM Transactions on Intelligent Systems and Technology* 7:3 (2016): Article 40.

[Frolov and Oseledets, 2016] Frolov, Evgeny, and Ivan Oseledets. "Tensor Methods and Recommender Systems." arXiv preprint arXiv:1603.06038 (2016).

[Ilarri et al., 2018] Ilarri, Sergio, Raquel Trillo-Lado, and Ramon Hermoso. "Datasets for Context-Aware Recommender Systems: Current Context and Possible Directions." *Proceedings of the IEEE 34th International Conference on Data Engineering Workshops* (2018).

[Palmisano et al., 2008] Palmisano, Cosimo, Alexander Tuzhilin, and Michele Gorgoglione. "Using Context to Improve Predictive Modeling of Customers in Personalization Applications." *IEEE Transactions on Knowledge and Data Engineering* 20:11 (2008): 1535–1549.

[Panniello et al., 2009] Panniello, Umberto, Alexander Tuzhilin, Michele Gorgoglione, Cosimo Palmisano, and Anto Pedone. "Experimental Comparison of Pre- vs. Post-Filtering Approaches in Context-Aware Recommender Systems." *Proceedings of the 3rd ACM Conference on Recommender Systems* (2009): 265–268.

[Suchman, 1987] Suchman, Lucy. *Plans and Situated Actions.* Cambridge, UK: Cambridge University Press, 1987.

[Wu et al., 2015] Wu, Hao, Kun Yue, Xiaoxin Liu, Yijian Pei, and Bo Li. "Context-Aware Recommendation via Graph-Based Contextual Modeling and Postfiltering." *International Journal of Distributed Sensor Networks* – Special Issue on Big Data and Knowledge Extraction for Cyber-Physical Systems (2015): Article 16.

[Zheng et al., 2015] Zheng, Yong, Bamshad Mobasher, and Robin Burke, "CARSKit: A Java-Based Context-Aware Recommendation Engine." *Proceedings of the 15th IEEE International Conference on Data Mining (ICDM) Workshops* (2015): 1668–1671.

Part 3

Fighting fraud

Fraud is as old as humanity itself and can take an unlimited variety of forms. According to PwC's 2020 Global Economic Crime and Fraud Survey (http://mng.bz/l2ny), 47% of global organizations have been the victim of a fraud (and many of the remaining 53% may have been without realizing it, so the number is almost certainly higher) for a total estimated loss of $42 billion. The European Central Bank reports (http://mng.bz/BK8J) that the total value of fraudulent card transactions annually amounts to €1.8 billion ($2 billion).

Fighting fraud, and more generally detecting anomalies in data, is a vital task that has enormous impact in multiple areas, such as finance, security, healthcare, and law enforcement. It has gained a lot of interest recently among machine learning practitioners. Whereas before, companies in most domains used a mix of human-based and fixed rules–based analysis, fraud detection is becoming more of an automated process, with machine learning playing a key role.

The second part of the book focused on a specific machine learning task: recommendations. The main goals of such a task are to gather data about user preferences, expressed implicitly or explicitly; create one or multiple models; and perform predictions to increase user satisfaction and business revenue. As we have seen, different techniques and approaches are available, but all of them have users as their target—that is, suggesting to them something that might be of interest. This focus on end users creates some constraints on how recommendation platforms are created and how the related infrastructure is defined, as well as on the types of algorithms to use. Considerations such as taking into account real-time, up-to-date preferences, prediction accuracy, and reduced impact on user experience drive the decision process at each step of the CRISP-DM process model. We have explored many of these constraints, specifically, discovering how graphs play a key role in solving some of the main challenges in such tasks.

Fighting fraud starts from a different perspective. It has different goals, and the analysis takes different approaches. One of the main differences between the analytic platforms for fighting fraud and the ones for recommendations has to do with the ultimate stakeholders. In the recommendations use case, the targets are the end users: the ones navigating the retail site or hotel booking site. In the fraud-fighting use case, the real stakeholders are the company's analysts, who have to spot issues in the fastest way possible and identify patterns to prevent the same frauds being perpetrated again.

Some of the techniques for fraud detection discussed in this part of the book (in particular in chapters 8 and 9) are borrowed from the more generic field of anomaly or outlier detection. An anomaly or outlier, in this context, refers to a data point that is significantly different from the others. In the context of fraud, we will see what this looks like for behaviors (such as transactions) that diverge from an individual's usual behavior, which can be an indicator of fraudulent activity. Rather than reasoning in generic terms, we will solve specific problems. Nonetheless, the approaches, algorithms, and methods described in these chapters can be applied in broader scenarios. In addition to revealing suspicious or abnormal behavior in financial contexts, anomaly detection is vital for spotting rare events such as rare disease outbreaks or side effects in the medical domain, with vital applications in medical diagnosis. Another application of anomaly detection is data cleansing, or the removal of erroneous values or noise from data as a preprocessing step to enable learning more accurate models of the data.

Chapter 10 takes a different approach to fraud detection, using social network analysis techniques to analyze how fraud affects people's behavior and how fraudsters could use other people in a social network to pursue their fraudulent goals.

Basic approaches to graph-powered fraud detection

This chapter covers

- An introduction to types of fraud in different domains
- The role of graphs in modeling data to reveal frauds faster and more easily
- Using a simple graph model to fight fraud

According to Van Vlasselaer et al. [2017]:

> *Fraud is an uncommon, well-considered, time-evolving, carefully organized and imperceptibly concealed crime that appears in many different types and forms.*

This definition highlights six characteristics of fraud that are associated with the challenges related to developing a fraud detection system:

- *Uncommon*—In almost all types of fraud and across domains, only a minimal portion of the data available is related to (or recognized to be related to) fraud. Detecting fraud is hard, and so is learning from historical cases (during the training phase).
- *Well-considered*—Frauds are planned with careful consideration; they don't just happen.
- *Carefully organized*—Frauds are generally well-organized crimes. Fraudsters often operate in large teams with well-defined roles. Moreover, some types of fraud, such as money laundering, involve complex structures that can take years to put in place.
- *Imperceptibly concealed*—Fraudsters spend a lot of effort hiding the fraud itself and applying techniques to make its recognition difficult.
- *Appears in many types and forms*—Fraudsters employ a wide range of techniques and approaches in a variety of domains. Many economic activities are susceptible to fraud.
- *Time-evolving*—The techniques fraudsters use evolve over time in response to the fraud detection methods applied to fight them, with parties on each side trying to stay one step ahead of their adversaries. New detection methods are constantly required to address new types of fraud.

For these reasons, fighting fraud is a challenging task for machine learning practitioners, but at the same time, it is fascinating. These considerations also mean that the techniques, constraints, and algorithms presented in this part have many differentiating aspects compared with those presented in part 2.

Why include the topic of fraud detection in a book on graphs? Akoglu et al. [2014] argue that graphs are "vital and necessary" for anomaly detection, for the following reasons:

- *Interdependent nature of the data*—Data objects are often related and exhibit dependencies. There are strong relationships among data instances in a huge variety of datasets and scenarios, including biological data such as protein-protein interaction networks, financial data such as credit card transactions, retail networks, and social networks.
- *Powerful representation*—Graphs naturally represent the interdependencies among related objects (nodes) through relationships (links or edges) that capture long-range correlations. Moreover, a graph representation lends itself to the representation of rich datasets by allowing the incorporation of node and edge attributes or types.
- *Relational nature of problem domains*—Anomalies are often relational in nature. Frauds are often perpetrated by a related group of subjects working in close collaboration. Another example, not related to fraud, can be found in the system-monitoring domain: the failure of one machine could cause other machines that depend on it to malfunction, or serve as an indicator of increased probability of the failure of other machines in close physical proximity because of environmental conditions.

- *Robust machinery*—Graphs are adversarially robust because they can provide a global view of the entire network. Fraudsters or other adversaries may be able to alter or fake certain behavioral clues, such as login times or IP addresses, but they likely won't be able to remove or conceal all the signs that graphs reveal about connections in the data. When the data is organized in graph structures, it is easier to inspect and navigate.

In the context of combating fraud, graph visualization can play critical roles in fraud detection and fraud investigation. The more autonomous transactional systems are, the harder it is to reveal fraud, which is where graph visualization comes in. It offers experts the opportunity to visualize and evaluate single transactions or many transactions through a quick view, allowing them to discover suspicious behaviors and investigate them further.

8.1 Fraud prevention and detection

Fighting fraud has some peculiarities that vary according to the domain, including the type of data, the dimensionality and variety of the data, and the final goals of the fraudsters. Nevertheless, it is possible to identify two main components that are essential parts of any effective strategy to fight fraud [Bolton and Hand, 2002]:

- *Fraud prevention* refers to measures that can be taken to prevent or reduce fraud, such as the use of fluorescent fibers, laminated metal strips, and holographs on bank notes; personal identification numbers for bank cards; internet security systems for credit card transactions; SIM cards and fingerprint sensors for mobile phones; and passwords for computer systems and telephone banking accounts. Each of these methods has drawbacks in terms of vulnerability, effectiveness, cost, and/or inconvenience for customers. A trade-off between pros and cons needs to be found.
- *Fraud detection* refers to the ability to recognize or discover fraud. It comes into play when fraud prevention has failed, but because it's not always obvious when that happens, fraud detection measures must be used all the time. We can do our best to prevent credit card fraud, but if a card's details are stolen, we need to be able to detect fraudulent use as soon as possible.

It is worth noting that preventive actions to fight fraud will cause fraudsters to adapt the strategies they use, which in turn will affect the effectiveness of the strategies used to detect fraud. The types of frauds that are perpetrated are dynamic, and so should be the fraud reduction systems in place. Although complementary, fraud detection and prevention have to be considered as a whole, not as independent and unrelated systems.

Surprisingly, one of the most common approaches to fraud detection is the classic expert-based approach, which relies on the experience, domain knowledge, intuition, and personal skills of the fraud analyst. These approaches are almost fully manual and human-based. The experts perform manual investigations of suspicious cases, generally signaled by other humans (such as customers complaining about being charged for transactions they did not initiate).

The result of this analysis can be the discovery of a new fraud mechanism being used by fraudsters. When such a mechanism is discovered, it is further analyzed and investigated to extend the existing fraud detection and prevention mechanism, which is often implemented by a rule-based engine. This engine consists of a set of rules, generally in the form of `if-then` statements, that are applied to every transaction or set of transactions that take place and trigger an alert or signal when they are matched. Figure 8.1 presents a mental model of this approach.

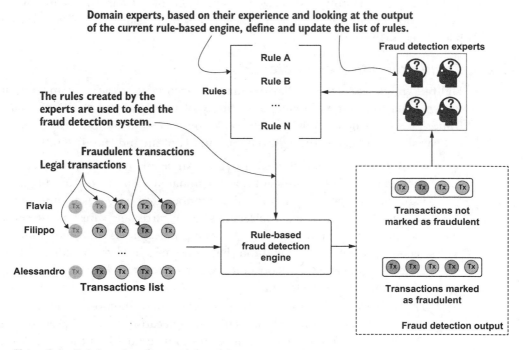

Figure 8.1   Rule-based engine mental model

A simple but effective set of rules for credit card fraud detection can be defined as follows:[1]

If

- The previous transaction was less than $15
- The previous transaction happened less than 2 hours ago
- The current transaction is more than $500

Then

- Set status to `declined`
- Set notification to a `large amount after a small transaction`

---

[1] Inspired by http://mng.bz/dmYQ.

This expert-based approach, even though it is useful and still common in many domains, suffers from several disadvantages:

- Rule-based engines are typically complex and therefore expensive to build because they require advanced manual input by fraud experts.
- This complexity makes them difficult to maintain and manage.
- Rules must be kept up to date because fraudsters are continually evolving their approaches and coming up with new ones. As soon as they discover the rules behind the fraud reduction system, they change their behavior to avoid being recognized.
- In most cases, these systems require further human follow-up, analysis, and investigation.

The biggest drawback of this approach is that because it involves a lot of human intervention for expert input, analysis, evaluation, and monitoring, it relies too much on individual contributions that are hard to share and maintain. The effectiveness of the fraud detection system is related to the availability of particular people with specific knowledge. So what happens when they go on holiday or retire?

In recent years, a shift has been taking place toward a data-driven, statistical, and machine learning–based fraud detection methodology. An automated approach is preferable to a pure human-based approach, for the following reasons as well as the ones mentioned previously [Van Vlasselaer et al., 2017]:

- *Precision*—An autonomous system can process massive volumes of data, uncovering fraud patterns that would be impossible for a human to recognize.
- *Operational efficiency*—Think about how many transactions a credit card issuer has to process every day, minute, and second. It would be impossible to have all transactions checked in real time by humans in the time constraints required by normal operation, but computers can handle this task easily. Furthermore, a machine-based approach can support the human-based approach by prefiltering, analyzing each transaction/operation and then sending only the most relevant or suspicious to a human for further investigation.
- *Cost efficiency*—As mentioned before, expert-based fraud detection systems are hard to implement and to maintain. A more automated, data-driven, and thus efficient approach is preferred.
- *Adaptation efficiency*—Some of the autonomous data-driven approaches are unsupervised (and will be highlighted in these chapters). This aspect allows them not only to be operationally and cost efficient, but also to adapt over time to the evolving characteristics of the frauds perpetrated and the fraudsters' behaviors.

To better illustrate the basic ideas behind fraud detection, let's consider a simple example from Fawcett and Provost [1997], illustrated in table 8.1.

Table 8.1   Example of anomaly detection for telecommunication

Call sequence	Date and time	Day	Duration	Origin	Destination	Fraud
1	2019-01-01 10:05:01	Mon	13 mins	Brooklyn, NY	Stamford, CT	
2	2019-01-05 14:53:10	Fri	5 mins	Brooklyn, NY	Greenwich, CT	
3	2019-01-08 09:42:15	Mon	3 mins	Bronx, NY	White Plains, NY	
4	2019-01-08 15:01:34	Mon	9 mins	Brooklyn, NY	Brooklyn, NY	
5	2019-01-09 15:06:54	Tue	5 mins	Manhattan, NY	Stamford, CT	
6	2019-01-09 16:28:20	Tue	53 sec	Brooklyn, NY	Brooklyn, NY	
7	2019-01-10 01:45:29	Wed	35 sec	Boston, MA	Chelsea, MA	True
8	2019-01-10 01:46:35	Wed	34 sec	Boston, MA	Yonkers, NY	True
9	2019-01-10 01:50:54	Wed	39 sec	Boston, MA	Chelsea, MA	True
10	2019-01-10 11:23:20	Wed	24 sec	White Plains, NY	Congers, NY	
11	2019-01-11 22:00:58	Thu	37 sec	Boston, MA	East Boston, MA	True
12	2019-01-11 22:04:00	Thu	37 sec	Boston, MA	East Boston, MA	True

The fraudulent calls are marked as fraud. They have been signaled by the customer, who complained about such calls because they didn't make them.

If you look at the table carefully, you'll notice that these calls have some characteristics that differentiate them from calls made by the real owners of the numbers. In particular, they are shorter, they happen during the night, and the source and destination are anomalous. An anomaly detection–based approach to fraud detection has great value here, especially compared with the expert systems techniques (the manual approach): it allows automatic detection of a significant fraction of fraudulent cases because those cases differ from the normal behavior evident from the historical examples.

One of the biggest challenges related to fraud detection is data management. The issues have been mentioned several times in the book in relation to big data; they include volume, velocity, variety, and veracity. Recall the diagram used in the first part of the book, repeated here in figure 8.2.

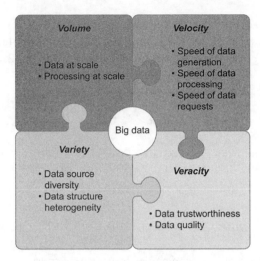

Figure 8.2 The four Vs of big data also apply in the context of fraud detection.

In this case, there are a few more challenges to handle, such as streaming data and data complexity. The datasets used as input for the fraud detection process are rich and complex in content, including user demographics, interests, and roles, as well as types of relationships. Incorporating these additional information sources makes data representation complex. As a result, methods that can scale to large datasets, update their estimations as the data changes over time, and effectively incorporate all the available and useful data sources are essential for anomaly detection.

Graph data models and analysis provide a set of valuable tools for dealing with such complexity. The schema flexibility allows data from a variety of data sources to be stored and provides multiple access patterns that scale quite easily even when the datasets are large. Graph-aided or -based algorithms make it easier to spot, analyze, and investigate relationships between events. The advantages provided by graphs in the context of fraud detection are highlighted in section 8.2 and explored further in the remainder of this chapter and in chapters 9 and 10.

Because fighting fraud is like any battle in which all the parties try to use any possible technique at their disposal to get ahead, analysts have to use all the tools available to them. It's important to recognize that these techniques are not mutually exclusive: they can be combined in an overarching system to reach the goal more easily, quickly, and effectively.

8.2 *The role of graphs in fighting fraud*

Graphs provide a powerful modeling and analysis tool for capturing long-range correlations among interdependent data objects, which makes them well suited to the fraud-fighting scenario. Our bank account and credit card transactions follow a logic related to what we do, where we live, what we like to buy, and so on. Moreover, fraud rarely happens in isolation: behind any fraud is a plan that involves preparation, which often requires cooperation among multiple fraudsters.

To better understand the value provided by graphs in terms of representation of the data (and, as we will see later, in terms of analysis), let's consider a simple example. Take a look at the transactional data source of a credit card fraud system in table 8.2.

Table 8.2   Example of credit card transaction data

Credit card	Merchant	Merchant category	Country	Amount	Date	Accept	Fraud
77777783427	207005	Clothes Shop	USA	120.00$	2019-01-11 00:12:01	TRUE	FALSE
47559798454	105930	Gas Station	ITA	50.00€	2019-03-12 08:01:30	TRUE	FALSE
25548837225	105930	Gas Station	ITA	20.56€	2019-04-23 10:10:20	TRUE	FALSE
18560530742	11525	Restaurant	BEL	50.00€	2019-05-01 15:00:12	TRUE	FALSE
37960598819	323158	Online Shop	USA	300.00$	2019-05-02 01:00:00	TRUE	TRUE
16307358365	11525	Restaurant	BEL	40.00€	2019-05-03 20:45:00	TRUE	FALSE

In this table, each line represents a money transfer between two actors: a credit cardholder and a merchant. The fifth transaction has been marked as fraudulent in the rightmost column because the card owner complained about it.

In this representation, with the data stored as a list of rows, the relationships between credit cardholders and merchants are hard to capture. Real-life data sources contain billions of transactions, making it impossible to extract correlations and useful insights manually. A possible representation of such data in a graph model is shown in figure 8.3.

In this graph, circles represent credit cards, and squares represent merchants. The relationships connecting the credit cards with the merchants represent the transactions. A bold line represents the fraudulent transactions. In this representation, it is evident that credit card Y has been stolen and that merchant 1 is acting suspiciously (processing a large number of fraudulent transactions). This trivial example shows clearly how graphs offer a powerful tool to make information that's hidden and hard to recognize in the original format more evident and easier to interpret and understand. Inspecting the visual representation of a graph can be a valuable part of the preprocessing phase: it familiarizes the analysts with the data and can quickly result in initial findings and insights. Moreover, the data is simple to query and analyze; we will see concrete examples in section 8.3. Then, during the postprocessing phase, graphs can provide a useful representation for verifying the obtained results and understanding the rationale behind them.

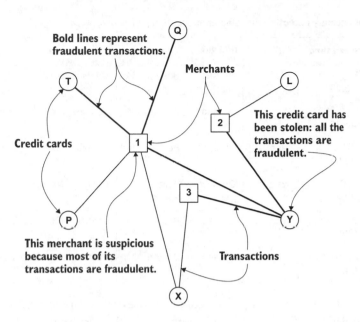

Figure 8.3 Graph representation of the credit card transactional data

These approaches are presented in section 8.3. The idea is to highlight how useful and flexible the graph representation can be; a single simple representation can serve different purposes.

The previous example is one possible way to convert data—specifically, transactional data to a graph model. A diametrically opposite approach consists of representing each transaction as a node and connecting the nodes according to some logic. The most common approach is based on similarity. The following example makes this approach clearer. Consider the call data we saw earlier, presented again in table 8.3.

Table 8.3 Example of anomaly detection for telecommunication

Call sequence	Date and time	Day	Duration	Origin	Destination	Fraud
1	2019-01-01 10:05:01	Mon	13 mins	Brooklyn, NY	Stamford, CT	False
2	2019-01-05 14:53:10	Fri	5 mins	Brooklyn, NY	Greenwich, CT	False
3	2019-01-08 09:42:15	Mon	3 mins	Bronx, NY	White Plains, NY	False
4	2019-01-08 15:01:34	Mon	9 mins	Brooklyn, NY	Brooklyn, NY	False
5	2019-01-09 15:06:54	Tue	5 mins	Manhattan, NY	Stamford, CT	False
6	2019-01-09 16:28:20	Tue	53 sec	Brooklyn, NY	Brooklyn, NY	False

Table 8.3 Example of anomaly detection for telecommunication *(continued)*

Call sequence	Date and time	Day	Duration	Origin	Destination	Fraud
7	2019-01-10 01:45:29	Wed	35 sec	Boston, MA	Chelsea, MA	True
8	2019-01-10 01:46:35	Wed	34 sec	Boston, MA	Yonkers, NY	True
9	2019-01-10 01:50:54	Wed	39 sec	Boston, MA	Chelsea, MA	True
10	2019-01-10 11:23:20	Wed	24 sec	White Plains, NY	Congers, NY	False
11	2019-01-11 22:00:58	Thu	37 sec	Boston, MA	East Boston, MA	True
12	2019-01-11 22:04:00	Thu	37 sec	Boston, MA	East Boston, MA	True

Using the graph construction techniques discussed in previous chapters, it is possible to convert such tabular data to a graph representation. In the resulting graph model, shown in figure 8.4, each call is represented as a node, and all the details are shown as related properties.

Using the properties and the related values, we can represent each node as a vector. Table 8.4 shows the process in detail.

Table 8.4 Sample table to convert the calls data to vectors

Sequence	Day of the week					Duration (minutes)			Origin (city/area)				
	Mon	Tue	Wed	Thu	Fri	[0, 1)	[1, 5)	>=5	Brook.	Bronx	Manhat.	Boston	W. P.
1	1	0	0	0	0	0	0	1	1	0	0	0	0
2	0	0	0	0	1	0	0	1	1	0	0	0	0
3	1	0	0	0	0	0	1	0	0	1	0	0	0
4	1	0	0	0	0	0	0	1	1	0	0	0	0
5	0	1	0	0	0	0	0	1	0	0	1	0	0
6	0	1	0	0	0	1	0	0	1	0	0	0	0
7	0	0	1	0	0	1	0	0	0	0	0	1	0
8	0	0	1	0	0	1	0	0	0	0	0	1	0
9	0	0	1	0	0	1	0	0	0	0	0	1	0
10	0	0	1	0	0	1	0	0	0	0	0	0	1
11	0	0	0	1	0	1	0	0	0	0	0	1	0
12	0	0	0	1	0	1	0	0	0	0	0	1	0

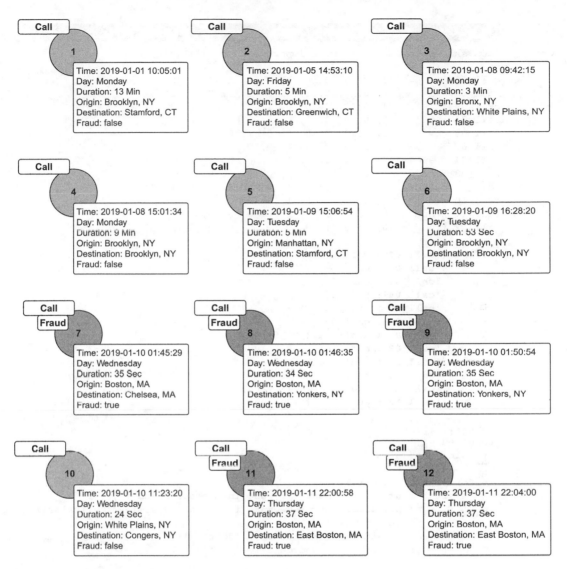

Figure 8.4 A first graph created from the data in table 8.3

Each property (each column of the original table) has been decomposed into the possible values, as we did for text to produce content-based recommendations. For the scalar properties (the duration, in this case), we have defined multiple ranges. This vector representation of each node is used to compute similarities, such as by using cosine similarity. The following listing shows how to do computation by using scikit-learn.

Listing 8.1   Code for computing similarities between the vectors

```python
from sklearn.metrics.pairwise import cosine_similarity

call_01 =        [1, 0, 0, 0, 0, 0, 0, 1, 1, 0, 0, 0, 0]
call_02 =        [0, 0, 0, 0, 1, 0, 0, 1, 1, 0, 0, 0, 0]
call_03 =        [1, 0, 0, 0, 0, 0, 1, 0, 0, 1, 0, 0, 0]
call_04 =        [1, 0, 0, 0, 0, 0, 0, 1, 1, 0, 0, 0, 0]
call_05 =        [0, 1, 0, 0, 0, 0, 0, 1, 0, 0, 1, 0, 0]
call_06 =        [0, 1, 0, 0, 0, 1, 0, 0, 1, 0, 0, 0, 0]
call_07_fraud = [0, 0, 1, 0, 0, 1, 0, 0, 0, 0, 0, 1, 0]
call_08_fraud = [0, 0, 1, 0, 0, 1, 0, 0, 0, 0, 0, 1, 0]
call_09_fraud = [0, 0, 1, 0, 0, 1, 0, 0, 0, 0, 0, 1, 0]
call_10 =        [0, 0, 1, 0, 0, 1, 0, 0, 0, 0, 0, 0, 1]
call_11_fraud = [0, 0, 0, 1, 0, 1, 0, 0, 0, 0, 0, 1, 0]
call_12_fraud = [0, 0, 0, 1, 0, 1, 0, 0, 0, 0, 0, 1, 0]

calls = {'call_01': call_01,
         'call_02': call_02,
         'call_03': call_03,
         'call_04': call_04,
         'call_05': call_05,
         'call_06': call_06,
         'call_07_fraud': call_07_fraud,
         'call_08_fraud': call_08_fraud,
         'call_09_fraud': call_09_fraud,
         'call_10': call_10,
         'call_11_fraud': call_11_fraud,
         'call_12_fraud': call_12_fraud}

print("....")
processed = []
for i in list(calls):

    for j in list(calls):
        if {'source': j, 'dest': i} not in processed and i != j:
            print("similarity between", i, j, cosine_similarity([calls[i]],
            ➥ [calls[j]]))
            processed += [{'source': j, 'dest': i}]
            processed += [{'source': i, 'dest': j}]
```

The output is shown in the following listing, with trailing zeros removed for brevity.

Listing 8.2   Output of listing 8.1

```
similarity between call_01 call_02 [[0.66666667]]
similarity between call_01 call_03 [[0.33333333]]
similarity between call_01 call_04 [[1.]]
similarity between call_01 call_05 [[0.33333333]]
similarity between call_01 call_06 [[0.33333333]]
similarity between call_02 call_04 [[0.66666667]]
similarity between call_02 call_05 [[0.33333333]]
similarity between call_02 call_06 [[0.33333333]]
similarity between call_03 call_04 [[0.33333333]]
```

```
similarity between call_04 call_05 [[0.33333333]]
similarity between call_04 call_06 [[0.33333333]]
similarity between call_05 call_06 [[0.33333333]]
similarity between call_06 call_07_fraud [[0.33333333]]
similarity between call_06 call_08_fraud [[0.33333333]]
similarity between call_06 call_09_fraud [[0.33333333]]
similarity between call_06 call_10 [[0.33333333]]
similarity between call_06 call_11_fraud [[0.33333333]]
similarity between call_06 call_12_fraud [[0.33333333]]
similarity between call_07_fraud call_08_fraud [[1.]]
similarity between call_07_fraud call_09_fraud [[1.]]
similarity between call_07_fraud call_10 [[0.66666667]]
similarity between call_07_fraud call_11_fraud [[0.66666667]]
similarity between call_07_fraud call_12_fraud [[0.66666667]]
similarity between call_08_fraud call_09_fraud [[1.]]
similarity between call_08_fraud call_10 [[0.66666667]]
similarity between call_08_fraud call_11_fraud [[0.66666667]]
similarity between call_08_fraud call_12_fraud [[0.66666667]]
similarity between call_09_fraud call_10 [[0.66666667]]
similarity between call_09_fraud call_11_fraud [[0.66666667]]
similarity between call_09_fraud call_12_fraud [[0.66666667]]
similarity between call_10 call_11_fraud [[0.33333333]]
similarity between call_10 call_12_fraud [[0.33333333]]
similarity between call_11_fraud call_12_fraud [[1.]]
```

Figure 8.5 shows the result if we define a threshold for similarity of 0.5 and store the relationships in the previous graph.

Looking at the distances between nodes, we see that the fraudulent calls are closer to other fraudulent calls than they are to normal calls. At this point, it is possible to use graph clustering algorithms such as community detection to group fraudulent calls and then use such a model to classify new calls as fraudulent or not, considering their distance from the groups created by the classification model. These approaches, presented in more detail in section 8.3, are close to other k-NN approaches presented in previous chapters. This recurring "pattern" shows again that graph-based techniques—in this case, graph construction based on nearest neighbor methods—are generic and can serve different analytical purposes. You can apply this mental pattern whenever you have to analyze data with a structure similar to that of table 8.3.

Another essential question when performing fraud analytics is whether the detection model might benefit from complex network analysis on social networks [Baesens et al., 2015]. In other words, do the relationships between people play an important role in fraud, and is fraud a contagious effect in the network? Are fraudsters randomly spread over the social network, or do observable effects indicate that fraud is a social phenomenon? That is, do fraudsters tend to cluster together? As stated earlier, fraud is rarely perpetrated by a single individual; complex and advanced schemes require the collaboration of many people, and fraudsters commonly use their social networks (friends, colleagues, and so on) to commit frauds. Therefore, social network analysis can help spot a community or organization of fraudsters.

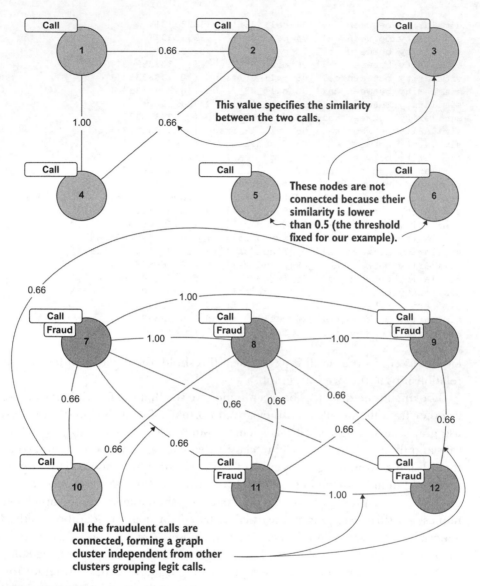

Figure 8.5   Graph of calls obtained via graph construction techniques

Fraudsters may be linked because they attend the same events/activities, are involved in the same crimes, use the same set of resources, or sometimes are the same person (in the case of identity theft), for example. Chapter 10 explores social network analysis as a supporting technique for fraud detection.

The concepts introduced here are a few of the possible ways to represent data as graphs to perform fraud detection. More advanced methods are presented in chapter 9.

8.3　*Warm-up: Basic approaches*

Let's start our war against fraud by considering a couple of approaches that are simple to understand and implement. Despite their simplicity, these techniques allow effective analysis in the cases mentioned and fit well in the graph space.

8.3.1　*Finding the origin point of credit card fraud*

Suppose that you would like to fight credit card fraud by identifying credit card thieves. This scenario is a classic one in fraud detection examples, especially in the graph space. In this case, the users (owners of credit cards) use their cards for several purchases, and at some point, their credit card details are stolen. The fraudsters use the stolen credentials to buy something or to transfer money between accounts. They typically test the card details by purchasing something with a low cost and then make a few big purchases before disappearing. The schema of this fraud is summarized in figure 8.6.

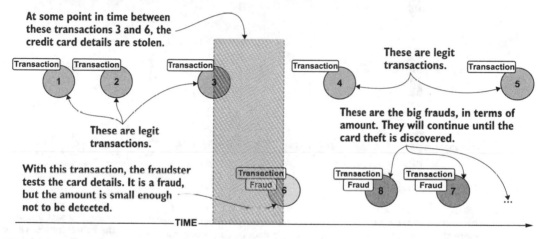

Figure 8.6　Credit card fraud schema

It's worth mentioning that the place where the credit card details are stolen can be a physical shop or an e-commerce site. In the latter case, a cyberattack commonly opens a breach, and all the credit card details of the registered users are copied.

The goal of this scenario is to identify in a sequence of transactions by multiple users the point where the credit card details were stolen. I took the inspiration for this approach and the one in section 8.3.2 from a couple of blog posts written by Max DeMarzi.[2] I like these ideas because they are effective and simple at the same time. Moreover, they show how by using the right graph data models, analyses that appear hard in traditional databases require a couple of queries on a graph. The examples in chapter 9 are more complex, but as this section's title suggests, the examples in this section will be helpful as a warm-up.

---

[2] See http://mng.bz/rmMX and http://mng.bz/VG65.

By considering only a specific user and their transactions, it would be hard to spot the point where the thieves acted. That transaction was accepted and valid; the issues (the fraudulent transactions) happen afterward. Luckily, if we consider the sequence of transactions by a lot of users, we can identify commonalities—shops or e-commerce sites—and start a deeper investigation. Figure 8.7 illustrates this concept.

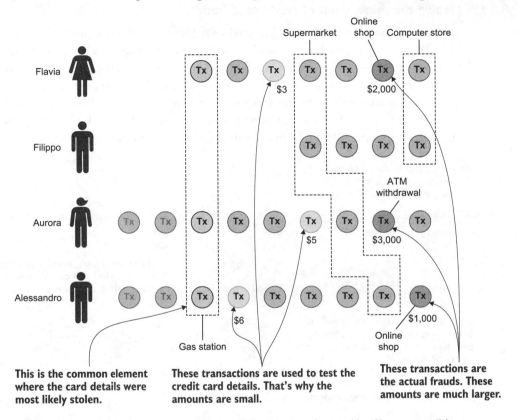

Figure 8.7   Combining data from multiple credit card transactions to identify commonalities

All the users who experienced issues with their credit cards used them at the same gas station. It is highly probable that the theft happened there. Moreover, it is clear that the cards were tested with small purchases to verify the details. Therefore, it is important to design a graph model that will make these facts evident and prompt further investigation.

How can we use a graph model to discover the transactions where the fraud originated? Let's start, as I always suggest in this book, with the available data, which may look something like table 8.5.

Table 8.5 Credit card transaction examples

Credit card	Merchant	Merchant category	Country	Amount	Date	Accept	Fraud
77777783427	207005	Clothes Shop	USA	120.00$	2019-01-11 00:12:01	TRUE	FALSE
47559798454	105930	Gas Station	ITA	50.00€	2019-03-12 08:01:30	TRUE	FALSE
25548837225	105930	Gas Station	ITA	20.56€	2019-04-23 10:10:20	TRUE	FALSE
18560530742	11525	Restaurant	BEL	50.00€	2019-05-01 15:00:12	TRUE	FALSE
37960598819	323158	Online Shop	USA	300.00$	2019-05-02 01:00:00	TRUE	TRUE
16307358365	11525	Restaurant	BEL	40.00€	2019-05-03 20:45:00	TRUE	FALSE

The data is a sample of transactions performed by the credit cardholders (enough to illustrate the concepts). The transactions are marked as fraudulent or not depending on whether the users complained about those purchases, so that information is available and accurate in most cases. The key elements that we would like to capture from the table for this specific scenario are

- The transactions made by the users, including details such as the amount and date
- The credit card identifier
- The identifier of the merchant where the purchase was made
- Information about the merchant type (not necessary but useful for simplifying our discussion)

A first attempt to design a graph model for this scenario is shown in figure 8.8.

The schema is definitely correct. What is missing is the order of the transactions for each user. As in figure 8.7, we need to consider the sequence of transactions, relating them to other users to find the point at which the credit card details were stolen. We can order the transactions by using the timestamp information, but that approach would make it hard to navigate them and find a common pattern. Hence, the next modeling step is to add a relationship between transactions to store the order between them explicitly. The extended model is shown in figure 8.9. This model considers the sequences of transactions for each user.

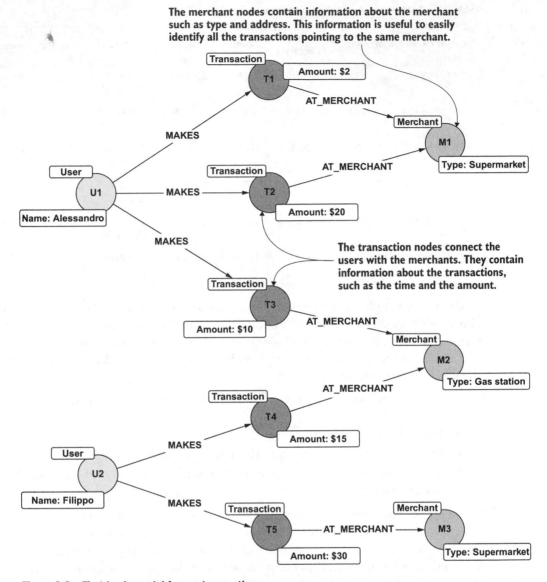

Figure 8.8   First basic model for our transactions

Now that we have our model, we can validate it by checking whether it can answer our question: where were the credit card details stolen? To follow along with this example, you'll need a sample dataset. In the code repository is a Cypher file (ch08/queries/ simple_fraud_dataset.cypher) containing a query to create a simple dataset that you can use for this purpose. In chapter 9, you will see how to create and import more complex datasets, but for the sake of simplicity, we'll start with a small one, finding all the complaints about fraudulent transactions made within the past week, and seeing

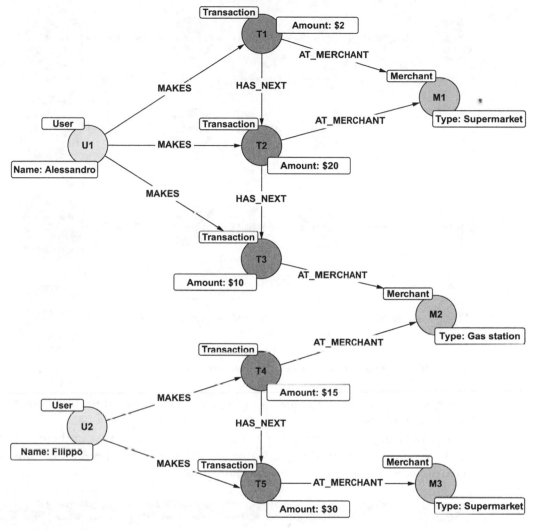

Figure 8.9 Extension of the basic model

which other transactions these users made within the past two weeks. We can use the HAS_NEXT relationship chain to go backward and find all the transactions.

```
MATCH p = (fraud:Fraudulent)<-[:HAS_NEXT*]-(tx:Transaction)
WHERE fraud.date > datetime() - duration('P7D') AND
NONE (tx IN nodes(p) WHERE COALESCE(tx.date, datetime()) <= datetime() -
⇒ duration('P14D'))
RETURN p
```

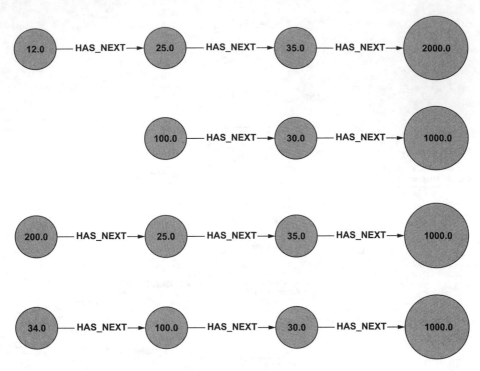

Figure 8.10   The biggest nodes are the fraudulent transactions.

This query shows only the sequences of transactions that lead up to a known fraud. The result looks like figure 8.10.[3]

The next step is identifying the common elements (patterns) in these sequences. To do so, we can extend the query a bit to find the stores where these transactions occurred and compute how often each store appears.

Listing 8.4   Top five common merchants in fraudulent transaction chains

```
MATCH p = (fraud:Fraudulent)<-[:HAS_NEXT*]->(tx)
WHERE fraud.date > datetime() - duration('P7D')
  AND NONE (tx IN nodes(p)
           WHERE COALESCE(tx.date, datetime()) <= datetime() -
➥ duration('P14D'))
WITH nodes(p) AS transactions
UNWIND transactions AS tx
WITH DISTINCT tx
MATCH (tx)-[:AT_MERCHANT]->(merchant)
RETURN merchant.name, COUNT(*) AS txCount
ORDER BY txCount DESC
LIMIT 5
```

---

[3] If you don't see the values in the Neo4j browser after the query, select the label Transaction below the query; then select amount as the attribute to visualize.

merchant.name	txCount
"Gas Station"	4
"Amazon"	4
"Supermarket"	2
"Jewelry Store"	2
"Toy Store"	1

Figure 8.11   Result of query 8.2

The result is shown in figure 8.11.

These results aren't bad, but they're not what we're looking for; some well-known online shops that everybody buys from appear in the list. We need to be careful: looking uncritically at these results, we might be tempted to say that the fraudsters are operating on Amazon, but because of that website's security measures, this is highly unlikely to be the case. Instead, we need to look at unusual common shops in the set of transactions we selected because they are more likely to be connected to the fraud.

We can take different approaches to achieve this goal. We could compare these results with the top merchants from the global list of transactions and mark as "not relevant" all the shops that appear at the top of both lists, for example. Instead, we will use a more sophisticated and interesting (as well as powerful) approach. We need to consider both sets of transactions:

- The global set containing data on all transactions, not only the transactions of people who were the victim of fraud. This dataset is our background set. We will get statistics about the occurrences of merchants in this set and use that information in our formula.

- The set of recent transactions by people complaining about a fraudulent charge. This dataset is our foreground set, representing our real target.

With these two sets in mind, our goal can be clearly stated as follows: find merchants that are uncommonly common[4] in the foreground dataset compared with the background dataset. This approach is used in search engines[5] to reveal significant terms in the search results, and we will borrow the related formula:[6]

---

[4] https://www.elastic.co/blog/significant-terms-aggregation
[5] http://mng.bz/A17W
[6] http://mng.bz/ZYvZ

$$score(merchantX) = \frac{foregroundPercentage(merchantX)^2}{backgroundPercentage(merchantX)} - foregroundPercentage(merchantX)$$

By applying this formula to the merchant list we obtained previously, we can reveal the merchants that appear more often than usual in the transactions of the set of people who were victims of fraud. This formula is simple, so we can convert the query to use it.

Listing 8.5   Query using the significance score to reveal fraud point

Computes the total number of transactions in the database. We could also consider the total number of transactions in the past 14 days because we consider that range in the analysis, but it doesn't matter with this small database. This value is used to compute the background percentage.

Computes the total number of transactions belonging to victims of fraud (the fraud chain). This value is used to compute the foreground percentage.

```
MATCH (t:Transaction)
WITH count(t) as txCount
MATCH p = (fraud:Fraudulent)<-[:HAS_NEXT*]-(tx)
WHERE fraud.date > datetime() - duration('P7D')
  AND NONE (tx IN nodes(p)
            WHERE COALESCE(tx.date, datetime()) <= datetime() -
            ➥ duration('P14D'))
WITH txCount, count(distinct tx) as txForegoundCount
MATCH p = (fraud:Fraudulent)<-[:HAS_NEXT*]-(tx)
WHERE fraud.date > datetime() - duration('P7D')
  AND NONE (tx IN nodes(p)
            WHERE COALESCE(tx.date, datetime()) <= datetime() -
            ➥ duration('P14D'))
WITH txCount, nodes(p) AS nodes, txForegoundCount
UNWIND nodes AS tx
WITH DISTINCT txCount, txForegoundCount, tx
MATCH (tx)-[:AT_MERCHANT]->(merchant)
WITH merchant, txCount, 1.0f*COUNT(tx)/txForegoundCount AS
➥ foregroundPercentage
MATCH (t:Transaction)-[:AT_MERCHANT]->(merchant)
with merchant, 1.0f*count(t)/txCount as backgroundPercentage,
➥ foregroundPercentage
RETURN merchant.name, backgroundPercentage, foregroundPercentage,
➥ (foregroundPercentage*foregroundPercentage/backgroundPercentage) -
➥ foregroundPercentage as score
ORDER BY score DESC
LIMIT 5
```

Gets the list of nodes in the fraud chains

For each merchant in the fraud chain, computes the foreground percentage (how often they appear in our foreground set)

Computes the score

Computes the background percentage

The results of the query are shown in figure 8.12.

The results are different and significant. From this list, it's evident where the fraudsters are operating and stealing credit card details.

Potential merchant where the card details could have been stolen

merchant.name	backgroundPercentage	foregroundPercentage	score
"Gas Station"	0.21052631578947367	0.36363636363636365	0.2644628099173554
"Jewelry Store"	0.10526315789473684	0.18181818181818182	0.1322314049586777
"Toy Store"	0.05263157894736842	0.09090909090909091	0.06611570247933884
"ATM"	0.05263157894736842	0.09090909090909091	0.06611570247933884
"Amazon"	0.3157894736842105	0.36363636363636365	0.05509641873278237

Figure 8.12 Results of query

When we have the list of merchants that are somehow related to a fraud, we can use this information to get a list of people—or, better, credit cards—that are at risk, including any cards used at that location within the past 14 days.

Listing 8.6 Query for getting potential victims

```
MATCH (merchant:Merchant {name:"Gas Station"})<-[:AT_MERCHANT] (tx)<-
➥ [:MAKES]-(user)
WHERE tx.date > datetime() - duration('P14D')
RETURN user.name
```

When we've identified the credit cards at risk, they can be blocked and the owners informed, or they can be monitored more closely to check whether other signals arise, such as small transactions with other merchants to test the cards.

It's important to note that the method presented here will not scale if the number of transactions is high. In particular, you may have a lot of transactions connected to some merchants, making their related nodes dense. Some techniques can be applied to mitigate such issues, such as splitting the dense nodes into multiple nodes, creating time-specific relationships (such as AT_MERCHANT_ON_2019_08_19), and so on. In chapter 9, we will consider techniques that can work at scale.

First, however, it's worth mentioning another scenario in which graph models provide a simple yet powerful and efficient representation that can spot a specific type of fraud. Even in this case, the analysis can be accomplished by using queries on the defined graph model.

8.3.2 Identifying a fraud ring

The steps of the particular fraud scheme we'll consider are summarized in the following list:

1 A large number of synthetic customer accounts is created at a financial institution (real accounts created for the purpose of committing the fraud).

2 For a long time, the accounts act like normal customers.

3 Over time, they request higher levels of credit, which they pay back on time, allowing them to gain credibility and trust with the bank.

4 In reality, the money is moved between the same set of accounts, using multiple and various hops to avoid recognition.

5 At some point, they all request the maximum credit they can get, take out the money, and disappear.

This specific type of fraud is called a *fraud ring* because the accounts, their details, and the money create a circle around the same set of people. A similar technique is used on a larger scale for money laundering. In this case, the money is moved from one account to another, generally in different countries, to clean money coming from illegal sources, to avoid paying taxes, or to finance terrorist or other illicit organizations. Let's see how we can fight this type of fraud, starting by defining the scenario.

Suppose that you would like to recognize the formation of a fraud ring as soon as possible, before the fraud is executed. The goal is to reveal the creation of the ring before it is too late. To understand the ring formation, consider the sample account holder details in table 8.6.

Table 8.6   Account holder details

Account ID	Username	Email	Phone number	Full name	Address
49295987202	alenegro	mpd7xg@tim.it	580-548-1149	Hilda J Womack	4093 Cody Ridge Road - Enid, OK
45322860293	jimjam	jam@mail.com	504-262-8173	Megan S Blubaugh	4093 Cody Ridge Road - Enid, OK
45059804875	drwho	mpd7xg@tim.it	504-262-8173	John V Danielson	4985 Rose Avenue - Mount Hope, WI
41098759500	robbob	bob@google.com	352-588-9221	Robert C Antunez	2041 Bagwell Avenue - San Antonio, FL

The products related to the accounts are listed in table 8.7. (The relational database will be more complex; this example is for purposes of illustration.)

Table 8.7   Products belonging to the accounts monitored

Account ID	Product type	Product ID
49295987202	Credit Card	793922
49295987202	Bank Account	896857
49295987202	Loan	885398

Table 8.7 Products belonging to the accounts monitored *(continued)*

Account ID	Product type	Product ID
45322860293	Credit Card	482513
45322860293	Bank Account	305693
45059804875	Credit Card	631264
45059804875	Bank Account	171215
45059804875	Loan	432775
41098759500	Bank Account	377703
41098759500	Loan	859916

If I asked you to model these tables in the form of a graph, which at this point in the book you should be able to do, you would most likely produce something like figure 8.13.

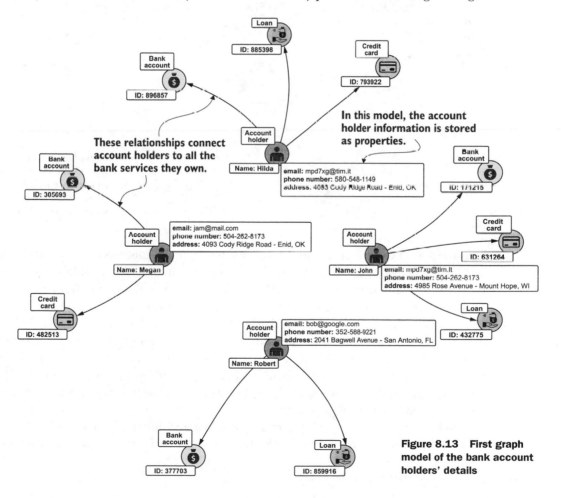

Figure 8.13 First graph model of the bank account holders' details

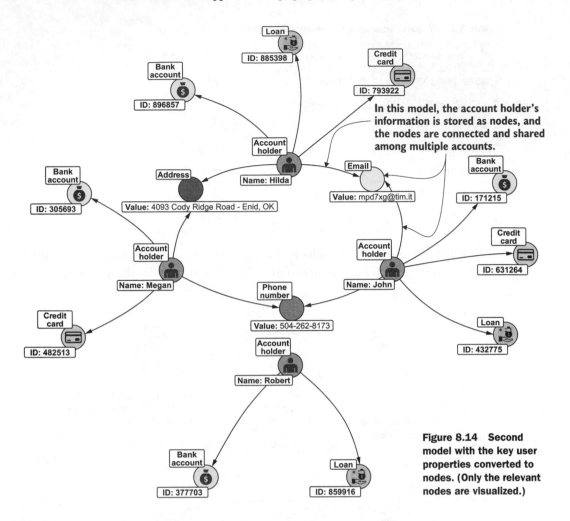

In this model, the account holder's information is stored as nodes, and the nodes are connected and shared among multiple accounts.

Figure 8.14 Second model with the key user properties converted to nodes. (Only the relevant nodes are visualized.)

This model is perfectly fine, especially considering the guidelines discussed so far, but to identify rings, we need to explode as much information as possible into separate nodes. Using this approach, you might create a graph like the one in figure 8.14.

Clearly, there is something strange about these bank accounts; the graph makes it obvious that they are well connected. The database is small, of course, so the links are easy to spot, but a mechanism allows us to inspect a graph of any size and search for connected components. A graph is considered to be connected (or strongly connected, if it is directed) if any pair of its nodes is linked by a path [Diestel, 2017]. In any graph (including unconnected graphs), a set of connected components known as a maximal connected subgraph can exist.

Luckily, we don't have to implement such an algorithm in Neo4j ourselves because it is already implemented and available as a plugin.[7] To try it, you need a simple

---

[7] https://github.com/neo4j/graph-data-science

graph; the Cypher queries necessary to create one are available in ch08/queries/ simple_ring_fraud.cypher.[8] Execute the queries, and install the plugin in Neo4j.[9] At that point, you can perform the following queries. The first query assigns the property partition to each user, specifying which cluster the user belongs to.

Listing 8.7 Queries to identify rings and assign users to them

```
CALL gds.wcc.write(
  {nodeQuery: "MATCH (p:User) RETURN id(p) as id",
   relationshipQuery: "MATCH (p1:User)--()--(p2:User) RETURN id(p1) as source,
   id(p2) as target",
   writeProperty: "partition"}
)
YIELD
  componentCount,
  createMillis,
  computeMillis,
  writeMillis
```

The next query shows the components of each cluster.

Listing 8.8 Query to visualize to which cluster each user belongs to

```
MATCH (n:User)
RETURN n.partition, COUNT(*) AS members, COLLECT(n.name) AS names
ORDER BY members DESC
```

The results are shown in figure 8.15.

n.partition	members	names
0	3	["Hilda J Womack", "Megan S Blubaugh", "John V Danielson"]
3	1	["Robert C Antunez"]

Figure 8.15 Result of the two preceding queries

These queries show exactly what we already knew: Hilda, Megan, and John form a cluster because they are connected via one or more properties, such as email address, phone number, and mailing address.

It looks as though Rob is out of the game, but the reality is a bit different: Rob is the head of the organization. (For purposes of this scenario, we can assume that we know this from other sources.) But he doesn't use any information in common with all the others. Smart guy! How can we capture his relationship in the ring?

---

[8] Tidy the database with the usual MATCH (n) DETACH DELETE n.
[9] Appendix B has instructions for installing and configuring the plugins.

One of the advantages of graphs, as mentioned previously, is that we can use the graph to merge data from different data sources. The bank account and credit card offer users the opportunity to connect to an online banking service. This system captures a lot of details about the user's browser, IP address, device, and so on that we aren't using. Let's consider only the IP information. Table 8.8 shows what this information might look like.

Table 8.8   Account connection information

Account ID	IP	Date
41098759500	166.184.50.48	2020-01-21
45059804875	166.184.50.48	2020-01-21
41098759500	208.125.140.154	2020-01-19
45059804875	74.248.71.164	2020-01-17
45322860293	208.125.140.154	2020-01-19

If we add this data source to our graph, we obtain the result in figure 8.16.

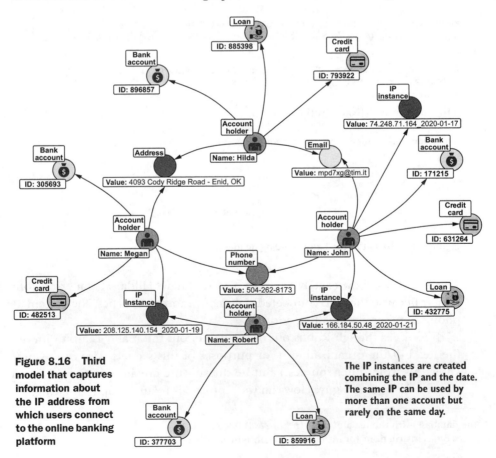

Figure 8.16   Third model that captures information about the IP address from which users connect to the online banking platform

The IP instances are created combining the IP and the date. The same IP can be used by more than one account but rarely on the same day.

Figure 8.16 illustrates our thesis: Rob is pulling the strings of everything. He is connecting as different account holders from the same places. Let's extend our database by using the queries available at ch08/queries/simple_ring_fraud_IP.cypher. Rerunning the queries in listing 8.7 gives us the result in figure 8.17.

n.partition	members	names
0	4	["Hilda J Womack", "Megan S Blubaugh", "John V Danielson", "Robert C Antunez"]

Figure 8.17 The result after merging the IP information

It's evident from these results that Rob is well connected to all the other accounts. Now human analysts can perform more in-depth investigations, the fraudulent accounts can be closed, and the people behind the accounts can be reported to the authorities and forbidden to open any other bank accounts in the country. Problem solved.

It's worth mentioning that the ring-detection approach can be used in contexts other than financial fraud, such as to identify multiple accounts belonging to the same user on a website. This problem is a common one in diverse scenarios, such as the following:

- Banned users trying to get new accounts
- On an auction site, the same user bidding with multiple accounts to increase the price of an item
- In a poker room, the same user playing with multiple accounts on the same table against other players
- A merchant on a marketplace such as Amazon paying people or other companies for posting fraudulent reviews to increase their product's credibility

In all these cases, finding rings helps us spot potential issues or discover suspect behaviors and fight them properly.

8.3.3 *Advantages of the graph approach*

This section introduced some simple yet powerful techniques for fraud detection. The scenarios presented fit well with a graph model: as you saw, with the appropriate model and queries, we can find insightful information about our data. These details would be hard to find in a large database if such relationships were not depicted explicitly. Specifically, in the case of credit card fraud, via a graph query, we were able to identify the uncommonly common pattern in a set of transactions that end up in a fraud. And in the ring example, graphs showed connections between people and accounts that would have been impossible to capture in a relational database.

Summary

This chapter introduced the basic concepts related to fraud and, more generally, outlier detection. Different approaches were presented in which the role of the graph is key to delivering high-quality analysis results and an infrastructure that can scale to real production-ready solutions. In more detail, you learned

- Types of fraud and how to deal with the most critical ones
- How to design a graph model capable of recognizing where users' credit card details were probably stolen
- How to identify rings in bank accounts based not only on the personal details provided, but also on information gathered from the multiple contact points users use to access the online banking system

References

[Akoglu et al., 2014] Akoglu, Leman, Hanghang Tong, and Danai Koutra. "Graph-Based Anomaly Detection and Description: A Survey." arXiv preprint arXiv:1404.4679 (2014).

[Baesens et al., 2015] Baesens, Bart, Veronique Van Vlasselaer, and Wouter Verbeke. *Fraud Analytics Using Descriptive, Predictive, and Social Network Techniques: A Guide to Data Science for Fraud Detection.* Hoboken, NJ: Wiley, 2015.

[Bolton and Hand, 2002] Bolton, Richard J., and David J. Hand. "Statistical Fraud Detection: A Review." *Statistical Science* 17:3 (2002): 235–255.

[Diestel, 2017] Diestel, Reinhard. *Graph Theory.* New York: Springer, 2017.

[Fawcett and Provost, 1997] Fawcett, Tom, and Foster Provost. "Adaptive Fraud Detection." *Data Mining and Knowledge Discovery* 1:3 (1997): 291–316.

[Van Vlasselaer et al., 2017] Van Vlasselaer, Véronique, Tina Eliassi-Rad, Leman Akoglu, Monique Snoeck, and Bart Baesens. "GOTCHA! Network-Based Fraud Detection for Social Security Fraud." *Management Science* 63:9 (2017): 3090–3110.

Proximity-based algorithms

This chapter covers

- Using advanced algorithms to fight fraud based on anomaly detection
- Using graphs for storing and analyzing the *k*-NN of transactions
- Identifying transactions that are anomalous

Chapter 8 introduced fraud detection techniques by showing two approaches based on identifying relationships that are explicit in the data. In the first case, each transaction connected the cardholder to the merchant where the card was used. In the second case, bank or credit card accounts were connected by the owner's personal or access details (phone number, address, IP, and so on). But in most cases, such relationships are not explicit, and in these circumstances, we need to do more work to infer or discover connections or relationships between data items to detect and combat fraud.

This chapter explores advanced algorithms for fighting fraud, borrowed from anomaly detection theory, that are capable of recognizing anomalous items in large transactional datasets in which the data points appear to be independent. As I touched on in chapter 8, anomaly detection is the branch of data mining concerned with discovering rare occurrences, or outliers, in datasets. When you're analyzing large and complex datasets, determining what stands out in the data is often at least as important and interesting as learning about its general structure.

Many techniques and algorithms have been developed to tackle the abnormality detection problem [Akoglu et al. 2014], focusing mainly on spotting anomalies in unstructured collections of multidimensional data points—that is, datasets in which each data point can be represented by a vector. These techniques treat data objects as independent points lying in multidimensional space, but the reality is that in a lot of scenarios, they may exhibit interdependencies that should be accounted for during the anomaly detection process. In a wide range of disciplines—such as physics, biology, the social sciences, and information systems—data instances are in fact inherently related. As we've seen, graphs provide a powerful tool for effectively capturing long-range correlations among interdependent data objects.

This chapter continues our investigation of the use of graphs in the anomaly detection space to fight fraud. First, we will use graph construction techniques to create a graph; then, we will analyze the graph to reveal anomalous transactions. The algorithms used here are not new, but the examples clearly show how graphs can help us visualize and navigate data better, simplifying the analysis process.

9.1   *Proximity-based algorithms: An introduction*

Suppose that you would like to identify suspicious credit card transactions to avoid customers being charged for payments they didn't authorize. In analyzing the operational data, you need to identify transactions that diverge from normal user behavior and mark them as potentially fraudulent.

At this stage, the scenario should be clear: you have been tasked with spotting fraudulent, or at least anomalous, transactions in a list of credit card operations. The goal is to go through the data and compile a list of transactions for further inspection. Conversely, when a new transaction has been requested, the system should evaluate whether to accept or reject it. It is worth noting that in this case, the data available is different from the scenarios we looked at in chapter 8. Here, we have a huge set of features for each transaction, whereas, before, we had only a few. This scenario is more realistic because, generally, credit card companies collect a lot of information about each transaction to enable them to classify a transaction as fraudulent as accurately as possible.

Even the purpose here is different. Previously, we were trying to pinpoint the location where users' credit card details were stolen or where purchases were made to test the stolen credentials. In this case, our goal is to identify anomalous transactions. When the system marks a transaction as suspicious, the card is blocked until further investigations and analyses are performed.

Clearly, this scenario requires a different approach. The data available is in the form of a sequence of transactions, described via a set of properties such as card ID, time, amount, location, merchant ID, and other information collected by the credit card system. Little or no information about the individual users and merchants is available. Furthermore, the volume of data is large compared with the earlier examples.

Because of the size of the data and the absence of explicit relationships, the techniques we explored in chapter 8 cannot be applied here. Instead, this chapter introduces a new technique for fraud detection that uses well-defined methods from the field of anomaly detection: *proximity-based approaches*. We will also use a graph representation to model and navigate the data and to improve the speed and performance of analysis. You'll find the approach used for modeling the graph from data to be familiar because it uses some of the graph construction techniques discussed earlier in this book. This chapter shows how flexible such approaches are and how they can be adapted to multiple contexts and use cases. I'll introduce the options quickly and then apply the most appropriate one to our scenario.

Proximity-based techniques define a data point as an outlier when it is uncommonly far from the other data points. A more sophisticated way of saying this is that its locality (or proximity) is sparsely populated. Different algorithms use different mechanisms for defining the proximity of a data point. These methods are subtly different, but the concepts behind them are similar enough to merit unifying them into a few groups. The most common ways to define proximity for outlier analysis are [Aggarwal, 2016]

- *Cluster-based*—The data points are split into clusters, using whatever technique is most appropriate, considering how the elements are represented and how accurate the algorithm should be. The outlier score is computed by using the nonmembership of a data point in any of the clusters, its distance from other clusters, the size of the closest cluster, or a combination of these factors. Points belong to clusters or should be considered to be outliers.

- *Density-based*—A local region is defined for each data point (perhaps based on grid position), and the number of other points in that region is used to define a local density value. This value can be converted to an outlier score, with elements with higher scores considered to be outliers. The basic assumption of density-based outlier detection methods is that the local density around a non-outlier object is similar to the local density around its neighbors, whereas the local density around an outlier object is significantly different from the local density around its neighbors. Whereas cluster-based methods partition the data points, density-based methods partition the data space.

- *Distance-based*—For each data point, the k-nearest neighbor (k-NN) network (yes, the same one we used earlier for recommendations) is computed. The outlier score is computed by using the distance of a data point to its k-nearest neighbors; the data points with the largest k-NN distances are marked as outliers. Distance-based algorithms typically perform better than the other methods presented here because they have higher granularity. In both clustering- and density-based methods, the data is aggregated before outlier analysis by partitioning the points or the data space, and the individual data points are compared with those distributions for analysis. In distance-based methods, the outlier score is based on the k-NN distance to the original data points. This greater granularity often comes at a significant computational cost, but that cost can be mitigated by using graphs and some other techniques.

All these techniques are based on some notion of proximity (or similarity, or distance) and are closely related. The major difference is in the level of detail in which this distance is defined.

We will focus on distance-based mechanisms because they are accurate compared with the others. Moreover, they fit well not only in the graph space, but also with the techniques I've presented so far. Although this chapter focuses on multidimensional numerical data such as credit card transactions, such methods have been generalized to many other domains, such as categorical data, text data, time series data, and sequence data.

Another takeaway in this chapter is the use of k-NN networks for a task different from recommendations, which shows the power of this technique for classification purposes. Earlier in this book, we explored the different uses and intrinsic flexibility of k-NN networks for solving disparate problems. This chapter completes the overview.

9.2   *Distance-based approach*

To illustrate the use of distance-based outlier detection methods, we will use a dataset of anonymized credit card transactions available on Kaggle.[1] The dataset contains credit card transactions made by European cardholders over two days in September 2013. There are a total of 284,807 transactions, of which 492 were fraudulent. The dataset is highly unbalanced: the positive class (frauds) accounts for 0.172% of all transactions. The dataset contains only numerical input variables, which are the result of a statistical transformation to make them uncorrelated, to better suit our scenario. Due to confidentiality issues, Kaggle cannot provide the original features and more background information about the data. The only features that have not been transformed are `Time` and `Amount`. The `Time` feature contains the seconds elapsed between each transaction and the first transaction in the dataset. The `Amount` feature is the transaction amount. The `Class` feature is the response variable; it takes the value `1` in case of fraud and `0` otherwise. The schema in figure 9.1 shows a high-level workflow with the subtasks necessary to identify outliers in such a list of transactions by using distance-based methods.

The first part, composed of two subtasks (extracting the data and storing it as nodes in a graph), is a classic graph construction technique. We've used it quite a bit in the book, so by now, you should be familiar with it. This first step creates a graph like the one in figure 9.2.

Let's take a closer look at what's involved here.

---

[1] https://www.kaggle.com/mlg-ulb/creditcardfraud.

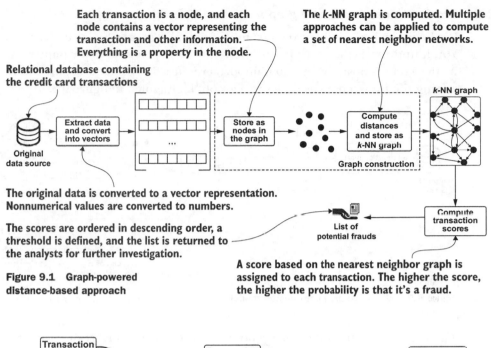

Figure 9.1 Graph-powered distance-based approach

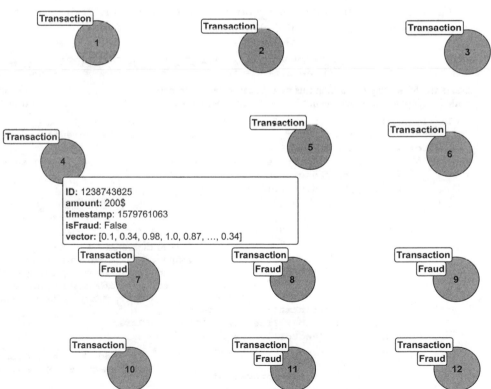

Figure 9.2 Transactions stored in the graph

9.2.1 Storing transactions as a graph

We begin by ingesting our data from its original format, CSV, as nodes in the graph. You'll find the Python scripts and the required dependencies for importing the data in the code repository, at ch09/import/creditcard. This step begins the process of storing the transactions as nodes in a graph, highlighted in figure 9.3.

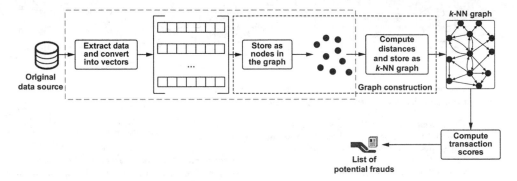

Figure 9.3   Where we are in our mental model

The next listing, from the code repository, shows how to ingest the dataset from Kaggle and convert the transaction data to vectors.

Listing 9.1   Code for importing transactions

Starts the 50 writing threads. In this case, because each transaction node is independent, there will not be any concurrency issues.

Reads from the transactions .csv file, using pandas

```python
def import_transactions(self, directory):
    transactions = pd.read_csv(os.path.join(directory, "creditcard.csv"))
    for k in range(50):
        writing_thread = threading.Thread(target = self.write_transaction)
        writing_thread.daemon = True
        writing_thread.start()

    j = 0;
    for index, row in transactions.iterrows():
        j += 1
        transaction = {
            'transactionId': j,
            'isFraud': row['Class'],
            'transactionDt': row['Time'],
            'transactionAmt': row['Amount']}
        vector = self.normalize(row, ['Time', 'Class'])
        transaction['vector'] = vector;
        self._transactions.put(transaction);
        if j % 10000 == 0:
            print(j, "lines processed")
    print(j, "lines processed")
    self._transactions.join()
    print("Done")
```

Iterates through the file, creating the parameter map

Creates the transaction vectors by removing useless columns and converting discrete/nonnumerical data to numbers (not necessary for this specific dataset, because the data is already normalized). See the code repository for the full implementation.

Adds the transaction object to the queue of elements to store

This join waits for all the elements to be processed.

```
def write_transaction(self):  ◁─────┐  Processes the queue elements by storing
    query = """                      │  each transaction as a node in the database
        WITH $row as map
        CREATE (transaction:Transaction {transactionId: map.transactionId})
        SET transaction += map
    """
    i = 0
    while True:
        row = self._transactions.get()
        with self._driver.session() as session:
            try:
                session.run(query, {"row": row})
                i += 1
                if i % 2000 == 0:
                    with self._print_lock:
                        print(i, "lines processed on one thread")
            except Exception as e:
                print(e, row)
        self._transactions.task_done()
```

The code in this listing should be easy to understand; it is similar to what we have done in other examples. The only relevant difference is that the vector for each node doesn't have to be computed later because it is already available in the data provided. The code extracts some data (like, time, is fraud, and so on) and makes it dedicated properties of the transaction nodes. The rest of the input data is put in the same nodes as a vector property, comprising the vector of floats so that we won't need to compute it ourselves.

> **WARNING** It is important to point out the use of multiple threads to write to Neo4j. This approach is a common one, but be careful: it can be used safely only when the queries don't cause any conflicts (in other words, when the queries act on different, nonoverlapping portions of the graph). This "isolation" will prevent any issue with serialization or, worse, deadlocks. The first type of problem can be solved with a delayed retry, but the second problem is not so simple to overcome, requiring the update operations to be written so that even though they run in parallel, they lock the nodes in the same order.

At the end of the ingestion, which should take a few seconds, your database will have 284,807 nodes and no relationships.

EXERCISE

After ingesting the data, run some queries on Neo4j (through the Neo4j browser) to see whether the ingestion succeeded. Here are some suggestions:

- Count how many transactions (with the label Transaction) have been inserted. Does this number match what you expected?
- Count the number of transactions labeled as fraudulent. Does this number match your expectations?

- Get 10 vectors from the nodes. Can you find the dimension of each vector?
- Get the top 10 transactions in terms of amount.

9.2.2 *Creating the k-nearest neighbors graph*

The second step (figure 9.4) is creating a *k*-NN graph by connecting the nodes using relationships that represent the distances between them.

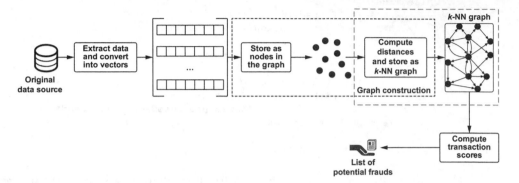

Figure 9.4   Where we are in our mental model

In the recommender systems we built earlier in the book, we used the concept of similarities, because we were looking for similar items or users. Here, we are considering distances, because we are looking for outliers that are far from the legitimate transactions. This change isn't a big one because the distance is related to the similarity by the following simple formula:[2]

$$distance = 1 - similarity$$

The formula states that when two data points are identical, their similarity is the highest possible: 1. As a result, their distance is 0. On the other hand, if they are fully distinct (perpendicular, if you prefer), the similarity is 0. In that case, the distance will be the highest possible: 1.

When the *k*-NN graph has been computed and stored, it is possible to find the outlier—in our case, the fraudulent transactions. Distance-based proximity methods usually produce output in the form of scores that represent the predicted probability that a data point (in this case, a transaction) is an outlier. By assigning a threshold, we can make a binary decision: whenever the score is higher than the fixed threshold, the transaction is considered to be an outlier.

---

[2] The formula can be used as though the similarity value is in the [0, 1] range. Otherwise, the similarity value has to be normalized by using, for example, *similarity/max(similarity values)*.

So far, so good, but as in the scenarios we've explored earlier in the book, the devil is in the details. Computing the k-NN graph is computationally expensive, requiring $O(N^2)$ time. Luckily, some techniques can make it faster; we will see a few of them when the time is right.

Now that we have all the transactions in the database as a set of nodes, we have to create the k-NN graph. To do so, we must compute the distance of each node from all the other nodes, using the `vector` property we created. These distances are ordered, and only the top k are stored as relationships in the graph. Each relationship also contains the distance value as its `weight` property. The result of this process is shown in figure 9.5.

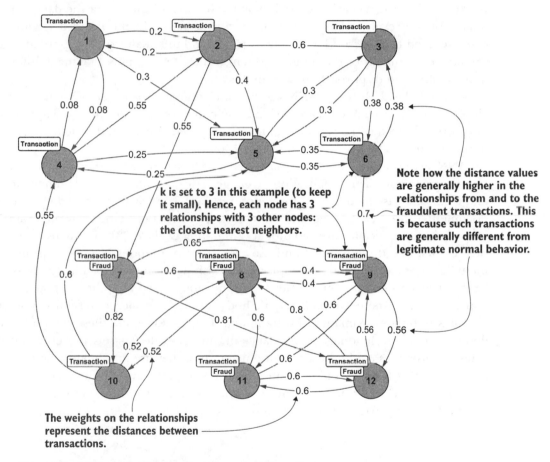

Figure 9.5 *k*-NN graph obtained using the vector information

As stated previously, and as we have seen in the recommendation scenarios, computing the k-NN graph is a tedious task because it requires computing the distances or similarities between every pair of transactions. That's why distance-based methods are less frequently used when there are a lot of data items (transactions, calls, and so on).

Creating a *k*-NN graph and persisting it as a real graph (an extension of the previous graph) has a lot of advantages in terms of accessing and analyzing your data, but it won't help during the computation of the similarities. I want to stress this point because, as I said at the beginning of the book, this book doesn't aims to solve only toy examples. Data scientists and data engineers have to solve real problems in which time, disk/memory space, and quality of results have to be taken into account.

In chapter 6, we explored a few techniques—locality-sensitive hashing (LSH) and Spotify's Annoy[3]—to compute an approximate nearest neighbor (ANN) graph, with good results. Now we're going to explore another interesting ANN approach that performs better than those two techniques. For the sake of clarity, the other approaches worked well in the scenario we used them for because of the size of the data and the quality of the results required by that specific scenario. In the fraud detection use case, we need to process a lot of dense vectors, and the quality of the approximation will affect the quality of the fraud detection results. I recommend taking a different, more sophisticated approach to ANN in this case.

Compared with the exact *k*-NN search, which searches the other elements for the *k* closest elements, the ANN search relaxes the conditions by allowing a small number of errors. It searches in a reduced set that is supposed to contain the elements closest to the specific vector used as the input for search.

ANN search has been a hot topic over the past few decades and provides fundamental support for many applications, from generic data mining to recommendations and from database indexes to information retrieval. For sparse discrete data (such as documents), the nearest neighbor search can be carried out efficiently on advanced index structures such as inverted indexes [Manning et al., 2008].[4] For dense continuous vectors, like those in our fraud use case, various solutions have been proposed, including tree structure–based approaches, hashing-based approaches (such as the LSH approach described in chapter 6), quantization-based approaches, graph-based approaches, and more. Graph-based methods have been proposed to reduce indexing complexity by approximating the traditional graphs. Recently, these methods have demonstrated revolutionary performance on million-scale datasets [Fu et al., 2019]. These approaches are interesting not only because they are graph-based, and hence relevant to this book, but also because in terms of performance, they represent the state of the art.[5] Without going into too much detail, I can describe the basic idea behind these approaches in two big steps:

---

[3] https://github.com/spotify/annoy.

[4] The inverted index data structure is the core component of all the typical search engine indexing algorithms. An *inverted index* consists of a list of all the unique words that appear in any document and, for each word, a list of the documents in which it appears. This data structure is also the most common one used in information retrieval processes.

[5] http://mng.bz/veDM.

1   Create a graph-based index structure. During this phase, a proximity graph (or neighbor graph) is created. In this graph, the nodes are the vectors in a multidimensional space, and the edges between the nodes are created by using some logic based on the specific distance function defined and the criteria for navigation. Two nodes are connected if it is probable that they are neighbors according to the distance function used.

2   Search for neighbors. Given a specific vector or search query, the proximity graph is navigated in different ways, according to the algorithm, to find the candidates to be the closest neighbors of the input vector.

I've chosen the Hierarchical Navigable Small World (HNSW) implementation [Malkov and Yashunin, 2016] as the ANN approach for this scenario. According to the benchmark available on Erik Bernhardsson's website and in Aumüller et al. [2018], it is one of the best, and the Python wrapper[6] is amazingly simply to use. The following listing shows how to compute and store the *k*-NN graph.

Listing 9.2   Computing and storing distances

Function for computing and storing the distance according to the set of parameters

```
def compute_and_store_distances(self, k, exact, distance_function,
    relationship_name):
    start = time.time()
    data, data_labels = self.get_transaction_vectors()      ← Function that creates the
    print("Time to get vectors:", time.time() - start)         vector used during the
    start = time.time()                                        distance computation

    if exact:                                               ← Switches between exact
        ann_labels, ann_distances = self.compute_knn(data, data_labels, k,
            distance_formula)                                  and approximate k-NN
    else:
        ann_labels, ann_distances = self.compute_ann(data, data_labels, k,
            distance_formula)

    print("Time to compute nearest neighbor:", time.time() - start)

    start = time.time()
    self.store_ann(data_labels, ann_labels, ann_distances, relationship_name)
    print("Time to store nn:", time.time() - start)

def store_ann(self, data_labels, ann_labels, ann_distances, label):   ←
    clean_query = """                                          Function that
        MATCH (transaction:Transaction)-[s:{}]->()             stores the
        WHERE transaction.transactionId = $transactionId       k-NN graph
        DELETE s
    """.format(label)

    query = """
```

---

[6] https://github.com/nmslib/hnswlib.

```
    MATCH (transaction:Transaction)
    WHERE transaction.transactionId = $transactionId
    UNWIND keys($knn) as otherSessionId
    MATCH (other:Transaction)
    WHERE other.transactionId = toInteger(otherSessionId) and
    ➥ other.transactionId <> {transactionId}
    MERGE (transaction)-[:{} {{weight: $knn[otherSessionId]}}]->(other)
""".format(label)

with self._driver.session() as session:
    i = 0;
    for label in data_labels:
        ann_labels_array = ann_labels[i]
        ann_distances_array = ann_distances[i]
        i += 1
        knnMap = {}
        j = 0
        for ann_label in ann_labels_array:
            value = np.float(ann_distances_array[j]);
            knnMap[str(ann_label)] = value
            j += 1
        tx = session.begin_transaction()
        tx.run(clean_query, {"transactionId": label})
        tx.run(query, {"transactionId": label, "knn": knnMap})
        tx.commit()

        if i % 1000 == 0:
            print(i, "transactions processed")
```

This code has been implemented in such a way that it allows the creation of both ANN and *k*-NN graphs. The credit card dataset is small enough to be manageable in the *k*-NN approach, so to test the different solutions, I ran the code in listing 9.2, using different distance functions and both approaches: approximate and exact. Table 9.1 contains brief descriptions of the functions.

Table 9.1   Different distance functions used during the tests

Name	Formula
Squared L2	L2 (also called Euclidean) distance is the straight-line distance between two points in Euclidean space. Squared L2 (the squared version of L2) is of central importance in estimating parameters of statistical models, where it is used in the method of least squares, a standard approach to regression analysis.
Mahalanobis[a]	Mahalanobis distance is the distance between a point and a distribution, not between two distinct points. It is effectively a multivariate equivalent of the Euclidean distance. It has excellent applications in multivariate anomaly detection, classification on highly imbalanced datasets, one-class classification, and more uncommon use cases.

[a]An interesting article about the importance and functionality of Mahalanobis distance is available at http://mng.bz/4MEV.

Listings 9.3 and 9.4 show in detail how the approximate and exact nearest neighbors computations were implemented. The switch is obtained by setting the `exact` parameter in the `compute_and_store_distances` function in listing 9.2.

Listing 9.3 Function that computes the approximate nearest neighbors

Initiates the index. The maximum number of elements should be known beforehand so that the index is computed on the data we have to load.

```
def compute_ann(self, data, data_labels, k, distance_function):
    dim = len(data[0])
    num_elements = len(data_labels)
    p = hnswlib.Index(space=distance_function, dim=dim)      # Declares the index
    p.init_index(max_elements=num_elements, ef_construction=400, M=200)
    p.add_items(data, data_labels)
    p.set_ef(200)
    labels, distances = p.knn_query(data, k = k)
    return labels, distances
```

Declares the index

Sets the query time accuracy/speed trade-off, defining the ef parameter that should always be > k and < num_elements. ef refers to the size of the dynamic list for the nearest neighbors (used during the search). Higher ef leads to more accurate but slower searches.

Query dataset, k number of closest elements (returns 2 numpy arrays)

Listing 9.4 Function that computes the exact nearest neighbors

```
def compute_knn(self, data, data_labels, k, distance_function):
    pre_processed_data = [np.array(item) for item in data]
    nbrs = NearestNeighbors(n_neighbors=k, algorithm='brute', metric=
    ➥ distance_function, n_jobs= 1).fit(pre_processed_data)
    knn_distances, knn_labels = nbrs.kneighbors(pre_processed_data)
    distances = knn_distances
    labels = [[data_labels[element] for element in item] for item in
    ➥ knn_labels]
    return labels, distances
```

After executing the code in listing 9.2 (the full code is available in the code repository) by using the parameters in table 9.2, you'll get your approximate nearest neighbor graph.

You can run a simple query from the Neo4j browser to inspect the new graph database.

Table 9.2 Parameter values used for creating the approximate nearest neighbor graph

Parameter	Value
exact	False
k	25
distance_function	L2
relationship_name	DISTANT_FROM

Listing 9.5 Visualizing a portion of the KNN (approximate) graph

```
MATCH p=(:Transaction)-[:DISTANT_FROM]-(:Transaction)
RETURN p
LIMIT 100
```

The result of the query will look like figure 9.6, a screenshot from the Neo4j browser.

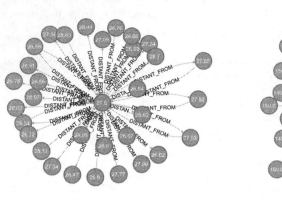

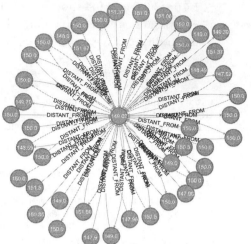

Figure 9.6   The result of listing 9.5

Before moving on, it is worth analyzing the differences between the approximate and exact nearest neighbor graphs. By running the Python script[7] in listing 9.2 with the parameters in table 9.3, you'll get an exact nearest neighbor graph.

The result of executing the script is a graph that contains both approximate and exact nearest neighbor graphs. (The approximate graph was computed with the previous run.) Now comparing the graphs is no more complex than running a simple query against it. The following listing shows the query to compare the graphs.

Table 9.3   Parameter values used for creating the exact nearest neighbor graph

Parameter	Value
exact	True
k	25
distance_function	L2
relationship_name	DISTANT_FROM_EXACT

Listing 9.6   Comparing the nearest neighbor graphs

```
MATCH (t:Transaction) with t
MATCH (t)-[r:DISTANT_FROM]->(ot:Transaction)
WITH t, r.weight as weight, ot.transactionId as otherTransactionId
ORDER BY t.transactionId, r.weight
WITH t, collect(otherTransactionId) as approximateNearestNeighbors
MATCH (t)-[r: DISTANT_FROM_EXACT]->(ot:Transaction)
WITH t.transactionId as transactionId, approximateNearestNeighbors, r.weight
➥ as weight,  ot.transactionId as otherTransactionId
ORDER BY t.transactionId, r.weight
```

---

[7] Depending on the hardware on which you'll run the script, it could take a long time to complete.

```
WITH transactionId, collect(otherTransactionId) = approximateNearestNeighbors
➥ as areNeighborsSimilar
WHERE areNeighborsSimilar = true
RETURN count(*)
```

If you don't want to wait to create the second graph and do the experiment yourself, I can reveal that this query will return a count higher than 230,000 (of a total 284,807 transactions), which means that accuracy is higher than 80%. This result is the percentage of times the list of neighbors produced by the approximate nearest neighbor computation for a node matches the exact one. If you check the remaining 20% or so, you'll see that the differences are minimal. What is not minimal is the time required to compute the exact nearest neighbor graph, which requires $N \times N$ distance computations. The ANN approach (specifically, the graph-based implementation of ANN provided by HNSW) not only performs well in terms of accuracy, but also dramatically reduces the time required for computing the nearest neighbor graph. Therefore, the approach proposed here is usable in a production environment with real datasets.

9.2.3 Identifying fraudulent transactions

The last step (figure 9.7) is identifying the fraudulent transactions. With the distance-based methods—specifically, the nearest neighbor approach that we are discussing in detail here—an observation (a transaction, in our scenario) is considered to be an outlier, or a possible fraud, if its neighbors are far away. Hence, a measure of outlierness—the outlier score—can be computed by using the distance of a node from its nearest neighbor(s): the higher the score, the higher the probability of an outlier.

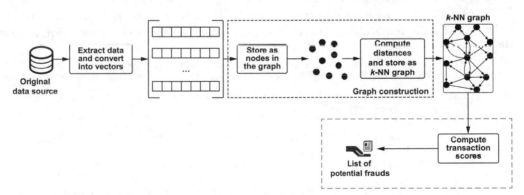

Figure 9.7 Where we are in our mental model

Different ways exist to measure the score for each observation based on its k-NN. There are two simple variations of this scoring mechanism:

- *Exact k-nearest neighbor score*—The outlier score of any data observation is equal to its distance from its *k*th nearest neighbor. So if *k* = 5 and the *k*-NNs of a transaction with ID 32 are [45: 0.3, 34: 0.45, 67:0.6, 50: 0.75, 21: 0.8], the 2-nearest neighbor score is 0.45 (the distance to the second node in the list), the 3-nearest neighbor score will be 0.6, and so on.

- *Average k-nearest neighbor score*—The outlier score of any observation is equal to the average distance to its *k*-nearest neighbors. So in the previous example, the score of the transaction with ID 32 would be 0.58 ((0.3 + 0.45 + 0.6 + 0.75 + 0.8) / 5).

In general—and trust me, this fact surprised me as well—if we know the correct value of *k* to use, looking at the exact *k*-NN score tends to give better results than the average *k*-NN score. In unsupervised problems like outlier detection, however, it is impossible to know the correct value of *k* to use for any particular algorithm, and an analyst might use a range of values of *k*. Moreover, when the dataset contains multiple clusters with different densities, defining a single ideal value for *k* is a complex (if not impossible) task.

At this stage, because the *k*-NN graph is stored in our graph database, computing the scores and evaluating the performance of the method proposed here are a matter of running a few queries. The focus should be on identifying the transactions that are potentially fraudulent and passing them to an analyst for further verification.

Before starting the deeper analysis, let's evaluate the overall results obtained by considering how the average distance of a node from its *k*-nearest neighbors is distributed across the entire dataset. Again, the graph representation—specifically, Neo4j with the APOC[8] plugin—can help a lot. Using the following queries, it is possible to export a .csv file with the transactions in one column and the average distance of each transaction from its *k*-nearest neighbors in the other. The queries show how to do this for the transactions that are identified as being likely and not likely to be fraudulent, respectively.

Listing 9.7 Creating a .csv with the average distance for fraudulent transactions

```
CALL apoc.export.csv.query('MATCH (t:Transaction)-[r:DISTANT_FROM]->
➥ (other:Transaction)
WHERE t.isFraud = 1
RETURN t.transactionId as transactionId, avg(r.weight) as weight',
➥ 'fraud.csv',
{batchSize:1000, delim: '\t', quotes: false, format: 'plain', header:true})
```

Listing 9.8 Creating a .csv with the average distance for nonfraudulent transactions

```
CALL apoc.export.csv.query('MATCH (t:Transaction)-[r: DISTANT_FROM]->
➥ (other:Transaction)
WHERE t.isFraud = 0
RETURN t.transactionId as transactionId, avg(r.weight) as weight',
➥ 'noFraud.csv',
{batchSize:1000, delim: '\t', quotes: false, format: 'plain', header:true})
```

---

[8] http://mng.bz/Q26j. Appendix B shows how to install and configure it.

The results have been analyzed with Microsoft Excel (the file is in the code repository at ch09/analysis/analysis.xlsx), and are shown in figure 9.8. The bar chart compares the distributions of the average distances across the two datasets (fraudulent versus nonfraudulent transactions). In general, we expect the average distances to be higher in the case of fraudulent transactions compared with nonfraudulent ones. In the figure, we should have higher values for fraudulent transactions on the right side (greater distances) and lower ones on the left (smaller distances).

DISTANCE DISTRIBUTION

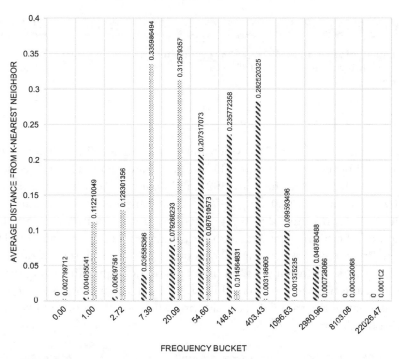

Figure 9.8 Chart comparing average distance distributions for fraudulent and nonfraudulent transactions

Reality meets our expectations in this case: the dotted bars, indicating nonfraudulent transactions, are higher on the left side, and the diagonally striped bars indicating fraudulent transactions are higher on the right side. Up to an average distance of about 20, the nonfraudulent bar is higher than the fraudulent one, and starting with the next value (54.6), the trend is inverted. The dotted bar's peak is at around 7, where we have 33% of the values (that is, one-third of the ~284,000 legitimate transactions have an average k-NN distance between 2.72 and 7.39). Approximately 78% of these transactions have an average score of between 2.72 and 20.09. The diagonally striped bar's peak is at 403, and we can see that 72% of the fraudulent transactions have an average *k*-NN distance of between 54 and 403. This result means that the non-fraudulent transactions have average distances from their nearest neighbors that are statistically lower than the average distances of the fraudulent transactions from their nearest neighbors.

Now that we are sure that the distance metric we are using is performing well and that the behavior of the data is in line with our expectations, let's move on to deeper analysis. The first query proposed for this purpose orders transactions by the minimum distance from the *k*-nearest neighbors, which means $k = 1$ in the *k*-NN score mechanism.

Listing 9.9   Computing potentially fraudulent transactions ordered by minimum distance

```
MATCH (t:Transaction)-[r:DISTANT_FROM]->(:Transaction)
WITH t, min(r.weight) as score, t.isFraud as fraud
ORDER BY score DESC
LIMIT 1000
WHERE fraud = 1
RETURN COUNT(distinct t)
```

This query returns a count of 118,[9] which means that of the first 1,000 transactions returned ordered by descending score, 11.8% were fraudulent. That value may seem to be low but isn't. Recall that there are 492 fraudulent transactions in the dataset of a total 284,807, which means that only 0.17% of the transactions are fraudulent. This result reinforces our intuition that the greater the distance a transaction is from its closest neighbor, the higher the chance that the transaction is fraudulent. This distance is the defined score from listing 9.9 onward as well as in the related descriptions. It will be computed in different ways, but in all cases, the higher the score, the higher the chance that the transaction is fraudulent. Following is a more generic query in which you can change the value of *k*, considering whatever element you like in the list of the nearest neighbors.

Listing 9.10   Computing potentially fraudulent transactions ordered by 4-NN distance

```
MATCH (t:Transaction)-[r:DISTANT_FROM]->(:Transaction)
WITH t.transactionId as transactionId, r.weight as weight, t.isFraud as fraud
ORDER BY transactionId ASC, weight
WITH transactionId, fraud, collect(weight)[3] as score      ◁————
ORDER BY score DESC
LIMIT 1000                                    3 can be any value less than k. (The vector
WHERE fraud = 1                               resulting from the collect starts from 0, so
RETURN COUNT(distinct transactionId)          k=1 is the element at 0, k=2 the element
                                              at 1 and so on.)
```

---

[9] The results can change a bit depending on the approximation used in the ANN.

In this query, we are fixing the vector position to 3 (which means the fourth element in our KNN, because the collect creates a 0-based vector). Hence, in this query, we are assigning the score based on the distance of each transaction to the fourth element in the KNN of the transaction itself. As a reminder, we set k (the number of nearest neighbors to consider) to 25 (see tables 9.2 and 9.3); the value can be any value lower than 25.

In this case, the query returns a count of 111, which means that 11.1% of the resulting list of transactions were fraudulent. This result is slightly lower than before but still much higher than 0.17%—the percentage of fraudulent transaction over the full dataset.

The results generated by these queries are good. For proof, run the following query, which generates a random score.

Listing 9.11 Generating a random list of 1,000 transactions

```
MATCH (t:Transaction)-[r:DISTANT_FROM]->(:Transaction)
WITH t, rand() as score, t.isFraud as fraud
ORDER BY score desc
LIMIT 1000
WHERE fraud - 1
RETURN COUNT(distinct t)
```

The query assigns a random score to each transaction, regardless of the distance from any element of the KNN. Because the list of transactions is generated randomly, the results of this query can vary, but you should find that the query usually returns 2 or 3, which is equivalent to 0.2% to 0.3%. That result is aligned with the distribution of the fraud transactions across the overall dataset, which is 0.17%.

This experiment sets our baseline. Let's try a few more experiments. Using the following query, we assign the score by using the average distance from all the k-nearest neighbors instead of picking the distance from one of the neighbors, as we have done before.

Listing 9.12 Computing the score of the transactions by using the average distance

```
MATCH (t:Transaction)-[r:DISTANT_FROM]->(:Transaction)
WITH t, avg(r.weight) as score, t.isFraud as fraud
ORDER BY score DESC
LIMIT 1000
WHERE fraud = 1
RETURN COUNT(distinct t)
```

The result is 86—worse than the result from listing 9.9, where the score used for the ordering was based on the minimum distance from the k-nearest neighbor, which was 118 in our test. This result is to be expected, because as I stated earlier, looking at exact *k*-NN scores usually gives better results than the approximate *k*-NN for most datasets. Still, this technique performs much better than selecting transactions randomly.

Graphs can help with deep analysis, and we can take this opportunity to discover more insights about the options available. An interesting possibility is to test listing 9.9 and listing 9.12 by using the exact *k*-NN graph. The following listings show how.

Listing 9.13   Computing the score by using the exact *k*-NN graph and minimum distance

```
MATCH (t:Transaction)-[r:DISTANT_FROM_EXACT]->(:Transaction)
WITH t, min(r.weight) as score, t.isFraud as fraud
ORDER BY score DESC
LIMIT 1000
WHERE fraud = 1
RETURN COUNT(distinct t)
```

Listing 9.14   Computing the score by using the exact *k*-NN graph and average distance

```
MATCH (t:Transaction)-[r: DISTANT_FROM_EXACT]->(:Transaction)
WITH t, avg(r.weight) as score, t.isFraud as fraud
ORDER BY score DESC
LIMIT 1000
WHERE fraud = 1
RETURN COUNT(distinct t)
```

These queries return 81 and 72, respectively, so the exact method returns worse results than the approximate one, perhaps because the graph-based approximation provided by HNSW removes some noise in the data.

EXERCISES

Try playing with the parameter values (k, exact, distance_function and relationship_name) and executing different queries to see whether you can get better results than the ones shown here. I did this experiment myself and found some interesting results. The following query, for example, considers scores from the 24th-nearest neighbors (k = 23), using the exact method and the Mahalanobis distance metric.

Listing 9.15   Computing the score by using the exact 24-NN distance with Mahalanobis

```
MATCH (t:Transaction)-[r:DISTANT_FROM_EXACT_MAHALANOBIS]->(:Transaction)
WITH t.transactionId as transactionId, r.weight as weight, t.isFraud as fraud
ORDER BY transactionId ASC, weight ASC
WITH transactionId, fraud, collect(weight)[23] as weight
ORDER BY weight DESC
LIMIT 1000
WHERE fraud = 1
RETURN COUNT(distinct transactionId)
```

The query returns 147, which means that 14.7% of the top results are potentially fraudulent transactions. This example shows once again that the *k*-nearest neighbor approach performs better than average distance score in the dataset we are considering, at least with the current value of k (25) and the current distance metric (Mahalanobis). I ran another interesting test with the parameters in table 9.4 to see what the effect of increasing k would be.

Table 9.4 Parameter values used for computing exact 400-NN with Mahalanobis

Parameter	Value
exact	True
k	400
distance_function	MAHALANOBIS
relationship_name	DISTANT_FROM_EXACT_400_MAHALANOBIS

Running the Python script will take a bit longer, due to the extra time required to store the *k*-NN in the graph, but now we can consider the 400 nearest neighbors for each transaction instead of 25. The following query uses the average score over the 400-item list of neighbors for each transaction to generate the list.

> **Listing 9.16 Computing the score by using average distance with Mahalanobis (k = 400)**

```
MATCH (t:Transaction)-[r:DISTANT_FROM_EXACT_400_MAHALANOBIS]->(:Transaction)
WITH t.transactionId as transactionId, avg(r.weight) as score, t.isFraud as
➥ fraud
ORDER BY score desc
LIMIT 1000
WHERE fraud = 1
RETURN COUNT(distinct transactionId)
```

The result is 183, which means that 18.3% of the top results are classified as fraudulent—definitely the best result so far! I also tested with L2 and the approximate nearest neighbor approach, and the result was 2. This example shows how much parameters can influence the results of your analysis.

You're probably thinking that these results aren't so great; you'd like to see much higher precision, around 80, which makes perfect sense. I had the same mindset at first. But it's important to consider how unbalanced the dataset is. We have more than 280,000 transactions, and only 492 are fraudulent. In these conditions, our queries can't perform much better. We can make the dataset more balanced, however, so that the number of fraudulent transactions is the same as the number of licit transactions. This approach enables us to better evaluate the quality of the scoring mechanism used so far. The following queries create a balanced dataset by taking only 492 (the number of fraudulent transactions) licit transactions randomly, among all the available, and adding to this dataset all the fraudulent transactions. The dataset is created by marking with a common label all the transactions in the dataset.

Listing 9.17   Generating a random set of transactions the same size as the fraudulent set

```
MATCH (t:Transaction)
WHERE t.isFraud = 0
WITH t, rand() as rand
ORDER BY rand
LIMIT 492
SET t:Test1
```

Listing 9.18   Assigning the fraudulent transactions to the same test set

```
MATCH (t:Transaction)
WHERE t.isFraud = 1
SET t:Test1
```

The previous queries can be run repeatedly to create multiple testing datasets (change Test1 to Test2, Test3, and so on). The result in each case is a homogeneous dataset of size 984, with the number of fraudulent and legitimate transactions balanced. Now, with a similar query, let's see how using the average distance allows us to catch the fraudulent transactions.

Listing 9.19   Assigning a score to the small dataset

```
MATCH (t:Test1)-[r:DISTANT_FROM]->(:Test1)
WITH t.transactionId as transactionId, avg(r.weight) as score, t.isFraud as
➥ fraud
ORDER BY score desc
LIMIT 100
WHERE fraud = 1
RETURN COUNT(distinct transactionId)
```

The result is 100. The first 100 transactions ordered by descending score are fraudulent.

All this evidence—the chart from figure 9.8, the tests over the top 1,000 transactions ordered by average and other metrics, and this last test on a reduced but balanced dataset—shows how the distance-based approach is capable of identifying fraudulent transactions. Bear in mind also that the so-called legitimate transactions are transactions *not proved to be fraudulent,* so the quality of the results could be even higher than presented here.

EXERCISE

I invite you to play with the parameters to find the best configuration for your dataset. Specifically, the distance function and the size of the k parameter affect the final results. In this sense, the graph approach will make all your analysis efforts pleasant and simple.

You can store and compare solutions, as we have done throughout this section. Playing with multiple *k*-NNs in the same graph is exciting—or at least it was for me!

This score-based approach can be easily converted to produce a binary output. In this case, instead of having a score that indicates how likely it is that a transaction is fraudulent, we can have a binary output that says "fraudulent" or "not fraudulent." Converting a score-based mechanism to a binary one is a trivial task. The two main approaches that have been proposed for this purpose are

- *Score threshold-based distance outliers* [Knorr and Ng, 1998]—An observation (in our case, a transaction) is an outlier if at least a portion *f* of the objects in the full dataset lie at greater than distance β from it. If the dataset has 100 transactions and $f = 0.1$ (10%) and $β = 0.5$, a transaction is an outlier if at least 10 other transactions have a distance higher than 0.5 from it. Note that the parameter *f* is virtually equivalent to using a parameter like *k* in the *k*-NN score. Instead of using a fraction *f*, we can use the exact *k*th-nearest neighbor distance by setting $k = \lceil N \times (1 - f) \rceil$. In this case, we can reformulate the condition as follows: an observation in a dataset is an outlier if its exact *k*th-nearest neighbor distance is at least β. See listing 9.20.
- *Rank threshold-based distance outliers* [Ramaswamy et al., 2000]—This second definition is based on top-*r* thresholding rather than the thresholding of the absolute values of the scores. This is exactly what we did in the preceding queries where we set our threshold to 1,000. The observations (again, transactions in our case) are ranked in decreasing order of the exact *k*-NN distance or the average *k*-NN distance. The top-*r* such data points are reported as outliers. Hence, the threshold is on the distance rank rather than the distance value. See listing 9.21.

It is worth mentioning that both of these variants are related to the distance-based approach. All that changes is the way in which the score or rank is computed for the outliers: the underlying neighborhood graph is still there as the base graph on which the computations are performed. The queries used earlier can easily be adapted to return rank threshold-based outliers, as follows.

Listing 9.20 Rank threshold-based query

```
MATCH (t:Transaction)-[r:SIMILAR_TO_EXACT_400_MAHALANOBIS]->(:Transaction)
WITH t.transactionId as transactionId, avg(r.weight) as score, t.isFraud as
➥ fraud
ORDER BY score desc
LIMIT 100
WHERE fraud = 1
RETURN transactionId
```

The threshold (the *r* value) is set to 100 in this query, but it can be anything you like. Regarding the score threshold-based outliers, the previous queries can be adapted as follows.

Listing 9.21 Score threshold-based query

```
MATCH (t:Transaction)-[r:DISTANT_FROM_EXACT]->(:Transaction)
WITH t.transactionId as transactionId, r.weight as weight, t.isFraud as fraud
ORDER BY transactionId ASC, weight ASC
WITH transactionId, fraud, collect(weight)[23] as weight
WHERE weight > 10
WITH transactionId, fraud, weight
ORDER BY weight DESC
LIMIT 100
WHERE fraud = 1
RETURN transactionId
```

As is evident from the previous discussions, the k-NN (exact or approximate) graph allows you to use multiple approaches on top of the same database with minimal effort and disk space.

9.2.4 *Advantages of the graph approach*

This section presented one of the most powerful proximity-based techniques for fraud detection. We have seen how a single graph model is capable of providing an effective support to multiple algorithms/approaches. In particular, graphs allow us to do the following:

- Properly index the k-NN graph by providing direct access to each of the k-nearest neighbors
- Store multiple k-NN graphs, exact and approximate, by using different distance functions and relationship types, making comparison and analysis simple
- Explore and evaluate multiple score mechanisms (thanks to the flexibility provided by the query and accessing mechanism), making it possible to identify the best one and use it for further analysis
- Use labels to mark different sets of nodes and use them to compute the accuracy of the models created

Proximity-based techniques are well-established techniques for outlier detection, and the examples in this chapter showed how to combine these classical techniques with graphs, making them even more powerful and easy to use.

Summary

This chapter introduced an advanced technique for fraud detection and analysis. A combination of graph construction techniques and anomaly detection highlights the value of graph models to support data investigation and deep analysis. Different approaches have been presented in which the role of the graph is key to delivering not only high-quality analysis results, but also an infrastructure that is ready to scale to real production-ready solutions. You learned

- How to construct a *k*-NN graph from transactions and how to use such techniques in a new domain for different tasks.
- How to use a graph model in a distance-based approach to outlier detection
- How to use several distance metrics and multiple approaches at the same time, combining the results in a single graph using different relationships
- How to recognize anomalous nodes in a graph by using different queries

The examples and code in this chapter illustrate an end-to-end approach, from data import to the final results of the analysis, using algorithms from outlier analysis theory.

References

[Aggarwal, 2016] Aggarwal, Charu C. *Outlier Analysis*. New York: Springer, 2016.

[Akoglu et al., 2014] Akoglu, Leman, Hanghang Tong, and Danai Koutra. "Graph-Based Anomaly Detection and Description: A Survey." arXiv preprint arXiv:1404.4679 (2014).

[Aumüller et al., 2018] Aumüller, Martin, Erik Bernhardsson, and Alexander Faithfull. "ANN-Benchmarks: A Benchmarking Tool for Approximate Nearest Neighbor Algorithms." arXiv preprint arXiv:1807.05614 (2018).

[Fu et al., 2019] Fu, Cong, Chao Xiang, Changxu Wang, and Deng Cai. "Fast Approximate Nearest Neighbor Search with the Navigating Spreading-out Graph." *Proceedings of the VLDB Endowment* (2019): 461–474.

[Knorr and Ng, 1998] Knorr, Edwin M., and Raymond T. Ng. "Algorithms for Mining Distance-Based Outliers in Large Datasets." *Proceedings of the 24th International Conference on Very Large Data Bases* (1998): 392–403.

[Malkov and Yashunin, 2016] Malkov, Yu. A., and D. A. Yashunin. "Efficient and Robust Approximate Nearest Neighbor Search Using Hierarchical Navigable Small World Graphs." arXiv preprint arXiv:1603.09320 (2016).

[Manning et al., 2008] Manning, C. D., P. Raghavan, H. Schutze, et al. *Introduction to Information Retrieval*. Cambridge, UK: Cambridge University Press, 2008.

[Ramaswamy et al., 2000] Ramaswamy, Sridhar, Rajeev Rastogi, and Kyuseok Shim. "Efficient Algorithms for Mining Outliers from Large Data Sets." *ACM SIGMOD Record* 29:2 (2000), 427–438.

Social network analysis
against fraud

This chapter covers

- Using social network analysis (SNA) to classify fraudsters and fraud risks
- Describing different graph algorithms for SNA-based fraud analytics
- Using a real graph database to perform a proper SNA

In this chapter, you will learn about techniques for combating fraud that approach the task from a different perspective. The techniques for fighting fraud presented in chapters 8 and 9 use different graph construction methods to create networks based on the information available in the transactions themselves and/or the users' accounts. In chapter 8, we created a graph connecting users with merchants by using transaction information, and we explored connecting nodes based on overlapping information (two accounts that use the same email address, for example). In chapter 9, you learned how to construct a graph (the k-NN graph) by computing distances between pairs of observations (each of which has been converted to a node) and storing the top k relationships.

In this chapter, we will consider the case in which a graph—specifically, a social network—exists either implicitly or explicitly in the data that we collect for fraud analysis. As you learned in the first part of the book, a graph is considered to be a social network if the nodes are people and the edges express relationships between people (friendship, family, work connections, and so on). Such networks can be imported from existing explicitly social networks, such as Facebook, LinkedIn, and Twitter, or they can be created from internal data. Telecommunications providers, for example, have massive transactional databases in which they record calls among their customers. Supposing that people with stronger relationships call one another more often than relative strangers do, it is possible to use such information to create a social network and assign strengths to the ties between people based on the frequency and/or duration of the calls. Other examples in which social networks can be inferred are the data collected by internet infrastructure providers (people connecting from the same IP address), banks (periodic recurrent transactions among people), retail organizations (one person sending deliveries to the address of another person), and the online gaming industry (people regularly playing from the same address or on the same team).

Whether the social network has been created implicitly or explicitly, the question is whether our fraud detection models might benefit from social network analysis (SNA) or complex network analysis (CNA). In other words, do the relationships between people play an important role in fraud, and is fraud a contagious effect in the network? Are fraudsters randomly spread throughout the social network, or are there observable effects indicating that social connections play a role in fraud attempts? Should we assume that the probability that someone will commit fraud depends on the people they are connected to? If John Smith has five friends who are fraudsters, what would you say about him [Baesens et al., 2015]? The goal is to determine which types of unstructured network information extracted from a social network (techniques related to SNA and CNA) can be translated into useful and meaningful characteristics of a subject (a fraudster, in our case), and how.

SNA—and link analysis in general as a tool for improving the quality of fraud detection systems—is a hot topic in the fraud-fighting software industry. Gartner Group fraud analyst Avivah Litan [2012] suggests a five-layer approach[1] to fraud detection and prevention, as illustrated in figure 10.1.

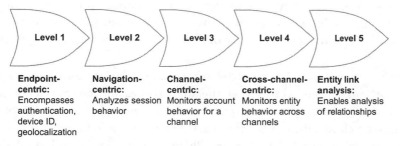

Figure 10.1   The five-layer approach to fraud detection proposed by Gartner

---

[1] https://www.gartner.com/en/documents/1912615.

In this model, each of the levels represents a specific type of customer activity and behavior:

- *Level 1* is endpoint-centric and includes user authentication, device, and geolocation information. It entails adding a set of authentication options for different customer access channels. For low-risk scenarios, all banks provide two-factor authentication, such as a combination of hardware or software ID and a personal identification number (PIN), or a user ID and password. For higher-risk scenarios, three-factor authentication (adding identity credentials from a third category, such as biometrics) is more secure but also more inconvenient. Out-of-band authentication, which requires separate information channels for authentication and access, is widely accepted as a defense against man-in-the-middle attacks. These controls sound fundamental, but many institutions are weak on monitoring even at this level [Barta and Stewart, 2008].

- *Level 2* is navigation-centric, which means that customer behavior during a particular session is analyzed for anomalies. The analysis includes real-time, dynamic capture of online customer and account activity. This information is used to build a customer profile to determine what is normal or abnormal for this customer, providing an enhanced view of the customer/account and forming the foundation for real-time decisions.

- *Level 3* is channel-centric. It focuses on analyzing account activity for anomalies. The idea is to have an end-to-end enterprise platform that can address a specific channel and provide extensibility across channels. In a banking context, a fraud prevention system might focus on Automated Clearing House (ACH) transactions. Thirty ACH transactions in one day would be considered to be abnormal if the customer usually makes one or two such transactions per month.

- *Level 4* is cross-product and cross-channel; it entails monitoring entity behavior across accounts, products, and channels. Transactions that initially look legitimate may appear to be suspicious when correlated with activities in other areas. A bank can monitor payments to credit card accounts made through telephone banking, online, by check, and by mobile device. Such a wide-spectrum transaction monitoring approach (rather than looking at a subset of transactions coming from a single source, as in the channel-centric approach) is important because it provides a global view of the subject's behavior. Fraudsters do a lot of system testing through low-dollar or zero-dollar transaction attempts that sampling may miss.

- *Level 5* is about entity link analysis, or evaluating connections between various users or transactions. At this level, the analysis goes beyond transaction and customer views to analyze activities and relationships within a network of related entities (such as customers who share demographic data or transaction patterns, or relationships among people generally). Entity link analysis helps detect and prevent fraud by identifying patterns of behavior that appear suspicious only when viewed across related accounts or entities, or by discovering the networks associated with a suspicious account, entity, or individual to determine whether a case is limited to an isolated individual or is part of a criminal conspiracy. In the automobile insurance industry, fraud detection systems may uncover staged accidents or false claims by identifying suspicious patterns or overlaps, such as cases in which an individual is the insured party in one case and a passenger in another, or the insured party and claimant have the same phone number, or there is repetitive use of the same body shops and medical professionals.

In this schema, the fifth level—the most advanced one—focuses on the use of graph analysis as a powerful tool for fighting fraud. The scenarios presented in chapter 8, in which graphs were used to create connections among people based on the information provided, also fall into this category. In that case, network analysis connects entities through demographic attributes such as address, phone number, employer, account ownership, IP address, and device ID.

This chapter focuses instead on SNA, which involves exploring explicit or implicit connections among users as a basis for performing fraud detection and prevention. We will consider various techniques for building a social network out of the data available and for identifying fraudsters or evaluating the risk of people being victims of fraud.

10.1 Social network analysis concepts

In general terms, we can say that network effects are powerful. This statement is commonly accepted as true and confirmed by a lot of concrete evidence. People tend to associate with other people whom they perceive as being similar to them in some way [Newman, 2010], such as race, religion, political affiliation, hobbies, socioeconomic status, or character. Thus, knowing certain characteristics of some nodes in a network (such as "honest" and "dishonest") will give us a decent chance of being able to guess the characteristics of the rest of the nodes [Koutra et al., 2011].

This concept is expressed by the term *homophily*, which boils down to the expression "Birds of a feather flock together." Friendships are mostly based on similar interests, origins, or experiences—including, conceivably, a shared tendency to commit fraud. Relationships determine which people are influenced by whom and the extent to which information is exchanged among them.

It is also important to note that not all social networks are homophilic. There are different ways to compute formally how much a network is homophilic, but broadly, we can say that a network is homophilic if nodes with label X (fraudster, New Yorker, doctor, and so on) are to a larger extent connected to other nodes with label X. In the context of fraud detection,

> *A network is homophilic if fraudulent nodes are significantly more connected to other fraudulent nodes, and as a consequence, legitimate nodes connect significantly more to other legitimate nodes [Baesens et al., 2015].*

More concretely, suppose that l is the fraction of legitimate nodes in the network, computed as the number of legitimate nodes divided by the total number of nodes, and f is the fraction of fraudulent nodes in the network, computed as the number of fraudulent nodes divided by the total number of nodes. In a purely random network—one in which the edges are created randomly between nodes without any internal or external influence—the expected probability that an edge connects two dissimilarly labeled nodes can be expressed as $2 \times l \times f$. These edges are called *cross-labeled edges*. A network is homophilic if the fraction of cross-labeled edges, computed as the ratio (r) between the number of cross-labeled edges and the number of all edges, is significantly less than the expected probability $2 \times l \times f$. Consider the social network shown in figure 10.2.

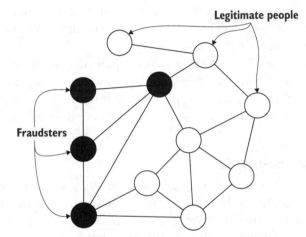

Legitimate people

Fraudsters

Figure 10.2   A toy example of a social network

The black nodes are the fraudsters, and the white nodes represent legitimate people. The network consists of 11 nodes, 7 legitimate and 4 fraudulent. In this example, the fraction l is 7/11, and the fraction f is 4/11. In a random network, the fraction of cross-labeled edges should be

$$2 \times l \times f = 2 \times 7/11 \times 4/11$$
$$2 \times 7/11 \times 4/11 = 0.462$$

The network has 4 cross-labeled edges, 5 edges between fraudulent nodes, and 9 edges between legitimate nodes, for a total 18 edges. So r (the observed fraction of cross-labeled edges) has a value of 4/18 (0.222), which is significantly less than (indeed, less than half of) the expected value in a random network. Thus, we can say that the network in figure 10.2 is homophilic. Using a formula, we say that the network is homophilic if

$$H: 2 \times l \times f \gg r$$

In marketing, the concept of homophily is frequently exploited to assess how individuals influence one another and to determine which people are likely responders and should be targeted with a marketing incentive. If all of Alessandro's friends use telecom provider X, for example, Alessandro is likely to sign a contract with the same provider.

The same reasoning holds in the context of fraud. We define a homophilic network as a network where fraudsters are more likely to be connected to other fraudsters and legitimate people are more likely to be connected to other legitimate people. Figure 10.3 demonstrates what such a network might look like.

The gray nodes represent fraudsters, and the white ones represent legitimate people. It is easy to see that the gray nodes are clustered into groups; this network has one large subgraph and a smaller one with three nodes. In the case of fraud analysis, such a group of fraudsters is called a *web of frauds*. Legitimate nodes are also clustered. As you can see, however, the network is not perfectly homophilic: fraudulent nodes are not uniquely connected to other fraudulent nodes but connect to legitimate nodes as

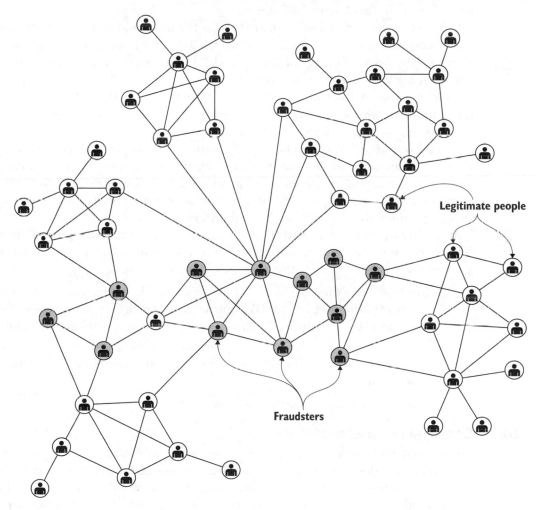

Figure 10.3 A web of frauds

well. By looking at this network, we can identify the legitimate nodes that have a high chance of becoming the victims of fraud attempts because they are the ones that are connected to a web of frauds.

EXERCISE

Use the formula given earlier to determine whether the network in figure 10.3 is homophilic. So far, we've been looking at snapshots of social networks, but by nature, social networks are dynamic and evolve rapidly. To conduct a proper analysis, our techniques must take this dimension into account—that is, we must consider how the network is evolving over time. A few fraudulent nodes popping up in the network together might indicate the emergence of a new web of fraud; subgraphs with many fraudulent nodes likely indicate more well-established systems. Preventing the growth of new webs and the expansion of existing webs are important challenges that need to be addressed in fraud detection models.

The relevance of social network analysis for fighting fraud is clear from the preceding discussion. Using the proper formula, we are capable of recognizing whether a social network exposes homophilic behavior. At this point, we can explore the SNA and CNA methods that are available to us.

Suppose that we have or can create a social network, which we verify to be a homophilic network, with some information about real or potential fraudsters. How can we use SNA to improve our fraud detection capabilities?

Fraudsters are often linked because they attend the same events and activities, are involved in the same crimes, use the same sets of resources, or are one and the same person (as evidenced by shared personal information). Guilt-by-association methods combine the available weak signals to derive stronger ones and have been used extensively for anomaly detection and classification in numerous settings (accounting fraud, cybersecurity, credit card fraud, and so on). So we can look for evidence that fraudsters are exchanging knowledge about how to commit fraud by using the social structure. We can use two types of approaches and techniques:

- *Score-based*—We analyze the social network node by node, assigning a score to each node using metrics that take into account the direct neighbors and the role of the node in the network (such as how many shortest paths pass through it).
- *Cluster-based*—Considering the relationships, we split the social network into multiple clusters (community) of nodes trying to derive some knowledge from these groups.

We'll begin by examining the score-based methods.

10.2 *Score-based methods*

Score-based SNA methods use metrics to measure the impact of the social environment on the nodes of interest. These metrics are assigned to each node, either alone or in combination, and analyzed to determine whether the unlabeled nodes are likely to be fraudulent. The resulting score indicates the probability or risk that a person (represented by a node in the social network) may be the target of a fraud or may be a

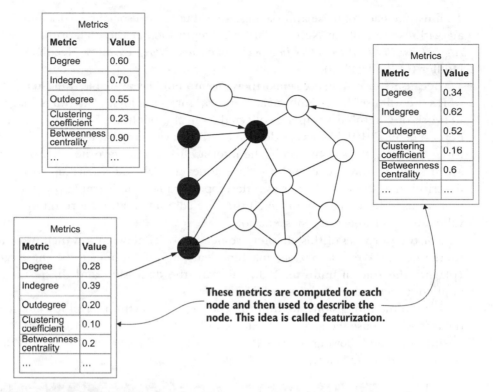

Figure 10.4 Featurization

fraudster. This idea of assigning a set of metrics to each node, as illustrated in figure 10.4, is called *featurization*.

Multiple types of metrics can be extracted from a network, some of them more relevant than others, depending on the circumstances. The network analysis techniques we use can be grouped into three main categories [Baesens et al., 2015]:

- *Neighborhood metrics*—Neighborhood metrics characterize nodes based on their direct connections, considering the *n*-order neighborhood around a node (which consists of the nodes that are *n* hops away from that node). Due to scalability issues, detection models often integrate features derived only from a node and its immediate contacts, known as the node's *first-order neighborhood*.
- *Centrality metrics*—Centrality metrics aim to quantify the importance of a node (here, an individual in a social network) [Boccaletti et al., 2006]. These metrics are typically based on a subgraph or the entire network structure.
- *Collective inference algorithms*—Given a network with known fraudulent nodes, collective inference algorithms attempt to determine the influence of these nodes on the unlabeled nodes in the network. The aim is to compute the probability that a node will be exposed to fraud and, thus, influenced by it (making the person identified by that node more likely to be a fraudster or the victim of fraud).

To illustrate each of these approaches, we will use a real social network and the graph algorithms available in Neo4.j[2] For an in-depth look at these algorithms, see *Graph Algorithms: Practical Examples in Apache Spark and Neo4j*, by Mark Needham and Amy Hodler (O'Reilly, 2019).

Because (for obvious reasons) there are no publicly available fraudster social networks, we will use the GitHub social network[3] for our analysis. GitHub is a large social network of GitHub developers, collected from the public API in June 2019 [Rozemberczki et al., 2019]. Nodes are developers who have starred at least 10 GitHub repositories (clicking the star button in the interface to save or "favorite" them), and edges are mutual follower relationships. The nodes are labeled according to job title or description and are marked as web developer or machine learning practitioner. The metrics used here, the way in which they are computed, and the resulting scores are valid and applicable to a real scenario.

For the purposes of this chapter, we need a social network in which two classes of users interact. We will consider machine learning practitioner to be the target class (playing the role of fraudsters). In this way, the discussion and the results can be applied directly to a fraudster social network.

Due to the dimensions, we don't need to create a Python script for importing the dataset; we can use the LOAD CSV feature in Neo4j. First, we need to import the nodes as shown in the following queries (after moving the dataset into the import directory of your Neo4j installation).

Listing 10.1   Creating the constraints

```
CREATE CONSTRAINT ON (g:GitHubUser) ASSERT (g.id) IS UNIQUE;
```

Listing 10.2   Importing nodes[4]

```
USING PERIODIC COMMIT 1000
LOAD CSV WITH HEADERS FROM 'file:///git_web_ml/musae_git_target.csv' AS row
CREATE (user:GitHubUser {id: row.id, name: row.name, machine_learning:
➥ toInteger(row.ml_target)})
```

Next, we have to import the relationships.

Listing 10.3   Importing relationships

```
USING PERIODIC COMMIT 1000
LOAD CSV WITH HEADERS FROM 'file:///git_web_ml/musae_git_edges.csv' AS row
MATCH (userA:GitHubUser {id: row.id_1})
MATCH (userB:GitHubUser {id: row.id_2})
```

---

[2] https://github.com/neo4j/graph-data-science.

[3] https://snap.stanford.edu/data/github-social.html.

[4] If you are using Neo4j desktop or the community edition, you need to prefix :auto before USING (here and in the next query) because Neo4J desktop uses the explicit transaction handler, which causes conflict with the "periodic commit" statement. With :auto, you can force Neo4J desktop to use the autocommit option rather than an explicit transaction handler. The same applies to the next query.

```
CREATE (userA)-[:FOLLOWS]->(userB)a
```

In a few seconds (or minutes, depending on the power of your computer), the graph database will be ready. As I have mentioned several times already, one of the advantages of graphs is that they allow us to gain insight into the data through visual inspection. Therefore, before using the graph, we should mark the nodes (GitHub users) with specific labels—WebDeveloper and MLDeveloper—so we can recognize them visually. The following queries serve this purpose, allowing us to recognize the nodes easily and simplifying the following analysis.

Listing 10.4 Marking the web developers

```
MATCH (web:GitHubUser {machine_learning: 0})
SET web:WebDeveloper
```

Listing 10.5 Marking the machine learning developers

```
MATCH (ml:GitHubUser {machine_learning: 1})
SET ml:MLDeveloper
```

The resulting graph is shown in figure 10.5. The blue nodes represent the web developers, and the red nodes the machine learning developers.

The use of labels here, instead of the value of the machine_learning property, will improve the results of later queries, in which we have to distinguish between machine learning and web developers.

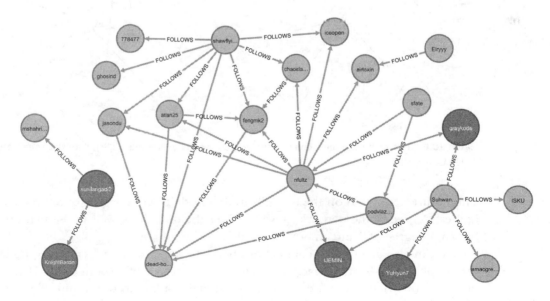

Figure 10.5 The graph database after the import

The selected social network seems to have the characteristics we need: machine learning developers (our target) are relatively infrequent in the graph and generally are connected to similar developers. Now we can compute the metrics we need.

10.2.1 Neighborhood metrics

Neighborhood metrics use direct connections and the *n*-hop neighborhood of a node to characterize the node itself. We can take different metrics into account, but in the context of fraud and for the purposes of this chapter, we will consider degree, triangles, and local cluster coefficient.

The *degree* of a node is formally defined as the number of connections the node has. Degree on its own does not take into account the direction of the relationship, but the related indegree and outdegree metrics do. *Indegree* counts the connections coming in, and *outdegree* counts those going out. The degree of a node summarizes how many neighbors the node has. In the context of fraud detection, it is also useful to distinguish between the number of fraudulent and legitimate neighbors a node has. We can refer to these metrics as the *fraudulent degree* and *legitimate degree*. To clarify, consider a simple social network with and without the directions of the relationships indicated (figure 10.6). In this graph, the red nodes (D and G) are fraudulent.

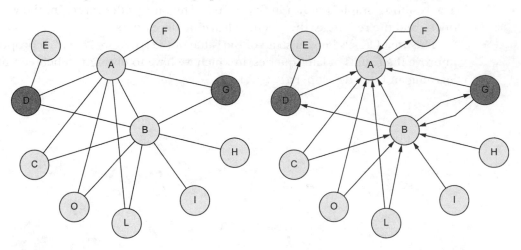

Figure 10.6   Two sample graphs, one undirected (left) and one directed (right), with two fraudulent nodes (D and G)

The undirected graph on the left tells us that node B has a degree of 8, which is the highest degree in the network. If we consider the directions, we can see that node B has an indegree of 6 and an outdegree of 3.

We can also analyze the connections between fraudulent and legitimate nodes in this graph. Nodes A and B each have a fraudulent degree of 2 (both G and D are connected to them) and thus are the nodes most highly influenced by fraud. The degrees of each node are listed in table 10.1.

Table 10.1   Degrees of the nodes in figure 10.6 (considering that D and G are fraudulent)

Node	Degree	Indegree	Outdegree	Fraudulent degree	Legitimate degree
A	8	7	1	2	6
B	9	6	3	3 (node G counts twice)	6
C	2	0	2	0	0
D	3	1	2	0	3
E	1	1	0	1	0
F	2	1	1	0	2
G	3	1	2	0	3
H	1	0	1	0	1
I	1	0	1	0	1
L	2	0	2	0	2
O	2	0	2	0	2

Let's compute the same metrics for the real network by using queries. The following listing shows how to compute the degree of a node (here, the GitHub user amueller).

Listing 10.6   Computing the degree of a node

```
MATCH (m:MLDeveloper {name: "amueller"})-[:FOLLOWS]-(o:GitHubUser)
return count(distinct o) as degree
```

Note that we use -[:FOLLOWS]- without an arrow here (<- or ->) because we are not interested in the direction of the relationship for computing the degree. In the case of a directed network, we can distinguish between the indegree and the outdegree. The indegree specifies how many nodes are pointing toward the target of interest, and the outdegree describes the number of nodes that can be reached from the target of interest. The following queries show how to calculate these metrics.

Listing 10.7   Computing the indegree of a node

```
MATCH (m:MLDeveloper {name: "amueller"})<-[:FOLLOWS]-(o:GitHubUser)
return count(distinct o) as indegree
```

Listing 10.8   Computing the outdegree of a node

```
MATCH (m:MLDeveloper {name: "amueller"})-[:FOLLOWS]->(o:GitHubUser)
return count(distinct o) as outdegree
```

We can easily compute the fraudulent (in our dataset, the connection with `MLDeveloper`) and legitimate (in our dataset, the connection `WebDeveloper`) degrees of a node (in our network, the meaning is slightly different, but the concepts hold) by using the following queries.

Listing 10.9 Computing the fraudulent (`MLDeveloper`) degree of a node

```
MATCH (m:MLDeveloper {name: "amueller"})-[:FOLLOWS]-(o:MLDeveloper)
return count(distinct o) as degree
```

Listing 10.10 Computing the legitimate (`WebDeveloper`) degree of a node

```
MATCH (m:MLDeveloper {name: "amueller"})-[:FOLLOWS]-(o:WebDeveloper)
return count(distinct o) as degree
```

For this user, the fraudulent (`MLDeveloper`) degree is 305, and the legitimate (`Web-Developer`) degree is 173. This result is not surprising: the GitHub user amueller is one of the authors of *Introduction to Machine Learning with Python: A Guide for Data Scientists* (O'Reilly, 2016), so clearly, he is a machine learning developer, and we would expect him to be more connected to other machine learning developers than to web developers. We can easily check whether this rule holds in general via the following query.

Listing 10.11 Computing the degrees for all machine learning developers

```
MATCH (ow:WebDeveloper)-[:FOLLOWS]-(m:MLDeveloper)-[:FOLLOWS]-
➥ (om:MLDeveloper)
WITH m.name as name,
count(distinct om) as mlDegree,
count(distinct ow) as webDegree
RETURN name, mlDegree, webDegree, mlDegree + webDegree as degree
ORDER BY degree desc
```

The results show that the same is true for all the machine learning developers in the network. So it seems that the dataset exhibits the features we described for the fraudulent social network.

The *degree distribution* of a network describes the probability distribution of the degrees in the network. In real-life networks, it generally follows a power law: that is, many nodes are connected with only a few other nodes, and only a few nodes in the network link to many other nodes. The next query allows us to compute the distribution of the degrees of the nodes.

Listing 10.12 Computing the distribution of the degrees

```
MATCH (m:GitHubUser)-[:FOLLOWS]-(om:GitHubUser)
RETURN m.name as user, count(distinct om) as degree
```

Degree distribution

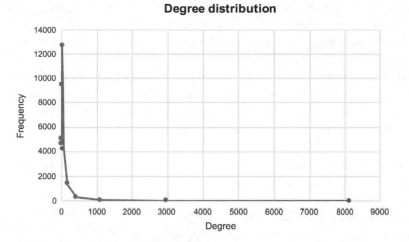

Figure 10.7   Degree distribution on the network used in the examples

The results can be downloaded as a CSV file and visualized, as in chapter 9. Figure 10.7 shows what the distribution will look like. (The Excel file is available in the code repository as ch10/analysis/DegreeAnalysis.xlsx.)

As you can see, the majority of the nodes have a degree of less than 100. Most of the values fall between 7 and 20.

EXERCISE

Explore the graph database you created by playing with listings 10.6 to 10.11 and changing them to consider web developers instead of machine learning developers. Identify some interesting web developers to use for these experiments.

The second neighborhood metric we will take into account is the *triangles count*: the number of fully connected subgraphs consisting of three nodes. Figure 10.8 shows an example of a fully connected subgraph, or triangle.

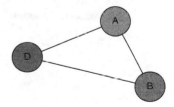

Figure 10.8   An example of a triangle

Looking at triangles is a way to investigate the influential effects of closely connected groups of people. It is related to the principle of *triadic closure*, which is a mechanism for making new connections [Rapoport, 1953]. In the context of social networks, it can be expressed as the idea that if two people have a friend in common, there's an increased likelihood that those two people will become friends themselves in the future. The term comes from the fact that if we have a simple network like the one in figure 10.9, the D-B edge has the effect of closing the third side of this triangle (as shown in figure 10.8).

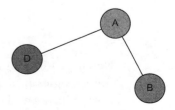

Figure 10.9   A simple network with one side of the triangle open

If we look at a social network at two distinct points in time, we will generally find that a significant number of new edges have formed thanks to this triangle-closing operation at the later point, as connections are made among people with a common neighbor [Easley and Kleinberg, 2010].

Nodes that are part of a group are affected by the other members of that group. In a social network, this effect extends to the beliefs, interests, opinions, and so on of the other members of the group. So in a fraudster network, it makes sense that if a node is part of many triangles in which the other two nodes are fraudulent, that node has a high chance of being affected by fraud itself (that is, of participating in fraud or being a victim of fraud). To compute such risk, we can distinguish between legitimate triangles and fraudulent triangles. If both the two other nodes in the triangle are fraudulent, we say that the triangle is fraudulent. If both nodes are legitimate, we say that the triangle is legitimate. If only one of the two nodes is fraudulent, the triangle is semifraudulent. Consider the toy network in figure 10.10.

Table 10.2 lists the triangle metrics for each node in this network that is part of at least one triangle.

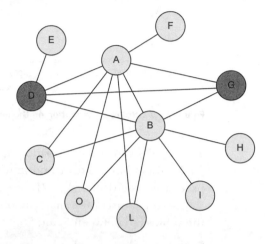

Figure 10.10   Sample fraudster network

Table 10.2   Triangle metrics for the network in figure 10.10

Node	Triangle	Fraudulent triangles	Legitimate triangles	Semifraudulent triangles
A	6	1	3	2
B	6	1	3	2
C	1	0	1	0
D	3	0	1	2
G	3	0	1	2
L	1	0	1	0
O	1	0	1	0

Neo4j provides in its graph data science library an easy procedure for computing all the triangles in a graph or those related to a particular node. Appendix B explains how to install and configure it. The following query demonstrates how.

Listing 10.13 Computing triangles for nodes

```
CALL gds.triangleCount.stream({
  nodeProjection: 'GitHubUser',
  relationshipProjection: {
    FOLLOWS: {
      type: 'FOLLOWS',
      orientation: 'UNDIRECTED'
    }
  },
  concurrency:4
})
YIELD nodeId, triangleCount
RETURN gds.util.asNode(nodeId).name AS name,
gds.util.asNode(nodeId).machine_learning as ml_user, triangleCount
ORDER BY triangleCount DESC
```

The basic role of triadic closure in social networks has motivated the formulation of simple social network measures to capture its prevalence. One of these measures is the *local clustering coefficient*. The clustering coefficient of a node A is defined as the probability that two randomly selected friends of A are friends with each other. In other words, the fraction of pairs of A's friends are connected by edges. Let's make this point clearer by again considering our toy network (figure 10.11).

The clustering coefficient of node A is 2/6, or 0.333, because among the six

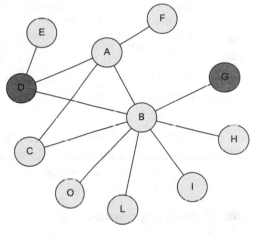

Figure 10.11 Sample graph

possible pairs of friends (B-D, B-C, B-F, C-D, C-F, and D-F), there are edges between C-B and D-B. In general, the clustering coefficient of a node ranges from 0 (when none of the node's friends are friends with each other) to 1 (when all the node's friends are friends with each other), and the more strongly triadic closure is operating in the neighborhood of the node, the higher the clustering coefficient will tend to be. In the fraud scenario, this metric is important because if a node has a low local clustering coefficient compared with the average clustering coefficient of the network, the node is connected to people who belong to independent groups. This anomalous condition can reveal a possible fraud risk, as the fraudster is joining groups of people to commit a crime. The formula for determining the local clustering coefficient of a node looks like this:

$$cl_A = \frac{\textit{number of pairs of neighbors of A that are connected}}{\textit{number of pairs of neighbors of A}}$$

The following query allows you to compute the clustering coefficients for each of the nodes in our network and store them as properties of the nodes.

Listing 10.14   Computing clustering coefficient

```
CALL gds.localClusteringCoefficient.write ({
  nodeProjection: 'GitHubUser',
  relationshipProjection: {
    FOLLOWS: {
      type: 'FOLLOWS',
      orientation: 'UNDIRECTED'
    }
  },
  concurrency:4,
  writeProperty:'clusteringCoefficient'
})
YIELD createMillis, computeMillis, writeMillis, nodeCount,
➥ averageClusteringCoefficient
RETURN createMillis, computeMillis, writeMillis, nodeCount,
➥ averageClusteringCoefficient
```

As you'll see from the result of this query when you run it, the average clustering coefficient is low: around 0.167.

EXERCISE

Explore the graph, checking the triangles of some nodes that have coefficient 0 or 1. You can use a query to find one or two such nodes and then use the Neo4j browser to navigate them. As a suggestion, I would create the query to avoid trivial nodes with only one or two followers.

10.2.2 *Centrality metrics*

Centrality metrics reveal central nodes in a graph or subgraph—that is, nodes that might have a strong effect on other nodes—by assigning to each node a score indicating how central it is to the flow of communication through the graph [Fouss et al., 2016]. In a social network, centrality metrics help us answer questions like these:

- What is the most representative node in a community?
- How critical is a given node with respect to the flow of information through the network?
- Which nodes are the most peripheral?

These metrics are useful in a fraud-fighting scenario; they can be used to prevent the expansion of future fraudulent activities by identifying the key actor in a web of frauds, who is likely to act as a central node and be heavily involved in communication regarding the organization of the frauds. Compared with neighborhood metrics, which take into account only the direct connections of a node to extract the value, these types of metrics consider the whole graph (or a large part of it). Hence, they take into account the role of the person in the entire network, not only in their ego network.[5]

The metrics we will consider include shortest path, closeness centrality, and betweenness centrality. For the purposes of demonstration, as with the neighborhood metrics, we'll use the GitHub network as a proxy for our hypothetical fraudster social network.

The *shortest path* is the minimum number of hops (geodesic distance) needed to reach a node from a target node. While computing these distances, the algorithm can take into account the weight of each relationship, which is particularly useful when you are using this metric to find the best route to take from one location to another. In other scenarios, such as ours, each relationship has the same weight: 1. In this case, the shortest path is determined by counting how many nodes (or relationships) you have to pass through to reach a target node from a source node. Figure 10.12 shows an example, identifying the shortest paths from node A to nodes G, I, and L.

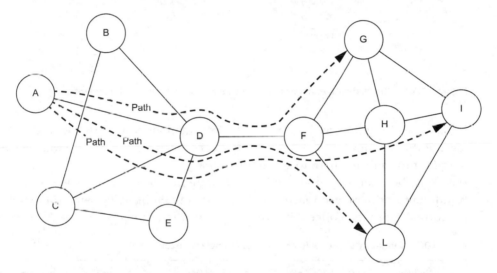

Figure 10.12 Shortest-path example

In the fraud context, the geodesic distance of a potential target from a fraudster can reveal the risk of their becoming a victim. The closer a legitimate node is to a fraudulent node, the greater the likelihood is that it will become a target. It is also interesting to know how many paths exist between fraudulent nodes and legitimate nodes: the more paths there are, the higher the chances are that the fraudulent influence will eventually reach the target node. In other words, if a fraudulent node is in a potential target's immediate subgraph (neighborhood), there is a better chance that it will be affected. Conversely, considering such distances can reveal the fraud potential of a

---

[5] *Ego networks* are social networks comprised of a node (a person, the ego) and all the other nodes (people) to which it is directly connected.

specific fraudster: how easy it is for that person to reach different victims directly or indirectly. Suppose that in our sample network, certain nodes have been identified as fraudulent, as shown in figure 10.13.

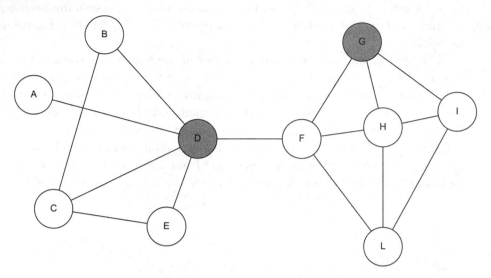

Figure 10.13   Shortest-path example in fraud use case. Dark nodes are fraudulent.

Looking at this graph, we can extract the information in table 10.3 to analyze the risk level of the legitimate nodes in the network. To calculate the risk, we will consider the length of the shortest path to a fraudulent node (column 2) as well as the n-hop paths that exist between that node and any fraudulent node—in other words, how many fraudulent nodes we can reach from the node in n hops. (The same fraudulent node is counted more than once if it is reachable by different paths.)

Table 10.3   Summary of geodesic distance to fraudulent nodes

Node	Geodetic path	1-hop paths	2-hop paths	3-hop paths
A	1	1	2	5
B	1	2	2	7
E	1	2	4	7
F	1	2	5	9
G	1	1	4	7
I	1	1	3	8
L	1	1	4	7

Many algorithms and techniques can compute the shortest path between two nodes, but that topic is beyond the scope of this book. Neo4j provides many solutions out of the box, and various libraries provide superoptimized algorithms for such well-known tasks. The following query shows how to use the Neo4j graph algorithms library to compute the shortest path for the database we imported.

Listing 10.15 Finding the shortest path between two nodes

```
MATCH (start:MLDeveloper {name: "amueller"})
MATCH (end:MLDeveloper {name: "git-kale"})
CALL gds.beta.shortestPath.dijkstra.stream({
nodeProjection: 'MLDeveloper',
relationshipProjection: {
FOLLOWS: {
type: 'FOLLOWS',
orientation: 'UNDIRECTED'
}
},
sourceNode: id(start),
targetNode: id(end)
})
YIELD index, nodeIds, costs
WITH index,
[nodeId IN nodeIds | gds.util.asNode(nodeId).name] AS nodeNames,
costs
ORDER BY index
LIMIT 1
UNWIND range(0, size(nodeNames) - 1) as idx
RETURN nodeNames[idx] as name, costs[idx] as cost
```

The results of this query are shown in figure 10.14. The cost is the number of hops it takes to get from the start node (amueller) to a specific node.

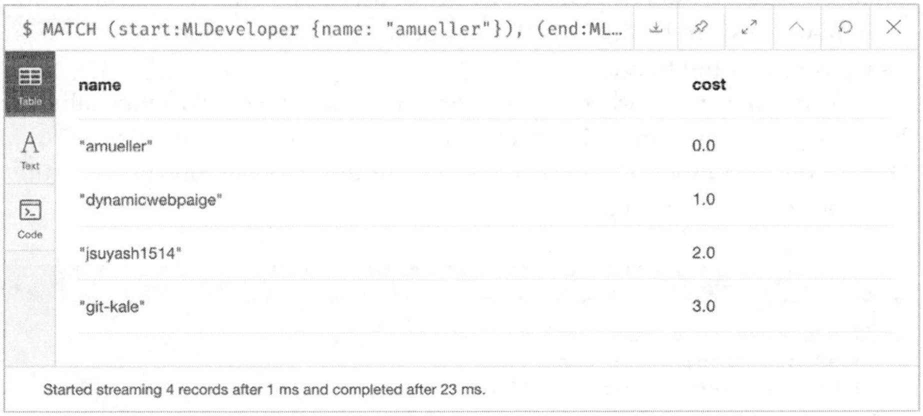

$ MATCH (start:MLDeveloper {name: "amueller"}), (end:ML...	
name	**cost**
"amueller"	0.0
"dynamicwebpaige"	1.0
"jsuyash1514"	2.0
"git-kale"	3.0

Started streaming 4 records after 1 ms and completed after 23 ms.

Figure 10.14 Results of listing 10.15

Closeness centrality is determined by considering all the shortest-path lengths linking nodes. Formally, it is the inverse of the mean distance of a node from all the reachable nodes in the network. The closeness centrality of a node a—cc_a—in a network G with n nodes is computed as

$$cc_a = \cfrac{1}{\cfrac{\sum_{b \in G,\, b \neq a,\, b \in reachable(a,\,G)} d(b,a)}{|reachable(a,G)| - 1}}$$

where

- $d(b,a)$ is the geodesic distance between the node a and the node b.
- $reachable(a,G)$ is the subgraph of G reachable from a.
- $|reachable(a,G)|$ is the number of nodes reachable by a.

The denominator is the average distance of the node a from all the nodes reachable from a. A high closeness centrality value indicates that the node can easily reach many other nodes in the network and thus has a strong impact on other nodes. We can see the logic of centrality this way: if a person is not central (has a low closeness centrality value), they have to rely on others to relay messages through the network for them or reach others. Conversely, a person who is central (has a high closeness centrality value) can easily spread a message across the network or reach others themselves without any (or few) intermediaries diluting their influence.

In the fraud use case, if a fraudulent node in a (sub)graph has a high closeness centrality value, fraud might easily spread through the (sub)network and contaminate other nodes. Being able to reach a high number of other nodes independently extends that node's reach. Furthermore, closeness centrality is useful beyond being a measure of the independence of a person in a social network. Researchers have also linked this metric with a person's ability to access information in the network easily, with power and influence. All these aspects can play a critical role in a fraudster's capacity to commit fraud.

We don't have to worry about computing closeness centrality values ourselves, because Neo4j and other libraries offer support for that task. The following query shows how to compute closeness centrality for the whole graph and store the values in each node for further analysis.

Listing 10.16   Computing and storing closeness centrality

```
CALL gds.alpha.closeness.write({
  nodeProjection: 'GitHubUser',
  relationshipProjection: 'FOLLOWS',
  writeProperty: 'closeness'
}) YIELD nodes, writeProperty
```

We can order the nodes by closeness centrality to find the machine learning developers with the highest values.

Listing 10.17 Getting the top 20 ML developers with the highest closeness centrality

```
MATCH (user:MLDeveloper)
RETURN user.name, user.closeness
ORDER BY user.closeness desc
LIMIT 20
```

The results of this query are shown in figure 10.15.

	user.name	user.closeness
1	"WillemJan"	0.40490843671124
2	"bradfitz"	0.40249188588998974
3	"antirez"	0.4017584057121543
4	"surajit-techie"	0.4010190622074717
5	"amiryeg"	0.40015072389929096
6	"iam-peekay"	0.4000870238891188
7	"jnunemaker"	0.3984884519845674
8	"jason9263"	0.39607694813040417
9	"manishmarahatta"	0.3922321409992301

Figure 10.15 Results of listing 10.17

Looking at the results, you'll notice that some users are prominent users who have a lot of followers and are working on highly relevant open source projects. But in our dataset, some of the top users would not be considered to be influential. The first one, WillemJan, has few followers but follows 33,000 GitHub users, bringing them to the top of the closeness centrality stack. This example shows that closeness centrality is biased by how many people you know (or how many you follow).

Betweenness centrality measures the extent to which a node lies on the shortest paths connecting any two nodes in the network. This metric can be interpreted as an indication of how much information passes through this node. A node with a high betweenness centrality may connect communities (subgraphs in the network). Consider the example shown in figure 10.16.

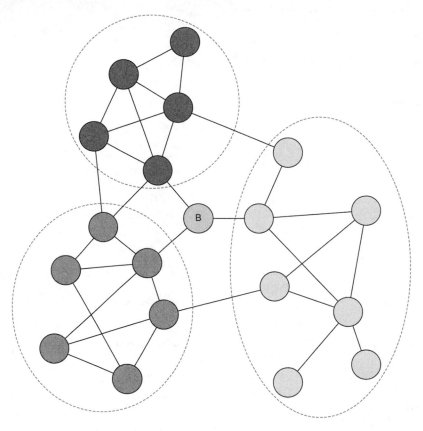

Figure 10.16   Sample graph with three almost-distinct clusters connected via one central node

In this figure, the central node B connects the almost-independent subgraphs. It's worth noticing that the node has a low closeness centrality value; it is directly connected to few nodes in the graph, and to reach the others, it has to pass through long paths. But it has a high betweenness centrality value because it is in the greatest number of paths.

This example is helpful for understanding the difference between these two concepts of centrality. Whereas closeness centrality measures how many people a person knows or how many people they can reach in few hops, betweenness centrality considers the position of the person in the entire network. In a communication network, betweenness centrality measures how much potential control a node has over the flow of communication.

This example gives us an idea of the value of those metrics when analyzing a social network to fight fraud. If node B in figure 10.16 is infected by fraud from one community, the fraud can easily pass on to the other communities. To prevent this contamination from occurring, one option is to remove this node from the network.

Betweenness centrality is a powerful measure in multiple domains. Perhaps a more intuitive example is the spread of disease. Within a large population, the nodes with high betweenness centrality have a high chance of transmitting the disease to a lot of people from different communities. By recognizing and isolating those nodes, it is possible to reduce the extent of the disease's outbreak. Similarly, in a terrorist network, the nodes with the highest betweenness centrality are key people for passing information, money, weapons, and so on across multiple cells or clusters. By identifying them, it is possible to identify more clusters, and by blocking them, we can affect the capacity of the entire network to operate.

The formula for computing the betweenness centrality of a node a takes into account for each pair of nodes the percentage of the shortest paths passing through a and sums all these percentages. Mathematically,

$$bc_a = \sum_{j < k} \frac{g_{jk}(a)}{g_{jk}}$$

where

- $g_{jk}(a)$ is the number of shortest paths between j and k passing through a.
- g_{jk} is the total number of shortest paths between j and k.

Like closeness centrality, this metric is fully supported by Neo4j and many other libraries. In our database, we can easily compute betweenness centrality by using the following query.

Listing 10.18 Computing the betweenness centrality of the nodes

```
CALL gds.betweenness.write({
  nodeProjection: 'GitHubUser',
  relationshipProjection: 'FOLLOWS',
  writeProperty: 'betweenness'
}) YIELD nodePropertiesWritten, minimumScore, maximumScore, scoreSum
```

Then we can order the nodes by betweenness centrality to find the machine learning developers with the highest values.

Listing 10.19 Getting the top 20 ML developers with the highest betweenness centrality

```
MATCH (user:MLDeveloper)
RETURN user.name, user.betweenness
ORDER BY user.betweenness desc
LIMIT 20
```

The results of this query are much more significant. Almost all the people in the list are highly relevant: they are authors of prominent books, or they contribute to a lot of open source projects in the machine learning space. Betweenness centrality, in this case, is capable of capturing better than closeness centrality the significance of people in the network. It represents a person's influence in the full network rather than in their circle of friends.

EXERCISE

In the preceding queries, we considered only machine learning developers to analyze their influence. Run the queries to search for the top web developers, considering betweenness and closeness centrality, and then look at their profiles on GitHub.

10.2.3 *Collective inference algorithms*

In the scenario considered in this chapter, a collective inference procedure infers the probability that a node could be affected by fraud—either becoming a fraudster or becoming the victim of a fraud—by taking into account the fact that inferences about nodes can mutually affect one another and that the propagation of the effect of such inference is proportional to the importance of a node. We will focus on PageRank, a powerful collective inference algorithm that we have seen in action earlier in the book.

PageRank [Page et al., 1998]—the basis of Google's famous search engine algorithm for ranking web pages—is perhaps the most popular technique for prestige computation today. It assigns a prestige score to each node *j* in a graph. Intuitively, the prestige score of a node must be higher if the node is linked to many nodes that are themselves important. This "prestige" can be seen the other way around in the case of fraud, of course. If a node is linked to a lot of prestigious fraudsters (well-known fraudsters who are marked as such in our semilabeled network), the chance of that node becoming involved in fraud (either as a perpetrator or victim) is high.

Our starting point is a semilabeled network with a few labeled legitimate and fraudulent nodes and many unlabeled nodes. Figure 10.17 represents our toy fraudsters network. Looking at this figure, what can we infer about the probability that node A is either a fraudster or the victim of a fraud, supposing that G and D are fraudsters?

Let's start our analysis by considering the scenario PageRank was introduced for and ignore the labels, treating all the nodes as equals. Assume for now that the nodes are web pages and that a surfer can browse to pages only by following the links on the page they are currently viewing.

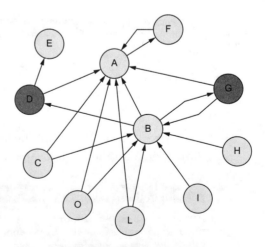

Figure 10.17 A simple directed fraud network in which D and G are fraudsters

The figure shows that web page A has seven incoming links. The probability that a surfer who is currently viewing web page B will visit web page A next is 1/3, or 33%, because web page B has three links to other web pages, one of which is web page A. Similarly, if a surfer is currently looking at web page C or D, there is a 50% probability in both cases that they will visit web page A next. The probability that a web page will be visited is called the *page rank* of that web page. To determine the page rank of web page A, we need to know the page ranks of web pages B, C, D, F, G, L, and O (the seven pages that link to A).

This process is collective inference: the ranking of one web page depends on the rankings of the other pages that link to it, and a change in the ranking of one of these pages might affect the rankings of all the others in a cascading fashion. Specifically, the main idea is that important web pages (pages that appear at the top of the search results) have many incoming links from other important web pages. Here's the basic approach to page ranking for any given page:

- The rankings of the web pages pointing to that page
- The outdegree of the pages that page is linked from

The initial page rank value of a node is set to the probability that a random surfer will start their navigation from that node—that is, 1/ *<number of pages>*. Then it iterates until some stopping criterion is met, generally when the change in the ranking at each iteration becomes marginal or when some defined maximum number of iterations has been reached. Figure 10.18 summarizes the algorithm with a concrete example.

At each iteration i, we can say that the page rank value of the node A, $PR(i,A)$, is computed as

$$PR(i,A) = \sum_{n \in N_A} \frac{PR(i-1,n)}{outdegree(n)}$$

where

- $PR(i-1,n)$ is the page rank value of the node n at the previous iteration.
- N_A are all the neighbors of A.

$PR(0,n)$ is the initial value for each node, representing the probability that a random surfer will start their navigation from that node. The assumption that a random surfer will visit pages only by following a random link on the web page they are viewing is not realistic, of course. Surfers' behavior is more random: rather than follow links on a web page, they might randomly visit other pages. Therefore, a more sophisticated PageRank algorithm must include the random-surfer model, which assumes that surfers often get bored and jump arbitrarily to another web page.

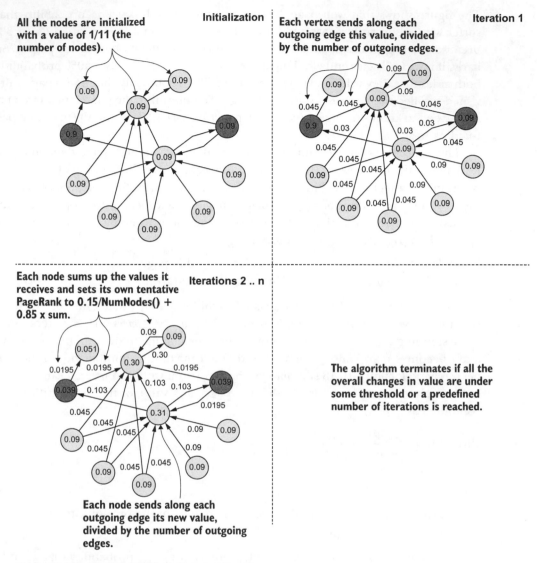

All the nodes are initialized with a value of 1/11 (the number of nodes).

Initialization

Each vertex sends along each outgoing edge this value, divided by the number of outgoing edges.

Iteration 1

Each node sums up the values it receives and sets its own tentative PageRank to 0.15/NumNodes() + 0.85 x sum.

Iterations 2 .. n

The algorithm terminates if all the overall changes in value are under some threshold or a predefined number of iterations is reached.

Each node sends along each outgoing edge its new value, divided by the number of outgoing edges.

Figure 10.18   PageRank initialization and iterations

Supposing that α is the probability that the surfer will follow a link on the web page they are currently viewing and $(1 - \alpha)$ is the probability that the surfer will visit a random other web page, a more advanced formula is

$$PR(i,A) = \alpha \sum_{n \in N_A} \frac{PR(i-1, n)}{outdegree(n)} + (1-\alpha)e_A$$

where $(1 - \alpha)$ is the *restart probability* and e_A is the *restart value* for web page A, which is often uniformly distributed among all web pages.

Starting from this advanced version, Page et al. introduced an extension of the PageRank algorithm by personalizing the search to the user. This personalization is done by changing the restart value from a uniform distribution across all nodes to a version that is tailored to a user's search interests. A higher restart value for a page X corresponds to the user's having a higher interest in that page.

This last version is well suited to our final use case: inferring the effect of fraudsters on an unlabeled node (which means that we don't know whether the person identified by that node is a fraudster or a victim of fraud). In this context, the PageRank algorithm can be seen as a propagation of node influence through a labeled network. (In our case, we know some of the nodes that are fraudulent.) We inject fraud into the network through the restart values in the following way:

$$e_A = \begin{cases} 0 \ \textit{if A is not a fraudulent nodes} \\ \dfrac{1}{\textit{number of fraudulent nodes}} \ \textit{if A is a fraudulent node} \end{cases}$$

At the end of the page rank computation, the top-ranked nodes are those most influenced by fraud. We can apply these ideas to our graph database. There are plenty of implementations of personalized page rank, and Neo4j has its own. The following query computes the personalized page rank for all the users, considering the machine learning developers as start values (specified here in the source nodes).

Listing 10.20 Computing personalized page rank for machine learning developers

```
MATCH (mlUser:MLDeveloper)
with collect(mlUser) as mlUsers #A
CALL gds.pageRank.write({
  nodeProjection: 'GitHubUser', #B
  relationshipProjection: 'FOLLOWS',
  maxIterations: 20,
  dampingFactor: 0.85,
  sourceNodes: mlUsers,
  writeConcurrency: 4,
  writeProperty: 'pagerank'
})
YIELD ranIterations, didConverge
RETURN ranIterations, didConverge
#A Computing the list of starting nodes, since we would like to consider the
➥ effect of this nodes on the network.
#B The page rank is computed on all the GitHubUsers
```

In this query, the `dampingFactor` is our α, and `sourceNodes` are the nodes used for the restart vector. When the scores have been computed, we can order the web developers by page rank value from highest to lowest by using the following query.

> **Listing 10.21   Sorting by page rank to find the most heavily influenced users**

```
MATCH (user:GitHubUser)
RETURN user.name, user.pagerank, labels(user)
ORDER BY user.pagerank desc
LIMIT 20
```

The top of the list returned by the previous query is occupied by the web developers who are most likely to be influenced by machine learning developers. If you would like to investigate further, you can use the following query to compute the sum of the page rank values of the followers of a particular machine learning developer.

> **Listing 10.22   Computing the sum of page rank for the followers of a developer**

```
MATCH (user:GitHubUser {name: "dalinhuang99"})<-[:FOLLOWS]-(follower)
WITH user, follower, follower.machine_learning as machine_learning,
CASE follower.machine_learning = 0
WHEN true THEN 0
WHEN false THEN follower.pagerank
END as mlpagerank,
CASE follower.machine_learning = 1
WHEN true THEN 0
WHEN false THEN follower.pagerank
END as webpagerank
RETURN user.pagerank, count(follower), sum(machine_learning),
➥ sum(mlpagerank), sum(webpagerank)
```

The results of this query show that this user has 1,000 machine learning developers following them out of a total of more than 7,000 followers, but the sum of those developers' PageRank values is higher than the sum of the web developers' rankings. This result means that the influence of machine learning developers on this user is greater than that of web developers, proving that the PageRank algorithm can be used to determine the effect of the network on a subject. Coming back to our fraud scenario, then, the PageRank value can measure the probability that a node (person) will be affected by fraud (participating in it or being targeted as a victim).

EXERCISE

Run the last two queries again, inverting machine learning developers and web developers, and explore the results.

10.3   *Cluster-based methods*

Social networks are powerful tools for revealing the relationships among people by means of the links in the network. In section 10.2, our analysis focused on extracting or computing features node by node, in most cases considering the directly connected neighboring nodes or the paths passing through each node. In such types of analysis, each node is considered individually, focusing on the role that it has in the network and its set of close connections. The resulting metrics are useful, but to have a good understanding of the effects that a social network has on a node (or, conversely, the effects of a node on the network), it is important to consider the node as part of a group of nodes rather than alone. Because of the dynamics of the network, it stands to reason that communities (groups of nodes within a network) that behave the same way or share an opinion or belief are likely to have a greater effect on the network than a single person and more influence in terms of information exchange. In the fraud use case, a group of fraudsters working together are likely to have a greater reach than one operating on their own.

In graph theory, a *community* is a subgraph or cluster in the network whose nodes are more strongly and densely connected than they are with the nodes in any other random subgraph in the network. All members of a community can be reached easily through other members of the same community (*connectedness*). At the same time, we expect nodes that belong to a community to have a higher probability of linking to the other members of that community than to nodes that do not belong to the same community (*local density*). So we can define a community more formally as a locally dense connected subgraph in a network [Barabási and Pósfai, 2016]. The graph in figure 10.19, for example, can be divided into three communities, in each of which there are many connections between nodes in the community and none or few outside it.

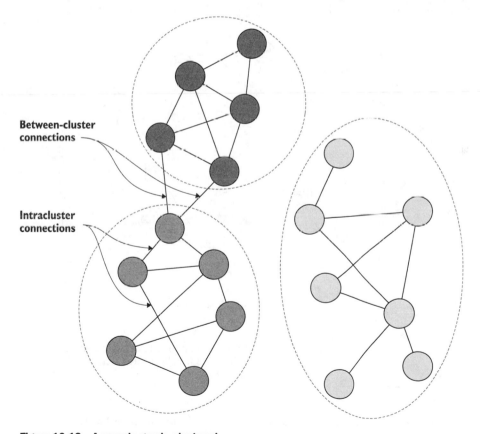

Figure 10.19   A sample graph, clustered

Fraudsters often work together as a group, sharing, reinforcing, and offering complementary ideas about how to perpetrate a fraud. Moreover, belonging to a group of fraudsters affects people's behavior, increasing the risk that they will also take part in a fraud (peer pressure at work). In this context, community mining aims to identify groups of fraudsters in the network to pinpoint subgraphs in which fraud is more likely to occur than in the rest of the graph. This information can help in the detection of hidden fraudulent structures. Bearing in mind that people are more likely to commit fraud if they are influenced by a whole community than by one fraudulent person, it can also be a useful way to identify people who are at risk of being drawn in to fraudulent activity and thus curtailing the growth of fraudulent groups [Baesens et al., 2015].

Communities are powerful mechanisms for identifying common behavioral patterns, even when the nodes are not connected in a classic social network. Figure 10.20 is a bipartite graph in which the nodes are stores and credit cards. The stores are connected to credit cards by fraudulent transactions.

As discussed in chapter 9, fraudsters tend to stick to the same behavioral patterns. They may use stolen credit cards in the same stores repeatedly, perhaps because staff at those stores are involved in the fraud or perhaps because previous attempts there

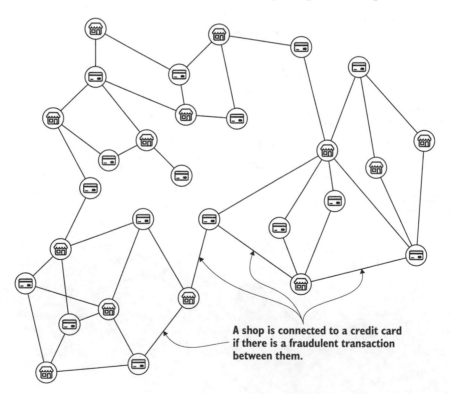

A shop is connected to a credit card if there is a fraudulent transaction between them.

Figure 10.20   **A bipartite graph with shops and credit cards connected by fraudulent transactions**

have been successful. We can project[6] the previous bipartite graph into a stores graph where two nodes are connected if they are linked to the same credit card node in the bipartite representation. The result will look like figure 10.21.

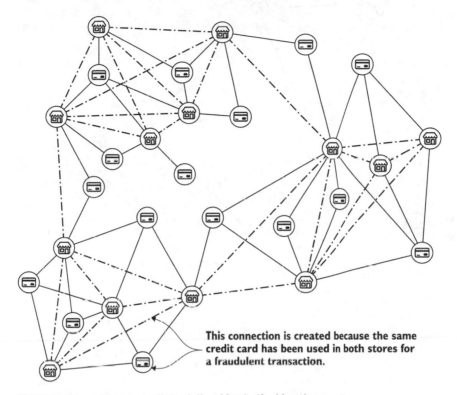

This connection is created because the same credit card has been used in both stores for a fraudulent transaction.

Figure 10.21 Adding projection relationships to the bipartite graph

It is easy to see that a few suspicious communities of stores are commonly used by fraudsters (figure 10.22). Discovering such communities reveals that some stores are more susceptible to being victims of fraud than others, and is a signal that those stores might be involved in the fraud themselves or may need to beef up their security.

A known pattern in credit card fraud is that the stolen card is used in many stores for small transactions. In this case, community mining exposes immediately which stores are often related to the same stolen credit cards—something that implementing fraud detection practices at the individual store level would not be able to reveal. The use of a card in more than one of these stores or multiple times in some of them can be used as a relevant signal that the card (detail) has been stolen. In many applications and contexts, the discovery of such communities through SNA can aid in the detection of fraudulent structures or the curtailment of fraud rings.

---

[6] Recall from chapter 5 that we can infer connections between nodes of the same type in a bipartite graph, creating a projection.

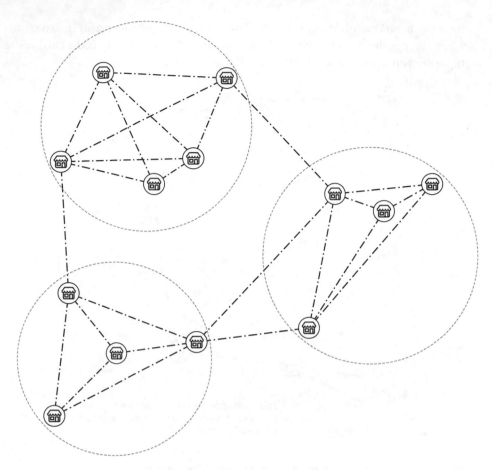

Figure 10.22   Clusters in the projection of the bipartite graph

A common technique for community mining is *graph partitioning*, also referred to as *node clustering*. The aim is to split the graph into some predetermined number of clusters by optimizing the ratio between the intracommunity and intercommunity edges. Different algorithms can be used to determine the optimal way to divide the graph. Among them, I would like to mention two opposite approaches:

- *Top-down* or *divisive*—These methods, also called *partitioning* or *splitting*, start from an initial situation in which all the nodes are considered as a single cluster. This cluster is split iteratively into pieces, trying to minimize intercluster connectivity, until a stable point is reached at which it is not possible to get a significant improvement.

- *Bottom-up* or *agglomerative*—These methods operate in the opposite way: they start by considering each node as an independent cluster and then recursively try to merge the nodes that are most similar or highly interconnected into clusters.

For our purposes, we will consider the second type of approach, which is also useful for detecting dense (highly interconnected) regions. Specifically, the algorithm used in the next examples is the Louvain method, introduced by Blondel et al. [2008]. This method is typically used to detect communities in large networks. Per the Neo4j documentation,[7]

> *It maximizes a modularity score for each community, where the modularity quantifies the quality of an assignment of nodes to communities. This means evaluating how much more densely connected the nodes within a community are, compared to how connected they would be in a random network. The Louvain algorithm is a hierarchical clustering algorithm, that recursively merges communities into a single node and executes the modularity clustering on the condensed graphs.*

For the sake of completeness, the implementation generally used is the parallel version introduced by Lu et al. [2015], which introduces some heuristics to break the inner sequential barrier.

You don't need to worry about the implementation of this algorithm, unless you would particularly like to implement it by yourself, because it is available in Neo4j and other libraries. The following query will perform Louvain community detection on our example network.

Listing 10.23   Executing Louvain community detection on the GitHub graph

```
CALL gds.louvain.write({
    nodeProjection: 'GitHubUser',
    relationshipProjection: {
        FOLLOWS: {
            type: 'FOLLOWS',
            orientation: 'undirected',
            aggregation: 'NONE'
        }
    },
    writeProperty: 'community'
}) YIELD nodePropertiesWritten,  communityCount, modularity
RETURN nodePropertiesWritten,  communityCount, modularity
```

As in the previous cases, the algorithm will store in each node a new property called community that contains the ID of the community the node belongs to. The following query will give you an idea of how Louvain splits our network into communities.

Listing 10.24   Retrieving the top 5 Louvain communities

```
MATCH (g:GitHubUser)
RETURN g.community,
count(g) as communitySize,
sum(g.machine_learning) as mlDevCount
ORDER BY communitySize desc
LIMIT 5
```

---

[7] http://mng.bz/XYy6.

g.community	communitySize	mlDevCount
36724	7846	373
3214	7769	5621
34977	6299	1133
4404	6091	867
34542	2588	129

Figure 10.23   Top five Louvain communities. (The results could be a bit different due to some random initialization.)

The result will look like figure 10.23.

Take a look at the number of machine learning developers in the first two communities. The first group is clearly a web developers' community (only 373 members are machine learning developers), and the second one is clearly a machine learning developers' community. The algorithm appears to have done a good job of recognizing groups of people with similar interests.

10.4   *Advantages of graphs*

In this case, we can't talk about the advantages of using graphs over some other approach, because the graph—specifically, the social network—is the core element of the approach described in this chapter. But we can recap the advantages of using a social network (and, thus, a graph approach) for fraud detection and prevention:

- Social networks provide an excellent source of knowledge for exploring and investigating frauds.
- Graphs are the best way to represent social networks.
- SNA, with different algorithms, offers a wide set of insights about the reach and influence of frauds and fraudsters.
- Graph algorithms are an awesome toolset for extracting insights from a graph and performing deep analysis of a social network, enabling us to recognize key people, groups of people, or nodes in the network.

Summary

Although much more could be said on the topic, this chapter completes our overview of fraud detection techniques that use a graph approach. Our focus here was on the role of social networks, and specifically SNA, in analyzing the behavior and influence of fraudsters within a network. In this chapter, you learned

- How to create a social network from different types of data sources
- How to use SNA methods to explore a web of frauds and fraudsters' influence within a network
- How to assign a set of features related to the network structure to each node
- How to use various graph algorithms to extract insights from a network (finding key influencers, computing clustering coefficients, counting triangles, and so on)
- How to group nodes into communities

It's worth mentioning that in this chapter, we were able to perform all our analyses by using only Neo4j and queries, using the available plugins without writing a single line of code. This fact demonstrates the power and flexibility of the graph approach and the libraries that exist today.

References

[Baesens et al., 2015] Baesens, Bart, Veronique Van Vlasselaer, and Wouter Verbeke. *Fraud Analytics Using Descriptive, Predictive, and Social Network Techniques: A Guide to Data Science for Fraud Detection.* Hoboken, NJ: Wiley and SAS Business Series, 2015.

[Barabási and Pósfai, 2016] Barabási, Albert-László, and Mártin Pósfai. *Network Science.* Cambridge, UK: Cambridge University Press, 2016.

[Barta and Stewart, 2008] Barta, Dan, and David Stewart. 2008. "A Layered Approach to Fraud Detection and Prevention: Increasing Investigator Efficiency Using Network Analytics." SAS Conclusions Paper.

[Blondel et al., 2008] Blondel, Vincent D., Jean-Loup Guillaume, Renaud Lambiotte, and Etienne Lefebvre. "Fast Unfolding of Communities in Large Networks." *Journal of Statistical Mechanics: Theory and Experiment* (2008): P10008.

[Boccaletti et al., 2006] Boccaletti, Stefano, Vito Latora, Yamir Moreno, Mario Chavez, and Dong-Uk Hwang. "Complex Networks: Structure and Dynamics." *Physics Reports* 424:4–5 (2006): 175–308.

[Easley and Kleinberg, 2010] Easley, David, and Jon Kleinberg. *Networks, Crowds, and Markets: Reasoning About a Highly Connected World.* New York: Cambridge University Press, 2010.

[Fouss et al., 2016] Fouss, François, Marco Saerens, and Masashi Shimbo. 2016. *Algorithms and Models for Network Data and Link Analysis.* New York, Cambridge University Press, 2016.

[Koutra et al., 2011] Koutra, Danai, Tai-You Ke, U. Kang, Duen Horng (Polo) Chau, Hsing-Kuo Kenneth Pao, and Christos Faloutsos. "Unifying Guilt-by-Association Approaches: Theorems and Fast Algorithms." *Proceedings of the European Conference on Machine Learning and Knowledge Discovery in Databases* (2011): 245–260.

[Litan, 2012] Litan, Avivah. "Who's Who and What's What in the Enterprise Fraud and Misuse Management Market." Gartner Resource ID G00230076 (2012).

[Lu et al., 2015] Lu, Hao, Mahantesh Halappanavar, and Ananth Kalyanaraman. "Parallel Heuristics for Scalable Community Detection." *Parallel Computing* 47: 19–37.

[Needham and Hodler, 2019] Needham, Mark, and Amy E. Hodler. *Graph Algorithms: Practical Examples in Apache Spark and Neo4j*. Sebastopol, CA: O'Reilly Media, 2019.

[Newman, 2010] Newman, Mark. *Networks: An Introduction*. New York: Oxford University Press, 2010.

[Page et al., 1998] Page, Larry, Sergey Brin, Rajeev Motwani, and Terry Winograd. "The PageRank Citation Ranking: Bringing Order to the Web." *Stanford InfoLab Technical Report*.

[Rapoport, 1953] Rapoport, Anatol. "Spread of Information Through a Population with Socio-Structural Bias I: Assumption of Transitivity." *The Bulletin of Mathematical Biophysics* 15:4 (1953): 523–533.

[Rozemberczki et al., 2019] Rozemberczki, Benedek, Carl Allen, and Rik Sarkar. "Multi-Scale Attributed Node Embedding." arXiv preprint arXiv:1909.13021 (2019).

Taming text with graphs

Text, text, and more text! We are surrounded by textual data. Much of the world's knowledge is stored and shared by using text in natural language. This has been true since the beginning of human history, when we started sharing knowledge in different languages—first by voice and later, to make it permanent, by writing.

Natural language is the main way in which we interact with other humans. We begin learning it as infants, yet understanding language is one of the most complex tasks a machine can do. Nevertheless, computer scientists, data scientists, and machine learning practitioners have worked hard to make machines capable of dealing with textual data, providing complex solutions that use text to offer advanced features to the final users.

In these last two chapters of the book, we will focus on the following aspects of this interesting research area:

- *Natural language processing (NLP)*—NLP aims at processing natural language (English, Italian, French, and so on) and converting it to data structures that a machine can understand and process. It extracts the hidden structure of the text, recognizing all the elements and the connections between them. This process allows machines to some extent to "understand" human language.
- *Knowledge representation, organization, and management*—NLP techniques provide the basis for harnessing the huge amount of data available to us and converting it to a useful source of knowledge for further processing. The output of this task, or set of tasks, has to be stored and organized properly so that it can be accessed and navigated easily. Regardless of the

context (such as a chatbot or question-answering system, or a company managing all its enterprise data), knowledge management is a key element in dealing with textual data (documents, speech, and so on) because it allows people to access information in an effective way.

These two tasks are strongly connected and constantly interacting, and both are huge topics. In chapters 11 and 12, we will see how to use NLP in combination with graph models and algorithms to extract meaningful information from text and store it in such a way that it can be accessed by multiple processes. Specifically, we will highlight the role and usefulness of graphs in helping practitioners deal with complex machine learning tasks.

Graphs provide a data model flexible enough to support many of the steps necessary to organize, access, and process textual data. In these chapters, because we are at the end of the book, we will take this concept to its extreme: the resulting graph will be the most complex one that we have discussed so far and also the most powerful. Storing your knowledge in a single connected source of truth containing a huge knowledge base will allow you to accomplish a huge range of tasks.

This topic is close to my heart: I'm one of the creators of, and for a long time was head of product for, GraphAware Hume (https://graphaware.com), a graph-powered insights engine. Hume is a software ecosystem that allows companies to collect all their enterprise data—structured and unstructured—from multiple data sources and convert it first to a knowledge graph and then to actionable insights.

Graph-based natural language processing

This chapter covers

- A simple approach to decompose a text and store it in a graph
- How to extract the hidden structure of unstructured data via natural language processing
- An advanced graph model for taming text

Let's start this new topic by considering the most common applications that deal with natural language (in different format) for providing services to end users. You likely use them every day, probably without even noticing how complex and useful they are.

Chapter 4 dealt with text to implement a recommendation engine that uses the content related to the items, such as the description of a product or a movie plot. In that case, this data was used to compare items or user profiles, find commonalities (specifically, similarities) among users or items, and use them to suggest something that might be of interest to the current user. Figure 11.1 presents the high-level structure of a content-based recommendation engine taken from chapter 4.

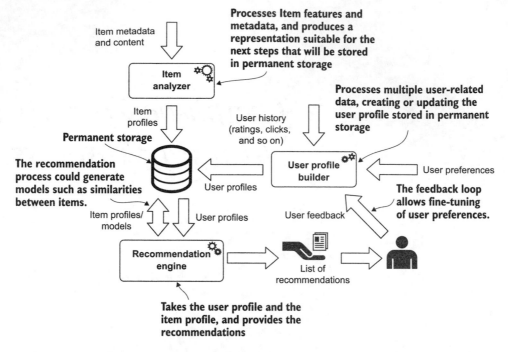

Figure 11.1   A content-based recommendation engine, as presented in chapter 4

The item analyzer and user profiles builder deal with text to make it available during the recommendation phase. The result of their analysis is stored in such a way that is it easy to access and query during the model generation and the recommendation process.

For many years now, the search engine has been perhaps the most critical type of application dealing with text, providing relevant results to users while they are looking for something. Think about Google and Yahoo! Without search engines like these two, the internet wouldn't have been the same; there would have been no useful way to discover new content or access the huge wealth of resources the internet offers, and as a result, it might never have grown to the scale it has. Searching is the most common technique we use to interact with a variety of content sources (news sites, retail sites, databases, and more). It helps us gain access to relevant data in an intuitive and effective way. Figure 11.2 shows a simplified schema of a search engine [Turnbull and Berryman, 2016].

The search engine is linked to a document store. It indexes the documents in that store in such a way that queries from users will be performed quickly, and the results will be accurate.

A more complex scenario occurs when an application gets a question in natural language and offers a reply or interacts with the user in some way. Most of us have experience with a digital voice assistant. You start a sentence with "Siri . . . ," "Okay Google . . . ," or "Alexa . . . ," and ask the assistant to perform some simple task such as

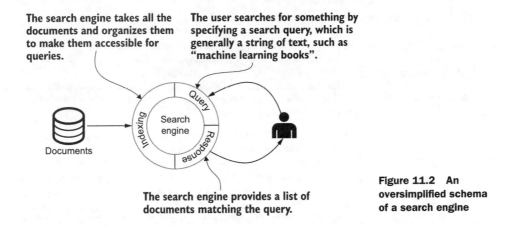

The search engine takes all the documents and organizes them to make them accessible for queries.

The user searches for something by specifying a search query, which is generally a string of text, such as "machine learning books".

The search engine provides a list of documents matching the query.

Figure 11.2   An oversimplified schema of a search engine

"Find the nearest restaurant," "Play a romantic song," or "Tell me the weather forecast." Excited by this new technology, you've probably experimented more, asking it to perform more complicated tasks and trying different questions in different formats. Chances are that you were frustrated by the agent's inability to deal with queries that go beyond the predefined set of skills.

These applications are doing their best, but the goal they are trying to achieve is difficult and complex. As figure 11.3 shows, answering even a simple question requires completing a whole set of tasks.

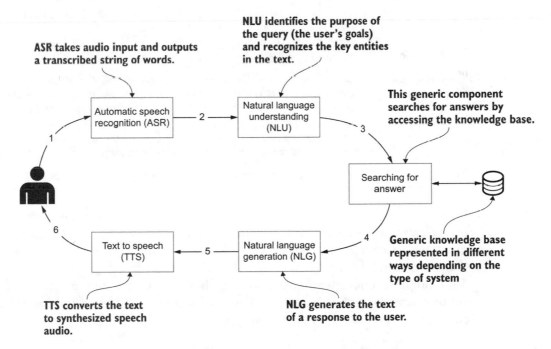

ASR takes audio input and outputs a transcribed string of words.

NLU identifies the purpose of the query (the user's goals) and recognizes the key entities in the text.

This generic component searches for answers by accessing the knowledge base.

Generic knowledge base represented in different ways depending on the type of system

NLG generates the text of a response to the user.

TTS converts the text to synthesized speech audio.

Figure 11.3   An example of the set of tasks performed by a conversational agent

These tasks are described in detail in table 11.1.

Table 11.1   Tasks performed by a conversational agent replying to a user query

Task/component	Description
Automatic speech recognition (ASR)	ASR takes audio (voice) input from the user and outputs a transcribed string of words that represent the query.
Natural language understanding (NLU)	The goal of the NLU component is to extract three things from the user's utterance. The first task is *domain classification*. Is the user (for example) talking about booking a flight, programming an alarm, or dealing with their calendar? this 1-of-n classification task is unnecessary for single-domain systems that focus only on, say, calendar management, but multidomain dialogue systems are the modern standard. The second task is *user intent identification*. What general task or goal is the user trying to accomplish? The task could be to find a movie, show a flight, or remove a calendar appointment. Finally, *entity extraction* entails extracting the particular concepts that the user intends the system to understand from their utterance with respect to their intent. These entities are used to circumstantiate the intent: Where would they like to book a flight to? Which event are they looking for in the calendar?
Searching for answer	This step is the meat of the process. The system, having received the domain, the intent, and the entities, accesses some knowledge base and determines a possible set of answers. Then it has to rank the answers and provide them as input to the following steps. In some cases, this process means finding passages in documents; in others, it means retrieving information that will be used to generate a proper answer.
	In this context, the knowledge base can be created from structured and unstructured data coming from multiple data sources.
	In conversational agents, this component also takes into account the previous questions from the user to narrow the context of the current question.
Natural language generation (NLG)	(Optional) Next, the NLG component generates the text of a response to the user. The task of NLG in the information-state architecture is often modeled in two stages: content planning (what to say) and sentence realization (how to say it).
	This component is optional. In most cases, the sentences are extracted as they are from existing documents in the knowledge base.
Text to speech (TTS)	TTS converts the answer to audio that the user can listen to instead of reading.

Due to the complexity of this scenario, it represents one of the most exciting and active research areas in machine learning. In the future, we will be able to interact with all the devices around us by using only our voices, but for now, this type of interaction is a dream.

Although recommendation agents, search engines, and conversational agents seem to be different, they have critical aspects in common. The underlying requirements can be summarized in the following way:

- The use of text for building a knowledge base.
  - Recommendation engines use item descriptions to create the recommendation model (for instance, identifying similarities among items).
  - Search engines preprocess the documents via indexing.
  - Chat bots and conversational agents create the knowledge base using unstructured data (documents and previous questions).
- A proper knowledge representation that stores all the information necessary for the scope of the application, providing efficient access to it.
- Interaction with the user, which in most cases happens via natural language.

The following sections and chapter 12 deal with those critical elements, proposing different graph-based approaches to accomplishing those tasks or tackling some of the related problems.

11.1 A basic approach: Store and access sequence of words

As usual, let's start with a basic graph model to illustrate the high-level concepts and the main issues related to graph-based natural language processing. Later in the chapter, starting in section 11.2, we'll discuss more advanced techniques and models.

It's worth noting that each graph model should be designed with the application's purpose in mind. Despite their simplicity, the models designed in this case are the right fit for the scope of the scenario described in this section. The models will serve their purpose appropriately without too many complications, showcasing a critical aspect of graph modeling: start simple and adapt by introducing new concepts and complexity only when necessary. With that said, it's time to begin our journey.

Suppose that you would like to implement a tool that supports message writing, suggesting the next word while you are typing. Moreover, suppose that you would like the tool to learn from you or from a specific set of documents. Such a tool could be useful not only for providing message-writing assistance, but also for supporting spell checking, extracting common phrases, summarizing, and so on.

The first step is splitting the input into words. The simplest approach in occidental languages is to use whitespace. (Other languages, such as Chinese, require different approaches.) When they are extracted, these words have to be stored in a way that keeps track of their order in the original text. The basic approach outlined here is inspired by a blog post[1] by Michael Hunger. A suitable graph model would look like figure 11.4 (using the sample phrase *you will not be able*).

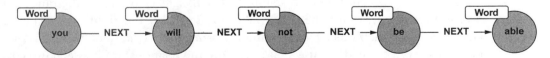

Figure 11.4   Basic schema applied to the phrase *you will not be able*

---

[1] http://mng.bz/y9Dq.

In this schema, the words themselves are considered to be unique, but not the relationships between the words, so if some words are used elsewhere in other sentences, they will not be replicated; instead, new relationships will be created. If we were to also process the phrase *you will be able*, the resulting graph would look like figure 11.5.

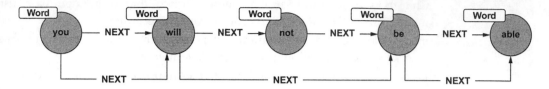

Figure 11.5   Our schema applied to the phrase *you will be able*

New relationships are created because of the new input but no new words are created, because we have already stored all these words. This model and approach, in which we keep the words unique and create new relationships for each sentence, has pros and cons that we are going to explore and analyze. The model may be useful in some cases but not in others. This example will illustrate how, in the evolution of your project, you can change your mind about certain aspects of your solution. Your needs may change, requiring you to develop a new schema that suits them better. Graphs are helpful for this purpose because they are flexible data structures that can evolve in response to your project's changing constraints and requirements. The following Cypher query shows how to process the text and obtain the expected graph database.

Listing 11.1   Splitting a sentence by using whitespace and storing it

```
WITH split("You will not be able to send new mail until you upgrade your
➥ email."," ") as words
UNWIND range(0, size(words)-2) as idx
MERGE (w1:Word {value:words[idx]})
MERGE (w2:Word {value:words[idx+1]})
CREATE (w1)-[:NEXT]->(w2);
```

In this query, the `WITH` clause at the beginning provides data to the next query statement. Note that `split()` defines the tokenization process based on whitespace, which is specified as the delimiter in the second parameter. The `range()` function creates a range of numbers, in this case from 0 to the size of the sentence—obtained by using the `size()` function on the text—minus 2. The `UNWIND` clause turns the range collection into result rows with the index value to use to get the right word. The `MERGE` clause, as usual, helps us avoid creating the same node (the same word, in this scenario) twice. At the end, we use `CREATE` to store the relationships between two consecutive words. As a side note, for `MERGE` to work efficiently, you would want to create a constraint in your graph, as in the following query.

Listing 11.2 Creating unique constraints for a word's value

```
CREATE CONSTRAINT ON (w:Word) ASSERT w.value IS UNIQUE;
```

If you would like to explore this first graph, the next query shows you the path.

Listing 11.3 Returning the path for the graph

```
MATCH p=()-[r:NEXT]->() RETURN p
```

The result will look like figure 11.6.

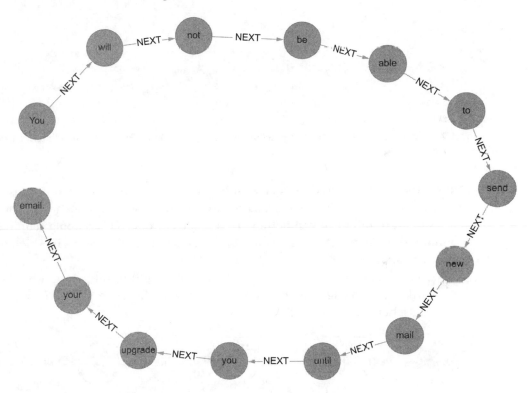

Figure 11.6 The resulting graph after processing the sentence "You will not be able to send new mail until you upgrade your email."

So far, so good—this result is exactly what we expected. But the model can be improved. As discussed previously, the same word can be followed by multiple other words in different sentences. By adhering to the model described, listing 11.1 produces multiple relationships between the same couple of words due to the last CREATE clause. If we ingest a new sentence like "He says it's OK for Bill and Hillary Clinton to send their kid to a private school," the resulting graph will look like figure 11.7.

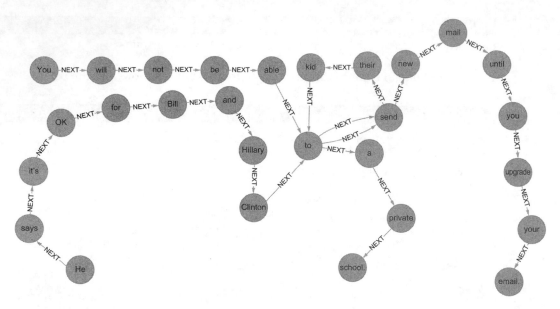

Figure 11.7   The resulting graph after also processing "He says it's OK for Bill and Hillary Clinton to send their kid to a private school."

Notice that we have multiple relationships between *to* and *send*. This result is correct and definitely useful in some scenarios, but in our case, we want to prioritize the words that are most likely to be next to the current one. This schema requires us to compute the number of relationships for each combination of words in which the current word appears first.

We can modify our graph model by adding a weight to the relationship between two words and making it unique when it connects the same couple of words. The resulting schema is shown in figure 11.8.

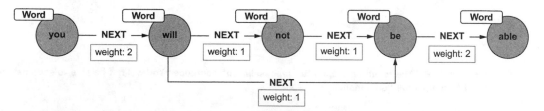

Figure 11.8   New schema model with weight property on the relationships

The new schema removes the need for multiple relationships by adding a `weight` property on the relationship connecting the words. This change in the schema requires a small change in the query.

Listing 11.4   Storing frequency of word pairs

```
WITH split("You will not be able to send new mail until you upgrade your
➥ email."," ") as words
UNWIND range(0,size(words)-2) as idx
MERGE (w1:Word {value:words[idx]})
MERGE (w2:Word {value:words[idx+1]})
MERGE (w1)-[r:NEXT]->(w2)
  ON CREATE SET r.weight = 1
  ON MATCH SET r.weight = r.weight + 1;
```

Note that the last CREATE has been replaced by a MERGE that either creates (ON CREATE) or updates (ON MATCH) the weight property on the NEXT relationship.

EXERCISE

Try the new query with the previous sentences, and check the resulting graph. Remember to clean up your database first.[2] Check the weight of the relationship between *to* and *send*.

With a proper model in hand, we can now approach our original problem. Because it would be hard for us now to train a model with our personal messages, let's use a generic dataset containing some text. We will use as a corpus the Manually Annotated Sub-Corpus (MASC) dataset,[3] a balanced subset of 500,000 words of written texts and transcribed speech drawn primarily from the Open American National Corpus (OANC). Table 11.2 shows a few examples of documents in the dataset. For space reasons, I've copied only the key columns.

Table 11.2   Sample items from the MASC dataset

Filename	Content
[MASC]/data/written/110CYL200.txt	It took some time and hard work, but with the help of Goodwill, Jerry was able to work out a payment plan with the prosecutor's office, find housing and conduct a more thorough job search.
[MASC]/data/written/111348.txt	The above figure was given to me as my share and to conceal this kind of money became a problem for me, so with the help of a British contact working with the UN here (his office enjoys some immunity) I was able to get the package out to a safe location entirely out of trouble spot.
[MASC]/data/written/111364.txt	Please I know very well that this mail might come to you as a surprise, I am rs Dagmar a dying woman who has decided to donate what I have to the Church, Mosque or any Charity Organization round your community through your assistance since I will not be able to do this here in my community for the reason which I will explain to you later.
[MASC]/data/written/111371.txt	Imagine the feeling of being able to offer your opportunity and products to millions of people in North America and other parts of the world from your own home-based niche.

---

[2] With MATCH (n) DETACH DELETE n.

[3] The file can be downloaded here: http://mng.bz/MgKn.

We will use only the tab-separated sentence dataset available in the file masc_sentences .tsv. For the following queries, please copy that file into the import directory in your Neo4j installation. To import all the sentences in the file and decompose them as described earlier, you'll need to run the following query (remembering to clean up your database first).

Listing 11.5 Importing the MASC dataset and processing its contents

```
:auto USING PERIODIC COMMIT 500
LOAD CSV FROM "file:///masc_sentences.tsv" AS line
FIELDTERMINATOR '\t'
WITH line[6] as sentence
WITH split(sentence, " ") as words
FOREACH ( idx IN range(0,size(words)-2) |
MERGE (w1:Word {value:words[idx]})
MERGE (w2:Word {value:words[idx+1]})
MERGE (w1)-[r:NEXT]->(w2)
  ON CREATE SET r.weight = 1
  ON MATCH SET r.weight = r.weight + 1)
```

PRO TIP   To go through the words in the sentence, this query replaces UNWIND with FOREACH (using the same range on the indices). The UNWIND clause turns the range collection into result rows and in this case returns a lot of data. FOREACH instead executes the MERGEs inside without returning anything. This clause simplifies execution and improves performance dramatically.

Let's take a quick look at the database. We can search for the 10 most frequent combinations of words via the following query.

Listing 11.6 Find the 10 most common pairs of words

```
MATCH (w1:Word)-[r:NEXT]->(w2)
RETURN w1.value as first, w2.value as second, r.weight as frequency
ORDER by r.weight DESC
LIMIT 10
```

The result is shown in figure 11.9.

Now we have all the components to satisfy our initial requirement: implement a tool that supports message writing, suggesting the next word. The idea is to take the current word and query our new graph to find the three most probable next words, using the weight on the relationship.

Listing 11.7 Query that suggests the most probable word

```
MATCH (w:Word {value: "how"})-[e:NEXT]->(w2:Word)
RETURN w2.value as next, e.weight as frequency
ORDER BY frequency desc
LIMIT 3
```

This query will give us the results shown in figure 11.10.

first	second	frequency
"of"	"the"	18824
"in"	"the"	13030
"to"	"the"	7126
"and"	"the"	4814
"]"	"."	4476
"on"	"the"	4397
"that"	"the"	4041
"to"	"be"	3761
"for"	"the"	3679
"of"	"a"	3259

Figure 11.9 The 10 most common pairs of words in the MASC dataset

next	frequency
"to"	294
"the"	185
"much"	129

Figure 11.10 The next most probable words to follow "how"

Apparently, the three best words to suggest to a user who wrote *how* as the last word are *to, the,* and *much.* Not bad!

EXERCISE

Play with the database, checking the results for other words. Do they make sense to you?

As you can see from the results obtained so far, the results are pretty good, but we can do better. Instead of considering only the last word, we can consider the previous two or even three words. This approach will give us the opportunity to improve the quality of the suggestions, but we'll have to change the structure of the database a little.

Again, there's nothing bad about changing your mind and refining the model of your database as you develop your solution. This situation happens quite often: you start with an idea in mind; design your model accordingly; and then realize that with a small change, you can get better or faster results, so you change the model and test. You should follow this process all the time; you shouldn't consider your model to be definitive. In this sense, graphs offer you all the flexibility you need. In some cases, you can even adapt your model without reingesting everything.

Let's try out this model refinement by considering the last two (or three) words the user wrote instead of only one. The idea for improving the quality of the recommendations by considering the two (or three) previous words can be formalized as follows:

1 Take the last two (or three) words the user wrote.
2 Search in the database for all sentences in which those words appear in the same order.
3 Find what the next possible words are.
4 Group the words and compute the frequency of each.
5 Order by frequency (descending).
6 Recommend the top three.

This process is illustrated in figure 11.11.

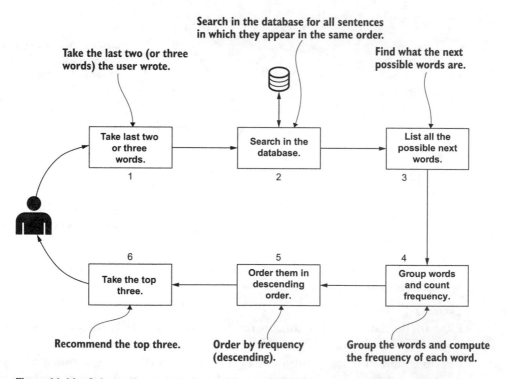

Figure 11.11 Schema for improving the quality of next-word recommendation

The new model should allow us to reconstruct sentences so that we can identify in which of them the words appear in the specific order we want. The current model cannot do this because it merges the sentences, updating only the weights. The original information is lost.

At this point, we have a few options. One option is to remove the unique constraint on Word and replicate all the words each time they appear (and do the same for the relationships), but this solution requires a lot of disk space without adding any concrete value. We can do better by using the model in figure 11.12.

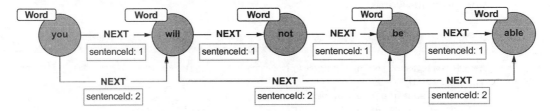

Figure 11.12   The third version of our schema

This model keeps the words unique but creates relationships specific to each sentence by adding an ID on the relationships. In this way, it is possible to reconstruct an original sentence by filtering the relationships by sentenceId. This approach uses less disk space than replicating the words, and the result obtained will be exactly the same. So let's clean up our database and reload with the new model. The query for cleaning up the database follows.

Listing 11.8   Cleaning up the database by using APOC's `iterate` procedure

```
CALL apoc.periodic.iterate(
"MATCH (p:Word) RETURN p",
"DETACH DELETE p", {batchSize:1000, parallel:true})
```

In this case, it's better to use `apoc.periodic.iterate` because the database is fairly big; removing it in a single transaction could take a while, and the transaction could fail. The `iterate()` function in the APOC plugin allows you to split the big commit into smaller commits, and the operations can be done in parallel, which will be much faster. When the graph database is empty, we can reimport and process the text.

Listing 11.9   New importing query that uses the sentence identifier

```
:auto USING PERIODIC COMMIT 100
LOAD CSV FROM "file:///masc_sentences.tsv" AS line
FIELDTERMINATOR '\t'
WITH line[6] as sentence, line[2] as sentenceId
WITH split(sentence," ") as words, sentenceId
FOREACH ( idx IN range(0,size(words)-2) |
```

```
MERGE (w1:Word {value:words[idx]})
MERGE (w2:Word {value:words[idx+1]})
CREATE (w1)-[r:NEXT {sentence: sentenceId}]->(w2))
```

As you can see, the MERGE used to create the relationships between words has been replaced by the CREATE we had in the first example. But in this case, a new property, sentence, contains a sentence identifier. If you look at the graph now, you'll see a lot of relationships coming out and in of almost every node. On the other hand, now you can execute a query like the following to suggest the next word based on the current and previous words.

Listing 11.10 Query to suggest the next word considering the last two words

```
MATCH (w2:Word {value: "know"})-[r:NEXT]->(w3:Word {value: "how"})-[e:NEXT]->
➥ (w4:Word)
WHERE r.sentence = e.sentence
RETURN w4.value as next, count(DISTINCT r) as frequency
ORDER BY frequency desc
LIMIT 3
```

To suggest a word based on the last three words, you can use a query like the following.

Listing 11.11 Query to suggest the next word considering the last three words

```
MATCH (w1:Word {value: "you"})-[a:NEXT]->(w2:Word {value: "know"})-[r:NEXT]->
➥ (w3:Word {value: "how"})-[e:NEXT]->(w4:Word)
WHERE a.sentence = r.sentence AND r.sentence = e.sentence
RETURN w4.value as next, count(DISTINCT r) as frequency
ORDER BY frequency desc
LIMIT 3
```

As expected, the quality of the suggestions is much higher, but at the cost of a bigger and more complex database. The last two queries search for specific patterns in the database. The Cypher language in this case helps you define at a high level the graph pattern you are looking for; the engine will return all the nodes and relationships matching that pattern.

It is worth mentioning a subtle drawback to the last schema we defined. The word nodes are unique, so if you have millions of sentences, this schema will create super-nodes—that is, nodes with millions of relationships coming in, going out, or both. In most cases, these dense nodes represent the so-called *stop words*: words that appear frequently in most texts, such as articles (*a*, *the*), pronouns (*he*, *she*), and auxiliary verbs (*do*, *does*, *will*, *should*). As mentioned previously, such dense nodes can be an issue during query execution because the time it takes to traverse them is high. For the purposes of this scenario and the solutions presented in this section, this situation will not be a big problem, but in section 11.2, we'll examine how to recognize and process these words properly.

11.1.1 Advantages of the graph approach

The first scenario showed how to represent text in the form of a graph. Sentences are split into simple tokens, these tokens are represented by nodes, and the sequence of words is maintained by relationships.

Despite its simplicity, the graph model designed in the end served perfectly the purpose we had in mind. You also saw how to evolve your model to respond to new needs or fulfill new constraints.

The last few queries showed how to search for specific patterns in the graph—an extremely powerful feature of graphs made available via a proper graph query language such as Cypher. With other approaches, such as a relational database, expressing the same concepts would have been much more complicated. Simplicity, flexibility (adaptability to changes), and power: these graph features emerged clearly in this simple scenario.

11.2 NLP and graphs

The basic approach discussed in section 11.1 has a lot of limitations, some of which we discussed along the way. It serves well the intended purpose of suggesting the next word based on the user's previous input, but it would not be suitable for advanced scenarios that require detailed analysis and understanding of the text, as in the case of the conversational agents, chatbots, and advanced recommendation engines mentioned in this chapter's introduction. Some of the aspects not considered in the previous examples are

- The words are not normalized to their base form (such as removing plurals or considering the base form of a declined verb).
- We are not taking into account dependencies among words (such as the connection between adjectives and nouns).
- Some words make more sense together because they represent a single entity. (*Alessandro Negro* is a person and should be treated as a single token, for example.)
- The stop words are not properly identified and (eventually) removed to prevent dense nodes. A few examples were given, but lists are available based on the language and the domain.
- Splitting by using only whitespace typically is not good enough. (Consider, for example, words like *can't* and all the types of punctuation that might be attached to the last word in a sentence.)

This section describes more sophisticated scenarios that require advanced NLP tasks. It walks through various techniques and tools for decomposing and properly analyzing textual data, as well as the graph models for storing the results of such analyses. This phase represents the fundamental step on top of which more advanced tasks can be accomplished.

Text is often thought of as being unstructured data, but free text has a lot of structure. The difficulty is that most of that structure isn't explicit, which makes it hard to search for or analyze information contained within the text [Grishman, 2015]. NLP uses concepts from computer science, artificial intelligence, and linguistics to analyze natural language, with the aim of deriving meaningful and useful information from text.

Information extraction (IE) is the first step in the process of understanding text and building a sophisticated, engaging machine learning application. It can be described as the process of analyzing text, decomposing it, and identifying semantically defined entities and relationships within it with the goal of making the text's semantic structure explicit. The results of this analysis can be recorded in a database for querying and inference or used for further analysis.

IE is a multistep process involving several analysis components that are combined to extract the most valuable information from text, making it available for further processing. Following are the main tasks, some of which we'll consider in detail in the remainder of this section:

- Tokenization, part of speech (PoS) tagging, stemming/lemmatization, and stop-word removal
- Named entity recognition (NER)
- Entity relationship extraction (ERE)
- Syntactic analysis
- Coreference resolution
- Semantic analysis

This list is not an exhaustive one—other tasks can be considered to be part of the core information extraction process—but those items are the most common and, I would say, the most valuable and useful in terms of the amount of information, structure, and knowledge they enable you to extract from the text. The results of each IE task have to be organized and stored properly so that they are useful for other processes and analyses or to be queried. The model used to store these results is critical because it affects the performance of the subsequent operations.

In this section, we will explore how graphs offer a perfect data model for taming text because they allow us to organize the structures and information within text so that they are immediately available for querying, analyzing, or extracting the sets of features necessary to feed other processes. For each task, a graph model is proposed to store the results properly. The proposed model will grow consistently from the first task to the last, and the resulting graph will incorporate all the knowledge that it is possible to distill from the text in a homogeneous data structure.

To simplify the description and make it more concrete, I will describe some of these tasks by starting with a real scenario that requires that technique. The process will be incremental: at each stage, new information will be added to the graph, and at the end, we will have the full corpus processed, structured, accessible, and ready for the next steps. Let's start our journey!

Suppose that you would like to decompose a text into its main elements (eventually normalizing them to the base form), get the role of each entity in the text, remove the useless words, and store the result in such a way that it is easy to navigate and query for searching purposes or for further analysis.

This scenario is quite common, because the first step of almost any IE process consists of breaking the content into small, usable chunks of text, called *tokens*. This process is called *tokenization*. Generally, tokens represent single words, but as you'll soon see, what constitutes a small, usable chunk can be specific to an application. As noted in section 11.1, the simplest approach to tokenizing English text is to split a string based on the occurrence of whitespace such as spaces and line breaks, as our simple tokenizer will do. Using this approach on the sentence

I couldn't believe my eyes when I saw my favorite team winning the 2019-2020 cup.

yields the following list:

["I", "couldn't", "believe", "my", "eyes", "when", "I", "saw", "my", "favorite", "team", "winning", "the", "2019-2020", "cup."]

This approach is exactly the approach we used earlier, but clearly, it is not enough. To have better tokenization, we need to handle things such as punctuation, acronyms, email addresses, URLs, and numbers. If we apply a more complex tokenization approach that uses token classes such as alphabetic, numeric, and whitespace, the output should be something like this:

["I", "couldn", "'", "t", "believe", "my", "eyes", "when", "I", "saw", "my", "favorite", "team", "winning", "the", "2019", "-", "2020", "cup", "."]

Much better!

In this example, we considered a single sentence, but in many scenarios, it is relevant to split the document into sentences first. In English, we can perform this task by considering punctuation such as periods and question marks. Tokenization and sentence splitting are greatly affected by several factors, the two most critical of which are

- *Language*—Different languages have different rules. These rules can dramatically affect the way in which you perform even a simple task like tokenization. There is no whitespace in between phrases in Chinese, for example, so splitting based on whitespace, as you'd do in English, may not work.
- *Domain*—Some domains have specific elements that have a specific structure. Consider molecular names such as *3-(furan-2-yl)-[1,2,4]triazolo[3,4-b][1,3,4]thiadiazole*[4] in the chemistry domain and sizes such as *60 in. X 32 in.* in a home improvement retail domain.

Even using the more sophisticated approach, tokenization on its own is not enough in most cases. When you have the list of tokens, you can apply multiple techniques to get a better representation. The most common techniques [Farris et al., 2013] are

---

[4] I explicitly searched for a complex name and found it here: http://mng.bz/aKzB.

- *Case alterations*—This task involves changing the case of the tokens to a common case so that the tokens are uniform. The process is often more complex than lowercasing everything, though: some tokens should have the first letter uppercased because they appear at the beginning of a sentence, and others should be capitalized because they are proper nouns (such as names of people or locations). A proper case alteration considers these factors. Note that this task is language-specific; in Arabic, for example, there is no lowercasing or uppercasing.

- *Stop-word removal*—This task filters out common words such as *the, and*, and *a*. Commonly occurring words like these often add little value (note that I didn't say *no* value) to applications that don't rely on sentence structure. This list of stop words is also application-specific. If you're processing a book like this one, you might want to filter out other words that add minimal value to the content but occur frequently, such as *chapter, section*, and *figure*.

- *Expansion*—Some tokens can be further extended or clarified by adding synonyms or expanding acronyms and abbreviations in a token stream. This task can allow applications to handle alternative inputs from users.

- *PoS tagging*—The purpose of this task is to identify a word's part of speech—whether it's a noun, verb, or adjective, for example. The task is highly valuable because it is used later in the process to enhance the quality of the results. PoS tagging can help determine the important keywords in a document, for example (we'll see how later in this section), or support proper casing (such as *Will* as a proper noun versus *will* the modal verb).

- *Lemmatization and stemming*—Suppose that you would like to search in a bunch of documents for the verb *take*. A simple string match will not work because, as you know, such a verb can appear in many forms, such as *take, took, taken, taking*, and *takes*. These forms are known as *surface forms*. The verb is the same, but it is conjugated in different ways according to the role it plays in the text and other syntactic rules. Lemmatization and stemming are tasks that allow us to reduce words to their root or base form, such as by converting all the surface forms of *take* to their root form. The difference between lemmatization and stemming is in the approach used to produce the root forms of words and the words produced. Generally speaking, stemming uses grammar rules, whereas lemmatization uses a dictionary-based approach. For this reason, stemming is faster but less accurate; lemmatization is slower but more precise.

For further reading, I recommend the excellent practical books on these topics mentioned in the references section at the end of this chapter [Lane et al., 2019; Farris et al., 2013]. The books cover broadly the steps outlined here, with concrete examples.

Figure 11.13 shows some of the tasks described in the preceding list applied to a simple sentence.

A lot of tasks seem to be involved in information extraction, but the reality is that (unless you would like to implement heavy customizations) plenty of software and

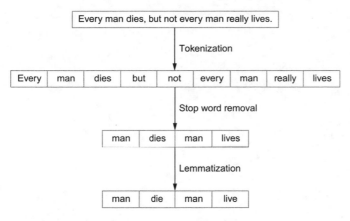

Figure 11.13 Tokenization, stop-word removal, and lemmatization applied to a sample sentence

libraries for various programming languages can perform all these tasks for you. The following example demonstrates the use of one of the most common libraries for such purposes: the spaCy[5] Python library.

Listing 11.12 Basic text processing with spaCy

```
import spacy

class BasicNLP(object):

    def __init__(self, language):          Prefers the GPU (which is
        spacy.prefer_gpu()          ◁───── faster) whenever possible

    def tokenize(self, text):
        nlp = spacy.load("en_core_web_sm")     ◁────── Loads the English-language model
        doc = nlp(text)
        i = 1
        for sentence in doc.sents:          Loops over the sentences
            print("-------- Sentence ", i,  "-----------")
            i += 1
            for token in sentence:          Loops over the tokens
                print(token.idx, "-", token.text, "-", token.lemma_)     ◁──

if __name__ == '__main__':                  Prints the index (the token start position),
    basic_nlp = BasicNLP(language="en")     the text as it is, and the lemmatized version
    basic_nlp.tokenize("Marie Curie received the Nobel Prize in Physics in
    ⇒ 1903. She became the first woman to win the prize.")
```

Processes the text ▷ doc = nlp(text)

This listing[6] implements a basic example that prints the result of the tokenization, which looks like this:

```
-------- Sentence 1 -----------
0 - Marie - Marie - NNP
6 - Curie - Curie - NNP
12 - received - receive - VBD
```

---

[5] https://spacy.io.

[6] The code is available in the book's repository, at ch11/basic_nlp_examples/01_spacy_basic_nlp_tasks.py.

```
21 - the - the - DT
25 - Nobel - Nobel - NNP
31 - Prize - Prize - NNP
37 - in - in - IN
40 - Physics - Physics - NNP
47 - in - in - IN
50 - 1903 - 1903 - CD
54 - . - . - .
-------- Sentence 2 -----------
56 - She - -PRON- - PRP
60 - became - become - VBD
67 - the - the - DT
71 - first - first - JJ
77 - woman - woman - NN
83 - to - to - TO
86 - win - win - VB
90 - the - the - DT
94 - prize - prize - NN
99 - . - . - .
```

How should we store the result of this first step in a graph model? As usual, there is no single right answer; the answer depends on what you want to do with it. What I'm going to present is the schema that we use in GraphAware Hume, which has proved to be flexible enough to cover a plethora of scenarios without any particular difficulties. The only issue is that it is quite verbose, in the sense that it stores a lot of data that is sometimes not required. As you'll see, it provides a starting point; you can prune some parts or add others.

The first schema presented is the minimum needed to fulfill a significant number of scenarios and requirements. The following aspects of this model are critical for many applications and uses:

- *Sentence nodes*—The main text is split into sentences, which are key elements in most text-analysis use cases (such as summarization and similarity computation).
- *TagOccurrence nodes*—These nodes contain details on how the tag appears in the text, such as start and end position, actual value, and lemma (PoS value).
- HAS_NEXT *relationships*—There are relationships of type HAS_NEXT between TagOccurrence nodes, which have the same scope as in section 11.1. In this way, this new schema incorporates—and heavily extends—the schema produced earlier so that the previous scenarios can also be resolved by using this new model.

Figure 11.14 shows the schema. The comments in it should help you read it properly, even though it may appear to be complex.

This schema can be improved slightly by adding Tag nodes to represent the lemmatized versions of the tokens. These nodes are unique; they are stored once, and all the sentences that contain such tags point to them via a TagOccurrence.

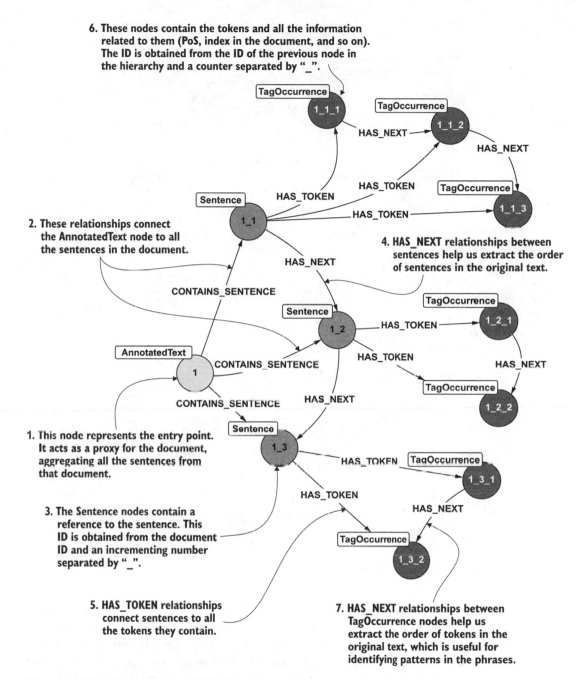

6. These nodes contain the tokens and all the information related to them (PoS, index in the document, and so on). The ID is obtained from the ID of the previous node in the hierarchy and a counter separated by "_".

2. These relationships connect the AnnotatedText node to all the sentences in the document.

4. HAS_NEXT relationships between sentences help us extract the order of sentences in the original text.

1. This node represents the entry point. It acts as a proxy for the document, aggregating all the sentences from that document.

3. The Sentence nodes contain a reference to the sentence. This ID is obtained from the document ID and an incrementing number separated by "_".

5. HAS_TOKEN relationships connect sentences to all the tokens they contain.

7. HAS_NEXT relationships between TagOccurrence nodes help us extract the order of tokens in the original text, which is useful for identifying patterns in the phrases.

Figure 11.14 First schema for dealing with text properly

For the reasons mentioned earlier, common words can generate dense nodes. To mitigate this issue, only non-stop words are stored as Tag nodes. The resulting model will look like figure 11.15.

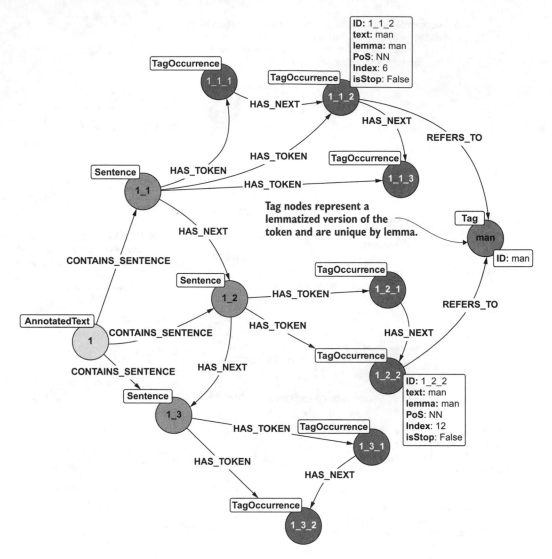

Figure 11.15   Extended schema with Tag nodes

The Tag nodes simplify navigation through the graph database when you would like to access it by using some key term(s) as an entry point. (Think about search, for example.) You could also achieve this task by using an index on the TagOccurrence nodes, but some queries are much easier to perform when you access Tag nodes directly and then use the relationships to TagOccurrence nodes. Because these nodes are not critical for our purposes, we will ignore them in our schema, examples, and exercises to make the graph easier to read, but keep them in mind as an option for specific access patterns.

With this new model in hand, we can extend our code for processing text and storing it in a graph. The following listing is a bit more sophisticated than listing 11.12, which converted the text to a graph by using the model described in figures 11.11 and 11.12.

Listing 11.13 Creating the first graph out of text

Loops over the processed docs. The pipe accepts a list of documents and returns a list of processed docs.

Processes the text without NER (improves performance)

```
def tokenize_and_store(self, text, text_id, storeTag):
    docs = self.nlp.pipe([text], disable=["ner"])   ◄──
    for doc in docs:
        annotated_text = self.create_annotated_text(doc, text_id)
        i = 1
        for sentence in doc.sents:
            sentence_id = self.store_sentence(sentence, annotated_text,
                text_id, i, storeTag)
            i += 1
```

The query for creating the AnnotatedText node is simple, storing only an ID to identify the original document.

Loops over the sentences, calling the store function on each

This function creates the main node with the label AnnotatedText, to which all the other nodes will be connected.

```
def create_annotated_text(self, doc, id):
    query = """MERGE (ann:AnnotatedText {id: $id})   ◄──
        RETURN id(ann) as result
    """
    params = {"id": id}
    results = self.execute_query(query, params)   ◄──
    return results[0]
```

This common function executes all the queries in the code. It requires the query and the parameters, and executes the query in a transaction.

```
def store_sentence(self, sentence, annotated_text, text_id, sentence_id,
    storeTag):
    sentence_query = """MATCH (ann:AnnotatedText) WHERE id(ann) = $ann_id
        MERGE (sentence:Sentence {id: $sentence_unique_id})
        SET sentence.text = $text
        MERGE (ann)-[:CONTAINS_SENTENCE]->(sentence)
        RETURN id(sentence) as result
    """
```

This function stores sentences along with the tag occurrences and the tags.

This query searches for the AnnotatedText node created by id, creates a sentence, and connects it to the AnnotatedText node.

```
    tag_occurrence_query = """MATCH (sentence:Sentence) WHERE id(sentence) =
        $sentence_id
        WITH sentence, $tag_occurrences as tags
        FOREACH ( idx IN range(0,size(tags)-2) |
        MERGE (tagOccurrence1:TagOccurrence {id: tags[idx].id})
        SET tagOccurrence1 = tags[idx]
        MERGE (sentence)-[:HAS_TOKEN]->(tagOccurrence1)
        MERGE (tagOccurrence2:TagOccurrence {id: tags[idx + 1].id})
        SET tagOccurrence2 = tags[idx + 1]
        MERGE (sentence)-[:HAS_TOKEN]->(tagOccurrence2)
        MERGE (tagOccurrence1)-[r:HAS_NEXT {sentence: sentence.id}]->
            (tagOccurrence2))
        RETURN id(sentence) as result
    """
```

This query stores the TagOccurrence nodes, connecting them to the sentence and to one another.

```
    tag_occurrence_with_tag_query = """MATCH (sentence:Sentence) WHERE
        id(sentence) = $sentence_id
        WITH sentence, $tag_occurrences as tags
```

```
FOREACH ( idx IN range(0,size(tags)-2) |
MERGE (tagOccurrence1:TagOccurrence {id: tags[idx].id})
SET tagOccurrence1 = tags[idx]
MERGE (sentence)-[:HAS_TOKEN]->(tagOccurrence1)
MERGE (tagOccurrence2:TagOccurrence {id: tags[idx + 1].id})
SET tagOccurrence2 = tags[idx + 1]
MERGE (sentence)-[:HAS_TOKEN]->(tagOccurrence2)
MERGE (tagOccurrence1)-[r:HAS_NEXT {sentence: sentence.id}]->
➥ (tagOccurrence2))
FOREACH (tagItem in [tag_occurrence IN {tag_occurrences} WHERE
➥ tag_occurrence.is_stop = False] |
MERGE (tag:Tag {id: tagItem.lemma}) MERGE
➥ (tagOccurrence:TagOccurrence {id: tagItem.id}) MERGE (tag)<-
➥ [:REFERS_TO]-(tagOccurrence))
RETURN id(sentence) as result
"""
```

Runs the query for storing the sentence

```
params = {"ann_id": annotated_text, "text": sentence.text,
➥ "sentence_unique_id": str(text_id) + "_" + str(sentence_id)}
results = self.execute_query(sentence_query, params)
node_sentence_id = results[0]
tag_occurrences = []
for token in sentence:
    lexeme = self.nlp.vocab[token.text]
    if not lexeme.is_punct and not lexeme.is_space:
        tag_occurrence = {"id": str(text_id) + "_" + str(sentence_id) +
        ➥ "_" + str(token.idx),
                          "index": token.idx,
                          "text": token.text,
                          "lemma": token.lemma_,
                          "pos": token.tag_,
                          "is_stop": (lexeme.is_stop or lexeme.is_punct
                          ➥ or lexeme.is_space)}
        tag_occurrences.append(tag_occurrence)
params = {"sentence_id": node_sentence_id,
➥ "tag_occurrences":tag_occurrences}
if storeTag:
    results = self.execute_query(tag_occurrence_with_tag_query, params)
else:
    results = self.execute_query(tag_occurrence_query, params)
return results[0]
```

Loops over the tokens extracted for each sentence and creates an array of dict to be used as a parameter for the query that stores the sentence

This filter avoids storing punctuation and spaces.

This query stores the TagOccurrence nodes, connecting them to the sentence and to one another and the Tag nodes. It is used as an alternative to the previous tag_occurrence_ query to store the Tag nodes.

Executes the query with Tag

Executes the query without Tag

In this code, with a single parameter (storeTag), it is possible to decide whether to store the Tag nodes. Because Tag nodes are not necessary in the rest of this section, this flag is set to false, which will result in a less verbose database and help us avoid dense node issues.

The tokenization breaks up the text according to specific splitting rules, which are generally a bit more complex than using whitespace and punctuation. Nevertheless, you might like to get more from your text. Tokens in a sentence are not isolated components; they are related through linguistic relationships. Syntactic relationships, for example, capture the role of a word in modifying the semantics of other words in the sentence and are helpful for determining the subject and predicate. In the example used earlier,

I couldn't believe my eyes when I saw my favorite team winning the 2019-2020 cup.

I is syntactically related to *believe* because it is the subject of that verb. Capturing these types of dependencies is critical for further understanding the text: they allow us to determine semantic relations (who did what to whom) later in the pipeline. Generally speaking, richer analysis at this stage simplifies the semantic analysis that follows.

So let's extend our previous scenario, adding a new requirement: you would like to recognize key syntactic elements in the text (such as verbs and their subjects and predicates) to improve understanding of the text for further analysis. Among the various parsing methods that have been proposed to date, dependency parsing—which is concerned with the identification of dependency structures in the text—has gained the greatest attention. Figure 11.16 shows the dependency parse obtained for our sample sentence by using the CoreNLP test service.[7]

Basic Dependencies:

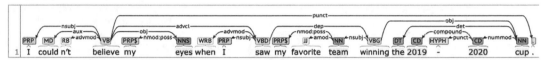

Figure 11.16 Dependencies among tokens obtained via `corenlp.run`

I hope that at this point in the book, you can recognize immediately where a graph can be applied. In this case, it is a special type of graph: a tree. In dependency parsing, each sentence is represented as a tree, which has as its root either the main predicate of the sentence or a dummy node labeled root with the main predicate as its sole child [Mihalcea and Radev, 2011]. Edges are used to connect each word to its dependency parent. In the sentence "John likes green apples," the predicate is *likes*. It takes two arguments: the liker (*John*) and the liked (*apples*). The word *green* modifies *apples*, so it is added to the tree as a child of *apples*. The final tree is shown in figure 11.17.

Adding these new syntactic relationships to our graph model is straightforward. Figure 11.18 shows how it could work.

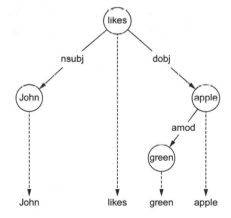

Figure 11.17 An example of a dependency tree

---

[7] http://corenlp.run.

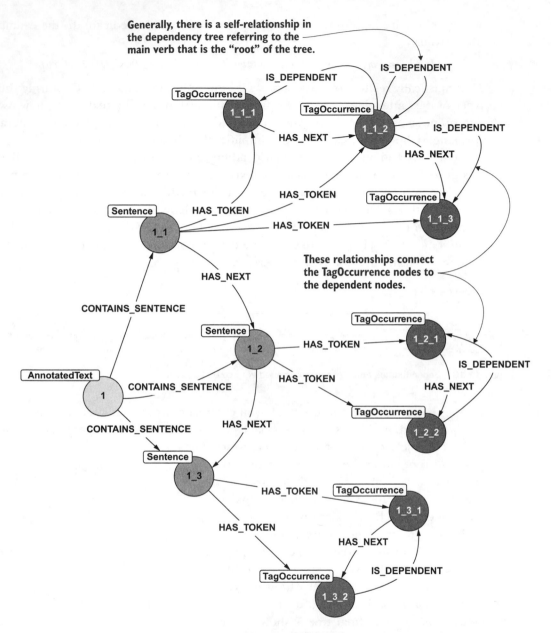

Figure 11.18   Extended schema with the dependency relationships

In the resulting graph model, the new relations connect TagOccurrence nodes to the dependent nodes. This connection is necessary because the same Tag can have different relationships in different sentences (*John* might be the subject in some sentences and the object in others), whereas a TagOccurrence represents the tag in a specific sentence context and can have only a specific role. The direction of the relationships follows the schema in figure 11.14, and the root (the main verb) of the dependency tree is recognizable via the self loop. The following listing is the code for extracting and storing the dependencies in the graph.

Listing 11.14 Extracting and storing the dependencies

```
def store_sentence(self, sentence, annotated_text, text_id, sentence_id,
    storeTag):

[... the same code as before ...]

    params = {"ann_id": annotated_text, "text": sentence.text,
        "sentence_unique_id": str(text_id) + "_" + str(sentence_id)}
    results = self.execute_query(sentence_query, params)
    node_sentence_id = results[0]
    tag_occurrences = []
    tag_occurrence_dependencies = []
    for token in sentence:
        lexeme = self.nlp.vocab[token.text]
        if not lexeme.is_punct and not lexeme.is_space:
            tag_occurrence_id = str(text_id) + "_" + str(sentence_id) + "_" +
                str(token.idx)
            tag_occurrence = {"id": tag_occurrence_id,
                              "index": token.idx,
                              "text": token.text,
                              "lemma": token.lemma_,
                              "pos": token.tag_,
                              "is_stop": (lexeme.is_stop or lexeme.is_punct
                                  or lexeme.is_space)}
            tag_occurrences.append(tag_occurrence)
            tag_occurrence_dependency_source = str(text_id) + "_" +
                str(sentence_id) + "_" + str(token.head.idx)
            dependency = {"source": tag_occurrence_dependency_source,
                "destination": tag_occurrence_id, "type": token.dep_}
            tag_occurrence_dependencies.append(dependency)
    params = {"sentence_id": node_sentence_id,
        "tag_occurrences":tag_occurrences}
    if storeTag:
        results = self.execute_query(tag_occurrence_with_tag_query, params)
    else:
        results = self.execute_query(tag_occurrence_query, params)
    self.process_dependencies(tag_occurrence_dependencies)
    return results[0]

def process_dependencies(self, tag_occurrence_dependencie):
    tag_occurrence_query = """UNWIND $dependencies as dependency
        MATCH (source:TagOccurrence {id: dependency.source})
        MATCH (destination:TagOccurrence {id: dependency.destination})
        MERGE (source)-[:IS_DEPENDENT {type: dependency.type}]->(destination)
        """
    self.execute_query(tag_occurrence_query, {"dependencies":
        tag_occurrence_dependencie})
```

> The piece of code affected by the changes to store the dependencies

> The dict with the dependency information is prepared and then appended to the list of dependencies.

> A specific function is called after the creation of the TagOccurrence nodes to store the dependencies among them.

> The query goes through the dependencies, searches for TagOccurrence nodes, and connects them.

At this stage, the resulting graph contains sentences, tokens—lemmatized, marked as stop words, and with PoS information—and relationships between tokens that describe their role in the sentence. That's a lot of information that can serve a wide range of use cases, such as the following:

- *Next-word suggestion*—As in section 11.1 with the next schema model, it is possible to suggest the next word considering the current one or any number of previous words.
- *Advanced search engines*—When we have the information about the order of the words together with dependencies among them, we can implement advanced search capabilities in which, apart from checking for the exact order of the words, it is possible to consider cases with some words between our target and provide some suggestion. A concrete example follows this list.
- *Content-based recommendation*—By decomposing the text into components, we can compare item descriptions (movies, products, and so on). This step is one of the first required for providing content-based recommendations. In this case, having the lemmatization and other normalization in place (stop-word removal, punctuation handling, and so on) will make the comparisons even more accurate.

With the schema in mind and the code in hand, let's try to accomplish a concrete task. Suppose that you have the following three sentences:

1 "John likes green apples."
2 "Melissa picked up three small red apples."
3 "That small tree produces tasty yellow apples."

EXERCISE

Import the three sentences into the graph, using listings 11.13 and 11.14. To look for all the documents containing the word *apples*, you can use the following query.

Listing 11.15   Searching for documents with the word *apples*

```
WITH  "apples" as searchQuery
MATCH (t:TagOccurrence)<-[*2..2]-(at:AnnotatedText)
WHERE t.lemma = searchQuery OR t.text = searchQuery
RETURN at
```

Easy—but you can do this with any search engine. Now let's consider a more complex use case: searching for *small apples*. With a search engine, you have two options: search for the words in that specific order, or search for both words in the document in any order. In the first case, you will not get any results (because *red* appears between the two words), whereas in the second case, you will get two documents (because both words also appear in the third document). This scenario is where the graph model we've created shows its power. Here is the query to perform this search.

Listing 11.16   Searching for *small apples*

```
WITH  "small" as firstWord, "apples" as secondWord
MATCH (t0:TagOccurrence)-[:HAS_NEXT*..2]-(t1:TagOccurrence)
WHERE (t0.lemma = firstWord or t0.text = firstWord) AND (t1.lemma =
➥ secondWord or t1.text = secondWord)
MATCH (t1)-[:IS_DEPENDENT]->(t0)<-[*2..2]-(at:AnnotatedText)     ◁
return at
```

> This line checks whether a syntactic dependency exists between the two tokens.

EXERCISE

With the graph, we can express queries in the same way we would in a search engine. Write the queries that find documents that contain the exact phrase *small apples* and find documents that contain those two words in any order.

Let's look at one more example that shows the power of NLP combined with a graph approach. As the following query demonstrates, we can use the graph to answer even more complex questions, forming the basis for applications such as information retrieval, chatbots, and conversational platforms.

Listing 11.17   Answering the question "What are the apples like?"

```
WITH  "apples" as searchQuery
MATCH (t0:TagOccurrence)
WHERE (t0.lemma = searchQuery or t0.text = searchQuery)
MATCH (t0)-[:IS_DEPENDENT {type: "amod"}]->(t1:TagOccurrence)
return t1.text
```

A graph is capable of answering complex questions without any human effort in terms of training. Decomposing the text and establishing the proper graph structure allow us to do a lot. Chapter 12 extends this idea by building a proper knowledge graph that provides support for more complicated scenarios.

11.2.1   Advantages of the graph approach

This section showed clearly how well NLP and graphs work together. Due to the highly connected nature of the data produced by NLP tasks, storing their results in a graph model appears to be a logical, rational choice. In some cases, as with syntactic dependencies, the relationships are generated as output of the NLP task, and the graph only has to store them. In other cases, the model has been designed to serve multiple scopes at the same time, providing easy-to-navigate data structures.

The graph model proposed here not only stores the main data and relationships extracted during the IE process, but also allows further extension by adding new information computed in a postprocessing phase: similarity computation, sentiment extraction, and so on. As a result, with relatively little effort, we can serve the word-suggestion use case as well as more complex search needs and even question answering ("What are the apples like?").

This model is further extended in chapter 12 to include more information extracted from the text and the results of postprocessing, allowing it to serve even more scenarios and applications.

Summary

This chapter introduced key concepts related to NLP and knowledge representation, matching them with graphs and graph models. The main point is that graphs can not only store textual data, but also provide a conceptual toolset for processing text and deliver advanced features—enabling complex search scenarios, for example—with minimal effort.

Topics covered included

- How to store text in the simplest way possible by decomposing it into chunks that are easy to navigate
- How to extract a meaningful set of information from a text
- How to design a powerful graph model for storing text and accessing it in different applications
- How to query a graph for different purposes such as search, question answering, and word suggestion

References

[Farris et al., 2013] Farris, Andrew L., Grant S. Ingersoll, and Thomas S. Morton. *Taming Text: How to Find, Organize, and Manipulate It.* Shelter Island, NY: Manning, 2013.

[Grishman, 2015] Grishman, Ralph. "Information Extraction." *IEEE Intelligent Systems* 30:5 (2015): 8–15.

[Lane et al., 2019] Lane, Hobson, Cole Howard, and Hannes Hapke. *Natural Language Processing in Action.* Shelter Island, NY: Manning, 2019.

[Mihalcea and Radev, 2011] Mihalcea, Rada, and Dragomir Radev. *Graph-Based Natural Language Processing and Information Retrieval.* New York: Cambridge University Press, 2011.

[Turnbull and Berryman, 2016] Turnbull, Doug, and John Berryman. *Relevant Search: With Applications for Solr and Elasticsearch.* Shelter Island, NY: Manning, 2016.

Knowledge graphs

This chapter covers

- Introducing knowledge graphs and their use
- Extracting entities and relationships from text to create a knowledge graph
- Using postprocessing techniques on top of knowledge graphs: semantic networks
- Extracting topics automatically

In this chapter, we'll continue the work started in chapter 11: decomposing a text into a set of meaningful information and storing it in a graph. Here, we have a clear goal in mind: building a knowledge graph.

In this way we will complete the journey we started 11 chapters ago, of managing and processing data by using graphs as a core technology and mental model. Knowledge graphs represent the summit of what has been discussed throughout the entire book. In previous chapters, you learned how to store and process user-item interaction data for providing recommendations in different shapes and forms, how to deal with transactional data and social networks to fight fraud, and more. Now we will dig deeper into how to extract knowledge from unstructured data.

This chapter is a bit longer than the others and quite dense. You'll need to read it as a whole to understand not only how to build a knowledge graph out of textual data, but also how to use it for building advanced services. Through diagrams and concrete examples, I've tried to make the chapter easier to read and understand; please look at them carefully as you read to be sure that you grasp the key concepts.

12.1 Knowledge graphs: Introduction

In chapter 3, I introduced the concept of using knowledge to transform data into insights and wisdom, using the series of images in figure 12.1. As you can see, the process is all about connecting information, and a graph is the ideal representation.

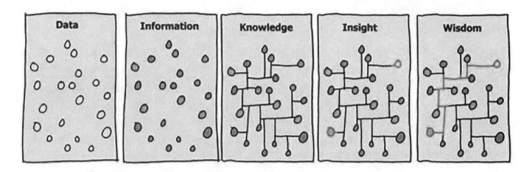

Figure 12.1 Illustration by David Somerville, based on the original by Hugh McLeod

Knowledge graphs solve, in an unbeatable way, the recurring problem in machine learning of knowledge representation (think about all the times I've spoken about knowledge representation in this book!) and provide the best tool for knowledge reasoning, such as drawing inferences from the data represented.

Knowledge graphs came into the limelight when Google announced, in a seminal blog post[1] from 2012, that its knowledge graph would enable users to search for *things, not strings*. Previously, the post explained, when a user searched for "Taj Mahal," this string was split into two parts (words) of equal importance, and the search engine tried to match them both with all the documents it had. But the reality in such a case is that the user isn't searching for two separate words but for a concrete "thing," be it the beautiful monument in Agra, an Indian restaurant, or the Grammy Award–winning musician. Celebrities, cities, geographical features, events, movies—these are the kinds of results users want to get when they are searching for specific objects. Getting back information that is really relevant to the query dramatically changes the user experience during search.

Google applied this approach to its core business, web search. Among other features, the most noticeable one from the user's perspective is that in addition to a ranked list of web pages resulting from the keyword (string-based) search, Google also shows a structured knowledge card on the right—a small box containing summarized information about entities that might correspond to the search term (figure 12.2).

---

[1] http://mng.bz/gxDE.

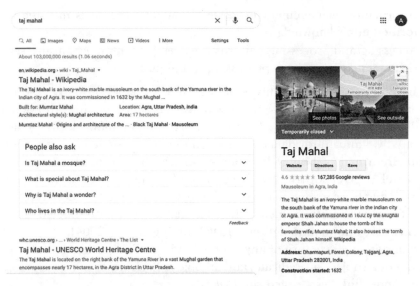

Figure 12.2 The current results for the string "taj mahal". Notice the box on the right.

Search was the beginning. A few years after Google's blog post, knowledge graphs started entering the field of information retrieval in general: databases, the Semantic Web, artificial intelligence (AI), social media, and enterprise information systems [Gomez-Perez et al., 2017]. Over the years, various initiatives have extended and developed the initial concepts introduced by Google. Additional features, new ideas and insights, and a range of applications have been introduced, and as a result, the concept of the knowledge graph has grown much broader, with new methods and technologies.

But what is a knowledge graph? What makes a normal graph a knowledge graph? There is no gold standard, universally accepted definition, but my favorite is the one given by Gomez-Perez et al.: "A knowledge graph consists of a set of interconnected typed entities and their attributes."

According to this definition, the basic unit of a knowledge graph is the representation of an entity, such as a person, organization, or location (such as the Taj Mahal example), or perhaps a sporting event or a book or movie (as in the case of a recommendation engine). Each entity might have various attributes. For a person, those attributes would include name, address, birth date, and so on. Entities are connected by *relations*. A person *works for* a company, for example, and a user *likes* a page or *follows* another user. Relations can also be used to bridge two separate knowledge graphs.

Compared with other knowledge-oriented information systems, knowledge graphs are distinguished by their particular combination of

- Knowledge representation structures and reasoning, such as languages, schemas, standard vocabularies, and hierarchies among concepts

- Information management processes (how information is ingested and transformed into a knowledge graph)
- Accessing and processing patterns, such as querying mechanisms, search algorithms, and pre- and postprocessing techniques

As we have done throughout this book, we will use a label property graph (LPG) to represent a knowledge graph—a break with usual practice, because knowledge graphs generally are represented with a Resource Description Framework (RDF) data model. RDF is a W3C standard for data exchange on the web, designed as a language for representing information about web resources, such as the title, author, and modification date of a web page or copyright and licensing information about a web document. But by generalizing the concept of a web resource, we can also use RDF to represent information about other things, such as items available from an online shop or a user's preferences for information delivery [RDF Working Group, 2004].

The underlying structure of any expression in RDF is a collection of triples, each consisting of a subject, a predicate, and an object. Each triple can be represented as a node-arc-node link, also called an *RDF graph*, in which the *subject* is a resource (a node in the graph), the *predicate* is the arc (a relationship), and the *object* is another node or a literal value. Figure 12.3 shows what this structure looks like.

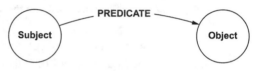

Figure 12.3   Simple RDF graph

RDF is intended for situations in which the information it encodes needs to be processed by applications, rather than being displayed only to people. It provides a common framework for expressing this information so that it can be exchanged between applications without loss of meaning. This framework makes it a bit more verbose and less readable by humans than an LPG, which is designed to store complex graphs by using relationships and nodes with their properties in a compact way. Take a look at the example in figure 12.4, from a blog post[2] by Jesús Barrasa.

LPGs are more flexible and powerful than RDF graphs for representing knowledge graphs. It's worth pointing out that this chapter focuses on how to build and access a knowledge graph created out of textual data. Building knowledge graphs from structured data is definitely a simpler task, and it's what we have done already in multiple scenarios covered so far.

When a knowledge graph is obtained from the text, using techniques that we will explore in this chapter, it is postprocessed or enriched to extract insights and wisdom. Figure 12.5 illustrates the whole process, which we will work through in this chapter.

The techniques for extracting structures out of text will be extended with the recognition of the key entities and the relationships among them. These techniques are critical for the creation of a knowledge graph. Because the same entities and relationships tend to recur in the documents belonging to a domain-specific corpus, it's

---

[2] http://mng.bz/eMjv.

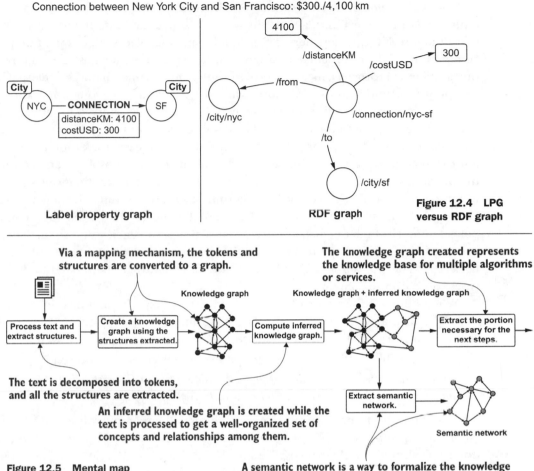

Figure 12.4 LPG versus RDF graph

Figure 12.5 Mental map of the whole process

important to infer a generic model that represents this information, abstracting from the instances appearing in the text. This model is known as an *inferred knowledge graph*. The result of this process represents the knowledge base that can be used in multiple advanced machine learning techniques or, more generally, AI applications. One of the most common approaches for representing the knowledge base is via a *semantic network*: a set of concepts and predefined connections among them.

12.2 *Knowledge graph building: Entities*

A key element for building a knowledge graph out of textual data is recognizing entities in the text. Suppose that you have a set of documents (from Wikipedia, for example), and you are tasked with finding the names of the people or other entities relevant to your domain in those documents, such as locations, organizations, and so on. When this information is extracted, you have to make it easily accessible via a graph for further exploration.

The task of *named entity recognition (NER)* involves finding each mention of a named entity (NE) in the text and labeling its type [Grishman and Sundheim, 1996]. What constitutes an NE type depends on the domain; people, places, and organizations are common, but NEs can include a variety of other structures, such as street addresses, times, chemical formulas, mathematical formulas, gene names, names of celestial bodies, products, and brands—in short, whatever is relevant to your application. In generic terms, we can define an NE as anything that can be referred to with a proper name that is relevant to the domain of analysis we are considering. If you are processing electronic medical records for some healthcare use case, for example, you may want to recognize patients, diseases, treatments, medicines, hospitals, and so on. As the previous examples suggest, many named entities have an extralinguistic structure, which means that they're composed according to rules that differ from general language rules. The term is also commonly extended to include things that aren't entities per se: numerical values (such as prices), dates, times, currencies, and so on. Each NE is related to a specific type that specifies its class, such as PERSON, DATE, NUMBER, or LOCATION. The domain is critical because the same entity can be related to different types based on the domain.

When all the NEs in a text have been extracted, they can be linked in sets corresponding to real-world entities, allowing us to infer, for example, that mentions of "United Airlines" and "United" refer to the same company [Jurafsky and Martin, 2019]. Suppose that you have the following document:

> *Marie Curie, wife of Pierre Curie, received the Nobel Prize in Chemistry in 1911. She had previously been awarded the Nobel Prize in Physics in 1903.*

The set of entities to extract would vary according to the relevant entities for your analysis goals, but supposing that we are interested in all the entities, a proper NE recognition result should be able to recognize and classify the names "Marie Curie" and "Pierre Curie" as person names, the names "Nobel Prize in Chemistry" and "Nobel Prize in Physics" as prize names, and "1911" and "1903" as dates. This task is straightforward for humans but not so simple for machines. You can try it by using an NE visualizer like the open source displaCy.[3] If you paste in the previous text and select all the entity labels, you'll get a result like figure 12.6.

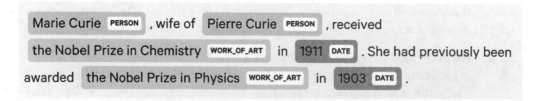

Figure 12.6   The results from the displaCy NE visualizer with our sample text

---

Interestingly, without any tuning, the service was able to recognize all the entities in the sentences (although the prizes are classified as "works of art").

Adding the NER task to the graph model is straightforward. As shown in figure 12.7, the best solution is to add new nodes with the label NamedEntity that contain the

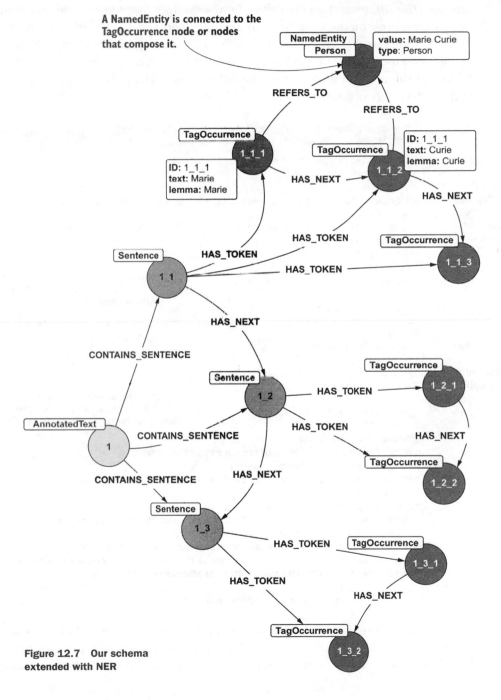

Figure 12.7   Our schema extended with NER

entities extracted from the document. These nodes are linked to any related TagOccurrence nodes ("Marie Curie," for example, is a single name composed of two TagOccurrence nodes, "Marie" and "Curie"). The NamedEntity nodes are created for each occurrence of the entities in the text, so "Marie Curie" can appear more than one time as different nodes. Later in this section, we will see how to link them to a common node that represents the specific entity that represents "Marie Curie" as a Person.

Extending our data model from chapter 11 for storing the results of an NER task in a graph is quite simple. The following listing contains the changes required to extract NEs from the text and store them. The full code is in ch12/04_spacy_ner_schema.py and ch12/text_processors.py files.

Listing 12.1   Adding the NER task to the model

```
def tokenize_and_store(self, text, text_id, storeTag):
    docs = self.nlp.pipe([text])
    for doc in docs:
        annotated_text = self.__text_processor.create_annotated_text(doc,
        ➥ text_id)
        spans = self.__text_processor.process_sentences(annotated_text, doc,
        ➥ storeTag, text_id)
        nes = self.__text_processor.process_entities(spans, text_id)
```

Adds the new step to extract and store the named entities → (points to the `nes = self.__text_processor.process_entities(spans, text_id)` line)

```
def process_entities(self, spans, text_id):
    nes = []
    for entity in spans:
        ne = {'value': entity.text, 'type': entity.label_, 'start_index':
        ➥ entity.start_char,
              'end_index': entity.end_char}
        nes.append(ne)
    self.store_entities(text_id, nes)
    return nes
```

The function takes the result of the NLP process and extracts the named entities. (points to the `def process_entities` line)

The function stores the entities in the graph. (points to the `self.store_entities(text_id, nes)` line)

```
def store_entities(self, document_id, nes):
    ne_query = """
        UNWIND $nes as item
        MERGE (ne:NamedEntity {id: toString($documentId) + "_" +
        ➥ toString(item.start_index)})
        SET ne.type = item.type, ne.value = item.value, ne.index =
        ➥ item.start_index
        WITH ne, item as neIndex
        MATCH (text:AnnotatedText)-[:CONTAINS_SENTENCE]->(sentence:Sentence)-
        ➥ [:HAS_TOKEN]->(tagOccurrence:TagOccurrence)
        WHERE text.id = $documentId AND tagOccurrence.index >=
        ➥ neIndex.start_index AND tagOccurrence.index < neIndex.end_index
        MERGE (ne)<-[:PARTICIPATES_IN]-(tagOccurrence)
    """
    self.execute_query(ne_query, {"documentId": document_id, "nes": nes})
```

The query loops over the entities, and for each, it creates a new node and links it to the tags composing the NE. (points to the `def store_entities` line)

As you can see, the changes required are minimal, both in terms of the pipeline and the code for saving the result of the NER task. spaCy has its own models for basic NEs, and these models are what we used in this code, but it also offers the opportunity to train new NER models by passing samples of annotated sentences. Refer to the spaCy documentation[4] to see how.

In written and spoken language, if a person, a location, or some other relevant entity is mentioned several times, later mentions often won't repeat the full name. Thus, in the example given earlier, we might see instead an abbreviated name ("Mme. Curie"), a pronoun ("she"), or a descriptive phrase ("the noted scientist"). The problem at this point is how to identify such relationships and extract them from plain text.

We can develop our scenario further by adding another requirement. Suppose that you would like to improve your access patterns by also considering all the mentions of named entities. As a concrete example, in the following text we would like to connect "she" with "Marie Curie":

> *Marie Curie received the Nobel Prize in Physics in 1903. She became the first woman to win the prize and the first person—man or woman—to win the award twice.*

In natural language processing (NLP), this task is accomplished by *co-reference resolution*, which is defined as the problem of identifying relationships between entity references in a text, whether they are represented by nouns or pronouns [Mihalcea and Radev, 2011]. Resolving pronoun references involves a combination of constraints and preferences: the antecedent must match the pronoun (in number, gender, and so on), and as antecedents, we prefer subjects over objects, words that are closer to the pronoun in the text, and words that can plausibly appear in the context of the pronoun [Grishman, 2015]. Typical algorithms for co-reference resolution attempt to identify chains of references by using rule-based systems, although the final criteria are based on gathering statistics over a large number of texts from the corpus or using machine learning classifiers.

Linking general co-referential noun phrases is a more difficult task. Some easy cases use the same noun several times, but most examples require some knowledge of the world, based on observing what phrases have been used elsewhere to refer to a specific entity. This approach allows us to resolve a phrase like "the noted Polish scientist" to "Marie Curie," or "the prize" to "the Nobel Prize."

Proposed graph-based approaches to co-reference resolution [Nicolae and Nicolae, 2006; Ng, 2009] use a graph-cut algorithm to approximate the correct assignment of references to entities in a text, but these methods are outside the scope of this book because the NLP libraries used in our codebase have their own implementations for co-reference implementation. The focus here is on how to model the results of such a task and get the most out of it.

Consider our sample text. Figure 12.8 shows the result obtained by using the Stanford CoreNLP test service mentioned in chapter 11.

---

[4] https://spacy.io/usage.

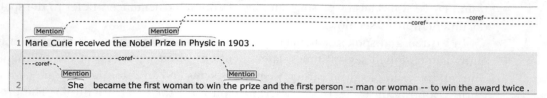

Figure 12.8   Co-reference results

We can represent these connections in our graph model by linking pronouns and other references to the real entities they are referring to. Figure 12.9 shows our model extended to include co-reference resolution. As usual, graphs provide the flexibility necessary to adapt the model to new needs with minimum effort while keeping the previous access patterns working effectively.

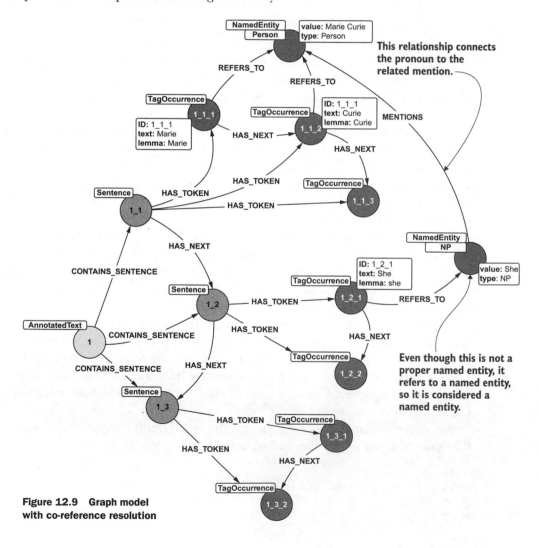

**Figure 12.9   Graph model
with co-reference resolution**

The extended graph model connects NamedEntity nodes by using the MENTIONS relationship. The changes in the code for storing the new co-references are shown in the following listing. The full code is in ch12/05_spacy_coref_schema.py and in ch12/text_processors.py.

Listing 12.2 Extracting co-references

Adds a new co-ref element in spaCy's **NLP pipeline**, a neural network implementation of co-reference resolution (see https://github.com/huggingface/neuralcoref).

```python
def __init__(self, language, uri, user, password):
    spacy.prefer_gpu()
    self.nlp = spacy.load('en_core_web_sm')
    coref = neuralcoref.NeuralCoref(self.nlp.vocab)
    self.nlp.add_pipe(coref, name='neuralcoref')
    self._driver = GraphDatabase.driver(uri, auth=(user, password),
        encrypted=0)
    self.__text_processor = TextProcessor(self.nlp, self._driver)
    self.create_constraints()

def tokenize_and_store(self, text, text_id, storeTag):
    docs = self.nlp.pipe([text])
    for doc in docs:
        annotated_text = self.__text_processor.create_annotated_text(doc,
            text_id)
        spans = self.__text_processor.process_sentences(annotated_text, doc,
            storeTag, text_id)
        nes = self.__text_processor.process_entities(spans, text_id)
        coref = self.__text_processor.process_co-reference(doc, text_id)

def process_co-reference(self, doc, text_id):
    coref = []
    if doc._.has_coref:
        for cluster in doc._.coref_clusters:
            mention = {'from_index': cluster.mentions[-1].start_char,
                'to_index': cluster.mentions[0].start_char}
            coref.append(mention)
        self.store_coref(text_id, coref)
    return coref

def store_coref(self, document_id, corefs):
    coref_query = """
        MATCH (document:AnnotatedText)
        WHERE document.id = $documentId
        WITH document
        UNWIND $corefs as coref
        MATCH (document)-[*3..3]->(start:NamedEntity), (document)-
            [*3..3]->(end:NamedEntity)
        WHERE start.index = coref.from_index AND end.index =
            coref.to_index
        MERGE (start)-[:MENTIONS]->(end)
    """
    self.execute_query(coref_query,
                       {"documentId": document_id, "corefs": corefs})
```

Extracts the co-references and stores them in the graph → (pointing to `coref = self.__text_processor.process_co-reference(doc, text_id)`)

Loops over the co-references found in the document and creates the dictionary for storing them in the graph → (pointing to `if doc._.has_coref:`)

The query connects the named entities via MENTIONS. → (pointing to `coref_query = """`)

The co-reference relationships are useful for connecting all the mentions of the key NEs to the sources, even when their canonical names are not used.

NEs and co-references play an important role in knowledge graph building. Both are first-class objects that represent occurrences in the text of relevant entities and their mutual relationships. But to improve the quality of the graph in terms of the knowledge we are able to extract from it, it is necessary to abstract from these occurrences in the text and identify the key entities that are referred to multiple times in the text. Natural language understanding systems (and humans) interpret linguistic expressions with respect to a *discourse model* [Karttunen, 1969]—a mental model that the system constructs incrementally as it processes text from a corpus (or, in the case of a human hearer, from a dialogue), which contains representations of the entities referred to in the text, as well as properties of the entities and relations among them [Jurafsky and Martin, 2019]. We say that two mentions co-refer if they are associated with the same entity.

The idea of the discourse model can be applied in the knowledge graph use case to simplify and improve access to the knowledge it embodies. As figure 12.10 shows, we can build a complement to the knowledge graph—the inferred knowledge graph mentioned in this chapter's introduction—that contains unique representations of the entities referred to in the processed text, as well as their properties and the connections among them.

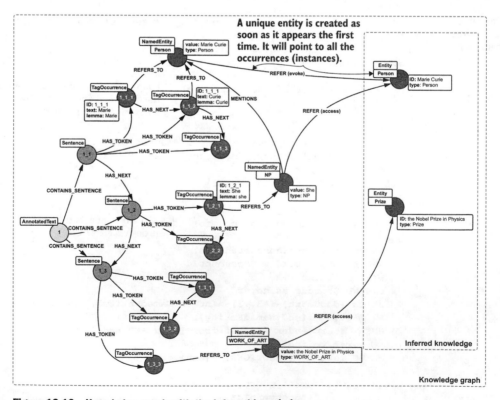

Figure 12.10   Knowledge graph with the inferred knowledge

Whereas the main body of the knowledge graph contains the decomposition of the text in the corpus and, eventually, the structured data reorganized in the graph model, this second part—connected to the first—distills key elements and relationships to provide answers to different questions and supports multiple services, eliminating the need to navigate the entire graph. This *inferred knowledge graph* contains an easy-to-share knowledge representation that is not directly connected to the specific instances (the documents) from which this knowledge is distilled.

The following listing shows how this inference is applied after the co-reference resolution task to build the second part of the knowledge graph incrementally. The function is in ch12/text_processors.py called from ch12/06_spacy_entity_relationship_extraction.py.

Listing 12.3 Creating the inferred knowledge graph

```
def build_entities_inferred_graph(self, document_id):
    extract_direct_entities_query = """
        MATCH (document:AnnotatedText)
        WHERE document.id = $documentId
        WITH document
        MATCH (document)-[*3..3]->(ne:NamedEntity)
        WHERE NOT ne.type IN ['NP', 'NUMBER', 'DATE']
        WITH ne
        MERGE (entity:Entity {type: ne.type, id:ne.value})
        MERGE (ne)-[:REFERS_TO {type: "evoke"}]->(entity)
    """

    extract_indirect_entities_query = """
        MATCH (document:AnnotatedText)
        WHERE document.id = $documentId
        WITH document
        MATCH (document)-[*3..3]->(ne:NamedEntity)<-[:MENTIONS]-(mention)
        WHERE NOT ne.type IN ['NP', 'NUMBER', 'DATE']
        WITH ne, mention
        MERGE (entity:Entity {type: ne.type, id:ne.value})
        MERGE (mention)-[:REFERS_TO {type: "access"}]->(entity)
    """
    self.execute_query(extract_direct_entities_query, {"documentId":
    document_id})
    self.execute_query(extract_indirect_entities_query, {"documentId":
    document_id})
```

The new step for extracting the inferred graph from the previous created graph

The first query creates entities out of the main named entities.

The second query creates connections to the main entities by using the co-reference connections available in the graph using **MENTIONS**.

With the code in listing 12.3, we have all the code necessary to extract the named entities and co-references in a text and to create this second layer of the knowledge graph. At this point, by using the code available in ch12/07_process_larger_corpus.py, you can import and process the MASC corpus we used in chapter 11 and start getting more insights out of it.

EXERCISES

With the graph database we've created, perform the following operations via queries:

- Find the distinct types of named entities created.
- Count the occurrences of each type, order them in descending order, and take the first three.
- Count the occurrences of the Organization entities in the inferred knowledge graph. How many are there? There should be fewer because the system should aggregate them when creating the inferred graph.

12.3 *Knowledge graph building: Relationships*

When the entities have been recognized, the next logical step is discerning relationships among the detected entities, which dramatically improves the quality of the knowledge graph in terms of the insights you can extract from it and the available access patterns. This step is key in creating a meaningful graph from a text because it allows you to create the connections between the entities and navigate them properly. The types of queries you can execute and, hence, the types of questions it can answer will increase significantly.

To decompose the text better and make it more understandable by machines and humans, suppose that you would like to identify relationships between the extracted entities that highlight connections among them—such as relationships between a prize and who it has been awarded to, or a company and who works for it.

Answering questions such as the most probable diagnosis is based on the symptoms a patient has, or who has won a Nobel Prize in Physics requires you to identify not only specific entities, but also the connections among them. Different techniques exist for performing this task; some are more complex than others, and some require supervision (labeling sample relationships to create a training set). The earliest, still-common algorithm for relation extraction is based on lexicosyntactic patterns. It involves mapping some of the aforementioned syntactic relationships among tokens or specific sequences of tags into a set of relevant (for the use case) relations between key named entities.

This task may seem to be a complex one, and in some circumstances, it is, but having a graph model helps a lot. A rough, simple approximation can be obtained by a set of semantic analysis rules, each of which maps a subgraph of the syntactic graph (such as a portion of the graph containing the syntactic relationships that relate key entities), anchored by some of the *entity* mentions, into a database relation applied to the corresponding entities. Consider, as a concrete example, the following sentence:

Marie Curie received the Nobel Prize in Physics in 1903.

The syntactic analysis determines that "received" has the subject "Marie Curie" and the object "the Nobel Prize." These dependencies can be visualized easily with the following code.

Listing 12.4 Visualizing dependencies

Annotates a simple sentence

```
import spacy
nlp = spacy.load('en_core_web_sm')
doc = nlp(u"Marie Curie received the Nobel Prize in Physics")
options = {"collapse_phrases": True}
spacy.displacy.serve(doc, style='dep', options=options)
```

This option allows us to merge, for example, "Marie Curie" into a single entity in the visualization.

Creates a server instance that will allow us to visualize the result

The result will look like figure 12.11.

Figure 12.11 Syntactic dependencies visualized with spaCy

A possible pattern would map this syntactic structure into the semantic predicate

```
(verb: receive, subject: p:Person, object: a:Prize) • (relationship:
RECEIVE_PRIZE, from: p, to:a)
```

Here, "receive" (considered in the lemmatized version) is an English verb, whereas RECEIVE_PRIZE is a relationship type (a semantic relation). Expressing these types of patterns is straightforward with a proper graph-based query language like Cypher. As an exercise, we will derive the graph we have. The sentence processed by the code we have produces the results shown in figure 12.12.

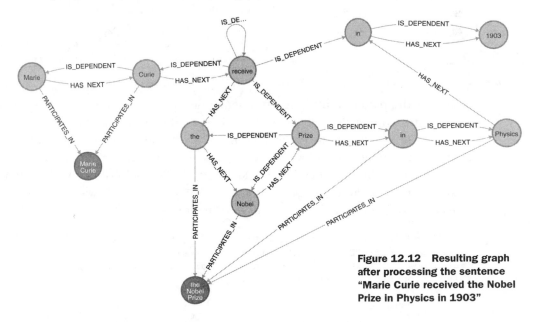

Figure 12.12 Resulting graph after processing the sentence "Marie Curie received the Nobel Prize in Physics in 1903"

The task of finding all the subgraphs respecting the pattern we are looking for can be performed with the following query.

```
MATCH (verb:TagOccurrence {pos: "VBD", lemma:"receive"})
WITH verb
MATCH p=(verb)-[:IS_DEPENDENT {type:"nsubj"}]->(subject)-[:PARTICIPATES_IN]->
➥ (person:NamedEntity {type: "PERSON"})
MATCH q=(verb)-[:IS_DEPENDENT {type:"dobj"}]->(object)-[:PARTICIPATES_IN]->
➥ (woa:NamedEntity {type: "WORK_OF_ART"})
RETURN verb, person, woa, p, q
```

The result in our knowledge graph will look like figure 12.13.

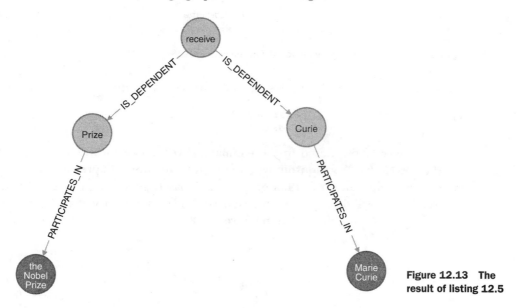

Figure 12.13   The result of listing 12.5

Note that the pattern must specify the semantic types of the subject and object—that is, the entity type, such as Person as the subject and Prize as the object. (In our example, the type is "work of art"; having a better NER model would help.) But "receive" conveys many relations, and we don't want instances of "receive" involving other types of arguments to be translated into the RECEIVE_PRIZE relationship. On the other side, large numbers of alternative patterns are needed to capture the wide range of expressions that could be used to convey this information, such as

```
(relationship: "win", subject: p:Person, object: a:Prize) →
  (relationship: RECEIVE_PRIZE, from: p, to:a)
(relationship: "award", indirect-object: p:Person, object: a:Prize) →
  (relationship: RECEIVE_PRIZE, from: p, to:a)
```

Note that in the latter example, the recipient appears as the indirect object ("The Committee awarded the prize to Marie Curie."). If we didn't include a syntactic regularization step to convert passive sentences to active ones, we would also require a pattern for the passive form ("The prize was awarded to Marie Curie."):

```
(relationship: "was awarded", object: a:Prize, indirect-object: p:Person) →
  (relationship: RECEIVE_PRIZE, from: p, to: a)
```

When these relationships have been extracted, they have to be stored in the graph model we designed. Figure 12.14 shows the changes to the schema required to add this new information.

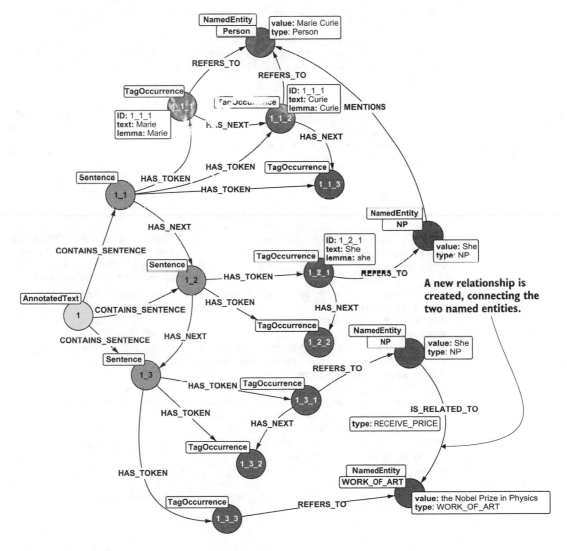

Figure 12.14 Extended model with the relationships

The following listing shows the changes that are needed to gather the syntactic relationships, convert them to relationships of interest, and store them in our graph model. The full code is in ch12/06_spacy_entity_relationship_extraction.py and in ch12/text_processors.py.

Listing 12.6   Extracting relationships from typed dependencies

```
def tokenize_and_store(self, text, text_id, storeTag):
    docs = self.nlp.pipe([text])
    for doc in docs:
        annotated_text = self.__text_processor.create_annotated_text(doc,
        ➥ text_id)
        spans = self.__text_processor.process_sentences(annotated_text, doc,
        ➥ storeTag, text_id)
        nes = self.__text_processor.process_entities(spans, text_id)
        coref = self.__text_processor.process_co-reference(doc, text_id)
        self.__text_processor.build_inferred_graph(text_id)
        rules = [
            {
                'type': 'RECEIVE_PRIZE',
                'verbs': ['receive'],
                'subjectTypes': ['PERSON', 'NP'],
                'objectTypes': ['WORK_OF_ART']
            }
        ]
        self.__text_processor.extract_relationships(text_id, rules)
```

An example of the possible rules that can be defined → (points to `]`)

The new step for extracting relationships from the existing graph based on the rules defined → (points to `self.__text_processor.extract_relationships(text_id, rules)`)

```
def extract_relationships(self, document_id, rules):
    extract_relationships_query = """
        MATCH (document:AnnotatedText)
        WHERE document.id = $documentId
        WITH document
        UNWIND $rules as rule
        MATCH (document)-[*2..2]->(verb:TagOccurrence {pos: "VBD"})
        MATCH (verb:TagOccurrence {pos: "VBD"})
        WHERE verb.lemma IN rule.verbs
        WITH verb, rule
        MATCH (verb)-[:IS_DEPENDENT {type:"nsubj"}]->(subject)-
        ➥ [:PARTICIPATES_IN]->(subjectNe:NamedEntity)
        WHERE subjectNe.type IN rule.subjectTypes
        MATCH (verb)-[:IS_DEPENDENT {type:"dobj"}]->(object)-
        ➥ [:PARTICIPATES_IN]->(objectNe:NamedEntity {type: "WORK_OF_ART"})
        WHERE objectNe.type IN rule.objectTypes
        WITH verb, subjectNe, objectNe, rule
        MERGE (subjectNe)-[:IS_RELATED_TO {root: verb.lemma, type:
        ➥ rule.type}]->(objectNe)
    """

    self.execute_query(extract_relationships_query, {"documentId":
    ➥ document_id, "rules":rules})
```

The query goes through the graph, navigating NEs and the relationships among the participants' tags, and extracts the desired relationships.

As the code shows, the rules for converting semantic relationships to the relationships of interest must be listed, but enumerating these patterns poses a dual problem:

- There are many ways in which semantic relationships can be expressed, making it difficult to get good coverage by listing the patterns individually.
- Such rules might not capture all the distinctions required for a particular predicate in different domains. If we want to collect documents about military attacks, for example, we probably want to include instances of "strike" and "hit" in texts about conflicts, but not in sports stories. We might also want to require some arguments and make others optional.

To get around these problems, other mechanisms may be used. Most of these approaches are supervised, which means that they require human support to learn. The most common approach is based on classifiers that determine the type of relationship (or lack of relationship) between NEs. It can be implemented by using different machine learning or deep learning algorithms, but what should the input to such a classifier be?

Training the classifier requires a corpus annotated with entities and relations. First, we mark the entities in each document; then, for each pair of entities in a sentence, we either record the type of relation connecting them or note that they aren't connected by a relation. The former are positive training instances, and the latter are negative training instances. After we've trained the classifier, we can extract the relationships in a new test document by applying it to all pairs of *entity* mentions that appear in the same sentence [Grishman, 2015]. Although it is effective, this approach has a big disadvantage related to the amount of data required during the training process.

A third approach combines the pattern-based approach with the supervised approach, using pattern-based as a bootstrapping process: the relationships are inferred automatically from the patterns, which are used to train the classifier.

Regardless of the approach you use for extracting the relationships, when they are stored as connections between the NEs in the knowledge graph representing the text, it is possible to project these relationships onto the inferred knowledge graph discussed earlier. In this case, the relationships should connect entities.

In the definition of the model, it's important to bear in mind that it is necessary to trace back why that relationship has been created. An issue is that in most graph databases available today, including Neo4j, relationships can connect only two nodes. But in this case, we would like to connect many more, to point back to the source of the relationship. This problem has two solutions:

- Add some information in the relationship as properties that will allow us to trace back to the origin of the connection between two entities, such as a list of IDs representing the NEs connected.
- Add nodes that represent the relationships. We can't connect to relationships, but these Relationship nodes will materialize the connections between entities, and we will be able to connect them to other nodes.

The first option is less verbose in terms of number of nodes but much more complex to navigate, which is why the proposed schema (figure 12.15) follows the second approach.

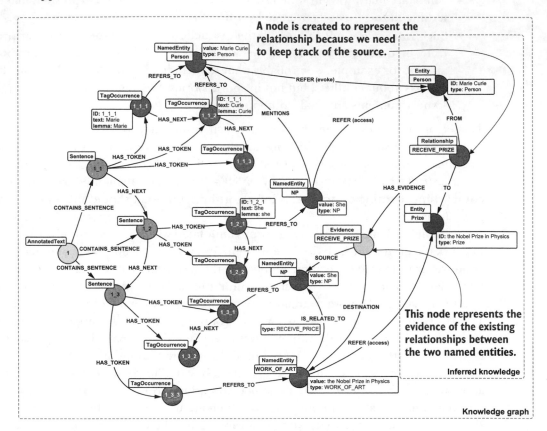

Figure 12.15   Extended inferred schema to include the relationships

The creation of an inferred knowledge graph has a great impact on the navigability of your graph and the types of access patterns it supports. Suppose that you've processed a large corpus of texts like the one in our example with Marie Curie, and you would like to know who has won a Nobel Prize in Physics.

The following listing shows how to extend the code we already have for extracting entities from the text to infer relationships among entities in the inferred knowledge graph. The full code is in ch12/text_processors.py called from ch12/ 06_spacy_entity_ relationship_extraction.py.

Listing 12.7 Extracting relationships and storing them in the inferred knowledge graph

The new step for extracting the relationships
of the inferred knowledge graph

```
def build_relationships_inferred_graph(self, document_id):
    extract_relationships_query = """                    ◁─────────────
        MATCH (document:AnnotatedText)
        WHERE document.id = $documentId
        WITH document
        MATCH (document)-[*2..3]->(ne1:NamedEntity)
        MATCH (entity1:Entity)<-[:REFERS_TO]-(ne1:NamedEntity)-
        ➡ [r:IS_RELATED_TO]->(ne2:NamedEntity)-[:REFERS_TO]->
        ➡ (entity2:Entity)
        MERGE (evidence:Evidence {id: id(r), type:r.type})
        MERGE (rel:Relationship {id: id(r), type:r.type})
        MERGE (ne1)<-[:SOURCE]-(evidence)
        MERGE (ne2)<-[:DESTINATION]-(evidence)      The query extracts the list of
        MERGE (rel)-[:HAS_EVIDENCE]->(evidence)     relationships created in previous
        MERGE (entity1)<-[:FROM]-(rel)              steps and creates the evidence
        MERGE (entity2)<-[:TO]-(rel)                and the relationships in the
    """                                             inferred knowledge graph.
    self.execute_query(extract_relationships_query, {"documentId":
    ➡ document_id})
```

At this point, after the text is processed and stored as described, the query needed to get the desired result will look like the following.

Listing 12.8 Getting the winners of the Nobel Prize in Physics

```
MATCH (nodelPrize:Entity {type:"WORK_OF_ART"})<-[:TO]-(rel:Relationship
➡ {type: "RECEIVE_PRIZE"})-[:FROM]->(winner:Entity {type: "PERSON"})
WHERE nodelPrize.id CONTAINS "the Nobel Prize in Physics"
RETURN winner
```

From the `rel` node, it is possible also to find all the text that makes this relationship evident.

The knowledge graph we have built represents the original content available in the corpus processed in a way that makes possible multiple types of searches and permits different access patterns and question answering. Most of these operations are impossible when we use the texts in their original format. Identifying NEs and the relationships among them enables queries that are not possible otherwise, and the inferred knowledge graph creates a second layer in which the distilled knowledge is easier to navigate. The graph is an abstraction that represents the key concepts in a text.

12.4 Semantic networks

The knowledge graph we've built so far contains a lot of information that has been extracted from the text and converted to knowledge that is ready to be used. Specifically, the inferred knowledge graph represents the distilled knowledge that has been extracted while more and more texts have been processed. At this point, it is relevant to investigate how concretely this knowledge graph can be used to deliver new advanced services to end users.

A knowledge graph is a representation of a knowledge base on top of which several types of automated reasoning and interesting features can be built. Knowledge representation and reasoning is a branch of symbolic AI that aims to design computer systems that are capable of reasoning (similar to humans) based on a machine-interpretable representation of the domain of interest. In this computational model, symbols serve as surrogates for physical objects, events, relationships, and other domain artifacts [Sowa, 2000].

One of the most common ways to represent such knowledge bases is to use *semantic networks*—graphs whose nodes represent concepts and whose arcs represent relations between those concepts. Semantic networks provide a structural representation of statements about a domain of interest, or "a means to abstract from natural language, representing the knowledge that is captured in text in a form more suitable for computation" [Grimm et al., 2007].

Typically, concepts are chosen to represent the meaning of nouns in such a text, and relations are mapped to verb phrases. Let's consider a concrete example we used earlier. The sentence

Marie Curie, the famous scientist, received the Nobel Prize in Physics in 1903.

should generate the semantic network shown in figure 12.16.

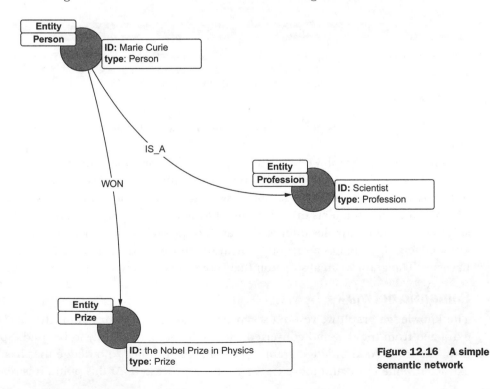

Figure 12.16   A simple semantic network

This structure is exactly the one created for the inferred knowledge graph. The only difference is that we materialized the relationships for keeping track of the sources, which is necessary if we want to know why such relationships are created. So the inferred knowledge graph is a semantic network—a simplified version of one because in our schema, we materialize the relationships to keep track of the source of each inferred relationship.

For that reason, in our mental map we consider extracting the semantic network from the inferred knowledge graph as a specific process (as shown in figure 12.17), removing all the overhead related to the mapping of relationships to the source and keeping only the concepts and relationships that are relevant, such as by considering how often they appear in the original corpus.

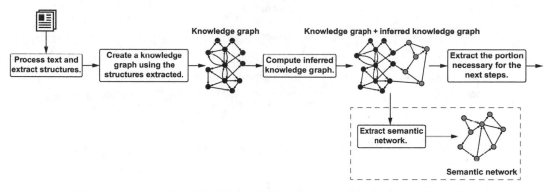

Figure 12.17   Mental map: extracting the semantic network

The content of a semantic network depends on the concepts and relationships that are relevant to the domain of interest and to the specific service the application should deliver at the end. In our case, the semantic network is the inferred knowledge graph extracted from the current big graph. During this process of extraction, it's possible to simplify the graph a bit, such as by removing the Relationship nodes and replacing them with proper relationships.

Sometimes, using the corpus you have is not enough to build a proper semantic network that can fulfill all your needs. Luckily, publicly available generic semantic networks exist. One of the most widely used is ConceptNet 5,[5] described by its creators as "a knowledge representation project, providing a large semantic graph that describes general human knowledge and how it is expressed in natural language" [Speer and Havasi, 2013]. The knowledge represented in the graph is collected from a variety of sources, including expert-created resources, crowdsourcing, and games. The aim of ConceptNet is to improve natural language applications by enabling them to better understand the meanings behind the words people use [Speer et al., 2017]. Figure 12.18, from the website, shows how it works.

---

[5] http://conceptnet.io.

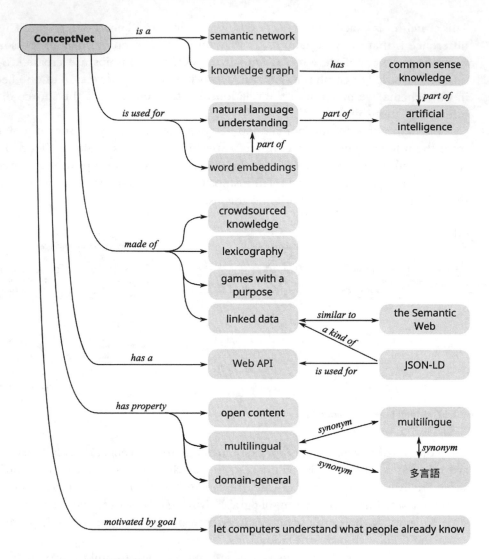

Figure 12.18   ConceptNet 5 as described on its website

The ConceptNet 5 API is quite straightforward to use. If you would like to know more about Marie Curie, for example, you can call the URL

```
http://api.conceptnet.io/c/en/marie_curie/
```

and get the following answer:

```
{
    "@id": "/a/[/r/Synonym/,/c/en/marie_curie/n/wn/person/,
    ➥ /c/en/marya_sklodowska/n/wn/person/]",
    "@type": "Edge",
```

```
    "dataset": "/d/wordnet/3.1",
    "end": {
        "@id": "/c/en/marya_sklodowska/n/wn/person",
        "@type": "Node",
        "label": "Marya Sklodowska",
        "language": "en",
        "sense_label": "n, person",
        "term": "/c/en/marya_sklodowska"
    },
    "license": "cc:by/4.0",
    "rel": {
        "@id": "/r/Synonym",
        "@type": "Relation",
        "label": "Synonym"
    },
    "sources": [
        {
            "@id": "/s/resource/wordnet/rdf/3.1",
            "@type": "Source",
            "contributor": "/s/resource/wordnet/rdf/3.1"
        }
    ],
    "start": {
        "@id": "/c/en/marie_curie/n/wn/person",
        "@type": "Node",
        "label": "Marie Curie",
        "language": "en",
        "sense_label": "n, person",
        "term": "/c/en/marie_curie"
    },
    "surfaceText": "[[Marie Curie]] is a synonym of [[Marya Sklodowska]]",
    "weight": 2.0
}
```

This answer tells you immediately that Marie Curie's other name is Marya Sklodowoska.

It's interesting to look at ConceptNet at this point in the chapter for a few reasons:

- It's created in exactly the same way described in the text, which validates our path so far. As you can see from the schema in figure 12.18, it integrates all the key concepts: the knowledge graph, the semantic network, AI, NLP, and so on.
- If you don't have enough information in your corpus to build a proper knowledge graph, and the domain you are referring to is a common one, you can use ConceptNet to fill the gaps. If you are processing news articles from online sources, and you get only the names of cities in the text, such as "Los Angeles," you can query ConceptNet to find the states where the cities are located (in this case, "California").[6]

---

[6] For this example, the query to use is http://api.conceptnet.io/query?start=/c/en/los_angeles&rel=/r/PartOf.

■ I love it. It's such a good resource for understanding text and extending a knowledge graph that I use it often, in many projects. It's simple and free to use, and quite fast: for the best speeds you can download it or, better, import it in a Neo4j instance.

Figure 12.19, from the paper by Speer and Havasi [2013] introducing the latest iteration of ConceptNet, describes the main relationships available and how they connect different components in the text. It clearly shows that the approach is similar to what it is proposed in this book. In this figure, *NP* stands for *noun phrase*, *VP* for *verb phrase*, and *AP* for *adjectival phrase*.

Relation	# edges	Sentence pattern
IsA	7,956,303	*NP* is a kind of *NP*.
PartOf	536,648	*NP* is part of *NP*.
AtLocation	535,278	Somewhere *NP* can be is *NP*.
RelatedTo	319,471	*NP* is related to *NP*.
HasProperty	303,921	*NP* is *AP*.
UsedFor	254,563	*NP* is used for *VP*.
DerivedFrom	242,853	*TERM* is derived from *TERM*.
Causes	233,727	The effect of *VP* is *NP*|*VP*.
CapableOf	167,405	*NP* can *VP*.
MotivatedByGoal	173,111	You would *VP* because you want *VP*.
HasSubevent	154,214	One of the things you do when you *VP* is *NP*|*VP*.
Desires	95,779	*NP* wants to *VP*.
HasPrerequisite	69,474	*NP*|*VP* requires *NP*|*VP*.
HasA	56,691	*NP* has *NP*.
CausesDesire	51,338	*NP* makes you want to *VP*.
MadeOf	43,278	*NP* is made of *NP*.
DefinedAs	39,406	*NP* is defined as *NP*.
HasFirstSubevent	35,242	The first thing you do when you *VP* is *NP*|*VP*.
ReceivesAction	24,609	*NP* can be *VP*.
LocatedNear	12,679	You are likely to find *NP* near *NP*.
SimilarTo	11,635	*NP* is like *NP*.
SymbolOf	11,302	*NP* represents *NP*.
HasLastSubevent	8,689	The last thing you do when you *VP* is *NP*|*VP*.
CreatedBy	1,979	You make *NP* by *VP*.

Figure 12.19   Table from Speer and Havasi [2013] showing which key relationships are available in ConceptNet 5

Accessing ConceptNet 5 via Python is quite simple, as shown in the following listing. You can use the `requests` library to get the content.

Listing 12.9   Accessing ConceptNet from Python

```
import requests

obj = requests.get('http://api.conceptnet.io/c/en/marie_curie').json()
print(obj['edges'][0]['rel']['label'] + ": " +
      obj['edges'][0]['end']['label'])
```

EXERCISES

Play a bit with the code in listing 12.9 to see different ways to process the results. The example given here is only a suggestion.

12.5   *Unsupervised keyword extraction*

NER is not the only way to recognize key elements in a text. Any text has certain words and phrases—not always related to NEs—that are more important than others because they express key concepts related to the content of the entire document, paragraph, or sentence. These words and phrases are generally referred to as *keywords*, and they provide enormous support in dealing with a big corpus.

Companies of any size have to manage and access huge amounts of data to provide advanced services for their end users or to handle their internal processes. The bulk of this data is usually stored in the form of text. The ability to process and analyze this enormous source of knowledge represents a competitive advantage, but often, even providing simple and effective access to it is a complex task due to the unstructured nature of the textual data and the size of the problem.

Suppose that you would like to provide effective access to a large corpus of documents (emails, web pages, articles, and so on) by identifying the main concepts, organizing indexes, and providing an adequate visualization. *Keyword extraction*—the process of identifying and selecting the words and small phrases that best describe a document—is vital to this task. In addition to constituting useful entries for building indexes for a corpus, the keywords you extract can be used to classify text and in some cases can serve as a simple summary for a given document. A system for automatic identification of important terms in text can be used for several purposes, such as

- Identifying named entities that a trained NER model is not capable of recognizing
- Creating domain-specific dictionaries (in this case, also using the extracted NEs)
- Extending the inferred knowledge graph with frequent and recurring keywords and connections with the entities
- Creating indexes and using the key terms to boost results when the user is looking for some specific keywords

Keywords play an important role in the process of building a knowledge graph, improving the quality (in terms of knowledge and access patterns) of the final result. So how do you get them? When you use unsupervised techniques, such as the one discussed in this section, the task of keyword extraction doesn't even require human support!

This section describes a method for keyword extraction[7] that uses a graph model representing the relationships between tags or concepts in the documents. The solution starts from a graph-based unsupervised technique called TextRank. Thereafter, the quality of extracted keywords is greatly improved by using a typed dependency graph and other tricks that are used to filter out meaningless phrases, or to extend keywords with adjectives and nouns to describe the text better. It is worth noting that although the proposed approach is unsupervised, the final results are comparable in quality to those achieved with supervised approaches. This algorithm is preferred in this book for a few reasons:

- It is purely based on graph techniques and algorithms that we've discussed already, such as PageRank.
- It uses syntactic dependencies that we analyzed in detail in chapter 11.
- The quality of the results is excellent, even when compared with supervised algorithms.

The TextRank algorithm, introduced by Mihalcea and Tarau [2004], is a relatively simple unsupervised method of text summarization that is directly applicable to the topic-extraction task. Its objective is to retrieve keywords and construct key phrases that are most descriptive of a given document by building a graph of word co-occurrences and ranking the importance of individual words by using the PageRank algorithm. Figure 12.20 shows how this co-occurrence graph is created.

The structure of the algorithm presented by Mihalcea and Tarau is summarized in figure 12.21.

---

[7] http://mng.bz/pJD8.

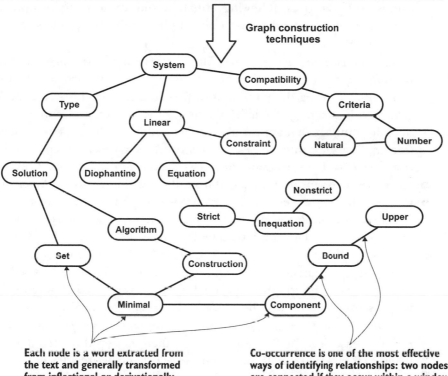

Compatibility of systems of linear constraints over the set of natural numbers. Criteria of compatibility of a system of linear Diophantine equations, strict inequations, and nonstrict inequations are considered. Upper bounds for components of a minimal set of solutions and algorithms of construction of minimal generating sets of solutions for all types of systems are given. These criteria and the corresponding algorithms for constructing a minimal supporting set of solutions can be used in solving all the considered types systems and systems of mixed types.

Graph construction techniques

Each node is a word extracted from the text and generally transformed from inflectional or derivationally related forms to a common base form.

Co-occurrence is one of the most effective ways of identifying relationships: two nodes are connected if they occur within a window of a maximum of *N* words.

Figure 12.20   The key concept in TextRank: converting the text to a co-occurrence graph

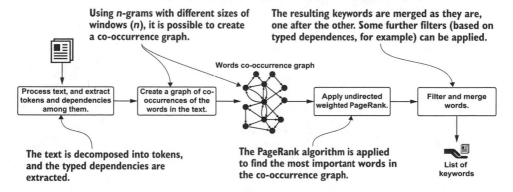

Using *n*-grams with different sizes of windows (*n*), it is possible to create a co-occurrence graph.

The resulting keywords are merged as they are, one after the other. Some further filters (based on typed dependences, for example) can be applied.

Words co-occurrence graph

Process text, and extract tokens and dependencies among them.

Create a graph of co-occurrences of the words in the text.

Apply undirected weighted PageRank.

Filter and merge words.

The text is decomposed into tokens, and the typed dependencies are extracted.

The PageRank algorithm is applied to find the most important words in the co-occurrence graph.

List of keywords

Figure 12.21   The key steps of the TextRank algorithm

The key steps of the algorithms are as follows:

1   Preselect relevant words from the NLP annotated text. Each document is tokenized and annotated. These processed words are basic lexical units, or tags. A configurable stop-word list and a syntactic filter are applied to refine the selection to the most relevant lexical units. The syntactic filter selects only nouns and adjectives, following Mihalcea and Tarau's observation that even human annotators tend to use nouns rather than verb phrases to summarize documents.

2   *Create a graph of tag co-occurrences.* Filtered tags are ordered based on their positions in the document, and co-occurrence relationships are built between adjacent tags, following the natural word flow in the text. This step introduces the relations between syntactic elements of the document into the graph. By default, only tags that appear next to each other can have a co-occurrence relationship. In the sentence "Pieter eats fish," no co-occurrence edge is created because "eats" is a verb that didn't pass the syntactic filter. But if the size of the co-occurrence window is changed from the default of 2 to 3, "Pieter" and "fish" will become connected. Finally, each co-occurrence edge is assigned a weight property indicating the number of times the two tags co-occurred within the given document. The graph obtained at this point looks like figure 12.20.

3   *Run undirected weighted PageRank.* The undirected PageRank algorithm is run on weighted co-occurrence relationships to rate nodes (tags) based on their importance in the graph. Experiments with unweighted PageRank show that weights are useful for bringing forward important keywords.

4   *Save the top one-third of tags as keywords and identify key phrases.* The tags are ordered based on the PageRank ratings; then the top third (configurable) are taken as final keywords. If some of these selected tags are adjacent, they are collapsed into a key phrase.

At the end of this process, the identified keywords and key phrases are saved to the graph database via a `DESCRIBES` relationship between a Keyword node and the AnnotatedText node. The resulting graph will look like figure 12.22.

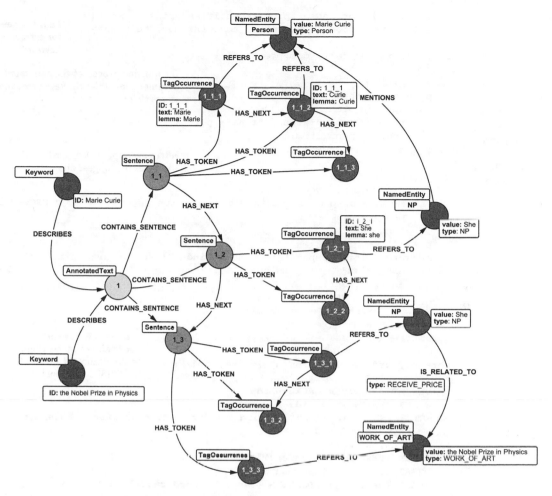

Figure 12.22 The graph model extended with keywords

Starting from the last version of the code that includes all the algorithms and techniques described so far, the following listing shows how to add this new algorithm to our growing project. The full code is in ch12/text_processors.py and ch12/ 08_spacy_textrank_extraction.py.

Listing 12.10   TextRank applied

```
def tokenize_and_store(self, text, text_id, storeTag):
    docs = self.nlp.pipe([text])
    for doc in docs:
        annotated_text = self.__text_processor.create_annotated_text(doc,
        ➥ text_id)
        spans = self.__text_processor.process_sentences(annotated_text, doc,
        ➥ storeTag, text_id)
```

```
        self.__text_processor.process_entities(spans, text_id)
        self.__text_processor.process_textrank(doc, text_id)    <-- Adds the new step for extracting keywords

def process_textrank(self, doc, text_id):    <-- The function processes the annotated document, identifies the keywords, and stores them.
    keywords = []
    spans = []
    for p in doc._.phrases:
        for span in p.chunks:    <-- Loops over the keywords found in the document, called chunks
            item = {"span": span, "rank": p.rank}
            spans.append(item)
    spans = filter_extended_spans(spans)    <-- Filters overlapping keywords and takes the longest one
    for item in spans:
        span = item['span'
        lexme = self.nlp.vocab[span.text];
        if lexme.is_stop or lexme.is_digit or lexme.is_bracket or "-PRON-" in
        ➥ span.lemma_:
            continue

        keyword = {"id": span.text, "start_index": span.start_char,
        ➥ "end_index": span.end_char}
        if len(span.ents) > 0:
            keyword['NE'] = span.ents[0].label_
        keyword['rank'] = item['rank']
        keywords.append(keyword)
    self.store_keywords(text_id, keywords)

def store_keywords(self, document_id, keywords):
    ne_query = """    <-- Creates new Keyword nodes and connects them to the document via DESCRIBES relationships
        UNWIND $keywords as keyword
        MERGE (kw:Keyword {id: keyword.id})
        SET kw.NE = keyword.NE, kw.index = keyword.start_index, kw.endIndex =
        ➥ keyword.end_index
        WITH kw, keyword
        MATCH (text:AnnotatedText)
        WHERE text.id = $documentId
        MERGE (text)<-[:DESCRIBES {rank: keyword.rank}]-(kw)
    """
    self.execute_query(ne_query, {"documentId": document_id, "keywords":
    ➥ keywords})
```

The preceding code uses an existing plugin for spaCy, called pytextrank,[8] that implements the TextRank algorithm properly. For this sentence,

The Committee awarded the Nobel Prize in Physics to Marie Curie.

it returns the following list of keywords (the numbers in parentheses are the rank assigned by the TextRank algorithm):

- The Committee (0.15)
- Marie Curie (0.20)
- The Nobel Prize in Physics (0.14)

[8] https://github.com/DerwenAI/pytextrank.

Not bad, especially considering that we're working with a single sentence. TextRank performs better on longer documents because it can consider how often specific words recur.

The initial results obtained with TextRank are quite promising, but the quality can be improved by using more insights about the text. At GraphAware, we have also implemented a TextRank algorithm, available in our open source NLP plugin for Neo4j.[9] The basic algorithm has been modified to take advantage of the typed dependency graph provided by Stanford CoreNLP.

To improve the quality of automatic keyword extraction, the extended algorithm considers the typed dependencies *amod* and *nn*. An adjectival modifier (*amod*) of an NP is any adjectival phrase that serves to modify the meaning of the NP:

```
"Sam eats red meat" -> amod(meat, red)
"Sam took out a 3 million dollar loan" -> amod(loan, dollar)
"Sam took out a $ 3 million loan" -> amod(loan, $)
```

A noun compound modifier (*nn*) of an NP is any noun that serves to modify the head noun:

```
"Oil price futures" -> nn(futures, oil), nn(futures, price)
```

These typed dependencies can be used to improve the results of the TextRank algorithm. Consider a concrete example. The following key phrase has been extracted by TextRank by using the standard approach:

```
personal protective
```

Clearly, this phrase means nothing because both words are adjectives; a noun is missing. In this case, the noun is *equipment*. This omission might have happened because the noun was ranked below the threshold of one-third of the top words in the documents considered, and during the merge, such words were ignored. As a result, documents discussing the same topic—"*personal protective equipment*"—were not assigned any common key phrase.

In this case, amod dependencies can help. In the text "personal protective equipment," there are amod dependencies among the three words:

```
amod(equipment, personal)
amod(equipment, protective)
```

Specifying these dependencies means that during the merge phase we also have to take "equipment" because it is connected to words that appear in the top third of the results. Typed dependencies can be used not only to complete existing key phrases with missing tags, but also to remove key phrases that have no mutual relationships of type COMPOUND or amod. Therefore, the improved TextRank algorithm introduces two new principles:

---

[9] https://github.com/graphaware/neo4j-nlp.

- All tags in a key phrase candidate must be related through COMPOUND or amod dependency.
- If a neighboring tag was not ranked highly enough to be included in a key phrase by the original TextRank but is connected to one or more top-scoring words by COMPOUND or amod typed dependencies, that tag is added.

The latter principle takes care of handling the previously mentioned shortcomings and also adds a higher level of detail.

With these small changes (and a few others not mentioned here, such as postfiltering based on tag part of speech or considering NEs and so on), the results obtained resemble the key phrases that many human annotators would use to describe given documents.

Thanks to its high accuracy, keyword extraction supports different types of analysis that can reveal a great deal of information about the corpus. The keywords extracted can be used in different ways to discover new insights about the documents in the corpus, including providing an index or even a summary of the contents of the documents.

To prove this concept, let's try working with the Wikipedia movie plots dataset.[10] This dataset contains descriptions of 34,886 movies from around the world, including summaries of their plots. You can use the code available in ch12/08_spacy_textrank_extraction.py to import the full dataset. The dataset is large, so it will take some time to process it and store the results. Then you can obtain a list of the most frequent keywords with the following query.

> **Listing 12.11   Get the list of the 100 most frequent keywords**

```
MATCH (n:Keyword)-[:DESCRIBES]->(text:AnnotatedText)
RETURN n.id as keywords, count(n) as occurrences
order by occurrences desc
limit 100
```

The results are shown in figure 12.23.

With even this simple query that considers the number of occurrences of keywords in the corpus, we can extract a lot of information about the content of our dataset:

- The dominant topic is "love," which appears as a keyword in a lot of plot summaries. This fact might reflect both the dominance of romance as a theme and users' enthusiasm about the films they're describing.
- The terms "film" and "story" appear quite often, which is to be expected because they are commonly used in describing the plot of a movie.
- The next-most-common keyword is "police," suggesting that movies about crime are quite common.
- Another interesting observation is that "man" appears to be much more common as a key component of the plot; "woman" is much lower in the ranking.

---

[10]http://mng.bz/O1jR.

keywords	occurrences
"love"	8365
"the film"	6844
"the story"	4554
"the police"	4130
"order"	3778
"time"	3599
"the house"	3133
"money"	3040
"the man"	3020
"a man"	2813
"the end"	2743

Figure 12.23   Results of executing listing 12.11 on the database

This simple example gives you an idea of how much information it is possible to extract about a corpus by considering only the keywords. In section 12.5.1, we'll develop this idea further, but first consider the following exercise.

EXERCISE

Play with the dataset, using not only the keywords, but also the NEs extracted from the text. Perform the same query by using NamedEntity instead of Keyword nodes. (Note that this change is not the only one you have to make in the query.) What observations can you make about the data?

12.5.1 *Keyword co-occurrence graph*

Keywords provide a lot of knowledge in themselves, but we can extend their value further by considering them in combination. Keywords can be connected via relationships by considering the documents in which they occur together. This approach generates a co-occurrence graph of keywords (in which we have only nodes of type Keyword and the connections among them).

The concept of a co-occurrence graph has been used as a technique for graph construction in other scenarios (specifically, in the recommendation chapters). The resulting graph is full of information that can be used to analyze the original graph itself. In the case we are considering—keywords—this graph will look like figure 12.24.

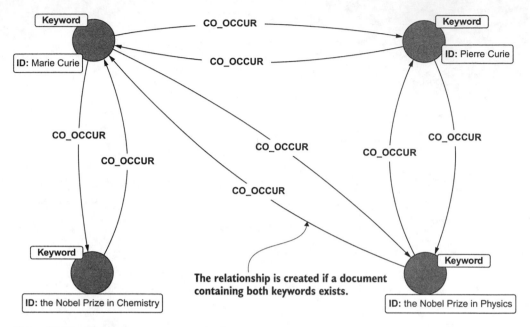

Figure 12.24   Keyword co-occurrence graph

Such a graph can be obtained by running a specific query on the original graph. Once again, graphs and the available plugins and libraries allow you to avoid writing code for recurring tasks. In the following example, we are using the APOC library for Neo4j that we have already used extensively.

Listing 12.12   Creating the co-occurrence graph

```
CALL apoc.periodic.submit('CreateCoOccurrence',
'CALL apoc.periodic.iterate("MATCH (k:Keyword)-[:DESCRIBES]->
   (text:AnnotatedText)
WITH k, count(DISTINCT text) AS keyWeight
WHERE keyWeight > 5
RETURN k, keyWeight",
"MATCH (k)-[:DESCRIBES]->(text)<-[:DESCRIBES]-(k2:Keyword)
WHERE k <> k2
WITH k, k2, count(DISTINCT text) AS weight, keyWeight
WHERE weight > 10
WITH k, k2, k.value as kValue, k2.value as k2Value, weight,
   (1.0f*weight)/keyWeight  as normalizedWeight
CREATE (k)-[:CO_OCCUR {weight: weight, normalizedWeight: normalizedWeight}]->
   (k2)", {batchSize:100, iterateList:true, parallel:false})')
```

> Depending on the size of the graph, this operation could take a long time. For this reason, I used apoc.periodic.submit, because it allows you to submit the following query as a background job. You can check the status by using "CALL apoc.periodic.list()".

In this query, note the combination of the `submit` procedure, which causes the query to execute in the background, disconnected from the browser request, and the `iterate` procedure, which allows you to commit the results periodically and avoid having a single big transaction. You can check the status of the background job by using `call apoc.periodic.list`.

Note also that we are filtering out the irrelevant keywords (those that appear fewer than 5 times, as specified by `WHERE keyWeight > 5`) and that we are considering the connections only if the pairs of keywords appear together at least 10 times (`WHERE weight > 10`). This approach allows us to create a proper co-occurrence graph in which the relevant information is even more evident.

EXERCISE

When the query has completed, explore the resulting knowledge graph by checking how the keywords are connected. You'll notice that the graph is much denser.

12.5.2 Clustering keywords and topic identification

The co-occurrence graph contains a lot of new information that can be used to extract knowledge from text. The goal in our case is to extract insights from the processed texts (the plot summaries). We've already used keyword frequency to get some insights about the content of our dataset, but with the keyword co-occurrence graph, we'll be better able to recognize the topics in the documents. Figure 12.25 provides an overview of the steps necessary to get the list of topics.

The co-occurrence graph connects keywords that appear together in the same graph, so it is capable of aggregating multiple keywords into groups that represent the same types of movies. At least, we would like to prove that idea. The filters we used to

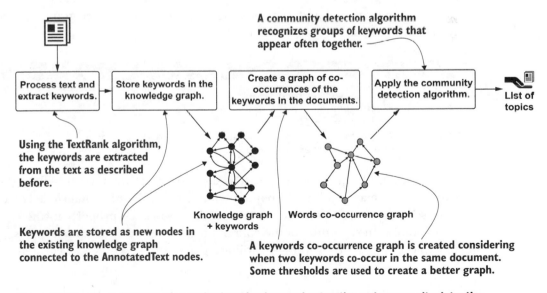

Figure 12.25 Steps for extracting topics by using keyword extraction and community detection

create the co-occurrence graph (relevant keywords and relevant connections) are helpful in this phase because they do a good job of isolating the keywords in the co-occurrence graph.

In chapter 10, I introduced a mechanism for identifying communities of people in a social network: the Louvain algorithm. The algorithm showed a high level of accuracy in identifying clusters, as well as high speed. Such an approach can also be applied to the co-occurrence graph to see what keyword clusters are the most relevant.

In this case, to simplify the query for running the Louvain algorithm, we split the operation in two. The first query creates a sort of virtual graph in which we specify only the part of the graph that we are interested in: the co-occurrence graph. (Remember that we do have the full knowledge graph!) In this way, we can specify where we would like to perform the community detection algorithm, ignoring all the rest.

Listing 12.13 Creating a virtual graph in the knowledge graph

```
CALL gds.graph.create(
    'keywordsGraph',
    'Keyword',
    {
        CO_OCCUR: {
            orientation: 'NATURAL'
        }
    },
    {
        relationshipProperties: 'normalizedWeight'
    }
)
```

With the virtual graph in hand, representing only the co-occurrence graph, it is possible to run the Louvain algorithm with the following simple query.

Listing 12.14 Revealing communities by using Louvain

```
CALL gds.louvain.write('keywordsGraph', {
    relationshipWeightProperty: 'normalizedWeight',
    writeProperty: 'community'
}) YIELD nodePropertiesWritten,  communityCount, modularity
RETURN nodePropertiesWritten,  communityCount, modularity
```

This query should be quite fast because, as discussed in chapter 10, this algorithm is amazingly performant, and the Neo4j implementation is highly optimized. The community assigned to each keyword is saved as the `community` property in the related node; it contains the identifier of the community. At the end of this process, it is possible to explore the results by using the following query.

Listing 12.15 Getting the communities and the top 25 keywords for each community

```
MATCH (k:Keyword)-[:DESCRIBES]->(text:AnnotatedText)
WITH k, count(text) as weight
WHERE weight > 5
with k.community as community, k.id as keyword, weight
order by community, weight desc
WITH community, collect(keyword) as communityMembers
order by size(communityMembers) desc
RETURN community as communityId, communityMembers[0..25] as topMembers,
  size(communityMembers) as size
```

The query first gets the list of **keywords** ordered by community (identified by the community identifier, `communityId`) and by frequency, then groups by community identifier, and takes only the top 25 **keywords** for each (the most relevant due to their frequency). The size of the community is used to order the final results, which are shown in figure 12.26. They might surprise you!

communityId	topMembers	size
180088	["France", "Germany", "the Germans", "Britain", "a spy", "the Americans", "Scotland", "Sgt", "british", "the Nazis", "World War I", "the Second World War", "the raid", "civilian", "the spy", "Pearl Harbor", "the Russians", "german", "the Duke", "the Allies", "the Pacific", "the duel", "Hitler", "Adolf Hitler", "the First World War"]	55
160926	["mankind", "the robot", "alien", "the universe", "Mars", "an alien", "the Moon", "the rocket", "a portal", "the spaceship", "outer space", "orbit", "the portal", "the human race", "a planet", "a rocket", "the galaxy", "a robot", "a spaceship", "the spacecraft", "NASA", "all life", "robot", "the pod", "deep space"]	36
179452	["the player", "the coach", "football", "the season", "baseball", "the final", "basketball", "player", "the championship", "the second half", "chess", "the first half", "the fan", "bat", "a player", "the locker room", "the other player", "the league", "the next game", "the final game", "a home run", "the championship game", "the New York Yankees", "halftime", "the playoff"]	25
180726	["the king", "the palace", "the castle", "the throne", "the kingdom", "the princess", "the King", "the prince", "the queen", "king", "the Queen", "a princess", "the Prince", "a king", "the emperor", "Queen", "the crown", "a castle", "incognito", "the royal family", "the knight", "the giant", "Transylvania", "the crown prince", "the moat"]	25
180051	["Tom", "Jerry", "pain", "the cat", "the mouse", "the cartoon", "a cat", "the corner", "cat", "mouse", "a mouse", "Butch", "Spike", "spike", "Tom 's head", "Tom 's tail", "cheese", "Tom 's face", "Tom 's mouth", "Mammy", "Mammy two Shoes", "Tom 's hand", "Jerry jump", "Tom 's friend"]	24

Figure 12.26   Results of the community detection algorithm applied on the co-occurrence graph

This example is only an extract, but it shows clearly the quality of the results. In each cluster, it's easy to recognize the topic: movies about the world wars, sci-fi movies, sports-related movies, medieval movies, and finally *Tom and Jerry* movies.

EXERCISE
Run listing 12.15, and explore the full list of results. Are you able to recognize the topics for all the results?

12.6 *Advantages of the graph approach*

The solution proposed in this chapter—the knowledge graph—cannot exist outside the context of a graph model, so we can't really talk about the advantages of the graph approach over other available approaches. But as you have seen, representing data and information in the form of a graph empowers a range of solutions and services by making it easy to explore the knowledge hidden in the data. This approach is the best way to deliver AI solutions.

Specifically, a knowledge graph is a natural way to represent data in textual format, which is typically thought of as unstructured and hence hard to process. When the data is stored in such a way, the amount of knowledge that can be extracted and the types of analyses that can be performed on that data are endless.

We have seen how simple it is to navigate among the relationships extracted or through the mentions, how to create hierarchies of concepts in a semantic network, and how to use automatic keyword extraction in the co-occurrence graph to extract topics from the movie plots in our dataset. The same concepts would hold for any other type of corpus.

Summary

This chapter is the last in the book; its aim is to show how what has been presented in this book finds its apotheosis in the knowledge graph. In this case, graphs are not a possible solution but the driving force, allowing information structuring, access patterns, and types of analysis and operations that would not otherwise be feasible.

Structured and unstructured data and information can coexist in this powerful knowledge representation, which can be used to feed more advanced services into your machine learning project than would be possible otherwise. The semantic network opens a whole range of new possibilities.

In this chapter, you learned

- How to extract NEs from a text and store them properly in a graph model
- How to extract relationships between the NEs and model them in a graph
- How to infer key entities and relationships from different instances in the text and create a powerful knowledge representation: a semantic network
- How to extract keywords from text in an unsupervised manner using a graph-based algorithm and store them in the knowledge graph you've created
- How to create a co-occurrence graph of keywords and process it
- How to identify key topics in a corpus by using only graph-powered techniques

I'd like to close by saying that this book is not the end of your journey—only the beginning of a new one. Now you have access to the main conceptual tools you need to use graphs properly in many contexts. This book cannot possibly answer all the questions you might have about graphs, of course, but I hope it has equipped you with the mental schemas necessary to approach machine learning projects from a different perspective.

References

[Gomez-Perez et al., 2017] Gomez-Perez, Jose Manuel, Jeff Z. Pan, Guido Vetere, and Honghan Wu. "Enterprise Knowledge Graph: An Introduction." In *Exploiting Linked Data and Knowledge Graphs in Large Organisations*. Switzerland: Springer, 2017: 1–14.

[Grishman, 2015] Grishman, Ralph. "Information Extraction." *IEEE Intelligent Systems* 30:5 (2015): 8–15.

[Grishman and Sundheim, 1996] Grishman, Ralph, and Beth Sundheim. "Message Understanding Conference - 6: A Brief History." *Proceedings of the 16th International Conference on Computational Linguistics* (1996): 466–471.

[Grimm et al., 2007] Grimm, Stephan, Pascal Hitzler, and Andreas Abecker. "Knowledge Representation and Ontologies." In *Semantic Web Services: Concepts, Technology and Applications*. Berlin, Heidelberg: Springer, 2007: 51–106.

[Jurafsky and Martin, 2019] Jurafsky, Dan, and James H. Martin. *Speech and Language Processing: An Introduction to Natural Language Processing, Computational Linguistics, and Speech Recognition*. Upper Saddle River, NJ: Prentice Hall, 2019 (3rd ed. draft, available at https://web.stanford.edu/~jurafsky/slp3).

[Karttunen, 1969] Karttunen, Lauri. "Discourse Referents." *Proceedings of the 1969 Conference on Computational Linguistics* (1969): 1–38.

[Mihalcca and Radev, 2011] Mihalcea, Rada, and Dragomir Radev. *Graph-Based Natural Language Processing and Information Retrieval*. New York: Cambridge University Press, 2011.

[Mihalcea and Tarau, 2004] Mihalcea, Rada, and Paul Tarau. 2004, July. "TextRank: Bringing Order into Texts." *Proceedings of the Conference on Empirical Methods in Natural Language Processing* (2004): 404–411.

[Ng, 2009] Ng, Vincent. 2009. "Graph-Cut-Based Anaphoricity Determination for Co-Reference Resolution." *Proceedings of Human Language Technologies: Conference of the North American Chapter of the Association of Computational Linguistics* (2009): 575–583.

[Nicolae and Nicolae, 2006] Nicolae, Cristina, and Gabriel Nicolae. "BESTCUT: A Graph Algorithm for Co-Reference Resolution." *Proceedings of the 2006 Conference on Empirical Methods in Natural Language Processing* (2006): 275–283.

[RDF Working Group, 2004] "RDF Primer: W3C Recommendation 10 February 2004." https://www.w3.org/TR/rdf-primer.

[Sowa, 2000] Sowa, John F. *Knowledge Representation: Logical, Philosophical, and Computational Foundations*. Pacific Grove, CA: Brooks Cole, 2000.

[Speer and Havasi, 2013] Speer, Robyn, and Catherine Havasi. "ConceptNet 5: A Large Semantic Network for Relational Knowledge." In *The People's Web Meets NLP: Collaboratively Constructed Language Resources*, edited by Iryna Gurevych and Jungi Kim. Berlin, Heidelberg: Springer, 2013: 161-176.

[Speer et al., 2017] Speer, Robyn, Joshua Chin, and Catherine Havasi. "ConceptNet 5.5: An Open Multilingual Graph of General Knowledge." *Proceedings of the 31st AAAI Conference on Artificial Intelligence* (2017): 4444–4451.

appendix A
Machine learning
algorithms taxonomy

Machine learning is a deep and wide domain. Consequently, there are many different branches of machine learning. The algorithms can be classified or organized into broad categories based on four criteria:

- Whether they are trained with human-provided labeled data
- Whether they can learn incrementally
- Whether they work by building a predictive model or by comparing new data points with known data points
- Whether the learner actively interacts with the environment or passively observes the information provided by the environment

This taxonomy provides an overview of the plethora of machine learning algorithms and is not exhaustive. Its purpose is to help you identify the right set of algorithms for your specific problem, considering also the data available and how it can flow into the system. Such a classification is useful for understanding

- The kinds of data needed and how to prepare the data
- How often and in which way to retrain the model (if at all)
- How the quality of prediction could be affected over time
- The architectural constraints of the solution to be designed

A.1 Supervised vs. unsupervised learning

Learning requires interaction between the learner and the environment. The first classification presented is based on the nature of this interaction during the training phase. Depending on the amount and type of supervision, we can distinguish between supervised and unsupervised learning.

If we look at learning as a process of using experience to gain expertise, *supervised learning* requires training examples/samples (the experience) that contain significant information explicitly. A typical example of this learning process is the spam filter. The learner requires labels, such as "spam" and "not spam" (the significant information), in the training dataset for each element (emails). It learns from these labels how to classify an email. These types of algorithms, generally speaking, have higher performance in terms of prediction accuracy. On the other hand, the effort required to provide labeled data is high and in some cases impossible to perform. Some of the most important supervised learning algorithms (some of which are covered in this book) are

- *k*-nearest neighbors (*k*-NN)
- Decision trees and random forests
- Bayesian networks
- Linear regression
- Logistic regression
- Support vector machines

At the other end of the spectrum, *unsupervised learning* doesn't require labeled data, so there is no distinction between training and test data. The learner processes input data with the goal of coming up with some insight about or a summary or compressed version of the data. Some of the most important unsupervised learning algorithms (again, some of which are covered in this book) are

- Clustering (*k*-means)
- Graph clustering
- Association rule mining
- PageRank

An intermediate learning process type can deal with partially labeled training data, usually composed of a mixture of labeled and unlabeled data. This process is referred to as *semisupervised learning*. Most semisupervised algorithms are combinations of supervised and unsupervised algorithms. An example of this type of algorithm is semisupervised label propagation.

An outlier of this classification criteria is *reinforcement learning*, in which the learner can only observe the environment (defined as the set of information available at the current time), select and perform actions, and get rewards in return. As a result of this interaction between the environment and the learner, the algorithm learns the optimal strategy (called a *policy*) to pursue to get the greatest reward over time. A policy defines the best actions for the system to perform given a specific condition of the environment. Reinforcement learning is used mostly for moving robots in a room or for playing chess and other games.

A.2   Batch vs. online learning

The second classification is based on the capability of the learner to adapt online, or in a short time, to streams of incoming data. Some algorithms, called *online learners*, can learn incrementally from new data as it comes. Others, called *batch learners*, need to use the whole dataset again, or a big portion of it, when data changes [Géron, 2017].

In *batch learning*, the system is trained with all the available data. Such a learning process can take a lot of time and computing resources, depending on the size of the data to be processed, so it is typically performed offline. For this reason, batch learning is also known as *offline learning*. To inform the batch learning system of new data, a new version needs to be trained from scratch on the full dataset. When the new model is ready for production, the old one can be replaced. Classical data mining processes, such as market-basket analysis,[1] belong to this category. The data miner has large amounts of training data to play with before having to output conclusions.

In *online learning*, the system is trained incrementally; data points are fed to it sequentially, one by one or in mini batches. In this case, the learning process is fast and cheap, and can be performed quite often. Online learning is great for systems that receive data continuously and need to adapt to changes rapidly and autonomously, such as a stock-prediction algorithm that has to make daily or hourly decisions based on stock prices collected so far.

Online learning can also be used to train a system by using large amounts of data that cannot fit in the resources available. This type of learning is called *out-of-core learning*. The algorithm loads mini batches of the data, performs a training step, purges the data, and proceeds to the next batch. Online learning is generally preferred (when applicable), for two reasons:

- It provides a better fit to the current data and current status.
- It is more efficient in terms of resource consumption.

Such learning is sensitive to bad data, however. To reduce the risk associated with bad data, it is necessary to monitor the system continuously and eventually switch off the learning. It is worth noting that online and offline learning algorithms can be supervised or unsupervised.

A.3   Instance-based vs. model-based learning

Another way to categorize learners is based on the capability of the system to generalize the data used during training to create a model for prediction. The two main approaches are instance-based and model-based learning [Géron, 2017].

In *instance-based learning*, the system first learns all the training examples; then, for new instances (data points), it finds the closest instances from the training examples. This approach requires a way to measure the distance between elements, such as

---

[1] Market-basket analysis is the process of analyzing customer buying habits by finding associations between the items that customers place in their shopping baskets. The discovery of such associations can help retailers develop marketing strategies by gaining insight into which items customers frequently purchase together.

calculating the cosine distance between vectors created with *TF-IDF*[2] or counting the number of words they have in common.

In *model-based learning*, the system builds a model from the training dataset that generalizes the training examples and then is used for making predictions. A typical example is the collaborative filtering technique for recommendation engines. Such algorithms use user-item interactions—buy, view, click, and so on—as training data to build a model. Then the model is used to predict the interest of users in unseen or unbought items and to promote the items with the highest predicted interest.

Using the training dataset to generalize a prediction model is generally a preferable solution in terms of prediction performance, defined in terms of response time and result quality. The issues related to this approach are

- The time required to build the model.
- Overfitting the training data, which happens when the training dataset doesn't contain examples that cover the spectrum of possible cases. In this case, the model knows only few examples and doesn't generalize enough to handle unseen samples properly.

A.4   *Active vs. passive learning*

Learning paradigms can also vary according to the role played by the learner during the training phase. *Passive learners* observe information provided by the environment. In the spam filter example, the passive learner would wait for the user to mark emails. *Active learners* proactively interact with the environment at training time by asking questions or performing experiments. In the spam filter example, the active learner would choose emails and ask the user to label them as spam or not. This approach may lead to better performance in terms of prediction quality, because the active learner can choose the right data to label (avoiding overfitting, for example), but the interaction with users or the environment affects the user experience.

Reference

[Géron, 2017] Géron, Aurélien. *Hands-on Machine Learning with Scikit-Learn and TensorFlow: Concepts, Tools, and Techniques to Build Intelligent Systems.* Sebastopol, CA: O'Reilly, 2017.

---

[2] TF-IDF refers to a vector in which each element represents a word and its value is the term *frequency-inverse document frequency*, a numerical statistic intended to reflect how important a word is for a document in a collection of documents (or *corpus*).

appendix B
Neo4j

Throughout this book, the **examples, code,** and exercises are based on a specific graph database: Neo4j. Nevertheless, all the theories, algorithms, and even code can easily be adapted to work with any graph database on the market now and (with a good approximation) in the future. I selected this database because

- I've worked with this **database** for the past 10 years (and know it inside out).
- It is a native graph **database** (with all the consequences that it brings, as explained throughout the book).
- It has a broad community of **experts.**

According to DB-Engines, Neo4j **has been** the most popular graph database management system (DBMS) for several years (http://mng.bz/YAMB; figure B.1).[1]

This appendix contains the minimum information necessary to get started with Neo4j, including a generic **introduction** to Neo4j, installation instructions, a description of the Cypher **language** (the language used to query the database), and the configuration of some **plugins** used in the examples.

---

[1] The score takes into account multiple factors, **such as** number of mentions of the database on websites, frequency of technical questions on Stack **Overflow and** Database Administrators Stack Exchange, job offers, and relevance in social networks.

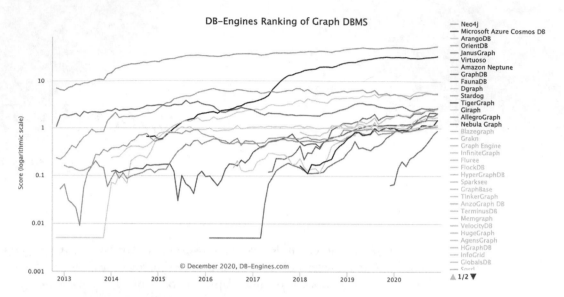

Figure B.1   DB-Engines ranking of graph DBMSes

B.1   *Neo4j introduction*

Neo4j is available as a GPL3-licensed open source Community Edition. Neo4j Inc. also licenses an Enterprise Edition with backup, scaling extensions, and other enterprise-grade features under closed source commercial terms. Neo4j is implemented in Java and accessible over the network through a transactional HTTP endpoint or the binary Bolt protocol.[2] We will use Neo4j throughout the book as our graph database reference implementation.

Neo4j has been widely adopted for the following reasons:

- It implements a labeled property graph database.[3]
- It uses a native graph storage based on index-free adjacency.[4]
- It provides native graph querying and a related language, Cypher,[5] that defines how the graph database describes, plans, optimizes, and executes queries.
- Every architecture layer—from the queries that use Cypher to the files on disk—is optimized for storing and retrieving graph data.
- It provides an easy-to-use developer workbench with a graph visualization interface.

Neo4j aims to provide a full-strength, industrial-grade database. Transactional support is one of its strengths, differentiating it from the majority of NoSQL solutions. Neo4j provides full *ACID* support [Vukotic et al., 2014]:

---

[2] https://boltprotocol.org.
[3] If you haven't read chapter 2 yet, see section 2.3.5 for details on label property graphs.
[4] See appendix D.
[5] https://www.opencypher.org.

- *Atomicity (A)*—You can wrap multiple database operations within a single transaction and make sure that they're all executed atomically. If one of the operations fails, the entire transaction will be rolled back.
- *Consistency (C)*—When you write data to the Neo4j database, you can be sure that every client accessing the database afterward will read the latest updated data.
- *Isolation (I)*—You can be sure that operations within a single transaction will be isolated one from another, so writes in one transaction won't affect reads in another transaction.
- *Durability (D)*—You can be certain that the data you write to Neo4j will be written to disk and available after database restart or a server crash.

The ACID support makes it easy for anyone who's used to the traditional guarantees of relational databases to transition to Neo4j, and makes working with graph data both safe and convenient. In addition to ACID transactional support, features to consider when choosing the right database for an architectural stack include

- *Recoverability*—This feature has to do with the database's ability to set things right after a failure. Databases, like all other software systems, "are susceptible to bugs in their implementation, in the hardware they run on, and in that hardware's power, cooling, and connectivity. Though diligent engineers try to minimize the possibility of failure in all of these, at some point it's inevitable that a database will crash. And when a failed server resumes operation, it must not serve corrupt data to its users, irrespective of the nature or timing of the crash. When recovering from an unclean shutdown, perhaps caused by a fault or even an overzealous operator, Neo4j checks in the most recently active transaction log and replays any transactions it finds against the store. It's possible that some of those transactions may have already been applied to the store, but because replaying is an idempotent action, the net result is the same: after recovery, the store will be consistent with all transactions successfully committed prior to the failure" [Robinson et al., 2015]. Moreover, Neo4j offers an online backup procedure that allows you to recover the database when the original data is lost. In such case, recovery to the last committed transaction is impossible, but it is better than losing all the data [Robinson et al., 2015].
- *Availability*—In addition to recoverability and to increase the chance of recoverability, "a good database needs to be highly available to meet the increasingly sophisticated needs of data-heavy applications. The database's ability to recognize and, if necessary, repair an instance after crashing means that data quickly becomes available again without human intervention. And of course, more live instances increases the overall availability of the database to process queries. It's uncommon to want individual disconnected database instances in a typical production scenario. More often, we cluster database instances for high availability. Neo4j uses a master/slave cluster arrangement to ensure that a complete

replica of the graph is stored on each machine. Writes are replicated out from the master to the slaves at frequent intervals. At any point, the master and some slaves will have a completely up-to-date copy of the graph, while other slaves will be catching up (typically, they will be but milliseconds behind)" [Robinson et al., 2015].

- *Capacity*—Another critical aspect is related to the amount of data it is possible to store in a database—in our specific case, a graph database. Thanks to the adoption of dynamically sized pointers in Neo4j 3.0 and later, the database can scale up to run any conceivable size of graph workload, with an upper limit "in the quadrillions" of nodes [Woodie, 2016].

Two excellent books on this topic are *Neo4j in Action* [Vukotic et al., 2014] and *Graph Databases* [Robinson et al., 2015]. At the time of writing, the latest version available was 4.2.x, so the code and queries were tested with that version.

B.2   *Neo4j installation*

Neo4j is available in two editions: Community and Enterprise. The Community Edition can be downloaded freely from the Noe4j website and used indefinitely for noncommercial purposes under the GPLv3 license.[6] The Enterprise Edition can be downloaded and tried for a limited amount of time and under specific constraints (because it requires you to buy a proper license). The book's code has been adapted to work perfectly with the Community Edition; I recommend using it, so that you have all the time you need. You can also use Neo4j packaged as a Docker image.

Another option is to use Neo4j Desktop,[7] which is a sort of developer environment for Neo4j. You can manage as many projects and database servers locally as you like and also connect to remote Neo4j servers. Neo4j Desktop comes with a free developer license for Neo4j Enterprise Edition. From the Neo4j download page, you can select the version to download and install.

B.2.1   *Neo4j server installation*

If you decide to download a Neo4j server (Community or Enterprise), installation is straightforward. For Linux or macOS, make sure that you have Java 11 or later installed, and then follow these steps:

1. Open your terminal/shell.
2. Extract the contents of the archive, using `tar xf <filecode>` (such as `tar xf neo4j-community-4.2.3-unix.tar.gz`).
3. Place the extracted files in a permanent home on your server. The top-level directory is NEO4J_HOME.
4. To run Neo4j as a console application, use `<NEO4J_HOME>/bin/neo4j console`.

---

[6] https://www.gnu.org/licenses/gpl-3.0.en.html.
[7] https://neo4j.com/developer/neo4j-desktop/.

5 To run Neo4j in a background process, use <NEO4J_HOME>/bin/neo4j start.

6 Visit http://localhost:7474 in your web browser.

7 Connect, using the username neo4j with the default password neo4j. You'll be prompted to change the password.

On Windows machines, the procedure is similar; unzip the downloaded file and proceed from there.

At the end of the process, when you open the specified link in the browser, you should see something like figure B.2.

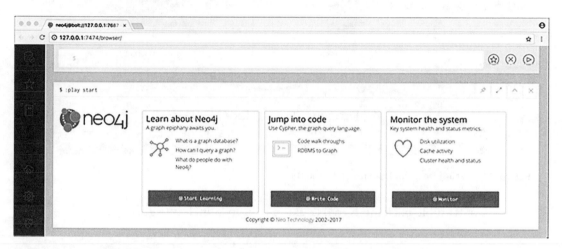

Figure B.2 The Neo4j browser

The Neo4j browser is a simple web-based application that allows the user to interact with a Neo4j instance, submit queries, and perform basic configurations.

B.2.2 Neo4j Desktop installation

If you decide to install the Desktop version for macOS, follow these steps to get it up and running quickly:[8]

1 In the Downloads folder, locate and double-click the .dmg file you downloaded to start the Neo4j Desktop installer.

2 Save the app to the Applications folder (either the global one or your user-specific one) by dragging the Neo4j Desktop icon to that folder (figure B.3).

---

[8] The installation procedure is taken from the installation guide, which is available when you download the software. Refer to that installation guide for directions for your operating system.

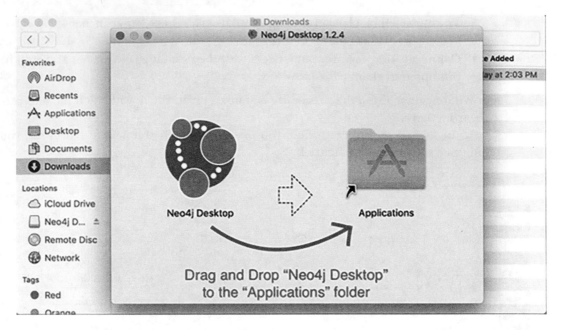

Figure B.3   Neo4j Desktop installation in macOS

3 Double-click the Neo4j Desktop icon to launch it (figure B.4).

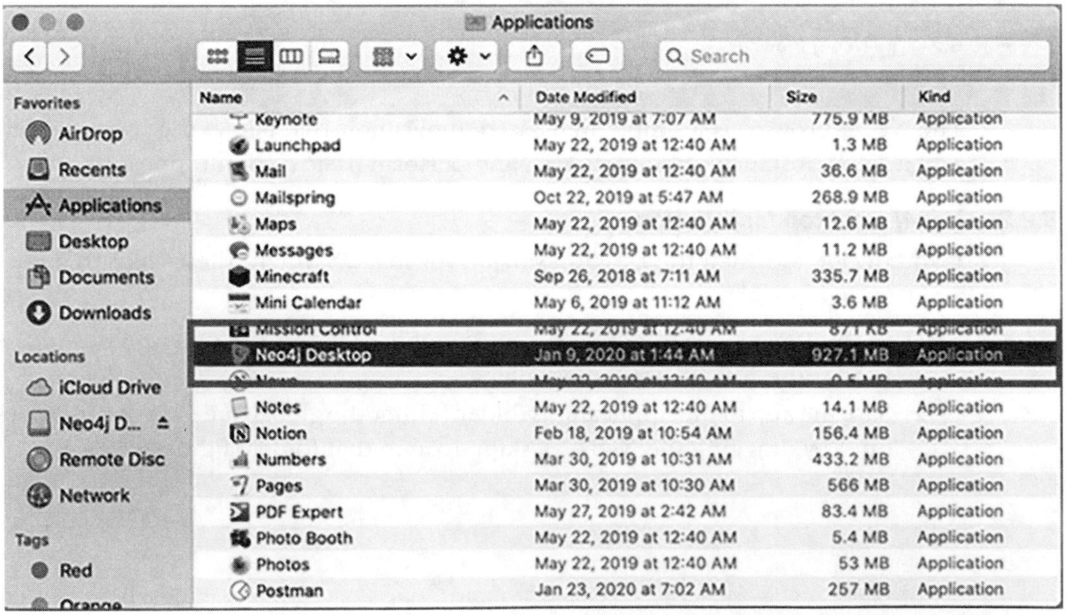

Figure B.4   Launching Neo4j Desktop

4 The first time you start Neo4J Desktop, you will be asked for the activation code
   you received upon downloading the software. Copy and paste the code into the
   Activation Key box. Alternatively, generate a key from within the app by filling
   out the form on the right side of the screen (figure B.5).

Software registration

Neo4j Desktop is always free. Registration lets us know who has accepted this gift of graphs.

Register yourself with the following contact
information.

Name *

    Name

Email *

    Email

Organization *

    Organization

Read about our privacy policy.

    Register later

Already registered? Add your software key
here to activate this installation.

Software key *

    eyJhbGciOiJQUzI1NiIsInR5cCI6IkpXVCJ9
    .eyJjYWxsYmFjayI6IiIsImVtYWsjoic2hyZ
    XlhbnMuZ2FuZGhpQG5sb3RlY2hub2xvZ3
    kuY29tIiwiZm9ybWF0IjoianNvbiIsIm9yZyI
    6Ik5lbzRqIiwicHViiLiojbmVVNGouY29tliwic
    mVniljoiU2hyZXlhbnMgR2FuZGhpliwic3Vi
    joibmVVNGotZGVza3RvcClsImV4cCI6MT
    YxMTYxMjQ2MSwidmVyljoiKiIsImIzcyI6Im
    5lbzRqLmNvbVhSIsIm5iZiI6MTU3OTk5MDA

OR

                                              Activate

Figure B.5   Activating the license in Neo4j Desktop

5 When the product has been activated (figure B.6), click the Add Graph button.
6 Select Create a Local Graph (figure B.7).
7 Enter the database name and password, and click the Create button (figure B.8).

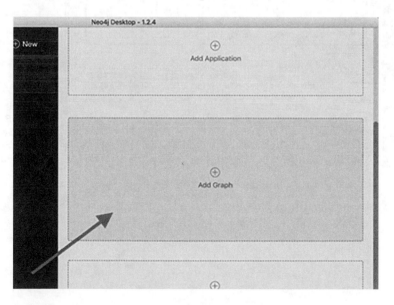

**Figure B.6
Adding a graph to
Neo4j Desktop**

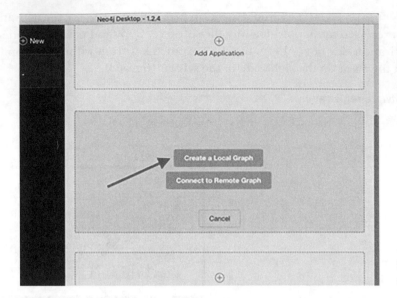

Figure B.7   Creating a new local graph

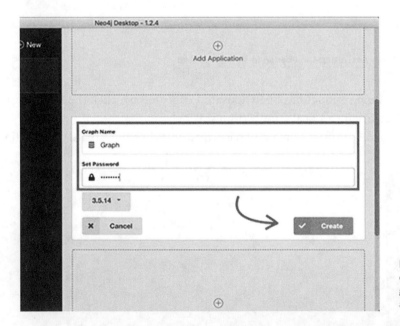

Figure B.8   In the case of a new local graph, create an admin password.

8   Start the new graph by clicking the Start button (figure B.9).

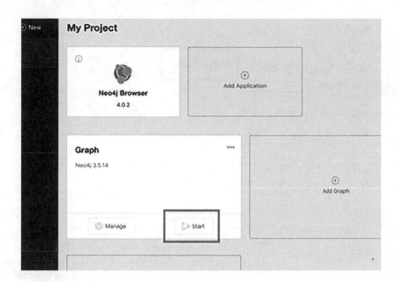

Figure B.9 Start the new created database instance.

9   Click the Manage button (figure B.10).

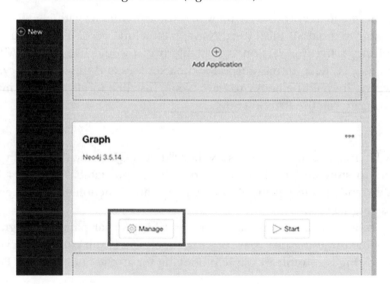

Figure B.10 Click Manage to operate the graph database.

10   In the next screen, click Open Browser to open the Neo4j browser in a new window (figure B.11).

Figure B.11 The Open Browser button opens the Neo4j browser.

You'll have access to the browser, from which you can interact with Neo4j.

If you want to avoid all this effort, Neo4j has a cloud version called Aura.[9] At the time of writing, a free-tier version is available if you would like to play with it a bit before jumping in. Keep in mind that for the exercises and the learning cycle in this book, however, it would be better to have Neo4j installed locally on your machine or wherever you can run the Python code.

B.3 Cypher

The query language used in Neo4j is Cypher.[10] Like SQL (which inspired it), Cypher allows users to store and retrieve data from the graph database. Cypher is easy to learn, understand, and use, yet it offers the power and functionality of other standard data access languages.

Cypher is a declarative language for describing visual patterns in graphs with ASCII-Art syntax. By using its syntax, you can describe a graph pattern in a visual, logical way. Following is a simple example of looking for all the nodes of type Person in a graph:

```
MATCH (p:Person)
RETURN p
```

This pattern can be used to search for nodes and relationships in the graph or to create them. It allows you to state what you want to select, insert, update, or delete from your graph data without describing exactly how to do it.

---

[9] https://neo4j.com/cloud/aura.
[10] https://neo4j.com/developer/cypher.

In addition to being used by Neo4j, Cypher has become open source. The open-Cypher[11] project provides an open language specification, technical compatibility kit, and reference implementation of the parser, planner, and runtime for Cypher. The project is backed by several companies in the database industry and allows implementors of databases and clients to freely benefit from, use, and contribute to the development of the openCypher language.

Throughout the book, you'll learn this language through examples and exercises. If you would like to learn more about Cypher, I recommend Neo4j's guide;[12] it's a good reference, full of examples.

B.4   *Plugin installation*

One of the great things about Neo4j is how easy it is to extend. Neo4j allows developers to customize it in multiple ways. You can enrich the Cypher language with new procedures and functions that you can call while querying the graph. You can customize the security with authentication and authorization plugins. You can enable new surfaces to be created in the HTTP API via server extensions.

Moreover, you can download, configure, and use a lot of existing plugins. The most relevant were developed by Neo4j and are supported by the entire community because they are open source. For the purposes of this book, we are going to consider two of them:

- *Awesome Procedures on Cypher (APOC)*—The APOC library is a standard utility library containing common procedures and functions. It contains more than 450 procedures and provides functionality for reading data from JDBC source or JSON, conversions, graph updates, and more. The functions and procedures are well supported and stable in most of the cases.
- *Graph Data Science (GDS) Library*—This library of procedures implements many common graph algorithms, such as PageRank, several centrality measures, similarities, and more recent techniques such as node embedding and link prediction. Because the algorithms run inside the Neo4j engine, they are optimized in reading nodes and relationships before analysis and storage of the results. This aspect allows this library to compute results quickly over tens of billions of nodes.

The next two sections describe how to download, install, and configure these plugins. I recommend doing all this before you start using Cypher queries in chapter 4.

B.4.1   *APOC installation*

Installing plugins in Neo4j is simple. Let's start with the APOC library. If you installed the server version, download the plugin from the related GitHub release page[13] (take

---

[11] https://www.opencypher.org
[12] https://neo4j.com/developer/cypher
[13] http://mng.bz/G6mv

*-all.jar to get the full library, and select the version that matches your version of Neo4j), and copy it to the plugins directory inside your NEO4J_HOME folder. At this point, edit the configuration file conf/neo4j.conf by adjusting or adding the following lines:

```
dbms.security.procedures.unrestricted=apoc.*
dbms.security.procedures.allowlist=apoc.*
```

Restart Neo4j, and open the browser. Run the following procedure to check whether everything is in place:

```
CALL dbms.procedures() YIELD name
WHERE name STARTS WITH "apoc"
RETURN name
```

You should see the list of APOC procedures.

If you are using the Neo4j Desktop version, the process is even simpler. After creating the database, open the Manage screen, click the Plugins tab, click Install in the APOC box, and wait to see the `Installed` message (figure B.12). For further details and explanations, see the official APOC installation guide.[14]

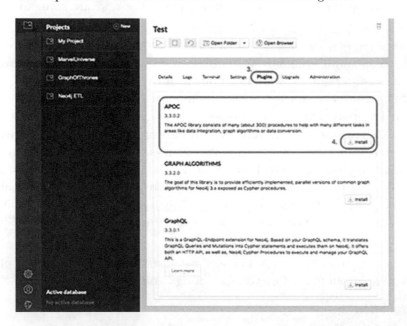

Figure B.12   APOC installation in Neo4j Desktop

---

[14] https://neo4j.com/labs/apoc/4.2/installation.

B.4.2 GDS Library

You can follow a similar procedure for the GDS Library. If you installed the server version, download the plugin from the related GitHub release page[15] (take *-standalone .jar), and copy it to the plugins directory inside your NEO4J_HOME folder. At this point, edit the configuration file conf/neo4j.conf by adjusting or adding the following lines:

```
dbms.security.procedures.unrestricted=apoc.*,gds.*
dbms.security.procedures.allowlist=apoc.*,gds.*
```

Restart Neo4j, open the browser, and run the following procedure to check whether everything is in place:

```
RETURN gds.version()
```

You should be able to see the version of the GDS you downloaded.

If you are using Neo4j Desktop, the process is even simpler. After creating the database, open the Manage screen, click the Plugins tab, click Install in the Graph Data Science Library, and wait to see the `Installed` message (figure B.13). After these steps, you will be ready to have fun with Neo4j and run all the examples and exercises in the book.

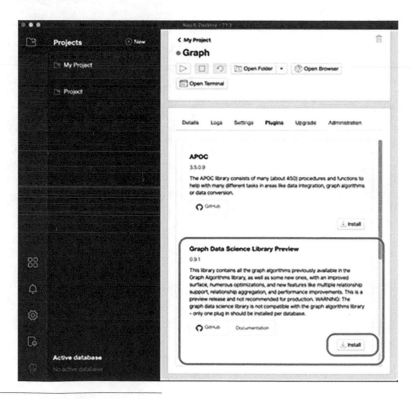

Figure B.13   GDS installation from Neo4j Desktop

---

[15] http://mng.bz/zGDB.

B.5   *Cleaning*

Sometimes, you need to clean a database. You can do this job by using the functions in the APOC library that you have installed into your database. To delete everything:

```
CALL apoc.periodic.iterate('MATCH (n) RETURN n', 'DETACH DELETE n',
➡ {batchSize:1000})
```

To drop all constraints:

```
CALL apoc.schema.assert({}, {})
```

References

[Robison et al., 2015] Robinson, Ian, Jim Webber, and Emil Eifrem. *Graph Databases*. 2nd ed. Sebastopol, CA: O'Reilly, 2015.

[Vukotic et al., 2014] Vukotic, Aleksa, Dominic Fox, Jonas Partner, Nicki Watt, and Tareq Abedrabbo. *Neo4j in Action*. Shelter Island, NY: Manning, 2014.

[Woodie, 2016] Woodie, Alex. "Neo4j Pushes Graph DB Limits Past a Quadrillion Nodes." *Datanami*, April 26, 2016. http://mng.bz/0rJN.

appendix C
Graphs for processing patterns and workflows

In many machine learning projects, including many of those described in this book, the graphs produced are large. The scale of these graphs makes processing them efficiently difficult. To deal with these challenges, a variety of distributed graph processing systems has emerged. In this appendix, we will explore one of these systems: Pregel, the first computational model (and still one of the most commonly used) for processing large-scale graphs.[1] This topic suits the purpose of the appendix for two main reasons:

- It defines a processing model that's useful for providing an alternative implementation of some of the algorithms discussed in this book (both graph-based and non-graph-based).
- It shows the expressive power of the graph and presents an alternative approach to the computation based on the graph representation of the information.

C.1 Pregel

Suppose that you would like to execute the PageRank algorithm on a large graph, such as the whole internet. As stated in section 3.3.1, the PageRank algorithm was developed by the founders of Google for their search engine, so the algorithm's primordial purpose was the same. We explored how the algorithm works in chapter 3, so let's focus now on how to solve a concrete problem: processing the PageRank values for such a large graph. This task will be complex to accomplish due to the high number of nodes (web pages) and edges (links between web pages), requiring a distributed approach.

---

[1] Its name honors Leonhard Euler; the bridges of Königsberg, which inspired Euler's theorem, spanned the Pregel River [Malewicz, 2010].

The input to a Pregel computation is a directed graph in which each node has a unique identifier and is associated with a modifiable, user-defined value that is initialized in some way (also part of the input). Each directed edge is associated with

- A source node identifier
- A target node identifier
- A modifiable, user-defined value

In Pregel, the program is expressed as a sequence of iterations (called *supersteps*), separated by global synchronization points, that run until the algorithm terminates and produces its output. In each superstep S, a node can accomplish one or more of the following tasks, conceptually conducted in parallel [Malewicz et al., 2010]:

- Receive messages sent to it in the previous iteration, superstep $S-1$
- Send messages to other nodes that will be read at superstep $S+1$
- Modify its own state and that of its outgoing edges, or mutate the graph topology

Messages are typically sent along outgoing edges (to the directly connected nodes), but a message can be sent to any node whose identifier is known. In superstep 0, every node is active; all active nodes participate in the computation of any given superstep. At the end of each iteration, a node can decide to deactivate itself by voting to halt. At that point it becomes inactive and will not participate in subsequent supersteps unless it receives a message from another node, at which point it is reactivated. After being reactivated, a node that wants to halt must explicitly deactivate itself again. This simple state machine is illustrated in figure C.1. The termination condition for the iterations is reached when all the nodes have voted to halt, so no further work is done in the next superstep.

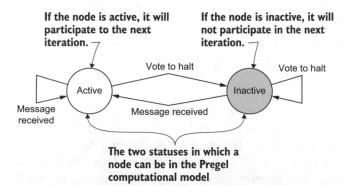

Figure C.1   Node statuses according to the Pregel computational model

Before applying the Pregel framework to our PageRank use case, let's consider a simpler example: given a strongly connected graph in which each node contains a value, find the highest value stored in the nodes. The Pregel implementation of this algorithm works this way:

- The graph and the initial values of each node represent the input.
- At superstep 0, each node sends its initial value to all its neighbors.

- In each subsequent superstep S, if a node has learned a larger value from the messages it received in superstep $S - 1$, it sends that value to all its neighbors; otherwise, it deactivates itself and stops voting.
- When all nodes have deactivated themselves and there are no further changes, the algorithm terminates.

These steps are shown in figure C.2 with concrete numbers.

Pregel uses a pure message-passing model, for two reasons:

- Message passing is expressive enough for graph algorithms; there is no need for remote reads (reading data from other machines in the processing cluster) or other ways of emulating shared memory.
- By avoiding reading values from remote machines and delivering messages asynchronously in batches, it's possible to reduce latency, thereby enhancing performance.

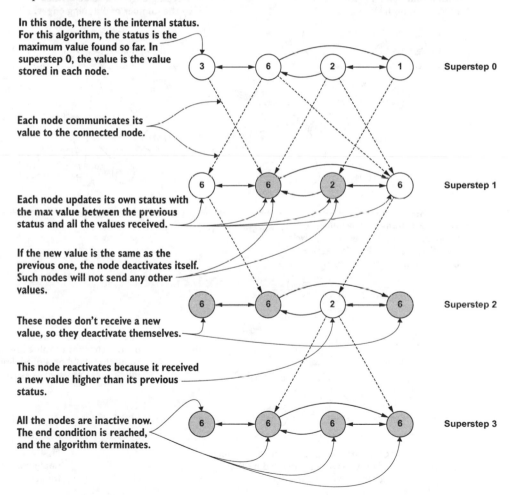

Figure C.2 Pregel implementation for finding the highest value stored in the nodes

Although Pregel's nodecentric model is easy to program and has proved to be useful for many graph algorithms, it is worth noting that such a model hides the partitioning information from users and thus prevents many algorithm-specific optimizations, often resulting in longer execution times due to excessive network load. To address this limitation, other approaches exist. This approach can be defined as a graphcentric programming paradigm. In this graphcentric model, the partition structure is opened to the users and can be optimized so that communication within a partition can bypass heavy message-passing [Tian et al., 2013].

Now that the model is clear, and the advantages and drawbacks have been highlighted, let's return to our scenario and examine the logical steps of the implementation of the PageRank algorithm using Pregel, which could look like figure C.3.

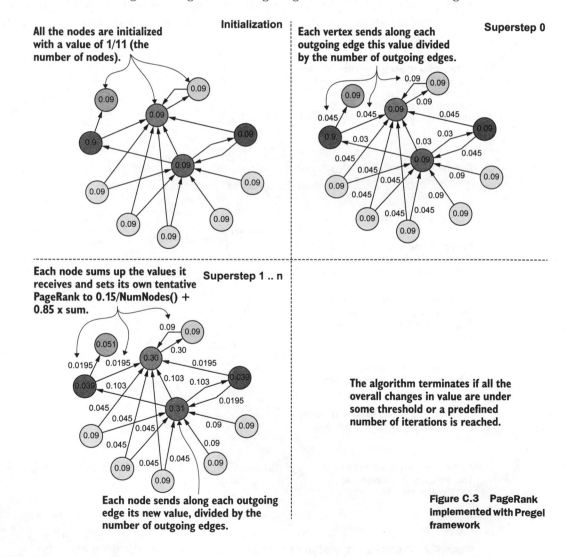

Initialization

All the nodes are initialized with a value of 1/11 (the number of nodes).

Superstep 0

Each vertex sends along each outgoing edge this value divided by the number of outgoing edges.

Superstep 1 .. n

Each node sums up the values it receives and sets its own tentative PageRank to 0.15/NumNodes() + 0.85 x sum.

Each node sends along each outgoing edge its new value, divided by the number of outgoing edges.

The algorithm terminates if all the overall changes in value are under some threshold or a predefined number of iterations is reached.

Figure C.3   PageRank implemented with Pregel framework

The schema in figure C.3 can be further described as follows:

- The graph is initialized so that in superstep 0, the value of each node is 1/NumNodes(). Each node sends along each outgoing edge this value divided by the number of outgoing edges.
- In each subsequent superstep, each node sums up the values arriving in messages into *sum* and sets its own tentative PageRank to 0.15/NumNodes() + 0.85 × *sum*. Then it sends along each outgoing edge its tentative PageRank divided by the number of outgoing edges.
- The algorithm terminates if all the overall changes in value are under some threshold or it reaches a predefined number of iterations.

The fun aspect of the Pregel implementation of the PageRank algorithm in the internet scenario is that we have a graph-by-nature dataset (internet links), a pure graph algorithm (PageRank), and a graph-based processing paradigm.

C.2 Graphs for defining complex processing workflows

In a machine learning project, graph models can be used not only for representing complex data structures, making it easy to store, process, or access them, but also for describing, in an effective way, complex processing workflows—the sequences of subtasks that are necessary to complete bigger tasks. The graph model allows us to visualize the entire algorithm or application, simplifies the identification of issues, and makes it easy to accomplish parallelization even with an automated process. Although this specific use of graphs will not be presented extensively in the book, it is important to introduce it because it shows the value of the graph model in representing complex rules or activities in contexts not necessarily related to machine learning.

Dataflow is a programming paradigm (often referred to as *DFP*, for *dataflow programming*) that uses directed graphs to represent complex applications and is extensively used for parallel computing. In a dataflow graph, nodes represent units of computation, and edges represent the data consumed or produced by a computation. TensorFlow[2] uses these graphs to represent computation in terms of the dependencies between individual operations.

C.3 Dataflow

Suppose that you are expecting a baby, and during your last visit, the doctor predicted the weight of the newborn to be 7.5 pounds. You would like to figure out how that might differ from the baby's actual measured weight.

Let's design a function to describe the likelihood of all possible weights of the newborn. You would like to know if 8 pounds is more likely than 10 pounds, for example [Shukla, 2018]. For this kind of prediction, the Gaussian (otherwise known as normal) probability distribution function is generally used. This function takes as input a number and some other parameters, and outputs a nonnegative number describing

---

[2] https://www.tensorflow.org.

the probability of observing the input. The probability density of the normal distribution is given by the equation

$$f(x|\mu, \sigma^2) = \frac{1}{\sigma\sqrt{2\pi}} e^{-\frac{(x-m)^2}{2\sigma^2}}$$

where

- μ is the mean or expectation of the distribution (and also its median and mode).
- σ is the standard deviation.
- σ^2 is the variance.

This formula specifies how to compute the probability of x (the weight, in our scenario) considering the median value μ (in our case, 7.5 pounds) and the standard deviation (which specifies the variability from the mean). The median value is not random; it is the actual average value of a newborn in North America.[3] This function can be represented in an XY chart, as shown in figure C.4.

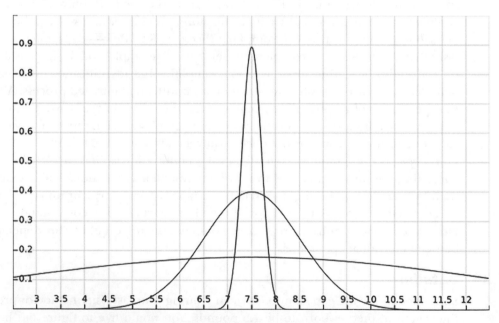

Figure C.4   Normal distribution curve (bell curve)

Depending on the value of σ (the standard deviation), the curve can be taller or fatter, whereas depending on the value of μ (the mean), it can move to the left or right side of the chart. Figure C.4 has the value of the mean centered to 7.5. According to the value of the standard deviation, the probability of the nearest values could be more or

---

[3] https://www.uofmhealth.org/health-library/te6295.

less distributed. The taller curve has a variance of 0.2, and the fatter one has a variance of 5. A smaller value of variance means that the most probable values are the closest to the mean (on both sides).

In any case, the graph presents a similar structure that causes it to be informally called the *bell curve*. This formula and the related representation mean that events closer to the tip of the curve are more likely to happen than events on the sides. In our case, if the mean expected weight of a newborn is 7.5 pounds, and the variance is known, we can use this function to get the probability of a weight of 8 pounds compared with 10 pounds. This function shows up all the time in machine learning, and it's easy to define in TensorFlow; it uses only multiplication, division, negation, and a few other fundamental operators.

To convert such a function to its graph representation in dataflow, it is possible to simplify it by setting the mean to 0 and the standard deviation to 1. With these parameter values, the formula becomes

$$f(x|\mu, \sigma^2) = \frac{1}{\sigma\sqrt{2\pi}} e^{-\frac{x^2}{2\sigma^2}}$$

This new function has a specific name: the *standard normal distribution*. The conversion to graph format requires the following steps:

- Each operator becomes a node in the graph, so we will have nodes representing products, power, negation, square root, and so on.
- The edges between operators represent the composition of mathematical functions.

Starting from these simple rules, the resulting graph representation of the Gaussian probability distribution is shown in figure C.5.

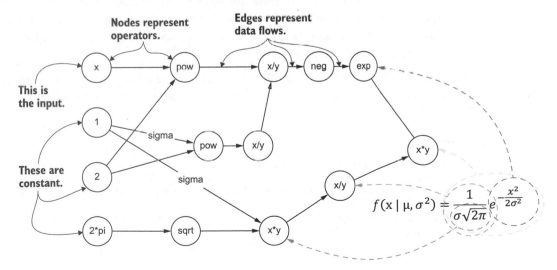

Figure C.5 A graph representation of the normal distribution in dataflow programming ($\sigma = 1$)

Small segments of the graph represent simple mathematical concepts. If a node has only an inbound edge, it is a *unary* operator (an operator that operates on a single input, such as negation or doubling), whereas a node with two inbound edges is a *binary* operator (an operator that operates on two input variables, such as addition or exponentiation). In the graph in figure C.5, passing 8 pounds (the weight we would like to consider for the newborn) as the input to the formula will provide the probability of this weight. The figure shows the different branches of the function clearly, which means that it is trivial to identify portions of the formula that can be processed in parallel.

In TensorFlow, this approach makes it easy to visualize and process even algorithms that appear to be quite complex. DFP was a commonly forgotten paradigm despite its usefulness in certain scenarios, but TensorFlow revived it by showing the power of graph representations for complex processes and tasks. The advantages of the DFP approach can be summarized as follows [Johnstonet et al., 2004; Sousa, 2012]:

- It provides a visual programming language with a simplified interface that enables rapid prototyping and implementation of certain systems. We've already discussed the importance of the visual sense and graphs as a way to better understand complex data structures. DFP is capable of representing complex applications and algorithms while keeping them simple to understand and modify.

- It implicitly achieves concurrency. The original motivation for research on dataflow was the exploitation of massive parallelism. In a dataflow application, internally each node is an independent processing block that works independently from all the others and produces no side effects. Such an execution model allows nodes to execute as soon as data arrives at them without the risk of creating deadlocks, because there are no data dependencies in the system. This important feature of the dataflow model can greatly increase the performance of an application being executed on a multicore CPU without requiring any additional work by the programmer.

Dataflow applications represent another example of the expressive power of graphs for decomposing complex problems into subtasks that are easy to visualize, modify, and parallelize.

References

[Malewicz, 2010] Malewicz, Grzegorz, Matthew H. Austern, Aart J. C. Bik, James C. Dehnert, Ilan Horn, Naty Leiser, and Grzegorz Cjajkowski. "Pregel: A System for Large-Scale Graph Processing." *Proceedings of the 2010 ACM SIGMOD International Conference on Management of Data* (2010): 135–146.

[Tianet et al., 2013] Tian, Yuanyuan, Andrey Balmin, Severin Andreas Corsten, Shirish Tatikonda, and John McPherson. "From 'Think Like a Vertex' to 'Think Like a Graph.'" *Proceedings of the VLDB Endowment* 7:3 (2013): 193–204.

[Johnston et al., 2004] Johnston, Wesley M., J. R. Paul Hanna, and Richard J. Millar. "Advances in Dataflow Programming Languages." *ACM Computing Surveys* (CSUR) 36:1 (2004): 1–34.

[Sousa, 2012] Sousa, Tiago Boldt. "Dataflow Programming: Concept, Languages and Applications." *Doctoral Symposium on Informatics Engineering* (2012).

[Shukla, 2018] Shukla, Nishant. *Machine Learning with TensorFlow.* Shelter Island, NY: Manning, 2018.

appendix D
Representing graphs

There are two standard ways of representing a graph $G = (V, E)$ in a suitable way to be processed: as a collection of adjacency lists or as an adjacency matrix. Each way can be applied to directed, undirected, and unweighted graphs [Cormen et al., 2009].

The *adjacency list* representation of a graph $G = (V, E)$ consists of an array *Adj* of lists, one for each vertex in *V*. For each vertex *u* in *V*, the adjacency list *Adj*[*u*] contains all the vertices *v* for which there exists an edge E_{uv} between *u* and *v* in *E*. In other words, *Adj*[*u*] consists of all the vertices adjacent to *u* in *G*.

Figure D.1(b) is an adjacency list representation of the undirected graph in figure D.1(a). Vertex 1 has two neighbors, 2 and 5, so *Adj*[1] is the list [2,5]. Vertex 2 has three neighbors, 1, 4, and 5, so *Adj*[2] is [1,4,5]. The other lists are created in the same way. It is worth noting that because there is no order in the relationships, there is no specific order in the lists; hence, *Adj*[1] could be [2,5] as well as [5, 2].

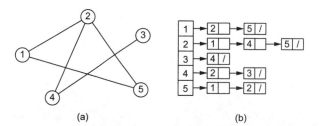

(a) (b)

Figure D.1 An undirected graph (a) and the related representation as an adjacency list (b)

Similarly, figure D.2(b) is an adjacency list representation of the directed graph in figure D.2(a). Such a list is visualized as a linked list in which each entry contains a reference to the next one. In the adjacency list for node 1, we have the first element as node 2; it also has a reference to the next one, the element for node 5. This approach is one of the most common for storing adjacency lists, because it makes elements such as addition and deletion efficient. In this case, we consider only the outgoing relationships, but we can do the same with the ingoing relationships; what is important is to choose a direction and keep it consistent during adjacency list creation. Here, vertex 1 has only one outgoing relationship, with vertex 2, so $Adj[1]$ will be [2]. Vertex 2 has two outgoing relationships, with 4 and 5, so $Adj[2]$ is [4,5]. Vertex 4 has no outgoing relationships, so $Adj[4]$ is empty ([]).

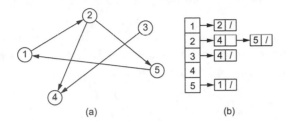

(a)   (b)

Figure D.2   A directed graph (a) and the related representation as an adjacency list (b)

If G is a directed graph, the sum of the lengths of all the adjacency lists is $|E|$. Because every edge can be traversed in a single direction, E_{uv} will appear only in $Adj[u]$. If G is an undirected graph, the sum of the lengths of all the adjacency lists is $2 \times |E|$ because if E_{uv} is an undirected edge, E_{uv} appears in $Adj[u]$ and $Adj[v]$. The memory required by an adjacency list representation of a directed or undirected graph is directly proportional to $|V| + |E|$.

Adjacency lists can be easily adapted to represent weighted graphs by storing the weight w of the edge E_{uv} in $Adj[u]$. The adjacency list representation can be similarly modified to support many other graph variants too.

A disadvantage of this representation is that it provides no faster way to determine whether a given edge E_{uv} is present in the graph than to search for v in the adjacency list $Adj[u]$. An adjacency matrix representation of the graph remedies this disadvantage, but at the cost of using asymptotically more memory.

For the adjacency matrix representation of a graph $G = (V, E)$, we assume that the vertices are numbered $1,2,...,|V|$ in some arbitrary manner and that these numbers are kept consistent during the life of the adjacency matrix. Then the adjacency matrix representation of a graph G consists of a $|V| \times |V|$ matrix $A = (a_{uv})$ such that $a_{uv} = 1$ if E_{uv} exists in the graph, and otherwise $a_{uv} = 0$.

Figure D.3(b) is the adjacency matrix representation of the undirected graph represented in figure D.3(a). The first line, for example, is related to vertex 1. This row in the matrix has 1 in columns 2 and 5 because they represent the vertices to which vertex 1 is connected. All the other values are 0. The second row, related to vertex 2, has 1 in columns 1, 4, and 5 because those vertices are the connected vertices.

Figure D.4(b) is the adjacency matrix representation of the directed graph represented in figure D.4(a). As for the adjacency list, it is necessary to choose one direction and use it during matrix creation. In this case, the first row in the matrix has 1 in column 2 because vertex 1 has one outgoing relationship, to vertex 2; all the other values

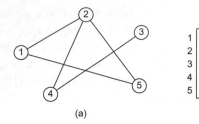

1 2 3 4 5
```
1 | 0 1 0 0 1
2 | 1 0 0 1 1
3 | 0 0 0 1 0
4 | 0 1 1 0 0
5 | 1 1 0 0 0
```

(a)   (b)

Figure D.3   An undirected graph (a) and the related representation as an adjacency matrix (b)

are 0. An interesting feature of the matrix representation is that by looking at the columns, it is possible to see the inbound relationships. Column 4, for example, shows that vertex 4 has two inbound connections: from vertices 2 and 3.

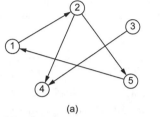

1 2 3 4 5
```
1 | 0 1 0 0 0
2 | 0 0 0 1 1
3 | 0 0 0 1 0
4 | 0 0 0 0 0
5 | 1 0 0 0 0
```

(a)   (b)

Figure D.4   A directed graph (a) and the related representation as an adjacency matrix (b)

The adjacency matrix of a graph requires memory directly proportional to $|V| \times |V|$, independent of the number of edges in the graph. In an undirected graph, the resulting matrix is symmetric along the main diagonal. In such cases, it is possible to store only half of the matrix, cutting the memory needed to store the graph almost in half.

Like the adjacency list representation of a graph, an adjacency matrix can represent a weighted graph. If $G = (V, E)$ is a weighted graph, and w is the weight of the edge, E_{uv}, a_{uv} will be set to w instead of 1.

Although the adjacency list representation is asymptotically at least as space efficient as the adjacency matrix representation, adjacency matrices are simpler, so you may prefer them when graphs are reasonably small. Moreover, adjacency matrices carry a further advantage for unweighted graphs: they require only one bit per entry. Because the adjacency list representation provides a compact way to represent *sparse* graphs—those for which the number of edges is less than the number of vertices—it is usually the method of choice. But you may prefer an adjacency matrix representation when the graph is dense—when $|E|$ is close to $|V| \times |V|$—or when you need to be able to tell quickly whether an edge is connecting two given vertices.

References

[Cormen et al., 2009] Cormen, Thomas H., Charles E. Leiserson, Ronald L. Rivest, and Clifford Stein. *Introduction to Algorithms*. 3rd ed. Boston, MA: MIT Press, 2009.

index

MANNING

The Manning Early Access Program

Don't wait to start learning! In MEAP, the Manning Early Access Program, you can read books as they're being created and long before they're available in stores.

Here's how MEAP works.

- **Start now.** Buy a MEAP and you'll get all available chapters in PDF, ePub, Kindle, and liveBook formats.

- **Regular updates.** New chapters are released as soon as they're written. We'll let you know when fresh content is available.

- **Finish faster.** MEAP customers are the first to get final versions of all books! Pre-order the print book, and it'll ship as soon as it's off the press.

- **Contribute to the process.** The feedback you share with authors makes the end product better.

- **No risk.** You get a full refund or exchange if we ever have to cancel a MEAP.

Explore dozens of titles in MEAP at www.manning.com.

 **MANNING**

Hands-on projects for learning your way

liveProjects are an exciting way to develop your skills that's just like learning on-the-job.

In a Manning liveProject you tackle a real-world IT challenge and work out your own solutions. To make sure you succeed, you'll get 90 days full and unlimited access to a hand-picked list of Manning book and video resources.

Here's how liveProject works:

- **Achievable milestones.** Each project is broken down into steps and sections so you can keep track of your progress.

- **Collaboration and advice.** Work with other liveProject participants through chat, working groups, and peer project reviews.

- **Compare your results.** See how your work shapes up against an expert implementation by the liveProject's creator.

- **Everything you need to succeed.** Datasets and carefully selected learning resources come bundled with every liveProject.

- **Build your portfolio.** All liveProjects teach skills that are in-demand from industry. When you're finished, you'll have the satisfaction that comes with success and a real project to add to your portfolio.

Explore dozens of data, development, and cloud engineering liveProjects at www.manning.com!